ALL THINGS HUMAN

STUDIES IN ANGLICAN HISTORY

Series Editor

Peter W. Williams, Miami University

A list of books in the series appears at the end of this book.

Sponsored by the Historical Society of the Episcopal Church

MICHAEL BOURGEOIS

All Things Human

HENRY CODMAN POTTER

AND THE SOCIAL GOSPEL

IN THE EPISCOPAL CHURCH

UNIVERSITY OF ILLINOIS PRESS

URBANA AND CHICAGO

Some of the material in chapter 3 was previously published
as "The Work and Well-Being of Women in American Social
Christianity: The Case of Henry Codman Potter (1835–1908),"
Union Seminary Quarterly Review 53, nos. 3–4 (1999): 125–51, and
is used here courtesy of *Union Seminary Quarterly Review.*

Library of Congress Cataloging-in-Publication Data
Bourgeois, Michael, 1956–
All things human : Henry Codman Potter and the social gospel
in the Episcopal Church / Michael Bourgeois.
p.   cm. — (Studies in Anglican history)
Includes bibliographical references and index.
ISBN 0-252-02877-5 (cloth : alk. paper)
1. Social gospel. 2. Potter, Henry Codman, 1834–1908.
3. Episcopal Church—Doctrines—History.
I. Title. II. Series.
BT738.B67   2004
261.8'092—dc21   2003007101

In memory of my parents, with love and gratitude

PETER W. WILLIAMS

Series Editor's Preface

Studies in Anglican History is a series of scholarly mono-
graphs sponsored by the Historical Society of the Episcopal Church and
published by the University of Illinois Press. It is intended to bring the
best of contemporary international scholarship on the history of the entire Anglican Communion, including the Church of England and the
Episcopal church in the United States, to a broader readership.

Michael Bourgeois teaches theology at Emmanuel College at the
University of Toronto and has now written this first major scholarly study
of Bishop Henry Codman Potter. As a priest of the Protestant Episcopal
Church from 1857 and bishop of its Diocese of New York from 1883 until
1908, Potter was a proponent and exemplar of the Episcopal Broad Church
movement and the American Social Gospel. *All Things Human* not only
recovers the memory of a neglected figure in American religious history
but also shows through Potter's life and work how he and other white
Protestants employed and reshaped antebellum religious and moral traditions as they engaged the evils of the American social order in the decades after the Civil War. Potter's emphasis on practical Christian living
and attention to human inequality, the work and well-being of women,
corruption and reform in political life, and the relations of labor and capital helped to shape a pattern of Christian life and thought that, while
not entirely successful in its aims, was vital in its engagement with the
world and comprehensive in its redemptive concern for all aspects of
human life.

Contents

Introduction

To the surprise of many contemporary observers, the Episcopal Church played a central role in the social awakening of white American Protestantism from the end of the Civil War to the start of World
War I, an awakening now regarded as continuous with the earlier revivals and awakenings of the eighteenth and nineteenth centuries and perhaps even as the "Third Great Awakening."[1] In his 1912 *Christianizing
the Social Order*, Walter Rauschenbusch looked back on the process by
which the social awakening of the churches had occurred and paid tribute to three early "pioneers of Christian social thought in America,"
Washington Gladden, Josiah Strong, and Richard T. Ely. He also reviewed
the steps by which social Christianity had "run beyond the stage of the
solitary pioneer" and had been "admitted within the organizations of the
Church." Rauschenbusch noted that although the Protestant Episcopal
Church had "failed to take any leading part in the older social conflicts
with alcoholism and with slavery," nevertheless "in the present struggle against industrial extortion it has furnished far more than its share
of workers and leaders." Rauschenbusch cited as evidence the 1887 formation of the Church Association for the Advancement of the Interests
of Labor (CAIL), "probably the first organization of social Christianity in
this country," and noted that "as early as 1901 the Protestant Episcopal
Church appointed a Standing Commission on Church and Labor, and
since 1907 Diocesan Commissions have been at work in a dozen dioceses." Among the "workers and leaders" of Christian social thought he
named were two Episcopalians: Richard T. Ely, economist, founder of the
American Economic Association, and member of the Christian Social

Union; and W. D. P. Bliss, priest, founding member of CAIL and the Society of Christian Socialists, editor of *The Dawn* and the landmark *Encyclopedia of Social Reform*, and secretary of the Christian Social Union.[2]

Rauschenbusch had served as pastor of the Second German Baptist Church in New York City from 1886 to 1897 and had devoted much of his energies to political and social questions. His assessment of the surprising activism of the Episcopal Church and its influence on the social awakening of white American Protestantism was undoubtedly influenced by his association with and respect for Ely and Bliss, as well as his high regard for the English Christian Socialists. His assessment was not, however, exaggerated. Both secular and religious contemporaries, as well as subsequent scholars, confirm Rauschenbusch's conclusion. In 1884, for example, Henry Ward Beecher, one of the period's most prominent Protestant ministers, praised the Episcopal Church's participation in temperance reform and hailed it as heralding the movement's success. "Few dared to hope, and none to prophesy, that we should see advancing at last the great Episcopal Church of the United States, with her bishops, her priests, her orderly Communion, her staunch and stable men not suspected of radicalism, but rather conservative in the public estimation. . . . [A] greater number would be willing to follow this orderly and most efficient institution, than, perhaps, would be willing to follow any other leadership." Ten years later the *New York Sun* observed: "The remarkable energy displayed by [Episcopal churches in metropolitan centers] of later years in pushing forward their religious and charitable enterprises [has] furnished an example which is now followed by Protestant churches generally." In 1905 the *Congregationalist* noted that while the leading exponents of social Christianity included more from among its own denomination than from the Episcopal Church, the latter "seems to get more of its clergy and laity interested in the practical workings of the new conception than we do." And, many years later, Henry May concluded, "Undoubtedly the Episcopal Church was the first major denomination to receive the new doctrines with any general welcome."[3]

The three Episcopal contributions to the social awakening cited by Rauschenbusch had in common one other "worker and leader" who played a pivotal role in the general welcome the Episcopal Church accorded the new doctrines. He was Henry Codman Potter, who served as rector of Grace Church, New York, from 1868 to 1883 and as bishop of New York from 1883 to 1908. Potter's 1886 pastoral letter to the clergy of the Diocese of New York, written in the midst of the uproar following the Haymarket Affair, challenged the prevailing view of labor as a commodity and inspired the formation of CAIL the following year. At the turn of the century CAIL, with Potter's participation and support, was instrumental in the establishment of the Joint Commission on the Relations of Capital and Labor and diocesan social service commissions.[4] Yet, unlike other proponents of social Christianity whose work has received considerable attention, Potter is little known today and seems to have faded from public memory shortly after his death. In the preface to his 1933 biography, *Henry Codman Potter, an American Metropolitan,* James Sheerin quotes the response of a "distinguished New York publisher and churchman" to the prospect of a book on the late cleric, who had died twenty five years earlier. "There is no use publishing any life of Bishop Potter," said the publisher; "he is entirely forgotten and the clergy no longer read books! Certainly they don't buy them!" Despite this discouragement, Sheerin wrote his book, noting that for him "such a warning only acts as a spur to do my bit to bring back some interest in 'a forgotten man' who is ecclesiastically and socially helpful to remember." Although limited in its treatment of Potter, subsequent scholarship substantiates Sheerin's contention. Earlier studies cite Henry Codman Potter as a significant figure in the development of Protestant social Christianity, particularly on the issues of industrialization and organized labor, and more recent works note Potter's contributions on these issues and others, including race relations and advancing social Christianity within the Episcopal Church. None, however, offers either a comprehensive review or even a complete analysis of his work on any one issue.[5] Similarly, some recent historical studies of the Episcopal Church mention Potter but do not examine his work in any detail.[6] While Potter may not be "entirely forgotten," he is certainly little known. The frequency with which these studies cite him and the significance they accord some aspects of his work, however, suggests that he and his work may be worth knowing.[7]

Historians of the Episcopal Church have sometimes remarked on its historical amnesia, whether general or selective. Recent studies of nineteenth-century Evangelical Episcopalianism, for example, rightly decry the extent to which the history of Evangelicalism's importance has been neglected.[8] I share such concerns and offer an illustration of the continuing need to recover neglected parts of the church's story. In December 1994, while in New York City for the defense of my doctoral dissertation (which is the basis for this book), I visited St. Paul's Chapel, the site of Henry Codman Potter's 1889 address at the celebration of the centennial of the inauguration of George Washington as the first president of the United States. On that occasion, Potter had delivered a stinging critique of the political corruption of the day. As I walked through St. Paul's, I observed glass cases at the rear that displayed material both from Washington's inauguration in 1789 and from an apparently uncritically festive bicentennial celebration during the presidency of George H. W. Bush in 1989. The display cases, however, held no material from the centennial celebrations in 1889. Whether intentionally or not, the material on display suggested that the only role that Christianity—or at least the Episcopal Church—has played in relation to government has been to bless the political status quo. Recollection of Potter's 1889 address at St. Paul's Chapel and of his wider work on political reform may help to correct this erroneous suggestion.

Recollection of Potter and his work as a whole may also help illuminate two larger concerns that have motivated and shaped my interest in and approach to Potter and his work. My first concern, in general terms, is the question of the relation of continuity, discontinuity, and faithfulness in religious traditions. What distinguishes legitimate change from illegitimate, fidelity from infidelity? To what extent are members of a religious tradition bound by it, and to what extent may they be free from it? In the study of American Protestantism in the nineteenth century, this concern is reflected in the discussion about whether the social gospel was primarily a response to external events or an extension of internal impulses of American Christianity. In the study of the Episcopal Church it is reflected in the question of the extent to which the liberal Broad Church movement of the late nineteenth century was a faithful expression of Episcopal Evangelicalism. As someone with predominantly liberal sympathies, I am fascinated with the common heritage of latter-day North American evangelicalism and liberalism and the story of how evangelicalism evolved into these related but divergent streams of Christianity. I also wish that evangelical and liberal historians and theologians might collaborate more to recover and reflect on their common heritage, and I hope that this study of one nineteenth-century evangelical liberal might be some small contribution toward that project.

My second concern is the relation of activity on social, political, and economic concerns to matters of theology and belief in Christianity's work. White and Hopkins, for example, discuss the debate about whether the social gospel was a theological movement or a social movement.[9] This debate has implications not only for scholarly assessments of more or less genuine expressions of Christianity, but also for how the churches organize their work: Arguments that the social gospel was primarily a social movement can be used to make social concerns marginal to Christianity, while arguments that it was a theological movement can be used to make them central. My concern also touches on the extent to which "practical Christianity" might shape the content of faith. The example of Henry Codman Potter suggests not only that the social gospel should not be undervalued because it emphasized practical Christianity rather than theology, but also that it should be valued in part because of its implications for theology.

————————

This study necessarily includes a considerable amount of biographical information about Henry Potter but is not a biography. Therefore a brief sketch of his family background, the course of his life, and some of the major religious, social, and political issues of the day may provide a helpful overview of Potter and his times. Henry Codman Potter was born on 25 May 1834 in Schenectady, New York, and died on 21 July 1908 in Cooperstown, New York. He was the fifth child of Alonzo and Sarah Nott Potter; his father was an Episcopal priest and a professor at Union College, and his mother was a daughter of Eliphalet Nott, a Presbyterian minister and president of Union College. At the time of Henry Potter's birth, Andrew Jackson was president of the United States, and Theodore Roosevelt was at the time of his death. The seventy-four years of his life were marked by dramatic changes and intense conflict in all aspects of American life—social, political, economic, scientific, and religious. The demographic and economic base of the country shifted from rural and agricultural to urban and industrial. Its population multiplied in large part through immigration, particularly by non-English-speaking Europeans. The conflict over slavery reached its peak in the Civil War and the "negro problem" continued through Reconstruction and in the wake of Reconstruction's failure. Conflict between labor and capital increased as the pace of industrialization quickened, as the newly wealthy flaunted their gains in opulent living, and as working people experienced dire suffering, particularly in the panics and depressions of the last quarter of the nineteenth century.[10]

The legacy of the evangelicalism of the Great Awakenings (1730–60 and 1800–1830) dominated Protestantism, but in the postwar period religious liberalism began to find expression through means other than Unitarianism and Universalism. This evangelical or Christocentric liberalism grew further in response to the need felt by many to reconcile Christianity with evolutionary theory and historical criticism. The evangelical Protestant vision of a Christian America continued unabated, strengthened as a result of its perceived success in ridding the country of slavery. In addition to ongoing concerns such as temperance reform and Sunday observance, the churches adapted older strategies as well as developed new ones to meet the challenges of immigration, industrialization, urbanization, and political corruption. Particularly important in the postwar period was the decreasing reliance on and, among some, ultimate rejection of traditional clerical support of laissez-faire economics and its corollary rejection of labor's right to organize.[11]

At the start of Henry Potter's life, the Protestant Episcopal Church was not a major force in American Protestantism. In the wake of the Revolutionary War, it had become marginalized because of its association with England and Anglicanism and its indifference or, among some, hostility to the Great Awakenings. At the start of the second quarter of the nineteenth century, it was preoccupied with internal disputes among High and Low Church parties, disputes that were only heightened by the impact of the Oxford Movement in the 1830s and 1840s. The slavery issue divided the Episcopal Church as it did other churches, but unlike others it never formally separated into northern and southern branches. Shortly before the war, however, the Episcopal Church began to show signs of vitality that by the last quarter of the century would propel it into leadership within the social awakening of American Christianity. Henry Potter's family heritage and early life are closely intertwined with the social and religious history of this period.[12]

The first of the Potters in North America was Robert Potter, who left England in the Puritan exodus and settled in Roxbury, Massachusetts, in 1634. He came under the influence of Anne Hutchinson and became "one of those who accepted her opinions, shared her condemnation, and followed her into exile." Among the charges against Hutchinson and her followers was that of propounding familism, "an assertion that love, not faith, is the most important part of the Christian religion. It was a protest against the prevailing emphasis on theological orthodoxy." Robert Potter removed to Portsmouth, Rhode Island, with other followers of Hutchinson. After further agitation, Potter and others were disenfranchised in 1642 and subsequently founded their own settlement. A later civic and ecclesiastical dispute led to Potter's imprisonment, but in the late 1640s and early 1650s he held various official positions in Warwick, Rhode Island, and "ended his life a peaceable citizen, dying in 1655."[13]

In subsequent generations the Potter family became members of the Society of Friends, an affiliation firmly established by the time of Joseph Potter, paternal grandfather of Henry Codman Potter. Born in 1757, Joseph Potter married Anna Knight and with her moved in 1792 to Beekman, New York, an area then being settled by Quakers. Joseph and Anna had nine children, the last of whom were Alonzo, born in 1800, and Horatio, in 1802; they were to become, respectively, the father and uncle of Henry Codman Potter. Joseph Potter was elected to the New York legislature in 1798 and in 1814 was visited in Albany by Eliphalet Nott, a Presbyterian minister and president of Union College. During that visit, Potter showed Nott a school paper written by his young son, Alonzo. Nott is reported to have responded: "I must have that boy; promise me that you will let me have him when he is old enough for college." Joseph Potter agreed, and Alonzo shortly commenced studies at Union College.[14]

Alonzo Potter graduated with highest honors from Union College in 1819, and thereupon he went to live and work with an older brother in Philadelphia. While there he became interested in the Episcopal Church. He was confirmed by Bishop William White, who had begun his own ministry in the years just prior to the American Revolution and who was responsible for the "astounding rescue of American Anglicanism" in the years after the Revolution.[15] Alonzo Potter decided to enter the church's ministry and undertook theological studies. In 1820 he was recalled to Union College to work as a tutor and was made professor of mathematics and natural philosophy in 1821. He continued to study theology and was ordained a priest of the Episcopal Church in 1824. He married Sarah Nott, daughter of Eliphalet Nott, in the same year. In 1826 he became rector of St. Paul's Church, Boston, where he remained until 1831, when he resigned for health reasons and returned to Union College as professor of moral and intellectual philosophy and political economy. During this period, in 1834, Sarah Nott Potter gave birth to their fifth child, Henry Codman Potter. In 1838 Alonzo Potter became Union College's vice president and was also elected, on separate occasions, bishop of the Eastern Diocese and of Western New York, both of which positions he declined. In 1839, while giving birth to their seventh child and only daughter, Sarah Nott Potter died. At her request, care of the children was entrusted to her first cousin, Sarah Benedict. Alonzo Potter married Sarah Benedict in 1840 and with her added another three children, all boys, to the family. In 1845 he accepted his election as bishop of Pennsylvania. Henry was five years old when his mother died and eleven when the family moved to Philadelphia.[16]

Although he had left the Society of Friends, Alonzo Potter retained a respect for his Quaker heritage. This respect he not only acknowledged but perhaps also embodied in his concern for both the bodily and spiritual welfare of the person and in his distaste for theological controversy and ecclesiastical partisanship. During Alonzo Potter's episcopate and early in Henry Potter's life, the Memorial Movement in the Episcopal Church reflected these dispositions. Several prominent clergy presented a memorial to the 1853 General Convention, the most important among them being William Augustus Muhlenberg. While rector of the Church of the Holy Communion, New York, Muhlenberg had founded St. Luke's

Hospital, the Sisterhood of the Holy Communion, and other charitable programs. Muhlenberg was one of the church's most distinctive figures of the time. Having come under the influence of the Oxford Movement in the 1830s, he later recognized the extremes to which it might lead and moderated his views. He described himself as an "Evangelical Catholic," holding Evangelical theological views while employing High Church ritual practices. Muhlenberg's charitable initiatives and conception of the church's social mission shaped the Episcopal Church in New York and, through the Memorial Movement and its supporters such as Alonzo Potter, the whole church.[17]

Alonzo Potter lived just long enough to see the end of the Civil War and the abolition of slavery, what he regarded as the "monster iniquity." He was a tireless worker, but his health suffered as a result. He died in July 1865, on a cruise that he had taken to recover from an illness. Having disembarked in Panama to consecrate a church there, he contracted malaria and died as the ship arrived at San Francisco.[18] William Reed Huntington, Henry Potter's successor as rector of Grace Church, New York, observed in a memorial address after Henry Potter's death in 1908 that one must look to Alonzo Potter in order to "rightly and deeply interpret" Henry Potter, for "it was as if the son had taken up the thread which fell from the father's hand at death and followed it as a clue."[19] Henry Potter also acknowledged his father's abiding influence on him. Speaking at the centennial of Union College in 1895, Henry Codman Potter described his father as having "sympathies as large and generous as were his intellectual endowments. The motto of Terence—'*Homo sum: humani nihil a me alienum*'—was as true of all that he was and did as if it had been his own."[20] This phrase, meaning "I am human: nothing human is alien to me," aptly describes the breadth of Alonzo Potter's sympathies, which included political economic theory, comprehensive ecclesiology, and the rationale and practice of religious charity. His practical concerns included women's work in the church, slavery and the "negro question," and temperance reform.

Alonzo Potter's younger brother, Horatio, followed him into the Episcopal Church and its ministry. He graduated from Union College in 1826, and, despite having no seminary training, was ordained in 1828. He worked as a parish priest for one year, then for five years as professor of mathematics and natural philosophy at Trinity College, Hartford. He became rector of St. Peter's Church, Albany, in 1833, where he served until elected bishop of New York in 1854.[21] Unlike his older brother, Horatio Potter was a High Church proponent, but like him he was generally moderate in his convictions and tolerant of some diversity in opinions and practices. He demonstrated no enthusiasm for the Memorial Movement and, in fact, clashed with Muhlenberg on cooperation with other Protestants and flexibility in worship. After the assassination of Abraham Lincoln, for example, Horatio Potter refused Muhlenberg's request to use, instead of one of those set out in the Book of Common Prayer, a prayer especially composed to mark the president's death in services at the Church of the Holy Communion. Nevertheless, he worked to strengthen financial support for mission churches in the diocese and praised Muhlenberg's charitable endeavors. He also wished to make the Episcopal Church accessible to the poor, to laboring classes, and to immigrants; and he cautiously supported the development of sisterhoods and deaconesses for the diocese's expanding extra-parochial work among these groups. Also during the episcopate of Horatio Potter the idea of a cathedral for New York took hold. He spoke in favor of it in an address to the diocesan convention, and in April 1874 a charter for it was granted by the State of New York, but little else was done until after his death. And he opposed the 1874 development of the Church Congress, issuing a pastoral letter against it and questioning the "use or safety of any general meetings of the clergy and laity for general debates on matters and things in general."[22]

Accounts of Henry Potter's youth suggest that he was a spirited child. Shortly after the family moved to Philadelphia, for example, he is said to have "suddenly developed a dislike for Latin declensions, and a habit of swearing, phenomena which were perhaps related," and to have been "helped over these hard places, mental and moral" by a summer of Latin tutoring and strict discipline. During this regimen he readily admitted to swearing, "having considered during the day that the satisfaction of using strong language was worth a whipping." He attended the Episcopal Academy, which his father had reopened in 1846, where his classmates included Henry George and R. Heber Newton. Upon completion of his studies, however, he neither enrolled at Union College, as had three of his older brothers, nor expressed any interest in the ministry. His interests were primarily social and he had "all the qualifications for successful secularity." At nineteen, he went into business and was employed at a Philadelphia wholesale dry-goods company.[23]

His life changed radically shortly after his twentieth birthday when, in August 1854, this self-described "wayward youth" had a conversion experience. Little is reported about the experience itself, but one important influence on it was M. A. de Wolfe Howe, rector of St. Luke's Church, Philadelphia. In a memorial sermon for Howe many years later, Henry Potter, referring to himself in the third person, noted the effect on him of a sermon Howe had preached many years earlier on the text "Young man, I say unto thee, Arise!"': "Its impression never left him—the clear, close, faithful message, searching, personal, awakening, starting in him a train of thought and emotion that, touched later by another hand, changed the whole current of his life." This "other hand" was Clara Boyd Jacobs, owner and general manager, by inheritance from her husband, of an iron mine and forge in Spring Grove, about fifty miles from Philadelphia. In addition to her business responsibilities there, "she instructed the children, advised their parents, dispensed medicines for their simple ailments, and . . . read the family prayers and had a Sunday School." While Alonzo Potter was bishop of Pennsylvania, the Potter family occasionally visited Spring Grove, and it was thus that Henry came into contact with her. "She was good as she was capable, pious, devout, living as naturally in the atmosphere of religion as in the pure air of the surrounding woods." Henry Potter credited Clara Jacobs with "turning his mind in the direction of religion." He also became engaged to her daughter, Eliza Jacobs.[24]

Potter began his studies at Virginia Theological Seminary in 1854, shortly after his conversion experience. His training for ministry thus occurred not only in the midst of continuing ecclesiastical tensions, but also of increasing political tensions that would shortly lead to the Civil War. One seminary classmate was Phillips Brooks, with whom he was to be a lifelong friend and later to participate in both political and ecclesiastical controversies. The growing conflict over slavery dominated the political context of this period. The Fugitive Slave Law, which in Alonzo Potter's view caused people in the North "to be converted into bloodhounds to run down the fugitives from bondage of the South," had been enacted in 1850. The Kansas-Nebraska Act, an abrogation of the Missouri Compromise allowing these territories to decide by popular vote whether to permit slavery within their boundaries, was enacted in 1854. The Republican party held its first national convention in Philadelphia in 1856, and in 1857 the Supreme Court issued its decision in the case of Dred Scott, ruling that slaves and their descendants had no standing in the federal courts. Virginia Seminary had students in approximately equal numbers from northern and southern states, and slavery was discussed and disputed among them.[25]

On one occasion during his seminary years, Potter was in New York on the Feast of the Epiphany and attended a service at the Church of the Holy Communion at which William Muhlenberg preached on missions. Potter later recalled, "I remember the vigor of that picturesque figure, a man whose enthusiasm was so pure, so vibrant, that it caught the young mind up into a state of interest in missions and made an impression never to be effaced." Potter completed his studies and graduated from Virginia Theological Seminary in 1857. Alonzo Potter ordained him to the diaconate on 27 May, and he began his ministry at Christ Church, Greensburgh, a mission church in a western Pennsylvania town with a population of about thirteen hundred. Charles Richards, another seminary classmate and friend, later wrote that Henry Potter, only recently removed from Philadelphia society, "found a surprising difference in the standards of life east and west of the Alleghenies. He had always thought that human nature was substantially the same everywhere, but now discovered that he could not speak the same language, nor appeal to the same motives which had been familiar to him. He must be made all over again before he could come in satisfactory touch with his people."[26]

In the fall of 1857 Henry Potter married Eliza Jacobs. Little of her is reported in the literature concerning Henry Potter, but Charles Richards described her as "a woman of strong character, outspoken, true, and with a keen sense of humor. She loved him with all her heart, and therefore was sensitive to any defects or weaknesses in the man she sought to idealize, and brave enough honestly to confront him with them. She was an invaluable wife, then and always." A letter to Henry from Alonzo Potter reinforces the impression that some viewed her largely in terms of her assistance to her husband's work. "She has great capacities for usefulness, and as she will feel very sensibly the absence of the large and lively circle at home, give her all the employment you can find in the Parish. . . . At the beginning of one's Ministry such help is especially important, that your time may not be too much frittered away in details. . . . This ought not to be so; and it would not if our profession . . . were less harassed by varieties of work much of which might be better done by Laymen and by the Pastor's wife." How Eliza Jacobs Potter regarded this conception of her purpose, or how Henry Potter regarded her, is not reported, but she did indeed participate in much of the work that constituted her husband's ministry.[27]

Potter's biographers' nearly exclusive focus on his public life has produced even less information about their children, but it is clear that Eliza Jacobs Potter bore and raised one son and five daughters. It is also clear that the Potters' family life was good, that Henry cared deeply for his children, and that they cared for and respected him. Writing later to her uncle, Frank Hunter Potter, Henry and Eliza's daughter Jane recalled

You asked for stories and happy recollections. Well, all the recollections are happy, and there were times of pure fun, full of the spirit of adventure and gaiety—in travels, in home life, in times of work and play. But as I look back these are not the times that made the deepest impression;

it was the way my father handled life—his skill with its technique—which always impressed me from my earliest childhood. . . . One could count on his love and kindness, on the wealth of his sympathy and large understanding and utter unselfishness, as surely as on the rising of the sun or the coming of the spring.

Her recollection also verifies the impression from accounts of Potter's public life that he was an extremely busy man. "I never remember a time when he was not overwhelmed with work, and from my earliest childhood I was conscious of the wonderful way he handled it." His work did not cause him to be a remote father. He liked to have the children in his study, kept scrap paper for them to draw on in his lower desk drawer, "and after the day was done used to romp with us and read us *Gulliver's Travels*." He let them play in the church "until one day a doll was found in the middle of the chancel during a Lenten service, and he had to conceal it in the sleeve of his surplice. After that he was forced to curtail our liberties." Jane also reported that her father disciplined the children by spanking, but only very rarely, as "the rest of his teaching of us was by the sheer force of his life and example." And she recalled that her father "was as full of fun as a child himself and loved to lead adventures, and was never happier than when taking us up the dark steeple ladder to the belfry of Grace Church, or teaching us to drive a fast and rather dangerous horse which he hired one summer for a very moderate sum because of its uncertain temper."[28]

In May 1859, after two years in Greensburgh, Potter became rector of St. John's Church in Troy, New York, which had been consecrated four years earlier by his uncle, Horatio Potter, in his second year as bishop of New York. During Henry Potter's tenure as rector there, the church's families increased from seventy to one hundred sixty and the communicants from one hundred fifty to three hundred five. Both Henry and Eliza Potter became involved in local charitable organizations. He worked with the Young Men's Christian Association and she became one of the founding trustees of the Children's Home Society, "the first corporate body composed entirely of women, which was legally constituted by the State Assembly to manage its own affairs."[29] The Potters remained in Troy until 1866 and from there witnessed the course of the Civil War. During this time Potter received two honorary degrees from Union College and declined several invitations to serve other churches.

In April 1866, however, he accepted a call to become assistant minister at Trinity Church, Boston. This position was in effect equivalent to that of rector, as Trinity was the church of the bishop, Manton Eastburn, who was occupied almost exclusively with diocesan business. An Evangelical, Eastburn had been bishop of Massachusetts since 1842 and was sixty-five years old when Potter came to Trinity. Shortly after beginning his brief tenure there, Potter returned to New York City after a trip to Europe and discovered that a seminary friend, Channing Moore Williams, was that morning at St. John's Chapel being consecrated as missionary bishop for China and Japan. Potter arrived in the middle of the service and was observed by Bishop John Williams of Connecticut, who then walked over to and conferred with Bishop Horatio Potter. Bishop Potter left his seat, walked to where his nephew was kneeling, leaned over the pew, and said "Henry, how would you like to be secretary of the House of Bishops?" Henry Potter held this position until his own consecration as bishop in 1883.[30] On Thanksgiving Day 1866, Potter addressed concerns of righteousness in political life in his sermon "Individual Responsibility to the Nation," which was subsequently published at the request of the congregation. This sermon was not Potter's only noteworthy service to Trinity Church: upon his departure to take up another position, he suggested that Trinity might find a suitable successor in his friend, Phillips Brooks.[31]

The Potters remained in Boston only two years. In April 1868, Henry Potter became rector of Grace Church, New York, and began a ministry in New York City that would last for forty years. His predecessor at Grace Church, Thomas House Taylor, had died eight months earlier and had been rector of the Low Church Grace since the year of Potter's birth. The congregation was wealthy, and Grace was considered the most fashionable of the city's Episcopal churches. The church relied on pew rents for its income, but during Taylor's tenure it had built two free chapels and initiated various mission activities. With a core of lay people already participating in the church's mission programs, and others constantly being recruited as well, Potter proceeded to develop a system of mission programs and organizations to minister to the "whole person," which, by the time he left Grace in 1883, addressed almost all aspects of human need. In 1870 Potter began planning for the construction of buildings suited to the needs of a modern institutional church. With the help of two substantial donations, and despite some setbacks, by 1882 four buildings had been completed for these purposes. Among them was a new Grace Chapel and adjacent hall, which was completed in 1876 and served as the hub of the church's programs. But it was not the buildings alone that increased. By 1883, the parish organizations had increased to sixteen, addressing a wide range of physical and spiritual needs.[32]

First expressed during the Panic of 1873–74, Potter's concern for the perils and proper stewardship of wealth reflects the economic location and consequent pastoral concerns of most members of the Grace Church congregation. In 1878 he warned that the possession of wealth "can benumb the conscience and brutalize the moral sense" but contended nevertheless that it "is not inconsistent with our Christianity nor alien from it."[33] Potter not only believed that the wealthy were responsible for using their resources to meet the needs of the poor; he also believed that they should do so in a way that decreased the dependence of the poor on help from others. He argued for the importance of discernment in charitable and philanthropic work in order to assure that those most in need received the assistance due them. While maintaining the need for some principle by which one might respond to requests for aid, Potter rejected the criterion of the "deserving poor." Potter's conviction of the necessity of charity properly implemented informed the manner in which the various parish organizations approached their work, leading to their emphasis on increasing self-sufficiency and decreasing pauperism.[34]

All these concerns were grounded in Potter's conception of Christianity's wider responsibilities to the world, and he regularly advocated the expansion of the church's programs to "reach and minister to the lowest and least cared for classes." His understanding of Christianity's mission to all human nature emphasized practical service to others: "Our Christianity must prove itself the helpful and saving power that it claims to be, or else it must get out of the way."[35] While rector at Grace Church, Potter sought to prove Christianity's helpful and saving power in part by preaching on issues such as the squalor of tenement housing, the scandal of child labor, the right of women to labor for self-support, the threats to Sunday observance, the evils of intemperance, and the neglect of those in prison. He also did so by participating in secular endeavors for human betterment, serving as a member of the jury for a model tenement design competition, on working committees and conferences of the State Charities Aid Association, and as a lifetime director of the American Colonization Society, which had been founded in 1816 for the purpose of settling freed blacks in Liberia.[36]

In September 1883, his health declining, Horatio Potter asked to be relieved of the administration of the diocese. The diocesan convention elected as assistant bishop Henry Codman Potter, who was consecrated in Grace Church the following month. Horatio Potter remained bishop of New York until his death four years later. On the evening of his consecration, Henry Potter visited the Midnight Mission of the Sisters of St. John the Baptist and the following day the prison on Blackwell's Island, indicating immediately his commitment to the mission work of the church.[37] He also quickly implemented new means or adapted earlier ones for this work, such as supporting the establishment of the Order of the Holy Cross in 1884 and the Advent Mission of 1885. As the former initiative had Anglo-Catholic associations and the latter Evangelical ones, Potter's support for these diverse approaches to the needs of the day also signaled his Broad Church inclination to employ whatever means might best meet those needs.[38]

The contemporary labor question featured prominently in both the work of the Order of the Holy Cross and the 1885 Advent Mission, reflecting the major social and economic changes of the mid-1880s and the emerging responses from a developing social gospel. Economist and Episcopal layperson Richard T. Ely founded the American Economic Association in 1885 to promote the study of German economics as an alternative to the prevailing Manchester economics; Congregationalists Lyman Abbott and Washington Gladden and Episcopalian R. Heber Newton were among its charter members. In the same year, Josiah Strong became pastor of Central Congregational Church, Cincinnati, and published *Our Country*. In June 1886 Walter Rauschenbusch became pastor of the Second German Baptist Church in the Hell's Kitchen district of New York. In May 1886 the Haymarket protests and resulting violence had provoked a groundswell of antianarchist and antilabor hysteria. In the pastoral letter he issued the week following Haymarket, Assistant Bishop Henry Potter called attention to the emerging "class conflict, whose proportions it is daily becoming more difficult to measure" but called upon the clergy to address the conflict's underlying issues and the responsibility of employers for causing and resolving the crisis. This letter signaled an important expansion of Potter's understanding of the nature of the social crisis and its potential solutions. It also represented a turning point in social Christianity's treatment of the demands of working people and the relation between labor and capital. Potter's letter stimulated discussion in the press, sermons on the labor problem in the churches, and as noted above, the formation the following year of the Church Association for the Advancement of the Interest of Labor. While not an early leader of CAIL, within a few years Potter's involvement increased.[39]

When Horatio Potter died in 1886, Henry Potter became bishop of New York, and his activities continued to show a catholicity of interests. In 1887 he delivered an address at Lambeth Palace commemorating the centennial of the organization of the Protestant Episcopal Church in the United States of America, and his *Addresses to Women Engaged in Church Work* was published. One week after the first meeting for CAIL, he presided at a meeting in the "interest of working men and women" at Chickering Hall. Late in that year and early the next, Potter participated in several meetings of the church's Commission for Church Work among Colored People and attended the annual meeting of the American Colonization Society. In early 1889 he met with the trustees of the proposed Cathedral of St. John the Divine to examine the architectural drawings that had been submitted. He worked to raise money for it, conceiving it as a free church and center for the mission work of the diocese, and presided when the cornerstone was laid in 1892. Potter's public appearances became less exclusively ecclesiastical during this time; for example, he spoke at Lehigh and Johns Hopkins Universities and offered prayers at a meeting of the American Association for the Advancement of Science and at the ceremony commemorating the centennial of the United States Constitution. Because of his oratorical skill, episcopal status, and social acceptability, Potter came to be ranked with Henry Ward Beecher and Lyman Abbott among the Protestant preachers of choice for major public functions.[40]

When in 1889 the time came to commemorate the centennial of the inauguration of George Washington, Potter was asked to provide the expected religious content at the public ceremonies. Benjamin Harrison, a Republican, was then president, having defeated Democrat Grover Cleveland in the previous election. Potter was a Republican, but disenchantment with political corruption had led him and other Mugwumps to vote for Cleveland in the 1884 election. In 1888 Potter voted for Harrison, but by the spring of 1889 he and many others were disappointed with the new administration's scant progress in reducing political patronage. Before an assembly at St. Paul's Chapel in New York that included the president and vice president, former presidents, and many other prominent national and local politicians, Potter delivered an address that praised Washington's integrity and implicitly but clearly criticized the dominant machine politics of the day. The press widely reported and debated Potter's remarks, and he became a national figure as a result of this timely plea for political righteousness.[41]

Two months after Potter's address at the Washington centennial, Andrew Carnegie's essay "Wealth" (later renamed and reprinted as "The Gospel of Wealth") appeared in the *North American Review*. Potter and Carnegie were probably already acquainted. Unlike some men of wealth, Carnegie cultivated cultural pretensions, and Potter had belonged to the city's leading cultural club, the Century Association, since 1868; Potter was also the association's president from 1894 to 1906, the first cleric to be elected to that position. In May 1891 Potter delivered an address at the dedication of Carnegie Hall in which he praised Carnegie's philanthropy. Also that month, the *North American Review* published Potter's

"Gospel for Wealth," a response to Carnegie's earlier essay, which Potter wrote at Carnegie's suggestion. Later that year Potter gave an address on the stewardship of wealth to the New York Chamber of Commerce.[42] The 1892 steel workers' strike against the Carnegie, Phipps, and Company plant in Homestead, Pennsylvania, began the third economic crisis of the late 1800s, a crisis that included the financial panic of 1893 and culminated in the Pullman Strike of 1894. From this period on, economic questions dominated Potter's activities. In 1892 he became an honorary vice president of CAIL and presided at and addressed a meeting of the Christian Social Union in Baltimore. In the following year he began mediating labor disputes through CAIL's Committee on Mediation and Conciliation, formed as a panel to which labor disputes could be referred with the consent of both employees and employer. In 1894 its membership was expanded and its name changed to the New York Council of Mediation and Conciliation. In this form the council continued its work throughout the 1890s, and Potter's work with CAIL continued and expanded in subsequent years.[43]

While Potter's work increasingly focused on the alienation of labor and capital, he did not neglect other concerns. In May 1892 *The Forum* published his article "The Significance of the American Cathedral," in which he articulated his rationale for the proposed Cathedral of St. John the Divine. This rationale included, among other arguments, the role of a free church, as he envisioned the cathedral, in alleviating class alienation. And in December of that year, he presided at the laying of the cornerstone for the cathedral. Potter was also elected president of the American Colonization Society in January 1892. The society was facing a crisis of mission and Potter, after he had returned from Europe and accepted the election, attempted to renew it and reorient its activities. He remained active in the society through 1896, but his efforts were unsuccessful.[44] His concern for political righteousness also continued unabated, and in the 1890s and early 1900s focused particularly on municipal government. He addressed civic reform organizations such as the City Club, the Good Government Club, and the City Vigilance League, and on Thanksgiving Day 1894 he delivered a sermon of public gratitude after the reform victory over New York's Tammany Hall political machine in the recent mayoral election. Potter would also later play a decisive role in the successful 1901 anti-Tammany campaign, in part because of his close association with the Stanton Street Mission in the city's east side tenement district.[45]

As the dire social consequences of the Panic of 1873 had caused Potter to address the question of the proper methods of providing charitable relief, so too did the consequences of the Panic of 1893. From 1895 to

1898, Potter made several addresses on this topic, particularly to the Charity Organization Society. Josephine Shaw Lowell had founded the society in 1882 to systematize the New York City's fragmented charitable programs, provide a means of distinguishing those truly in need from those who were not and assist those in need in attaining self-sufficiency. The society's aims, then, were congenial to Potter's own views, and he continued to argue against indiscriminate relief and for expanded programs of education and employment. In the 1890s he began, however, to base his argument not simply on proper stewardship but also on the demands of justice and on the need to alleviate class alienation.[46]

In 1897 Potter's *Scholar and the State* was published, which included his address at the centennial of the inauguration of George Washington and several other essays and addresses. It received wide attention and favorable reviews and renewed Potter's national stature as a social critic. In the previous year he had delivered an address on civil service reform, continuing his earlier critique of patronage appointments to government posts. In 1895 he criticized the Cleveland administration for interference in the boundary dispute between Venezuela and British Guiana and two years later gave a public address on international arbitration.[47] Before the 1898 Spanish-American War and even after what he regarded as the "colossal blunder" of American annexation of the Philippines, Potter publicly argued against American territorial expansion on the grounds that the country was neither practically prepared to assume government of the Philippines nor morally justified in doing so. Acknowledging the country's additional lands, however, the General Convention of 1898 established the Commission on the Increased Responsibilities of the Church and appointed Potter to it. In the following year he publicly supported the anti-imperialist Continental League and delivered an address against imperialism at the meeting of the Church Congress. At the end of 1899, on behalf of the Commission on the Increased Responsibilities of the Church, he embarked on a fact-finding mission that took him to Hawaii, the Philippines, Japan, and India. By the time he returned he had altered his position, arguing—to the great and vocal dismay of his anti-imperialist friends—that although the annexation of the islands was a blunder, it was the country's duty to execute its responsibilities honorably.[48]

Shortly after returning in March 1900 from his travels in Asia and the Pacific, Potter was faced with an egregious case of civic corruption. In the late summer of 1900 Robert Paddock, vicar of the Cathedral Mission in Stanton Street, rescued a fourteen-year-old girl from a brothel to which she had been taken by force. Receiving abuse rather than aid from the police, Paddock reported the incident to Bishop Potter, who investigated the matter and presented it to the diocesan convention in September. With the convention's approval, Potter investigated further and wrote a letter to the New York mayor, a Tammany Hall functionary, Robert Van Wyck. Potter's letter, in which he decried the outrages visited upon the women and children of New York's Lower East Side, was printed in newspapers throughout the country as well as the city. One week later Potter preached the sermon "God and the City" in a service at St. Paul's Chapel that, according to the *New York Times,* was "crowded to the doors" with men and women of diverse classes and stations. Although he declined to assume a formal leadership role in the resulting reform campaign, Potter supported and spoke in favor of the various reform efforts that led to the election of reform candidate Seth Low as mayor of New York in 1901.[49] On the same day and same page that the *Times* quoted Potter's prediction of Seth Low's victory in the upcoming election, it also quoted his response to President Theodore Roosevelt's recent dinner with Booker T. Washington, in which Potter noted that Washington had been "on a number of occasions a guest at my table." Potter seems to have become interested in Washington's work at about this time, perhaps after he became disillusioned with the approach of the American Colonization Society. Washington later spoke warmly of Potter in a memorial address he delivered after Potter's death.[50]

Shortly before the municipal election, in late June 1901, Eliza Jacobs Potter died. She had been ill for some time but, as Hodges notes, became "alarmingly worse" on the evening of 29 June. Henry Potter was called away from a celebration of the fiftieth anniversary of the ordination of five New York priests to be with her, and she died that night. As Hodges explains, "It was no longer the custom, as in the days of the Bishop's father, to publish affectionate appreciations of the departed members of one's family. Bishop Potter endured his grief in silence." Her funeral was held on 2 July at Grace Church, which was "crowded to utmost capacity"; among those attending, "the poor were there in large numbers, and their sorrow was genuine and sincere."[51] In October 1902, to the apparent surprise of many, Henry Potter married Elizabeth Corning Clark, a wealthy widow who had financially supported some of his episcopally initiated mission enterprises and financed the construction and operation of an East Side settlement house. Some newspapers criticized Potter for his remarriage, but it is not clear whether they took offense at Mrs. Clark's wealth or at the fact of a bishop remarrying.[52]

Potter also faced criticism for his views on temperance at this time. In an 1878 address he had said that he was a total abstainer, but he seems to have become a temperate drinker later. He was a founding member of the Church Temperance Society, an Episcopal alliance of total abstainers and temperate drinkers, and in 1893 he became a member of New York's Committee of Fifty on the Drink Problem. In early 1899, speaking at a benefit for the Church Temperance Society's proposed saloon substitute, the Squirrel Inn, Potter observed that the saloon was a social necessity and, as he had in earlier addresses on temperance, argued that working people deserved places of recreation just a surely as people of wealth had their private clubs. His remarks were quoted and misquoted in the press; prohibitionists took offense and criticized him, and advocates of "rational temperance reform" defended him. Potter was undaunted, however, and in a December 1901 speech to the Church Club, in his 1902 address to the diocesan convention, and in remarks he made in 1904 while presiding at the dedication of a reformed saloon, the Subway Tavern, he maintained that places of recreation that embodied what was good in the saloon were necessary to combat what was evil in it.[53]

Potter's involvement in the relations between labor and capital intensified further in the last years of the nineteenth and early years of the twentieth century. He continued his work with CAIL and the New York Council of Mediation and Conciliation. On the CAIL Labor Sunday in May 1898, he preached on the application of Christian principles to the labor question. He maintained that the interests of labor and capital were identical, as the two are dependent on each other, thus assuming labor's equality with capital and right to organize, and that the trade union movement had made a great contribution toward educating capital and the public on this point.[54] Shortly after this sermon, he became involved with another organization with a similar orientation to labor, the National Civic Federation, which had been formed by the reforming journalist Ralph Easley. Easley had noticed Potter by May 1898. In January 1901 Potter joined a National Civic Federation committee on industrial conciliation with representatives of capital, labor, and the general public. The federation became involved in mediating, with mixed success, several major labor disputes, including the steel strike of 1901 and the anthracite coal strike of 1902–3. Potter played a key role in the attempts to settle these strikes, served on the federation's executive committee until his death, and regularly participated in its meetings and conferences.[55] In addition to such practical activity, Potter also most completely expressed his views on the relations of labor and capital. In a series of addresses delivered at Kenyon College in November 1901, subsequently at Yale University in April 1902, and published later in 1902 as *The Citizen in His Relation to the Industrial Situation,* Potter outlined the current industrial situation and the various responsibilities of citizens, corporations, and the state. He argued that the church was rightly concerned with economic matters and that in Christianity would be found the solution to the labor question. He supported the organization of labor as the only means of assuring that employers would give workers their due and trade unionism as invaluable in providing training in self-government. He held that communism was untenable, but also that all laissez-faire economic theories were "of the devil, and deserve, as Jesus did with devils, to be cast out."[56]

In these same years Potter also helped to institutionalize the social gospel within the Episcopal Church. During the 1901 General Convention, he attended and addressed a mass meeting convened by CAIL, shortly after which the convention passed a resolution forming the Joint Commission on the Relations of Capital and Labor. Potter was appointed to the commission and designated its chairman, and he wrote and presented its report to the next General Convention in 1904. During Potter's tenure as chair, the General Convention voted in 1904 to continue the joint commission and in 1907 to make it permanent. In 1907 CAIL formally recommended to the General Convention, through Potter, the establishment of diocesan social service committees. That year's report of the joint commission, presented by Potter, also made this recommendation so that the church's various social service efforts might be better coordinated. Shortly thereafter, in November 1907, the Convention of the Diocese of New York established its Social Service Commission, with Bishop Potter as its chair.[57]

In 1902, having suffered a collapse about one week after completing his Yale lectures, Potter requested assistance in fulfilling his manifold responsibilities. The election for an assistant bishop at the diocesan convention the following year included three candidates. On the first ballot the convention elected David Hummel Greer, rector of St. Bartholomew's Church. Potter gave Greer responsibility for visitations to the city churches and retained that for the rural churches, but he did not immediately decrease his activities in other areas. His most important work with the Joint Commission on the Relations of Capital and Labor followed, and he continued his involvement with the National Civic Federation. During the next few years he also delivered addresses on temperance, child labor, municipal reform, international arbitration, and labor and capital.[58]

In October 1906 Potter's third daughter, Lena, then aged 44 and married to businessman Winthrop Cowdin, committed suicide after a year as a patient at a private sanitarium in Cromwell, New York. According to a contemporary report, she had been ill with "necrosis of the jaw" since the time of the Spanish-American War, during which she had organized a group of nurses to work with the Red Cross in Cuba. In the months preceding her death, the cancer had spread to and affected her brain so that "this in conjunction with her suffering prompted her to take her life."[59] As in the case of the death of Eliza Jacobs Potter, Henry Potter seems to have borne this grief privately.

In early 1907 Potter published three articles on women and domesticity in *Harper's Bazar*, and in early 1908 he addressed the New York Women's Trade Schools and the Women's Press Club. He presided at the April 1907 Peace Congress held at Carnegie Hall, as well as at a January 1908 meeting there concerning constitutional government in Russia. In March and April 1908 he presided at the first meetings of the New York Diocesan Social Service Committee. Potter intended to attend the Church Congress in June and the Lambeth Conference in July 1908, but in May he suffered another collapse and instead withdrew to convalesce to the summer home in Cooperstown, New York, owned by Elizabeth Clark Potter. His health, however, did not return. He was critically ill, suffering from arteriosclerosis, an embolism in his right leg, and a "prolonged attack of stomach and liver trouble" due to overwork. He died on 21 July. Family and friends attended a private funeral in Cooperstown, after which Potter's body lay in state at Trinity Church in New York. On 20 October, the twenty-fifth anniversary of his consecration as bishop, a public funeral was held at Grace Church and his body was interred in the crypt of the Cathedral of St. John the Divine. His body was later moved to the Cathedral's Chapel of St. James; the construction was funded by a gift from Elizabeth Clark Potter. She died on 4 March 1909, less than a year after Henry Potter's death.[60]

Numerous memorial services were held and memorial essays published for Henry Codman Potter. Those who paid tribute to Potter—for example, William Reed Huntington, John Mitchell, Booker T. Washington, Seth Low—represented the broad range of his interests and activities. Friends associated with the City and Suburban Homes Company raised money for construction of two model tenements known as the Bishop Potter Memorial.[61] In his address to the 1908 New York diocesan convention, Bishop David Hummel Greer honored Potter and characterized his significance, maintaining that "whosoever hereafter shall undertake to tell the story of the Church for the past forty years, not only in this city and this Diocese, but elsewhere in the land, and throughout the whole scope and compass of its work, must of necessity tell the story of his life, as that of one of the leading and conspicuous figures in it."[62]

1   A Many-Sided Mission

In 1857, twenty-three years old and the son of the Evangelical bishop of Pennsylvania and nephew of the High Church bishop of New York, Henry Potter began his ministry not in an established urban congregation in Philadelphia but at Christ Church, Greensburgh, a mission church in a small western Pennsylvania town.[1] After the American Revolution the Low Church and High Church parties had achieved a reasonable working relationship, upon which the survival of the beleaguered church depended. By the second decade of the nineteenth century the Evangelical movement in the Church of England and the dominant evangelicalism of American Protestantism, however, had generated an Evangelical party that had begun to displace the older Low Church party, offer an alternative vision of the place of the church in the new American republic, and initiate a rejuvenation of the Episcopal Church. In spite of the resistance of many Episcopalians to evangelical enthusiasm, revivalism, and sectarianism, by 1820 the Evangelical party was playing a major role in the church and by 1844 it included two-thirds of Episcopal clergy. Episcopal Evangelicals sought to be both evangelical and episcopal, to foster true religion within the forms and practices of the Episcopal Church. They endeavored to cooperate with High Churchmen on matters of common concern while working to keep the church faithful to its Reformation heritage; and they sought to cooperate with other evangelical Protestants while retaining their loyalty to orderly worship and episcopal church governance. Through both disagreements and compromises, by the 1830s the two parties were working together in relative peace. The 1833 start of the Oxford Movement, however, began a process that would break that peace. Many Evangelicals were initially favorably disposed to the movement because of its call for religious renewal. With the publication of the first *Tracts for the Times*, however, by 1837 most began to see the movement's threat to their understanding of the church. As more *Tracts* appeared, as John Henry Newman and others renounced Anglicanism and joined the Roman Catholic Church, and as the movement inspired an increasing emphasis on ritual and the development of the Anglo-Catholic party, Evangelical fears were confirmed.

When Henry Potter began his ministry shortly after midcentury, the influence of the Evangelical party was declining, but its members continued the contest for the identity of the Episcopal Church for another twenty-five years. Evangelicalism was itself transformed by that contest, as well as by the contemporary challenges of the Civil War and abolition, industrialization and urbanization, with consequences including the fracturing of Evangelicalism's moderate and radical wings, the 1873 schism that produced the Reformed Episcopal Church, and the subsequent disappearance of the Evangelical party from the Episcopal Church. Such consequences may be taken as evidence that Evangelicalism lost the contest for Episcopal identity, but the decreasing number of those who considered themselves Evangelical nevertheless maintained important elements of antebellum Evangelicalism even as they moved nearer to fundamentalism by the end of the century. More important for the emerging postwar identity of the Episcopal Church, key elements and methods of antebellum Evangelicalism were also maintained by the growing number of those against whom radical Evangelicals struggled during this time—members of the Broad Church movement. The Evangelical party lost the contest for the identity of the Episcopal Church and, in the process, ceased to be a significant factor in that struggle, but after the Civil War the Broad Church movement picked up some of the Evangelical party's main emphases and worked them into a new synthesis that Broad Church adherents regarded as responsive to the emerging needs of the day. While radical Evangelicals regarded the Broad Church movement and its associated theological liberalism as a threat to Reformation orthodoxy, many moderate Evangelicals consciously relied on evangelical traditions and became key leaders in the development of the new synthesis and early members of the Broad Church movement. Henry Codman Potter retained and reinterpreted the Evangelicalism of Alonzo Potter, two key elements of which were, first, the vision of a comprehensive church and, second, the centrality of the practical application of the Christian faith.[2]

Toward a Comprehensive Church

Alonzo Potter was decidedly Evangelical, but not dogmatically so. He began his episcopate in the Diocese of Pennsylvania in 1845 in the midst of the disputes about Tractarianism and in the same year as John Henry Newman's departure to the Roman Catholic Church. Unlike High Churchmen and Anglo-Catholics for whom salvation was mediated primarily by the church and its rituals and forms, for Evangelicals salvation was mediated primarily by faith, conversion, and holy living. High Churchmen and Anglo-Catholics appealed not only to the Bible but also to various parts of Christian tradition for authority for their beliefs and practices, but Evangelicals maintained the Reformation principle of *sola scriptura.* Until the 1870s, Episcopal Evangelicalism included within itself both moderates and radicals. The radicals tended toward sectarianism in polity and perfectionism in faith and practice while the moderates valued loyalty to and the unity of the Episcopal Church and professed tolerance of diverse beliefs and practices. In the antebellum period Evangelical millennialism contained both premillennial and postmillennial elements. After the war, however, radicals embraced premillennialism more exclusively, looking to Christ's return to establish God's reign on earth, while moderates shifted more toward postmillennialism and continued to expect the growth of righteousness on earth until the start of Christ's millennial reign.[3]

The Diocese of Pennsylvania had its share of partisans in the disputes about Tractarianism. In his first addresses to the diocesan convention, Alonzo Potter warned against the dangers of extreme ecclesiasticism and articulated principles for a comprehensive ecclesiology tolerant of diversities of belief and practice. In 1847 he argued that the church must "recognize practically the broad and comprehensive principles on which the Reformation and re-organization of the Anglican Church were conducted, and thus be tolerant of diversities in doctrine and practice which always prevailed, and which are not likely to disappear except before the fires of a ruthless intolerance."[4] In the years that followed, he developed his view of a comprehensive church further. In an 1854 letter to Henry, then studying at Virginia Theology Seminary, Alonzo Potter cautioned his son on two points: first, "lest you crowd too many studies in each day, a course dangerous to health of body and health of mind"; and, second,

> Lest the type of your theology and piety be narrow. A tendency to narrowness, to party views and censorious judgment of those who differ from us, is one of the dangers of our profession, and I have noticed more of it

than I could wish among the graduates of [General Theological Seminary]. There are few things which I would cultivate more assiduously and anxiously than the ability to see and appreciate good in all classes of men, as far as they have it, and to use charity in our surmises respecting their motives. All this I hold to be perfectly consistent with fixed opinions and unwavering loyalty to them.[5]

And in an 1857 essay entitled "Church Comprehension and Church Unity," he maintained:

> The theory of our Church recognizes the cardinal fact that large diversities of opinion are compatible with loyalty to a common Saviour. It calls us to consider Christianity as a *life,* not as a mere collection of *dogmas;* it asks how men live, soberly or sensually, righteously or unrighteously, godly or ungodly, rather than what in all particulars, speculative as well as practical, they may happen to think. She does not underrate the importance of the faith once delivered to the saints, but she would secure it by moral rather than by intellectual means, by proper culture and training in the duties of life, and in the hopes and services of religion, rather than through theological controversies.
>
> Would that her practice might in every respect accord with her theory![6]

Like many of his evangelical contemporaries in the Episcopal Church as well as in others, Alonzo Potter's vision of a comprehensive church thus entailed not only a tolerance of diversity in theological belief and liturgical practice, but also the primacy of the practical embodiment of Christian convictions in personal and institutional life.

In contemporary American Protestantism similar views were being expressed, notably in the comprehensive ecclesiology articulated by Horace Bushnell. By the 1840s, New England Protestantism had been assailed by three divisive theological conflicts revolving around issues of the Trinity, the person of Christ, human depravity, and the atonement. The first of these, waged by Congregationalist liberals and conservatives in the late eighteenth and early nineteenth centuries, led to the liberals' control of Harvard College, the conservatives' establishment of Andover Theological Seminary, and ultimately the formation of a new denomination allied with Unitarianism. In the late 1820s, the second conflict broke out over interpretations of human depravity between Congregationalists Nathaniel Taylor and Bennet Tyler; this dispute peaked in the early 1830s while Bushnell was a student at Yale Divinity School and was still raging as he began his ministry after graduation. And in the 1830s and 1840s the work of transcendentalists Ralph Waldo Emerson and Theodore Parker, which rejected some basic elements of Unitarian belief at that time, provoked the third conflict.[7]

In the midst of bitter Congregationalist and Unitarian partisan disputes and of the particular Taylorite/Tylerite divisions in his own congregation, in the 1830s Bushnell began to advocate a "comprehensive method" for uniting the church that assumed that both sides of the dispute contained elements of truth and error. He first published the principles for this method in 1848 in his essay "Christian Comprehensiveness." In this essay, relying on the work of French philosopher Victor Cousin and illustrating his case with examples from Christian history, he sought "to show that all the Christian truths stand in opposites, or extremes that need to be comprehended" in a broader, deeper understanding of Christian truth. Citing some of the more apparently irreconcilable opposites of competing Christian discourses, he argued: "Let Calvinism take in Arminianism, Arminianism Calvinism; let decrees take in contingency, contingency decrees; faith take in works, and works faith; the old take in the new, and the new the old—not doubting that we shall be as much wiser as we are more comprehensive, as much closer to unity as we have more of the truth."[8]

Alonzo Potter had also begun articulating principles for a comprehensive ecclesiology not later than 1847, the year before Bushnell's essay was published. Perhaps Bushnell's work reinforced the elder Potter's later statements on comprehensive ecclesiology, but it seems not to have been the source of those views. Alonzo Potter may not have been aware of and influenced by Bushnell's work, but Henry Codman Potter certainly was at least by the time he began his work at Grace Church in 1868. At various points, Henry Potter favorably cited Bushnell on Christian nurture, Anglo-Saxon superiority, and the importance of recreation for human well-being, but nowhere did he cite Bushnell on Christian comprehensiveness. On this matter his primary influence seems to have been Alonzo Potter. It seems likely, then, that by midcentury many in white American Protestant churches had become disillusioned with various doctrinal, liturgical, and ecclesiastical squabbles. Based on their common experiences in their diverse denominations, they may have independently come to share convictions about the importance of comprehensiveness. For example, William Sparrow, a member of the faculty at Virginia Seminary where Potter and Phillips Brooks were students in the mid-1850s, taught that Christians should "eschew all dogmatic questions, and ecclesiastical questions, and all other questions that might call attention" from the person of Christ.[9] Bushnell, then, may simply have given persuasive expression to views already widely held by the time his writings on comprehensive ecclesiology were published. Nevertheless, as Bushnell's influence on many church leaders of Henry Potter's generation was great and as Potter provides evidence of Bushnell's influence on him in other matters, it seems likely that Bushnell's views on Christian comprehensiveness reinforced the comprehensive ecclesiology advocated by Alonzo Potter and other Evangelicals of his generation and provided a wider theological justification for it within American Protestantism.

Alonzo Potter expressed his vision of a comprehensive church at a time when the Evangelical party was on the defensive in its struggles with Tractarianism. This vision may have been, in part, one element of the broader strategy to secure a place for Evangelical belief and practice within the Episcopal Church. Nevertheless, it also reflected the growing commitment of many American evangelicals to tolerance of diversity as an alternative to the theological and ecclesiastical partisanship that threatened the peace and unity of the churches. Within the Episcopal Church, as seen in Alonzo Potter's appeal to the "broad and comprehensive principles" of Anglicanism and earlier in the Low Churchmanship of William White, this vision also expressed the sense in which for at least moderate Evangelicals, Episcopal identity itself required such tolerance of diversity. The true Episcopal Church was a comprehensive church.[10]

Among the most significant contributions to the Evangelical vision for a comprehensive church was the memorial, drafted by William Augustus Muhlenberg, presented at the 1853 General Convention. In a book published near the end of the century, Henry Codman Potter described Muhlenberg as "the most picturesque and original figure in the history of our American Christianity." Potter's assessment may exaggerate Muhlenberg's importance for American Christianity, but it does accurately reflect his importance for Potter as "the man who more than any other, except his own father, was the pattern of his ministry."[11] Muhlenberg was raised in a wealthy Lutheran family in Philadelphia but, because the local Lutheran church for a time refused to offer services in English, he and his siblings attended the Episcopal United Parish whose rector was Bishop William White. Muhlenberg greatly admired White, who ordained him to the diaconate in 1817 and to the priesthood in 1820. From early in his ministry, at first with White at the United Parish, Muhlenberg was interested in liturgical, educational, and humanitarian reform. His fundamental religious orientation was Evangelical, but he was sympathetic to the Oxford Movement in its early years and throughout the partisan controversies he maintained friendships with colleagues of all parties.[12]

In 1845 he became pastor of the Church of the Holy Communion in New York City, the construction of which had been financed by his sister in order to provide a venue where he might put in practice his commitment to free churches, his interest in liturgical reform, and his vision for the church's wider social ministry. His innovations in ritual in the worship at Holy Communion led some who did not know him well to conclude that he was a Tractarian, but the breadth of his interests and activities soon demonstrated that he fit within no contemporary party. He was best described in his own term as an Evangelical Catholic. Holy Communion was not only a free church, with no rented pews, but with programs that included a dispensary, an infirmary, an employment agency, and prison and hospital visitation; it was also one of the earliest examples of what later came to be called an institutional church. Muhlenberg established in 1845 the Sisterhood of the Holy Communion to undertake the church's educational and health work, and in 1858 St. Luke's Hospital, which was initially operated by the sisterhood. In 1851 he also began publication of a newspaper, the *Evangelical Catholic*, to provide a forum for nonpartisan discussion of theological and ecclesiastical issues and reporting on "matters of Practical Christianity," namely, the domestic missions and charitable work that he regarded as central to the church's work and unity. One unsigned article, likely by Muhlenberg, reported favorably on the growth of the Broad Church movement in England and prophesied: "The exclusive, the self-satisfied, will stand by their old favorite formulas on the one side and on the other, while the fresher stream of life in the Church will sweep by in its force and leave them 'High and Dry' or 'Low and Slow.'" Although it ceased publication after only two and one-half years, the *Evangelical Catholic* promoted the Evangelical vision of a comprehensive church that would shortly lead to the development of the Broad Church movement in the Episcopal Church.[13]

The memorial to the 1853 General Convention, drafted by Muhlenberg, was perhaps his most important expression of church comprehensiveness. Twelve Evangelical or Low Church clergy signed it without qualification and five High Church clergy signed it with some reservations, and together they presented it to the House of Bishops. Against the background of the dramatic successes of revivals and reform societies of other Protestant churches from the 1820s through the 1840s, and the ecclesiastical partisanship of the 1840s that had impeded the growth and threatened the unity of the Episcopal Church, the memorial called the church's attention to the "great moral and social necessities of the day" and asked whether

the period has not arrived for the adoption of measures, to meet these exigencies of the times, more comprehensive than any yet provided in our ecclesiastical system: in other words, whether the Protestant Episcopal Church, with only her present canonical means and appliances, her fixed and invariable modes of public worship and her traditional customs and usages, is competent to the work of preaching and dispensing the Gospel to all sorts and conditions of men, and so adequate to do the work of the Lord in this land and in this age?

The memorialists answered their own question negatively and suggested that the Episcopal Church could be made more competent for this work by a more flexible approach to its ministry, one by which the Episcopal Church would ordain not only its own members but also other Protestants "who could not bring themselves to conform in all particulars to our prescriptions and customs, but yet sound in the faith, and who, having the gifts of preachers and pastors, would be able ministers of the New Testament." But the "ultimate design" of the memorial, which such flexibility in ordination was intended to serve, was for the House of Bishops to take steps to move the church toward "some ecclesiastical system, broader and more comprehensive than that which you [the bishops] now administer, surrounding and including the Protestant Episcopal Church as it now is, leaving that Church untouched, identical with that Church in all its great principles, yet providing for as much freedom in opinion, discipline and worship as is compatible with the essential Faith and order of the Gospel." Finally, they asked that their concerns be referred to a commission for further consideration.[14] After debate, the House of Bishops formed the requested commission to study the memorial and report at the next General Convention. Alonzo Potter, who supported the memorial in the debate on the floor, was appointed to the commission. He worked diligently to advance the memorial's cause in the Episcopal Church, drafting the detailed questionnaire distributed to clergy in the Episcopal Church and other churches, and collating and publishing their responses. M. A. de Wolfe Howe (who signed the memorial and later wrote Alonzo Potter's biography) described Potter as one of the Memorial Movement's "earliest, most efficient and most liberal friends." In the three years following the 1853 General Convention, Potter's work and Muhlenberg's publications clarified and expanded the concerns behind the memorial, demonstrating the relationship between the greater flexibility in worship, ministry, and methods it advocated to the broader mission of ministering to poor and working people.[15]

Writing almost twenty years later about the importance of the memorial, Howe pointed to "that revival which dates from 1853, and which places the Episcopal Church in the forefront of those Christian bodies that are abroad, under the Master's mandate, in the highways and hedges, with the sweet constraint of Divine love compelling as many as they find to come in to the marriage-feast." Some later historians of the Episcopal

Church have tended to confirm this view.[16] More recent studies, however, argue that the memorial failed, particularly as an attempt to secure a unity of American evangelicals, and correctly observe that its only direct concrete consequence was the church's formation of the standing Commission on Church Unity that had little real authority. The memorial also failed as a strategy to secure greater liberty for Evangelical methods and to thwart the spread of Tractarian beliefs and practices.[17] Nevertheless, the Memorial Movement signaled a turning point in the Episcopal Church's efforts to respond to the needs of the time. The revival of the Episcopal Church to which Howe referred did in fact occur, and in the Diocese of Pennsylvania Alonzo Potter continued to be in the forefront of that revival, initiating new programs and establishing new institutions to make the Episcopal Church "competent to the work of preaching and dispensing the Gospel to all sorts and conditions" of people. He supported the development of domestic and foreign missions and the revival of nonclerical ministries such as deacons, deaconesses, and sisterhoods. Potter also initiated various programs and institutions for education, particularly religious instruction for young men and women. He was instrumental in the establishment of the Hospital of the Protestant Episcopal Church in Philadelphia; its program for "training of nurses was engrafted at his suggestion, and the entire system of organized female effort for the spiritual and temporal relief of the suffering peculiarly his own."[18]

Ultimately, in spite of the lack of formal action by the church's General Convention, the memorial led to liberalized liturgical practice, increased ecumenical dialogue, and the implementation of new means of reaching those outside the church and meeting their needs, whether spiritual or physical. Through his example and his influence on the next generation of church leaders, Muhlenberg also helped lay the foundation for the development of the American Broad Church movement and the social awakening of the Episcopal Church. As Alvin Skardon argues:

> Many of Muhlenberg's activities qualify him as a pioneer of the social Gospel but his influence is broader. . . . The fact that his activities were centered in New York, then the center of the church as well as of the secular affairs of the nation, made him an influence throughout the entire country. And this influence was strengthened by the manner in which the memorial was presented, the questionnaire sent out, and the ensuing controversy conducted. But his most notable achievement was that he profoundly influenced a group of younger men who were to play an important part in the life of the Episcopal church in the years after the Civil War. He left behind no party in the church nor any group in-

doctrinated with partisan principles. The men whom he influenced were instead imbued with his concern for social justice and his belief in the comprehensive character of the church.[19]

For Henry Codman Potter and the Episcopal Church, the 1853 memorial was a primary channel by which antebellum Evangelical convictions flowed to the changing context of the postwar period. Of course, as Potter and his contemporaries applied these convictions in this changing context, the character of those convictions shifted and developed in response to the new needs. Nevertheless, the conviction to engage the evils of the postwar social order remained fundamentally continuous with that of antebellum Evangelicalism. Henry Codman Potter employed the vision of the Memorial Movement throughout his work. As minister at St. John's Church, Troy, he began to demonstrate a concern for ministry to the whole person that flowered in his ministry at Grace Church, New York. Later, as bishop of New York, he continued to heed the memorial's call for the "adoption of measures, to meet these exigencies of the times," during times when some of the same exigencies prevailed and some new exigencies had emerged.[20]

While at Grace Church, he also indicated his commitment to a comprehensive church by attending, with Phillips Brooks, Bishop Thomas Clark, and others, the May 1874 planning meeting for the American Church Congress. Modeled on the English organization of the same name, the Church Congress was conceived as a forum in which clergy and laity could freely discuss matters of concern in church and society. This freedom of discussion among persons from various church parties reflected the program of the Broad Church movement. With immediate antecedents in the work of F. D. Maurice in England and William Muhlenberg in the United States, the Broad Church movement was characterized by its emphasis on the practical work of the church, tolerance of diverse theological beliefs and liturgical practices, and vigorous pursuit of religious truth. As a result, it helped shift the Episcopal Church's attention from partisan disputes among those within to addressing the manifold needs of those without. Although not all its proponents were social gospelers, their general acceptance and advocacy of social Christianity contributed greatly to its spread in the Episcopal Church and, as a result of the Episcopal Church's leadership, more widely in American Protestantism. Although members of various church parties presented papers and participated in its discussions, the Church Congress was, in effect, both a product of and a platform for the Broad Church movement. Members of the Broad Church movement such as Phillips Brooks, William Reed Huntington, W. S. Rainsford, and Edward A. Washburn constituted the majority of the leadership of the Congress, particularly in its early years. Probably out of deference to Bishop Horatio Potter's opposition to the formation of the Church Congress, however, Henry Potter did not attend its first meeting in New York in 1874 and did not play a prominent role in its first several years. He began regularly attending its annual meetings no later than 1882, when he delivered the address "Christianity and the Criminal," and after he became bishop he was one of the few bishops who participated regularly in the Congress. Further, Potter was bishop for the second and third decades of the life of the Congress and supported and collaborated with the many prominent Congress leaders who were clergy in the Diocese of New York.[21]

Henry Potter's commitment to the principles of a comprehensive church appeared more clearly in his episcopate, especially when seen in light of the change in the Diocese of New York that it represented. For most of the nineteenth century the Diocese of New York suffered from the same ecclesiastical partisanship that affected other parts of the Episcopal Church and American Protestantism at large. Since the 1810–30 episcopate of John Henry Hobart, whom Allen Guelzo describes as "the most splenetic and provocative spokesman for High Church principles in the nineteenth century," that party had been dominant in the diocese and the source of all its bishops. Notable conflicts erupted in 1843 when Bishop Benjamin Onderdonk ordained Arthur Carey, to whose Tractarian sympathies some Evangelicals strongly objected, and in 1845 when Onderdonk himself was indefinitely suspended for sexual impropriety. While Onderdonk was certainly guilty of what today would be called sexual harassment, it was his Evangelical enemies who collected the evidence and brought the charges against him. The indefinite suspension left the diocese divided and without a bishop, and it was not until 1850 that the General Convention adopted legislation enabling election of a provisional bishop. Because of continuing divisions, however, the diocese failed to elect a bishop in two attempts. It was only in 1852 and after eight ballots that it finally settled on Jonathan Wainwright, who unfortunately died two years later. In a special convention in 1854, the diocese again undertook the process and again cast eight ballots before electing Horatio Potter.[22]

Although regarded as moderate in his High Church views, Horatio Potter strictly interpreted and enforced the church's prohibition of preaching by Episcopal clergy in the churches of other Protestant denominations. As a result, he became embroiled in controversies with Evangelical Episcopalians, notably over his censure of Stephen H. Tyng Jr., who in 1867 had accepted an invitation to preach in a Methodist church, and of R. Payne Smith, dean of Canterbury, who assisted at a service in a Presbyterian church while in New York for an 1873 meeting of the Evangelical Alliance. By this time Evangelical Episcopalians had long been discontent with the lack of liberty granted them by the Episcopal Church in their efforts to cooperate with evangelicals of other churches, and with the continuing influence of Tractarianism and the growth of Anglo-Catholicism. Potter's censure of Smith, while only the last in a series of Evangelical grievances, seems to have been the precipitating cause of the schism wherein Bishop George Cummins and twenty-six other Evangelical Episcopalians formed the Reformed Episcopal Church in December 1873.[23]

In September 1883 Horatio Potter proposed, because of diminished health, his "complete withdrawal from the administration of the Diocese" in a manner to be determined by the diocesan convention. Rather than request the bishop's resignation so that a successor might be elected, the convention chose to elect an assistant bishop to whom would be entrusted all responsibility for administration of the diocese. Faced with the task of electing an assistant and eventual successor to Horatio Potter, the convention chose, from a slate of fourteen candidates and after three ballots, Henry Codman Potter. The other leading candidate had been Morgan Dix, High Church rector of Trinity Church. In fact, with the exception of Horatio Potter, all the diocese's previous bishops had been associated with Trinity. Voting in 1883 generally followed party lines, with the Low and Broad Church advocates supporting Potter and the High Church proponents and Anglo-Catholics supporting Dix. Potter received a plurality of votes from clerical and lay delegates on the first and second ballots, after which Dix's name was withdrawn. On the third ballot, Potter received 54 percent of the clerical vote and 70 percent of the lay vote. The convention thereupon passed a motion to make unanimous Potter's election as assistant bishop. While it may have seemed to some that he was born to be bishop, and while the effort to elect him was well organized, the relatively easy election of the Broad Church rector of Grace Church was of great significance. The dominance of the High Church and the prevalence of party strife in New York had ended and the era of the Broad Church had begun. Henry Potter was consecrated assistant bishop in Grace Church in October 1883, and Horatio Potter remained bishop in name until his death in January 1887. On the evening of his consecration, in his first official act, Henry Potter visited the Midnight Mission of the Sisters of St. John the Baptist. The mission, in the establishment of which Muhlenberg had played a role over twenty years earlier, offered sanctuary from New York's brutal prostitution traffic to women who had been forced into the streets. The next day, Potter visited the prison on Blackwell's Island and preached to the four hundred men there; "I thank God," said the bishop, "for the privilege of beginning my work as a missionary."[24]

One year later, Potter gave the opening address at the October 1884 Church Congress and in it offered a rationale for the organization's existence and work.

> It is well that there should be an arena where the utmost openness and candor of discussion should prevail, and where the unity should be rather that of one purpose, to seek and to find the truth, and the peace that of a large charity than of a restricted and enforced uniformity. The church has many wants to-day, but none of them is more real than the want of a tribune of the people, where voices, diverse it may be, but honest and reverent, may be heard, and when themes not always accounted appropriate to the pulpit may be frankly and courageously discussed.

At the 1889 Congress, he participated in a discussion on social issues with Bishop Frederic Dan Huntington and R. Heber Newton, rector of All Souls Church, New York, and in subsequent years continued to be active in the Church Congress.[25] Potter's commitment to the unity of truth seeking and the peace of a large charity, as well as his sense that the pulpit is not the appropriate forum for fearless truth seeking, were nevertheless sometimes sorely tested. Two such tests came shortly after his election as assistant bishop, one brought on by R. Heber Newton and the other by Arthur Ritchie. Although the issues in the two cases were very different (in the one clerical intellectual liberty and higher biblical criticism and in the other extremes of High Church ritualism), Potter responded to them similarly and demonstrated both his evenhandedness and the limits of his comprehensiveness. A contemporary editorial in the *New York Tribune* observed,

> Assistant Bishop Potter is fast gaining a reputation as an ecclesiastical diplomat. Having quietly, but firmly, repressed the too liberal utterances of the Rev. R. Heber Newton, he has now persuaded the rector of St. Ignatius' Church to give up the Benediction Service, which, evangelical churchmen hold, savors of Rome. . . . A less careful, or a tactless bishop would long ago have brought scandal on the church by hasty or arbitrary action at All Souls' or St. Ignatius'. The wisdom of Dr. Potter's course is manifest.[26]

Potter's disciplining of Newton might suggest a timid commitment to truth seeking, but his action must be seen in light of both his view of his episcopal role as keeper of the ecclesiastical peace and his contention that the pulpit was not the appropriate place for fearless truth seeking. He did not ask Newton to cease publication of his work on the new biblical criticism, only to cease elaborating it from the pulpit. Further, he shielded Newton from the heresy hunters who sought stronger action against him.

Potter's support of Newton and, later, biblical scholar Charles Augustus Briggs also reflects a key element of the Broad Church movement and one of the ways in which it, like contemporary liberal evangelical movements in other Protestant churches, differed most significantly from both antebellum evangelicalism and conservative postwar evangelicalism. While the latter steadfastly adhered to the Reformation doctrine of *sola scriptura*, after the war liberal evangelicals began to reconsider the status of biblical authority. Liberal evangelicals employed emerging literary and historical scholarship for this task, but they had taken up the task in no small measure because of their recent experience of the ease with which proslavery forces had been able to marshall scriptural arguments in its support and, likewise, the difficulty with which antislavery forces had been able to argue against slavery from the Bible. As chapter 2 will discuss, in 1863 Alonzo Potter and several of Henry Potter's friends and colleagues in the Diocese of Pennsylvania had been involved in a controversy over Bishop John Henry Hopkins's defense of slavery, in which Hopkins had relied heavily on scriptural arguments. Although Henry Potter was working in Troy, New York, at the time, he certainly would have been aware of the controversy. More important, this incident is but one example of the use of scripture in the struggle against slavery that ultimately led many Protestants to reevaluate their convictions about biblical authority and embrace higher biblical criticism.[27]

Potter further demonstrated his Broad Church sympathies when, at the request of Phillips Brooks, he preached at Brooks's controversial consecration as bishop in October 1891. High Churchmen and Anglo-Catholics tended to regard Brooks's criticism of apostolic succession as making him ineligible for the episcopate and opposed his consecration. Unlike them, Potter maintained that Brooks's position was acceptable for those serving the church; but unlike Brooks and some of his other supporters, Potter endorsed apostolic succession with some qualifications. Because of the depth of their friendship and their shared commitment to a comprehensive church, Brooks and Potter could publicly disagree on a contentious issue while publicly supporting each other. For his part, Potter expressed his views on the matter in his address to that year's diocesan convention, arguing that the

> endeavor to force the view of one party or school as a finality upon the whole Church is simply so much partisan intolerance. . . . We may re-

gret, dear brethren, as I am quite free to say I do, that any man called to a high and sacred office does not see its sanctions and trace its authority along the lines that seem so clear to us. But an intelligent recognition of the relations of the clergy to questions of ecclesiastical order in our time demands that we must recognize the liberty, as well as the limitations, which pertain to every man among them.[28]

Also in 1891, Potter faced a dispute over invitations by some Episcopal clergy to other Protestant ministers to speak in their churches, a practice some High Church partisans regarded as a violation of canon law. To this open pulpit dispute Potter responded by advocating, unlike his uncle before him, a broad reading of the relevant canons. He did so in part out of a desire to be evenhanded (some High Church partisans, after all, had previously invited Orthodox and Old Catholic clergy to speak from their pulpits), but more importantly because the principle on which he wished to "govern and guide this great Diocese" was "that it may realize its utmost possibilities of service to the whole Body of Christ." At the close of his convention address that year, he summarized his view of Christian comprehensiveness:

> In a body which, while, as we rejoice to believe, under divine guidance and inspiration, is still made up of very frail and faulty members, led by very fallible and often very imperfectly formed guides, no graver or more perilous situation could come to pass than that in which the due proportion of the faith and the due balance of opposite aspects of the one truth were no longer maintained by the differing and sometimes apparently dissonant voices of its teachers. The moment that we have affirmed a truth we are bound to admit that there are, and rightly ought to be, various standpoints from which to look at it. There are those to whom, constitutionally, such a statement is intolerable; but that does not alter the fact. And, because it is the fact, the Church's duty in our time is clear. . . . There is a divine doctrine, but let us take care that in defining it we do not make it narrower than Christ Himself has made it! There is a divine order, but let us not seek only so inexorably to enforce it that, like those iron images of the middle ages, it shall crush the life out of the victim whom it embraces.[29]

In support of his reasoning Potter cited early Christian theologians Origen, Tertullian, Gregory of Nazianzus, and John Chrysostom and contemporary Anglican theologians Charles Gore, B. F. Westcott, and Walter Locke.[30] By drawing on early Christian theologians and Anglo-Catholic scholarship, Potter made his case agreeable to those of a High Church or Anglo-Catholic persuasion. The motion to reprint the bishop's 1891 address for wider circulation came from High Church proponent Morgan Dix.

As in the Newton case, Potter demonstrated his support for those advancing higher biblical criticism by ordaining Charles A. Briggs a priest of the Episcopal Church. A Presbyterian minister and pioneer in biblical studies, Briggs taught at Union Theological Seminary, New York, where his work had aroused considerable opposition. In proceedings that attracted widespread public attention, the New York Presbytery twice acquitted him of heresy, but the Presbyterian Church's General Assembly suspended him from ministry in 1893. Briggs's interest in Protestant ecumenism had already inclined him to be favorably disposed to the Episcopal Church, especially after the House of Bishops adopted in 1886 William Reed Huntington's quadrilateral proposal for Christian unity, and he corresponded with Potter during his trials. Responding to Potter's congratulations upon the outcome of one of the cases before the Presbytery of New York, Briggs wrote: "I gladly recognize you as my bishop, although your hands have not been put upon me. I would not hesitate to ask that also, were it not plain that, for the present, I can do no more for the unity of Christ's church by working among the Presbyterians. But would that this city were under your episcopal guidance."[31] Ultimately Briggs did ask Potter to lay hands on him, a request that he welcomed. In 1898 Potter ordained Briggs as deacon without incident, but Briggs's scheduled ordination to the priesthood provoked vociferous protest and a formal request that Potter investigate Briggs's alleged heresy. B. F. DeCosta, who in 1887 had helped found the Church Association for the Advancement of the Interests of Labor, threatened to take up heresy charges against Briggs, and Bishop Nicholson of Milwaukee went so far as to threaten ecclesiastical action against Potter. As in earlier disputes, Potter disregarded the controversy and no action was initiated against either Briggs or himself. On 14 May 1899 he ordained Briggs at the Stanton Street Mission, which in 1893 had been adopted as a mission of the Cathedral of St. John the Divine. Potter later named Briggs a canon of the cathedral and defended his orthodoxy when his 1904 address on ecumenism to the Church Club of New York proved too sympathetic to Roman Catholicism for many Protestants.[32]

In addition to tolerance of diversity and vigorous theological inquiry, and again reflecting the influence of the Evangelicalism of Alonzo Potter, William Augustus Muhlenberg, and the Memorial Movement, the Broad Church movement was also noted for its concern for making the church more accessible and responsive to poor and working people. As I noted earlier, in his visits to the Midnight Mission and Blackwell's Island immediately after his consecration, Henry Potter signaled his intent to emphasize the practical work of Christianity, his concern for the poor and outcast, and his support for those ministering to them. He later institutionalized his concern for the imprisoned by regular visits to Blackwell's Island and by incorporating a visit there into the retreats he annually conducted for the diocese's candidates for ordination. In the three years after his consecration, he also gave a series of devotional and inspirational addresses to women in church work, which were later published. And, as I will discuss further, the coercion of women and children into prostitution would command his attention in a particularly important way seventeen years later.[33]

In the early years of his episcopate Potter also presided at the 1884 anniversary meetings of the New York City Mission Society and the Church Temperance Society (of the latter of which he had been a founder); delivered two addresses at the 1884 Church Congress and several other public addresses on various topics; and presided at the 1886 meeting of the American Colonization Society and was elected one of its vice presidents. Potter also quickly implemented new means of enlivening the church and making it more effective, demonstrating his continuing concern to implement the comprehensive vision of the Memorial Movement. Two instances of this innovation are notable: the 1884 establishment of the Order of the Holy Cross and the 1885 Advent Mission.[34]

In late 1881 three young Anglo-Catholic priests began to live in community and work among the poor of New York's East Side tenement district. They adopted a communal rule and received approval for it from Bishop Horatio Potter. Their leader was James Otis Sargent Huntington, son of Bishop Frederic Dan Huntington and later founding member of the Church Association for the Advancement of the Interests of Labor. Huntington and his colleagues Robert S. Dod and James G. Cameron labored in obscurity for three years and also received the support of Assistant Bishop Henry Potter. Eventually they decided to establish a religious order, the Order of the Holy Cross, to which they would make a formal profession and take vows of poverty, chastity, and obedience. Since Cameron disagreed over the vows to be taken and Dod's health permitted his admission only as a novice, Huntington alone made his formal profession in a service held in November 1884. Bishop Huntington, his father, attended the service and Assistant Bishop Potter presided.

Alarmed responses appeared within a month. Presiding Bishop Alfred Lee, an ardent Low Church partisan, criticized in a public letter to Potter the "Romish" character of the order and the service admitting Huntington to it. He argued that Potter's action in presiding at the service was unprecedented and that in it "the whole monastic system was sanctioned . . . [and] attributed to divine inspiration." The fruits of monasticism, in Lee's view, were "evil and pernicious." He regarded the legacy of sacerdotal celibacy as "a history of shame, suffering and sin," and maintained that the "corrupt morals of the priesthood wherever Romanism is in the ascendant is a notorious fact." In closing, Lee invoked the memory of Alonzo Potter (and, by implication, his opposition to Romish practices) by signing his letter "your own friend and your father's friend."

In his response, Henry Potter defended both his actions and the order. He argued, first, that the ecclesiastical support for sisterhoods implied the same support for "Brotherhoods established for the same purpose." More important, however, was his view of the order as an alternative to "the profound and widespread apathy" of the church to the tenement districts, "schools of poverty, misery and almost inevitable vice" to which the church's missions were as yet a meager response. Huntington and his colleagues had proposed to live among those whom they sought to serve, and to do so under the circumstances of tenement life required that they "be willing to be poor, to live alone, to obey a fixed rule (or regimen) of life." Responding to Presiding Bishop Lee's implied appeal to Alonzo Potter, Henry Potter acknowledged his father's opposition to extreme ecclesiasticism but claimed as justification for the order the late bishop's concern for adapting the work of the church to contemporary conditions.

> I revere my father's memory as that of the noblest prelate and the wisest man I ever knew. . . . He dreaded the taint of Roman error and I do. But he believed that things that had been abused were not necessarily evil in themselves. And had he lived on and into the new conditions and sore needs of our day, he would have owned, I think, that an Order of Men under obligations in no essential different from those Orders of Women might do a John the Baptist's work if need be, crying in the wilderness of a great city's sin that men should repent and open in their hearts a highway for their Lord. If I did not think that he would have thought so, you may be sure that I would not have done what I have.

Bishops, clergy, and laypeople took sides on the Order of the Holy Cross, and Potter's clarification appeased some early opponents to some extent. Presiding Bishop Lee responded at length to Potter's letter but took no formal action against him. One supporter was R. Heber Newton, whom Potter had only recently asked to cease his controversial lectures on biblical criticism. Newton wrote in part: "I have shown you a year ago my readiness to go all lengths possible to support you, and you will find no warmer backer in any troubles that you may get into out of this affair than myself. While I am utterly opposed to the revival of a system which has been tried and condemned by history, I will for one be behind you with a stout club, where all your other loyal presbyters will be, if the dear Papa of Delaware [Bishop Lee] attempts to call you in question before the church for your liberty and right as a bishop." The order continued its work in New York for several years, as George Hodges observed, "without justifying either the fears of those who were alarmed by its appearance, or the hopes of those who found in it a new service of the poor." Ultimately, the order withdrew from New York's tenement district to a rural area north of the city, an action that certainly "dulled the point of some of the most convincing paragraphs" of Potter's defense. Nevertheless, the brief history of the order's work among New York's poor exhibits the strength of Potter's commitment to that work and his eagerness to employ various, if sometimes controversial, means of accomplishing it.[35]

A second instance of Potter's use of new means of enlivening the church was the 1885 Advent Mission. Some clergy of the Church of England had for some time been conducting revivals, calling them instead missions to avoid the negative connotations of revivalism among Anglicans. Shortly before Potter's election as assistant bishop, a committee was formed to plan for such a mission in New York and Potter worked closely with it. In a May 1885 pastoral letter Potter articulated his rationale for the upcoming mission, acknowledging the legitimate fear of "mistaking excitement for profound moral conviction, and exalted feelings for a deep, settled purpose," but noting that the church had "reason to dread lest the use of accustomed means shall content us with perfunctory service and superficial results" and that it should welcome any means, "from whatever quarter it may come," that might help it address the needs of the day.

In addition, as an editorial in that month's *Churchman* observed, the organizers of the mission had commendably given prominence to the labor question, since the disaffection between labor and religion was of alarming proportions. "The alienation has been allowed to progress too far already," the editorial continued, "and the situation is one that must enlist our best energies, if we do not wish the Church to suffer for generations." It thus looked to the Advent Mission as a promising means of alleviating that alienation. Thus, while the Order of the Holy Cross demonstrated Potter's willingness to embrace and adapt Anglo-Catholic traditions to enliven and make more effective the church's response to the needs of the day, the Advent Mission showed a similar willingness to embrace and adapt evangelical methods as well.[36]

Practical Christianity

In support of their program of doctrinal and liturgical tolerance, vigorous truth seeking, and emphasis on the practical work of the church, some proponents of the Broad Church movement often offered an explicit theological rationale for their views. This work, too, had its antecedents in the religious and moral reform convictions that, in the Episcopal Church, gave rise to the Memorial Movement. In April 1851, in the course of his labors to establish the Episcopal Hospital in Philadelphia, Alonzo Potter presented a report to the committee of clergy and laity convened for that purpose. In it he gave a rationale not only for this particular work, but also for all religious charitable endeavors.

> The Church, in her collective and corporate capacity, owes a debt not only to the destitute sick, but also to the fatherless, to the widow, to the stranger and to the vicious who are without friends. . . . Her debt can be adequately paid only when, in addition to the casual charities of her individual members, she adds the systematic and well-directed efforts of institutions administered on religious principles, and in such a way as to effect with the least means the greatest possible amount of good. Experience teaches that much of the charity which is directed exclusively to the bodies of men contributes, in the end, to increase the evil it attempts to cure; and a like experience shows that when we could combine with such charity, moral and religious culture, that culture will make a deep and lasting impression on the character and habits. . . .
>
> There are few duties of our Church more imperative, and none perhaps which at this time is more imperfectly discharged, than the duty of *hospitality to the poor.* . . . Institutions . . . are needed, not to supersede private beneficence on the part of our Pastors and people, but rather to guide and encourage them. Much the largest proportion of cases must always be met by individuals. It is for the benefit alike of those who give and of those who receive that it should be so. But associated effort is also requisite. . . . In rearing an institution for the relief of human misery in any of its forms, the Church holds out a solemn challenge to all her members not to forget the poor.[37]

This lucid statement of Alonzo Potter's theory of social ministry contains several emphases central to his practice of religious charity: the church's responsibility to the poor; the necessity of systematic, institutional charities; the dangers of ill-conceived charities; the importance of personal charitable work; and the mutual benefit of such work to the donor and the recipient. In all these, his concern was for Christianity's ministry to the whole person, regarding its appropriate work as "ministering at once to the bodies, the minds, the social requirements and the spiritual needs of people."[38] With these basic convictions Alonzo Potter approached a wide range of religious and social concerns.

Clearly and consciously influenced by his father's view of religion and social ministry, from very early in his work as a priest Henry Potter exhibited his conviction of the need to adapt the church's methods to the new challenges it faced. While rector at St. John's Church in Troy, New York, for example, Potter made a special effort to work with young people in his congregation. He also cooperated with the Troy Young Men's Christian Association and represented it at the 1864 national convention in Boston. In his address to the convention, he recalled the YMCA's purpose of providing shelter and help to young men, especially those in the cities and separated from their rural homes, and his address discussed the methods appropriate to that purpose. He argued that any program or system for meeting the needs of these young men "will be incomplete, which does not take in the 'whole man'—which does not recognize all the various needs of a youth in a great city, and seek to answer and meet them." In this way, he reflected and sustained his father's vision of Christianity's ministry to the whole person and signaled a principle by which he would organize his own understanding of the church's ministry.[39]

After becoming rector of Grace Church in April 1868, Potter participated in many of the early developments of social Christian ministry. On the foundation laid by his predecessor, Thomas House Taylor, Potter helped build an impressive edifice of parochial mission work that advanced the development of "institutional" churches in American Protestantism. The example of Grace illustrates the judgment of C. H. Hopkins that the "institutional church was primarily an effort to recoup the ground lost by Protestantism when its churches moved out of the crowded working-class areas of the great cities and at the same time betrayed the confidence of those classes." Institutional churches were thus one strategy by which Protestants responded to the needs of those in the urban centers, particularly the poor and immigrants, who were not church members. As such, institutional churches constituted a central component of what Aaron Abell terms "the Protestant religio-social system." Episcopal churches in New York City were among the first to develop institutional programs, in part because they had relocated from working-class neighborhoods but also because of the influence of Muhlenberg and, later, Stephen H. Tyng Jr. Potter's tenure at Grace nearly coincided with Tyng's as rector of Holy Trinity Church, New York, a church described by Abell as "one of the great mission churches of America." Tyng's work at Holy Trinity was so successful that, when the church faced financial troubles in 1878, "New York philanthropists endowed it with an annual income for the 'support of undenominational, evangelistic and humanitarian work among the poor of New York City.'" New Yorkers' aid to Holy Trinity may also have provided Potter with a precedent for his later appeal to them for support of the Cathedral of St. John the Divine.[40]

Historians of American social Christianity have neglected the importance of both Potter and Grace Church in the 1860s and 1870s for the development of institutional churches. The literature emphasizes the contributions of antebellum pioneers such as William Muhlenberg and Congregationalist Thomas K. Beecher and of those working in the 1880s after the term *institutional church* became commonly used, such as New York Episcopalians William S. Rainsford and William Reed Huntington. Indeed, Rainsford at St. George's, Huntington at Grace, Percy S. Grant at Ascension, and David H. Greer at St. Bartholomew's all led important Episcopal institutional churches from the 1880s through the early 1900s. They did so, however, only after Potter's tenure at Grace Church and, perhaps more important, during his tenure as bishop of New York. While work such as that carried out at Grace in the 1870s was not called institutional until some years later, Grace Church was, during the rectorate of Henry Potter, an institutional church in both form and intent.[41]

Like all other Manhattan Episcopal churches and many of those of other denominations, the church's pews were rented. The church had been relocated from a site in lower Manhattan in 1846, whereupon Thomas House Taylor campaigned for the construction of a free mission chapel. He was successful, and the chapel eventually became an independent church. Taylor then set about to build another free chapel, which was completed in 1853. From this chapel were conducted the church's mission activities, including an industrial school, founded by Mrs. Taylor, which taught sewing to and provided clothing for poor children. In Potter's first year there Grace Church added three new outreach programs: the Ladies' Benevolent Society, which provided not only employment for poor women by giving them sewing to do at home, but also clothes for charitable institutions by donating to them the garments made by the women; the Ladies' Domestic Missionary Relief Association, which collected and dispersed clothes and other items to domestic missionaries and their families; and the St. Luke's Association, which provided free medical aid to the poor, including doctors' visits, nursing, medicines, food, and clothing. In addition, the parish visitor, who was responsible for the families served by Grace Church's free chapel, coordinated his pastoral activities with the work of the various programs.[42]

Because the existing Grace Chapel building was inadequate for the work of these programs, in 1870 Potter and others at Grace began to plan for buildings from which the church's programs might better be operated. The plan was advanced in 1872 by a donation of property from Levi P. Morton, banker and vestry member, in memory of his wife, Lucy Kimball Morton, who before her death had taken great interest in Potter's idea. Levi P. Morton also worked with Potter in New York's Charity Organization Society and later became governor of New York and, from 1889–1893, vice president of the United States under Benjamin Harrison. The property he donated consisted of the abandoned Calvary Chapel; it or the proceeds from its sale were to be used as the authorities of Grace Church saw fit to further their plan. Before Potter's plan could be realized, however, it received two setbacks. The first was the destruction of Grace Chapel by fire in December 1872, leaving the parish ministries without a building. As a result, Grace Memorial House, as Morton's donation came to be known, came into immediate and unanticipated use. The second setback was the financial panic of 1873–74, which resulted in thousands of business failures, widespread destitution, and curtailed charitable contributions. Nevertheless, three of the four envisioned buildings, including a free chapel and adjacent hall and parsonage, were completed by 1876. The fourth, known as Grace House and in which most of the parish organizations were accommodated, was completed in the following year. In 1882 yet another Grace House was formally opened in order to meet the needs of the parish's increasing work. This last building was funded by a donation from Catherine Lorillard Wolfe, one of the most generous supporters of Potter's work at Grace.[43]

By this time the church's outreach work had also multiplied. Notable among the new organizations were a German mission, which within three years of its establishment expanded from two Sunday services in Grace Hall to occupancy of its own church; a day nursery, providing care, meals, and instruction to children of working women; a diet kitchen, providing meals to the poor when ill; Grace-House-by-the-Sea, a summer country haven for poor children; a young people's club, providing entertainment and companionship for young men and women living on their own; and a free reading room for working men, presumably conceived as an alternative to saloons. The aim in all these programs, as Potter expressed it in speaking of the young people's club, was "to *illustrate* the spirit of a kindly and brotherly Christianity [rather] than formally to inculcate it," with the hope that this approach would "help to win those who are now indifferent to all religious claims, first, to understand the spirit of Christ and His Church, and then to welcome their teachings."[44]

The focal point for these programs was Grace Chapel, the free chapel that Grace Church had supported, in various incarnations, since 1849. Free *chapels* were supported by churches with rented pews, with the result that the rich worshiped in the churches and the poor in the chapels; free *churches* were churches that derived their support from sources other than pew rents, with the result that all worshiped together. This distinction, however, should not be drawn too sharply, for some churches with rented pews reserved some for those who could not afford the rents. Nevertheless, the system had unfortunate consequences for relations among classes and for Protestantism's ability to minister to the poor. Again, it was William Muhlenberg who pioneered the Episcopal free church movement with the establishment of the Church of the Holy Communion, New York, as a free church in 1845. Support for free chapels and churches grew over the next three decades, and in 1874 some of the movement's proponents formed the Free Church Association. In 1883, with W. S. Rainsford as rector, St. George's became the first major New York Episcopal church to abandon pew rental.[45]

While maintaining a free chapel since 1849, Grace Church was committed to and dependent on pew rents. Potter regarded this two-tiered system as a proximate good at best. He believed free churches were important not only as a means of providing religious services for those who could not otherwise afford them (the dominant rationale of early free church advocates), but also as a means of alleviating the alienation among classes. The rich, he argued, needed to worship in free churches as much as, perhaps more than, did the poor. It was not within his power as rector to terminate the church's pew rental system, but he regularly exhorted the congregation to support Grace Chapel. He also preached in support of free churches and other measures, such as common worship on special occasions, for the alleviation of class alienation.[46]

This latter concern he also expressed in his May 1877 sermon at the annual meeting of the Free Church Association, "The Free Church a Witness to the Brotherhood of Humanity." Potter began with a somewhat defensive response to a newspaper report that he "ministered to the most exclusive congregation, who themselves worshiped in the most expensive pews, to be found in any church in the land." He acknowledged, nevertheless, that the report accurately indicated the popular conviction of "the inconsistency of all pewed churches, however hospitable their welcome or inexpensive their accommodations, with the Church's doctrines and her Master's teachings." With this conviction he was in basic agreement. Potter's rationale for free churches combined an appeal to the "brotherhood of humanity in the liberating and ennobling bond of a common Saviour and Redeemer," the threat of potentially dire social consequences of unchecked class alienation, and recognition of the evil, albeit unintended, of perpetuating class distinctions within the churches.[47]

As to the realization of free churches, Potter acknowledged that the impediments were many and included irrational and prejudicial feelings. Recognizing these realities, he argued, in a clear statement of his gradualist approach to both ecclesiastical and social reform, that one could not "drive the plough-share of revolution through cherished and inherited prejudices without turning up something else than a kindly soil in which to sow the seeds of reform. Wrongs must sometimes be righted by revolution, but evils will be corrected just so fast as, and no faster than, you can enlighten and educate any prejudiced mass of people to a clearer vision of the truth." This recognition of the limits to reform, however, did not dim his vision of or enthusiasm for free churches. "If they for whom Christ died are brethren, then let those who say so show the world that they believe it. No mere toleration of the poor or the unrefined or the uneducated will do this. No mere spasm of occasional condescension, whether in church or out of it, will do it either. Nothing will do it save a new and mightier baptism of that Divine Spirit of love and self-forgetfulness for which even now the Church is waiting!"[48]

Potter carried his commitment to free churches and concern about class alienation into his episcopate, particularly through his campaign for construction of the Cathedral of St. John the Divine. The idea of a cathedral for New York had arisen in the first quarter of the century. No serious action was taken until the episcopate of Horatio Potter, when a board of trustees was formed in 1873. Henry Potter, however, was to put his distinctive stamp on this project. In 1887 he issued an appeal, "To the Citizens of New York," for their support of the cathedral as "a people's church," a "centre of practical philanthropies," and a pulpit for "the best preachers . . . from all parts of the land and of various schools of thought." In May 1892 *The Forum* published his article "The Significance of the American Cathedral," in which he articulated his rationale for the proposed Cathedral of St. John the Divine. In December 1892, he presided at the laying of the cornerstone for the cathedral.[49]

It was Potter's vision of the cathedral's mission that also motivated him in the summer of 1895 to take up residence for six weeks at the Stanton Street Mission. The mission had been operated by St. George's Church and staffed by the Brotherhood of St. Andrew, but by 1893 St. George's was unable to support the mission. The brotherhood approached Potter for help, proposing that operation of the mission be assumed by the cathedral. The idea appealed to Potter's vision for the cathedral and sense of the importance of direct personal contact in mission and charitable work. He endorsed the plan and commended it to the 1893 diocesan convention, noting that while the mission would need money it would "most need men and women who will go down and live, in turn, for a while, in the Mission House, and work with and among the people whom they are trying to serve." In the summer of 1895, Potter took his own advice, sent the mission's minister on vacation, and from 10 June to 8 August 1895 assumed charge of the mission himself. The newspapers sensationalized his visit, but he insisted that he was simply attempting to obtain firsthand information about this field of mission work and to demonstrate his idea of the cathedral as a free church.[50]

Henry Potter's attempts to address class alienation and meet the material and spiritual needs of the poor took place in the context of the postwar economic expansion, during which, by the 1870s, wealth and its uses had become critical religious and moral issues. In the decade immediately after the war, white American Protestants were largely convinced of the basic goodness of the social and economic order and tended to bless the economic expansion and the unprecedented fortunes amassed. The religious political economy advocated by Alonzo Potter and others persuaded many that the extremes of wealth and poverty produced by the new industrial age were ordained by God. In its extreme form, this ethic regarded business success and Christian living as nearly synonymous. More commonly, Protestant clerics exhorted those who possessed wealth to use it for the common good. It was not until the advent of widespread corruption and the onset of the economic crises of the last quarter of the century, beginning with the Panic of 1877, that a significant number of Protestants began to question the adequacy of the ethic of the "stewardship of wealth." Even in the face of these crises, however, most failed to question the socioeconomic order.[51]

To his Grace Church congregation, Henry Potter preached the stewardship of wealth, qualified only by some attention to wealth's dangers as well as its duties. He warned that the possession of wealth "is fraught with peril" because of its tendency to desensitize one's conscience but maintained that it is not in itself inconsistent with faithful living. Indeed, he argued that, properly used, wealth has a highly positive social role.

> Wealth has duties to perform in the constitution of our modern society, that poverty could never perform. The progress of science, of the arts, of higher education, the organized efforts of philanthropy, require capital in the hands of a few, just as truly as trade requires capital. And wealth thus used by the wealthy becomes a permanent and inestimable factor in the elevation of men. Nay, more, if in deference to any narrow and superficial interpretation to Christ's language, a man should take his

wealth and distribute the whole of it in largesses to the poor to-morrow, he would be doing the poor an incalculable evil and not a benefit.[52]

Potter amplified this statement on wealth and its duties throughout his work at Grace Church. The congregation's wealth was one factor in his discussion of this issue. Wealth was a problem for Protestants of all mainline denominations, but perhaps especially for Episcopalians because of their church's high proportion of wealthy members. The stewardship of wealth was an ethic for those who were both rich and Christian and who wished to remain both. Such observations, however, do not require that one regard Potter and his contemporaries as hypocrites. Many and perhaps most worked honestly to live a faithful response to the needs of the times in the context of what they saw as a basically good socioeconomic order. That some had a great deal of money and others very little they believed to be an unfortunate but inevitable outcome of that order.

Like many of his generation, however, Potter later began to question the goodness of that order. The way for Potter's later thinking was paved by the interaction of his religious convictions and the social and economic crises of the late nineteenth century. By the middle of the 1880s, however, he was assistant bishop of New York and his congregation was the whole of the diocese. His perspective remained that of a pastor ministering to those who controlled wealth and counseling them on its just use. Indeed, Potter was acquainted and even friends with many of New York's wealthiest men, including J. P. Morgan, Andrew Carnegie, and William Waldorf Astor. As George Hodges observed, "Bishop Wilberforce, after a good deal of experience, came to the conclusion that society could not be saved by dining with it. Bishop Potter was not so sure." Potter certainly used his influence with such men and women to solicit funds for charitable work and to mediate labor disputes. Because his perspective was basically theirs, his economic ethic, like other aspects of his ethic, was essentially paternalistic.[53]

Although by the late 1880s Potter's work on economic issues focused on the relations of labor and capital, his response to Andrew Carnegie's 1889 essay "Wealth" demonstrated his continuing reliance on the stewardship of wealth. It also highlighted an important aspect of Potter's ethic, namely, the necessity of direct personal involvement in charitable and philanthropic work. In his essay, first published in the *North American Review* in June 1889, Carnegie expounded an ethic of stewardship similar to that preached in pulpits and publications since the end of the Civil War. Carnegie's starting point was the problem of the alienation of rich and poor. Assuming the inevitability of an unequal distribution of wealth, he argued that the rich were responsible for administering their surplus wealth for the greater public good. As the rich had demonstrated their administrative skill through their accumulation of wealth, they were better able than their heirs or the state to disburse this wealth. For Carnegie, it was indisputable that "there is no mode of disposing of surplus wealth creditable to thoughtful and earnest men into whose hands it flows, save by using it year by year for the general good." Such stewardship, he believed, would solve the problem of class alienation while leaving intact social and economic individualism and the "laws" of accumulation and distribution, thus making it a strategy realizable in the contemporary context.[54]

Reaction to Carnegie's essay was mixed, an indication that by the 1890s many were questioning the economic order and the inevitability of inequitable wealth distribution. Carnegie, who saw himself as a thinking person's industrialist committed to the common welfare, was surprised by the criticism of his essay. While most wealthy industrialists and financiers maintained that God had given them their wealth to dispose of as they saw fit, Carnegie contended that "amassing wealth is one of the worst species of idolatry" and that "few millionaires are clear of the sin of having made beggars." Perhaps it was his own guilt at having made beggars, a guilt that seems to have bothered few of his peers, that compelled Carnegie to adopt a different view and argue it publicly. On the other hand, labor practices at Carnegie's mills and factories, especially in the Homestead Strike of 1892, cast some doubt on the sincerity of his concern about the sin of "creating beggars." In any event, Carnegie responded to the criticism of his "Wealth" in two ways. First, he wrote a rejoinder entitled "The Advantages of Poverty," published by the *Nineteenth Century* in March 1891. Second, he initiated a symposium on "Wealth" in the *North American Review*, the first installment of which was written by Henry Codman Potter.[55]

In May 1891, the same month that Potter delivered an address at the dedication of Carnegie Hall in which he praised Carnegie's philanthropy,[56] Potter's essay "The Gospel for Wealth" appeared in the *North American Review*. While some American Protestants, such as liberal Congregationalist William Jewett Tucker and Episcopal Christian socialist W. D. P. Bliss, denounced Carnegie's paternalism and offered alternative strategies on the distribution of wealth, Potter largely accepted Carnegie's assumptions and conclusions. But while Carnegie's essay was "concerned with wealth as a means of contributing to the happiness of those in whose behalf it is expended," Potter's was concerned with "what wealth may become to those who worthily employ it." He warned of the corrupting influence of wealth not only on those who possess it but also on those who emulated them, maintaining that the responsibility of the rich included both themselves and others influenced by them. More important, he argued that possessors of wealth must use it to combat the insidious tendency to the hardening of their sympathies.

> One's own life must somehow reach over into, and be qualified by, the struggles and interests of other lives. In the case of the poor this is made inevitable by the hard conditions of their poverty. As in an open boat, with half-rations, all must learn self-restraint for the good of all, so it is in the sorrows, hardships, and struggles that come to the men and women who live on a day's wage. . . . But it is the tendency of a well-clad, well-fed, comfortable, and sheltered life to make such care and concern for others more and more impossible, save as it resolutely seeks opportunities for its exercise.

The personal exercise of care for others was, for Potter, essential to charitable and philanthropic endeavor, and thus to the correct stewardship of wealth. He noted, however, that most charitable work regrettably separated the giver from the recipient: "Unfortunately, at this point, a conspicuous tendency of our modern philanthropy interferes in a most discouraging way. That tendency, whether in the case of long-existing evils or of exceptional emergencies, is to deal with the problems which confront it vicariously." Further, Potter maintained that personal involvement in charity was not only more effective for the recipient than institutionally implemented strategies but also the means for the giver to attain "the deepest joy and the highest happiness of which the human heart is capable." Among the examples of useful service he mentioned was the need to reform local police courts: "What an opportunity here for the personal intervention of those whose means and position make them strong enough to insist that it shall be listened to!" Potter thereby combined his concern for political righteousness with his stewardship ethic in a way typical of Progressive Era political reform.[57]

Potter's ethic of stewardship, then, while predominantly paternalistic, was not entirely so, as this emphasis on the personal element in charity entailed an element of mutuality not present in other contemporary versions of the "gospel of wealth." As with his conviction that the rich needed to worship in free churches perhaps more than the poor, Potter believed that the rich needed to give of their wealth perhaps more than the poor needed to receive it. Potter believed not only that those with material blessings were responsible for meeting the needs of the poor and for involving themselves directly in this work, but also that they should do so in ways that decreased the dependence of the poor. Indeed, these three principles were central to his view of the way in which all charitable and philanthropic work, including that of the church, should be implemented. Here again, Potter echoed concerns common among his Protestant contemporaries as they struggled to meet the needs of the day.

At midcentury, white American Protestants tended to believe that, just as the wealthy deserved their riches, the poor deserved their privation. Some regarded pauperism and vagrancy as crimes, some saw in the poor a blessed opportunity for the exercise of Christian service, and most viewed poverty as an inevitable and permanent condition of human life in this world. In the face of the various economic crises of the last quarter of the century, some responded by repeating the traditional line. Others, like Henry Potter, began to adjust their thinking and, as a result, the thinking of the churches, to better address the new conditions.[58]

Potter first spoke of helping the poor in ways that decreased their dependence in the wake of the Panic of 1873–74. While arguing for discrimination in charitable efforts to assure that those most in need received the assistance due them and maintaining the need for criteria on which to evaluate requests for aid, Potter rejected the criterion of the so-called deserving poor. "The deserving poor are almost as hard to find as the deserving rich," he pointed out and suggested that if this principle had been applied by "the Divine Friend who supremely helps us all, the infinite pity and succor of Calvary would never have been vouchsafed to anybody." Based on a contemporary sociological study and his experience of Grace's charitable organizations, however, he distinguished "chronic idlers" and "hereditary paupers" from those whose poverty was either no fault of their own or the result of betrayal by "false friends or their own appetites." This latter group had "the clearest claim on our sympathy and help," while the former group deserved "a treatment partly reformatory and partly punitive," not "indiscriminate benefactions." Although he made such distinctions, Potter nevertheless maintained that "the sentimentalism of indiscriminate and thoughtless charity" was far better than "the cynicism and indifference which sneers at all charity alike."[59]

Potter returned to these concerns in the wake of the Panic of 1893 in several addresses delivered from 1895 to 1898 and in his work with New York's Charity Organization Society. Many Protestants supported the society's efforts, intended to aid only the truly needy and assist them in attaining self-sufficiency, but not all did. The New York Society of Christian Socialists, for example, criticized the society's effort to identify the "truly needy," one aspect of which was to arrest and prosecute "professional beggars." In 1890 the Christian socialists reported that the Charity Organization Society's officers arrested as many as seven hundred twenty-five beggars a month and asked, "Is there no better work for the charity organization society to do than to set the police on the poor people who ask the rich people to give them something, and to send the poor people to prison, where they cannot bother the rich?"[60]

Potter nevertheless supported the society's aims and continued to speak against indiscriminate relief and for the development of new strategies for education and employment, such as trade and industrial schools. In the 1890s, however, he appealed not simply to the demands of proper stewardship but also to the demands of justice for the poor and unemployed and to the need to alleviate class alienation. In December 1898, speaking at a monthly conference of the Charity Organization Society, Potter warned that "the rumbling thunders" of social unrest would not be silenced by indiscriminate relief or by programs that maintained dependence. Only "justice to the poor and unfortunate," providing employment and enabling self-sufficiency, would resolve the growing alienation between rich and poor, capital and labor.[61]

The base from which Potter addressed various particular concerns was his understanding of Christianity's wider responsibilities to the world. In his 1870 case for the expansion of Grace Church's programs to "reach and minister to the lowest and least cared for classes," he argued that Christianity's mission "must be a *many-sided* mission, having something to say to those to whom it comes, not only on Sundays, but on week-days; something to say to the bodies of those whom it would fain care for, as well as their souls; something to *do* for their physical and intellectual pains and hungers, as well as for that other and deeper hunger of the soul for the Bread of Life. No truly Christian endeavor can leave these physical and intellectual wants out of account; Christ never did; His Church may never dare to." Christianity's mission to all human nature, in Potter's view, emphasized concrete action, helpful service to others, rather than belief or worship. Potter did not neglect these latter aspects of Christian life, but he valued them according to their ability to nurture a life of service to others. It was such service, he believed, not theological argument or liturgical practice, which witnessed to the truth of Christian beliefs. Observing that Jesus Christ had inaugurated a fellowship that ought to have a word of hope to all people oppressed by sorrow and want, he argued that it was the church's business "to take that word and carry it to men and translate it into deeds which they can not fail to understand. If this is not its business, then it has no business at all."[62]

As shown in his Grace Church sermons on tenement housing, women's and children's labor, immigration and Sunday observance, the evils of intemperance, and care for those in prison, Potter translated that word of hope into concern for all human suffering.[63] Again like Muhlenberg before him, he also translated it into direct participation in endeavors for the alleviation of suffering organized outside church structures. One organization with which he worked was the State Charities Aid Association, which sought to support and reform public charities by holding them accountable to taxpayers. Potter chaired the association's special committee on the construction of a new Bellevue Hospital; was a member of its committees on Hospitals and Adult Able-Bodied Paupers; and, at its 1880 conference, presided at a session on care for the insane and delivered the closing address. At the association's 1875 annual meeting, members heard addresses by both Potter and William Cullen Bryant, a prominent opponent of slavery, cofounder of the Republican party, and editor of the reform-oriented *New York Evening Post*. Other noteworthy New York leaders with whom Potter served in the association were Levi P. Morton, financier and member of Grace Church; Frederick Law Olmstead, architect and designer of New York's Central Park; Abram Hewitt, elected mayor of New York in 1886 in a race against Henry George and other candidates; the Rev. Edward McGlynn, noted Roman Catholic social reformer and supporter of Henry George; and Theodore Roosevelt, whose 1886 bid for the New York mayor's office was also thwarted by Hewitt. Henry Potter's older brother, Howard, a financier and philanthropist, also served on the association's executive committee.[64]

In 1879 Potter served on a jury for a model tenement design competition sponsored by a building trade journal, the *Plumber and Sanitary Engineer*. Other jury members were Charles Chandler, president of the New York City Board of Health; Robert Hatfield, president of the New York chapter of the American Institute of Architects; John Hall, minister at Fifth Avenue Presbyterian Church; and Robert Hoe, printing press manufacturer and art patron. This group was asked to determine, from one hundred ninety designs submitted for a tenement on a twenty-five-by-one-hundred-foot lot, the design that best combined maximum profit for the investor with maximum safety and convenience for the tenants. In its judgment, the jury "emphatically declare[d] that in their view it is impossible to secure the requirements of physical and moral health within these narrow and arbitrary limits," concluded that the problem of tenements could be solved only by statutory reform, and declared the competition void. Nevertheless (and, in light of later events, unfortunately) the jury went on to commend those plans that came closest to meeting the competition's aims. It awarded first prize to a design for a dumbbell-shaped structure, which in subsequent years became notorious for its various deficiencies.

> Situated on a pinched 25 x 100 foot lot, the dumb-bell was usually five or six stories high and contained fourteen rooms to a floor, seven on ei-

ther side running in a straight line. . . . [It] harbored four families to a floor. . . . Of the fourteen rooms on each floor, ten depended for light upon the narrow air shaft. This was an indentation at the side of the building about twenty-eight inches wide and enclosed on all sides. It proved to be not only inadequate for the purpose of providing light and air, but a positive hindrance to the health and comfort of the tenants. The shaft was a fire hazard, acting as a duct to convey flames from one story to the next. It became a receptacle for garbage and filth of all kinds.[65]

The competition also engendered wider interest in tenement reform. An 1879 conference of clergy and laypeople, attended by Potter, resolved that the clergy would preach on the subject on Sunday, 23 February. In the following weeks, three public meetings were held, at the last of which the Committee of Nine was formed to introduce legislation to reform the state tenement house law. The new law, enacted in 1879, virtually assured the widespread adoption of the dumbbell design. It would take later reform efforts to undo the damage done, despite the jury's disclaimer, by its perceived endorsement of the twenty-five-by-one-hundred-foot lot and the dumbbell design.[66]

In his sermon "The Homes of the Poor," preached at Grace Church on the agreed Sunday, Potter described in some detail the conditions of tenement houses and their effects on the people living in them. While decrying the assault by tenement living on the bourgeois values of privacy and modesty, he also argued that tenements were evil because they dehumanized their residents.

> For, in order to appreciate the situation of our tenement house population, you must add to the inevitable evils that come from over-crowded, ill-ventilated, viciously-arranged apartments, those others that come from intemperance and crime and neglect. Over against this wretched life, so scanty and uninviting in its home-aspects, stands the gin-palace and the corner grocery, in which heartlessness and greed conspire to demoralize the parents and rob the children. And so it comes to pass that there are men and women, aye, and children, too, living in this New York of ours, who are gradually losing all trace of the humanity with which God endowed them.[67]

As for the church's response to the evils resulting from tenement living, Potter defined its role as that of informing and educating those individuals who own and manage this housing and affirmed its responsibility for addressing what some would regard as worldly or secular affairs.

> Managing real estate is not the calling of the Church, and few institutions are so poorly adapted for such a task as would be a parish or congregation.

But managing real estate is the business of the individual citizen, and as to the moral bearings of that or any other earthly business, the Church, as the witness and messenger of an eternal moral Governor, nay, as the messenger, most of all of a God once incarnate in our common humanity, must needs, if it has any business at all in the world, have a good deal to say.[68]

Henry Codman Potter continued not only to insist that the incarnate God had a good deal to say about all the world's affairs but also to articulate and demonstrate just what he thought God might say about some of those affairs. In doing so he reflected, and helped to advance, the rise and development of American social Christianity after the Civil War. He also brought to that work the vision of a comprehensive church and the commitment to the practical work of the church derived from evangelicalism in the Episcopal Church and in wider American Protestantism. In the Episcopal Church, Alonzo Potter and William Muhlenberg mediated these traditions to Henry Potter as they and other moderate Evangelicals did to other younger church leaders who, shortly after the war, would become associated with the Broad Church movement. That influence demonstrates Henry Potter's appreciation of the vitality and flexibility of Evangelical traditions. His work shows also the comprehensiveness, or many-sidedness, of those traditions, including tolerance of diverse theological and liturgical expression, in part to avoid any damaging ecclesiastical disputes and in part to refocus the church's labors on the practical work of Christian life. As developed by the Broad Church movement, this agenda came to include the vigorous pursuit of theological inquiry, especially higher biblical criticism. Although Potter's role as bishop caused him to tread more cautiously in the realm of biblical criticism than some of his contemporaries, he nevertheless clearly supported this effort and those who engaged in it.

Attempting to reach more effectively those outside the churches, Potter encouraged the adaptation of older means, such as religious orders and revivals, without regard for their association with particular ecclesiastical parties. His enduring concern was with their potential for effectiveness in meeting the needs of the day. Similarly, during his tenure at Grace Church, he was directly involved in the early development of a new means for such work, the institutional church, which was itself many-sided in its ministering to the various needs of church members and nonmembers alike. As bishop, Potter continued to support the development of other institutional churches in the Diocese of New York. Indeed, his vision for the Cathedral of St. John the Divine owed much to the theory and practice of both the earlier comprehensive church and the later institutional church.

Related to the institutional church movement, and expressed through Potter's vision for the cathedral, was the free church movement. Originally motivated by the need to respond to the alienation of working classes from Protestantism by Christianizing them, both the institutional and free church movements maintained this motive well into the late nineteenth century. With Potter, as with others, however, these movements came to include the motive of Christianizing the middle and upper classes as well. Realizing that class alienation in church and society was not resolvable by a one-sided strategy, Potter argued that Christians had to prove their religion's worth to poor and working people before Christians could reasonably expect them to embrace it. Thus, while maintaining a conservative stewardship-of-wealth ethic, Potter insisted on direct personal involvement in charitable work. He did so not only because he believed this approach more effective than an impersonal institutional approach for those it sought to aid, but also because he believed it was necessary for maintaining Christian sympathies in those who sought to give aid, especially in light of the desensitizing effects of wealth. As the misuse of accumulated wealth was also one of the chief causes of political corruption in the postwar period, his concern about the perils of wealth also provided the foundation for Potter's concern for political righteousness. Further, Potter both argued and demonstrated that the effort to address the needs of poor and working people included participation in programs initiated by churches and nonreligious agencies alike.

The Protestant vision of a Christian America, originating in the earliest days of the European conquest of North America, developed and adapted to the changing conditions of life throughout the eighteenth and nineteenth centuries. Henry Codman Potter applied this vision, derived from the variation of it employed by antebellum Evangelical Episcopalians, to several specific social issues that dominated his activity: racial reform and immigration; the work and well-being of women; the ethics of political life, both domestic and international; and the relations of labor and capital. In each of these areas, Potter relied on the religious traditions of previous generations but also helped to reshape those traditions—in dialogue with emerging theological perspectives, developing social and economic theories, and challenging social events—to better meet the changing conditions of life in the late nineteenth century.

2 *Brotherhood and Inequality*

One critical set of issues facing American Christians in the nineteenth century was that encompassing slavery, emancipation, and postwar racial reform; rising immigration by people of other than northern European ancestry and other than Protestant religious affiliation; increased contact with non-European-American peoples as a result of territorial acquisitions; and (to a lesser extent in the consciousness of white social gospelers) ongoing interaction with aboriginal Americans. Henry Potter and his white contemporaries addressed these concerns with common assumptions and convictions, rooted in various aspects of American religious and social thought, about the "fatherhood of God and brotherhood of humanity," the inevitability of human social inequality, and the responsibility of the more favored to the less favored. Some of these convictions appear contradictory today, but they nevertheless established the broad framework within which Potter and others worked as they attempted to bring the gospel to bear on the needs of their day.

Slavery and Emancipation

Within the framework of antebellum race relations, Alonzo Potter was typical of moderate antislavery reformers. In his memorial sermon for Henry Codman Potter, W. R. Huntington observed that Alonzo Potter "felt a keen sympathy for the negro, in the old slavery days. I do not know that he was accounted an Abolitionist, but he was distinctly 'Anti-Slavery.'"[1] M. A. DeWolfe Howe reported that Alonzo Potter's sympathy and care for black people "had been manifested in his boyhood, at his

58

brother's house in Philadelphia, and again in his ministry to the colored people while a Professor at Schenectady." Writing after the Civil War, Howe might understandably have exaggerated Alonzo Potter's efforts in this area, but he remarked only that "intense as were his feelings of re-pugnance to the enslavement of any human being, he made no factious assault upon the institution of slavery as it existed under the laws of our country."[2] While Potter's respect for law and view of the limits of cleri-cal involvement in public issues prevented him from publicly condemn-ing slavery, he nevertheless strongly opposed it and worked for the wel-fare of black people, especially within the Episcopal Church and its Diocese of Pennsylvania.

By 1830 the population of Philadelphia included 15,000 blacks, about 1,000 of whom had achieved sufficient economic and social success to be regarded as middle class. Although a black Methodist church with a black pastor had been established in 1794, Howe reports that the black population of Philadelphia "had been so utterly neglected by all Chris-tian people that they might have pleaded, in excuse for any measure of moral degradation, 'No man cared for my soul.'" In 1843, during the epis-copate of Henry U. Onderdonk, the Pennsylvania diocesan convention adopted a resolution that denied representation in the convention to black congregations. From the start of his episcopate in 1845, Alonzo Potter supported and participated in efforts, led by a few lay Episcopalians, to provide worship services and Sunday school to black Philadelphians. These efforts resulted in the formation of a black Episcopal congregation, the Church of the Crucifixion, and ultimately to the construction of a church building and the parish's admission into the Pennsylvania dioce-san convention. In the admission process the church's organizers neglect-ed to call attention to the fact that its members were black, and because blacks were excluded from the convention, the Church of the Crucifix-ion was to be represented there by white men. As another black Episco-pal congregation existed with black deputies who had been excluded from the diocesan convention, the representation for the Church of the Cru-cifixion seems to have been not primarily an example of white paternal-ism. Rather it was a deliberate strategy to circumvent the diocesan rule and assure representation for the congregation in the convention to which it had been duly admitted.[3]

The nature of the congregation's membership became generally known before its white representatives appeared at their first diocesan convention. Some of the other delegates objected to this representation of the Church of the Crucifixion, and not because they advocated per-mitting black delegates to represent their own church. The convention debated the matter but reached no resolution. Perhaps because Alonzo Potter preferred a consensus-building mode of leadership and because he was an interested party in the case, "for several successive Conventions it was re-opened, and long and excited debates were had whether white men representing a congregation of blacks should be permitted to sit in the councils of the Church and take part in the enactment of the laws of the Diocese." When the issue was finally to be decided, however, Bishop Potter, normally acutely attentive to correct procedure, took two unusual procedural steps. First, rather than temporarily ceding his position as chair to another convention member so that he might speak on this matter, he addressed the convention from the chair and

> with a freedom, decision and manliness not often exhibited by those in high places . . . poured forth the honest and almost impassioned recoil of his soul from that measure of prejudice and injustice, that would not only deny to men of the proscribed race liberty to appear for themselves in the councils of the Church, but also the privilege of being represented by men of the dominant race, though occupying the foremost rank in the social circle. The Bishop did not refrain from abjuring that peculiar type of Christian charity which would both—hold the African in legal disability to confer with brethren in the household of Christ on matters of common interest—and also repel from counsel any who with generous fraternity had braved the rebuke of the community and sought to do him good.

In a second procedural irregularity, Bishop Potter altered the voting procedure by calling his own name first rather than last.[4]

While generally restrained in his public utterances, Alonzo Potter expressed his views clearly in private correspondence. On 11 May 1861, one month after the attack on Fort Sumter, South Carolina, he replied to a letter from a friend who was rector of an Episcopal church in Washington, D.C., where slavery was not made illegal by Congress until the following year. After expressing his concern for his friend and the residents of Washington generally, he wrote, "What is before the whole country the All-seeing alone can say. We have been a haughty, arrogant, self-relying people, idolizing our institutions, ourselves, our great country and our 'manifest destiny;' and this, with the 'monster iniquity,' has deserved, if it has not provoked, God's heaviest judgments. Oh that prayer and humiliation might avert the blow."[5] As the subsequent months and years revealed, the blow was not averted, for, in the minds of many, God's heaviest judgment was pronounced on the nation for the "monster iniquity" of slavery and its other sins.

During the war, "ardently as he desired that in some way under the ordering of Divine Providence the war might bring about the extinction of slavery, he did not vex the public ear with popular harangues against the institution." In late 1863, however, Alonzo Potter was provoked to depart from his customary public restraint. John Henry Hopkins, bishop of Vermont, had in 1861 published a pamphlet on the biblical view of slavery, arguing that it should be gradually abolished with respect for the rights of southern states, but that abolition had no biblical or theological warrant. In May 1863, soon after the Emancipation Proclamation and just before a Pennsylvania election seen as potentially indicating the state's level of support for the federal government, Hopkins permitted his pamphlet to be reprinted and circulated by the government's opponents. Hopkins again claimed to support complete but gradual abolition and to be both ignorant of and disinterested in the political affiliation of those who requested the republication of his pamphlet—by his own account, Philadelphia "Episcopalians of high character." Nonetheless, many in Pennsylvania regarded the pamphlet's appearance as a defense of slavery and the rebellion.[6]

It cannot be known whether Alonzo Potter's response combined a profound moral disagreement with a justifiable objection to what he may have regarded as Hopkins's undue encroachment of proper diocesan authority. In any case, in September 1863, Bishop Potter and a majority of one hundred sixty-three clergy of the Diocese of Pennsylvania issued a protest. In it they, while disavowing any desire to become embroiled in politics, argued that they felt compelled "to deny any complicity or sympathy" with the position of the bishop of Vermont.

> This attempt not only to apologize for slavery in the abstract, but to advocate it as it exists in the cotton States, and in States which sell men and women in the open market as their staple product, is, in their judgment, unworthy of any servant of Jesus Christ. As an effort to sustain, on Bible principles, the States in rebellion against the government, in the wicked attempt to establish by force of arms a tyranny under the name of a Republic, whose "corner-stone" shall be the perpetual bondage of the African, it challenges their indignant reprobation.[7]

As strongly as he felt about the evil of slavery, however, Alonzo Potter was also concerned about the danger of clerical demagoguery. The following month, he sent a letter to the diocesan clergy urging them "to remember that as Ministers of the Prince of Peace it is our duty as far as possible to avoid all unseemly exhibitions of feeling and to bear with serene patience any seeming provocation that may be presented."[8] Among the clergy who signed the protest were three of Henry Codman Potter's schoolmates and friends: Phillips Brooks, who later joined him in criticizing the Episcopal Church on the ease with which it reunited after the war; Leighton Coleman, who was later bishop of Delaware and a colleague of Henry Potter's in the Church Temperance Society; and R. Heber Newton, later a prominent proponent of social Christianity and the Broad Church movement. A fourth noteworthy signatory was Eliphalet Nott Potter, Henry Potter's next-younger brother, whom Alonzo Potter had ordained to the diaconate the previous year at St. John's Church, Troy, where Henry Potter was then rector. Had Henry Potter himself been serving in the Diocese of Pennsylvania, as he had been from 1857 to 1859, he too would certainly have signed the protest. As noted in the previous chapter, Hopkins's pamphlet and the controversy it provoked reflect the broader challenge to evangelical Protestant convictions about scriptural authority posed by the ways in which many Christians used the Bible to support the continuing existence of slavery.

George Hodges observes that despite Henry Potter's opposition to slavery and support for the national government during the war, the subjects of his sermons from this period, which he spent at St. John's Church, "are curiously devoid of allusion to current events."[9] A fugitive slave was arrested in Troy in 1860 but was rescued by a mob and sent on to Canada. Abraham Lincoln passed through Troy in February 1861 on his way to his inauguration. Potter's older brother, Robert, commanded a New York division in the war, distinguishing himself in several battles and being twice wounded. In July 1863 Henry Potter visited the battlefield at Gettysburg before the dead were buried; with 51,000 combined Union and Confederate killed and wounded in three days of fighting, the stark reality of the war would have been all too clear in these southeastern Pennsylvania fields and hills. Potter recalled later: "I never witnessed such a sight, and I received a physical shock from which it took me a long time to recover. I came back to Troy, and was for a long time laid up with a serious illness." His convalescence coincided with the draft riots of 1863 and, as Potter discovered only later, local rioters threatened to destroy the house of the friend in which he was recuperating because they disapproved of its owner's politics. His experience at Gettysburg, however, did not shake Potter's conviction of the righteousness of the cause of abolishing slavery and restoring the union.[10]

The Episcopal Church's treatment of slavery and the war helps to illuminate not only Henry Potter's apparent lack of reference to the war and its causes during this period, but also his unambiguous criticism of the church after the war. Unlike other Protestant denominations with national constituencies, the Episcopal Church did not formally divide over the slavery issue. By 1861, however, it was divided in fact when Episcopalians in the seceded states organized the Protestant Episcopal Church in the Confederate States of America. Nevertheless, throughout the war leaders of the Protestant Episcopal Church in the United States of America (PECUSA) proceeded as if their southern counterparts remained full members. At the 1862 and 1865 PECUSA General Conventions, the roll call included the names of all dioceses, and the convention floor included seats for all delegates, south and north. Southern Episcopalians were explicitly invited to attend the 1865 General Convention, held in Philadelphia six months after Appomattox, and a few did. In its 1862 General Convention and bishops' pastoral letter, the PECUSA addressed the political and ecclesiastical crisis for the first time. Significantly, neither the deliberations of the convention nor the pastoral letter addressed the issue of slavery; the delegates' concerns were confined to the civil rebellion and the ecclesiastical schism.[11]

In the pastoral letter, the bishops decried the "stupendous rebellion" and considered it in light of both human agency and divine providence. They regarded the war as God's judgment on the nation for its sins, but, unlike Alonzo Potter, they did not include slavery among the sins that warranted such chastisement. Further, they argued that the rebellion was both a sin and "*a great crime* before the laws of God, as well as man," thereby justifying the federal government in acting to maintain political union. They did not, however, make any similar argument for a justification of the federal government's actions based on the sin of slavery. The attitude of the convention was likely influenced by Bishop John Henry Hopkins, who served as presiding bishop *pro tempore.* Hopkins also prepared a draft of the pastoral letter that made no reference to the war and absented himself when the revised letter, written by Bishop Charles McIlvaine, was read. Hopkins's influence was also felt after the war at the 1865 General Convention, at which he was presiding bishop. The convention adopted a thanksgiving "for peace in the country and union in the Church" but declined to include a "thanksgiving for the restoration of union in the nation, and for the removal of the curse of slavery."[12]

Phillips Brooks expressed indignation at the convention's action, as did his friend Henry Codman Potter. The following month, in a sermon on Thanksgiving Day that he entitled "Thanks for Victory," Potter explicitly linked the outcome of the war and the justice of God. In it he urged his congregation at Troy to give thanks to God through Jesus Christ, for it was the principles and teachings of the gospel of Christ that had prevailed. "If it is only brute force which has won us peace, and there has been no triumph of those divine facts of justice and truth and the sacredness of humanity which Christ brought into the world, then we had better stop right here and go home. I have no business to speak or you to listen." Further, he specifically cited the convention's action, denying that it "represented fairly the mind of the constituencies behind it" and criticizing "that timid and unmanly temper which has, among so many of our Northern People, too long sacrificed principle to expediency." The St. John's congregation had Potter's sermon printed, under the title "Our Threefold Victory."[13]

In the years that followed, Potter maintained that the victory over slavery was a victory for divine justice. In 1893, in an address delivered at Gettysburg at the dedication of a monument to the New York soldiers who had died there thirty years earlier, he conceded that certain divisive rancors are best forgotten in the interests of the country but avowed

> We may never forget that the struggle of which these graves are the witnesses was a struggle for the eternal righteousness. We may never forget that the cause which was substantially decided here was the cause of freedom, and justice, and the everlasting equities, as against a despotism which, however amiable its ordinary exhibitions, had in it . . . the essence of that "crime that degrades men." We may never forget that behind the question of the Union was the question of unpaid labor, of bartered manhood, of a traffic which dealt in human hearts.[14]

Potter maintained a concern for the welfare of black people all his life. As was the case with many of his predecessors and contemporaries, however, Potter's concern was moderate. W. R. Huntington observed only that, like Alonzo Potter "Bishop Henry Potter's feeling for the negro was also keen. One of the early acts of his episcopate was the taking a prominent part in the Consecration, here in this very church where we are gathered, of the negro Bishop of Cape Palmas [Liberia]. And only a year ago he incurred odium at Richmond [during the General Convention held there in 1907] by asking a colored clergyman to be a guest at his table."[15] Even in Potter's own day such actions hardly constituted a comprehensive program for racial reform, but he did participate in some contemporary racial reform strategies.

After the Civil War, white religious and secular reformers employed three basic strategies for racial reform: first, advocacy of civil rights for blacks; second, education for blacks in the southern states through domestic missions and philanthropic agencies; and third, support for the colonization or resettlement of blacks in Africa, especially in Liberia. Of these three, Henry Codman Potter was prominently involved in the colonization movement, and he provided some support for religious and

philanthropic educational work by and for blacks. Potter did not, however, participate in advocacy of civil rights for blacks. Those postwar
social Christians who advocated civil rights as the next step after emancipation, such as Jesse Henry Jones and Thomas Wharton Collens, were
heirs of the abolitionist tradition. Alonzo Potter had been antislavery but
was not an abolitionist, and Henry Potter's moderate concern with racial reform is continuous with the moderate antislavery tradition of the
prewar period. While he addressed many public issues during his forty
years in New York, there is no record of any comment on racial reform
matters such as the passage of the Civil Rights Act of 1875 or its over-
turning by the Supreme Court in 1883; the Compromise of 1877 and
subsequent "retreat from Reconstruction"; the rise of Jim Crow laws and
lynchings in the 1880s and 1890s; the *Plessy* v. *Ferguson* case, culminating in the Supreme Court's "separate but equal" ruling of 1896; or the
Brownsville incident of 1906. Potter only once referred to the lynchings
of blacks in the late nineteenth century. In 1898 in the context of an argument against U.S. administration of the Philippines in the wake of the
Spanish-American War, he maintained that the record of U.S. treatment
of "subject races" was thoroughly shameful and dishonorable. "The story in every case, in greater or lesser degree, has been one long record of
cruelty, rapine, lust, and outrage. 'The best Indian,' an army officer has
been quoted as saying, 'is a dead Indian'; and the best negro or Chinaman
apparently is one who has been strung up at a lamp-post or grilled alive
on a village bonfire." His awareness of such racial violence, however,
seems not to have led him to support more progressive strategies for racial reform.[16]

Potter was typical of moderate white social gospelers in his neglect
of civil rights for blacks. Those of his contemporaries who developed a
commitment to progressive strategies of racial reform, such as Josiah
Strong and Washington Gladden, did so late in their lives and as a result
of their recognition of the failure of earlier efforts. Others, such as Lyman
Abbott, became more conservative. While it is not true that social gospelers in general, and Potter in particular, neglected racial reform as such,
it is certainly true that most neglected civil rights as a means of achieving that reform. Potter's involvement in postwar education for blacks was
only slightly greater, and may have been limited by the scant involvement of the Episcopal Church. The General Convention established the
Freedmen's Commission in 1865 and five years later made it the permanent Commission on Home Missions to Colored People but in 1878 de-
moted the commission to a subcommittee. Potter attended the subcommittee's meetings and preached in support of its work in late 1887 and

early 1888. Other denominations were undertaking substantial campaigns in education for blacks. Notable among such efforts was the American Missionary Association, a cooperative effort of Congregationalist, Methodist, Baptist, and Presbyterian churches. In the Episcopal Church, however, such work seems to have had little support. The only other evidence that Henry Potter was involved in this work early in his life is Booker T. Washington's later report that Potter had attended the Hampton Institute graduation ceremonies in 1875, the year in which Washington had graduated. Many years later, Potter did play at least a supporting role in Washington's later industrial education work.[17]

In the years following emancipation, Potter was nearly alone among white reformers in his support for colonization. His prominence in this area in the mid-1890s, however, was not entirely by his choice. While blacks in North America had long talked of returning to Africa, colonization (as distinguished from emigration) had been conceived primarily by whites as a solution to the race problem. This strategy's most important organization was the American Colonization Society (ACS), founded in 1817. The ACS sent its first black settlers to Liberia in 1820, and by the outbreak of the Civil War it had sent more than twelve thousand. Evangelical Episcopalians, including William Muhlenberg and William Meade, were among the society's strongest early supporters, and the church's unofficial association with the ACS was strengthened by its establishment of a mission in Liberia in 1835. From its inception the ACS was controversial. Its stated purpose was to "put free blacks where they could best use their civilized talents for the benefit of themselves and Africa." The dual nature of this purpose was upheld by ACS advocates even after Emancipation and the end of the war. In 1889 one supporter wrote, "I believe the redemption of Africa, through the aid and efforts of the educated descendants of the African slaves of the United States, will prove the most efficient means to settle the race question in the United States."[18] Many in the country saw colonization nevertheless as a means of putting free blacks where whites would not have to deal with their just demands. Before the war, the ACS was criticized by blacks who feared that all free blacks would be coerced to emigrate to Africa, by white abolitionists who feared colonization was an effort to make slavery more secure, and by slaveholders who feared the promise of freedom for blacks in Africa would undermine the institution of slavery. After the war, it was criticized for diverting attention from the problem of racial reform in the United States. When treatment of blacks worsened as the century waned, however, both emigration and colonization again became attractive alternatives for blacks seeking some measure of real freedom.[19]

In 1891 the ACS was the only organization that had the means to assist those interested in emigration. At the same time, however, it faced a crisis of mission. After emancipation, the society's fortunes had risen and fallen in inverse relation to those of black people in the United States. At a low ebb in the decade after the war's end, interest in colonization rose again with the retreat from Reconstruction in the late 1870s. This interest rose yet again in the early 1890s as a result of the deteriorating racial and economic situation and the advocacy of emigration by Bishop Henry M. Turner of the African Methodist Episcopal Church, who had been involved with the ACS since the late 1870s. When the society's long-serving president died in 1891, its members "looked for a new president from the ranks of long-time members," hoping to find "a leader who could generate favorable public opinion in both the black and white communities and attract donations from the new class of wealthy philanthropists." At its January 1892 annual meeting, the ACS elected as its president Henry Codman Potter.[20]

Potter had become a lifetime member of the ACS in 1871, his third year as rector of Grace Church. In 1886, while assistant bishop, he presided at the ACS's annual meeting in Washington and became one of its vice presidents but was otherwise inactive in the society. Potter's initial interest in the ACS was probably due to both the tradition of ACS support among Evangelical Episcopalians and his own commitment to employing various means to address particular social needs. Both his extant addresses on the subject and his support for other measures of racial reform demonstrate that, unlike some white supporters of colonization, Potter never regarded colonization as the sole or primary solution to race relations in the United States. At the same time, his views seem not to have been directly influenced by black colonization advocates such as Bishop Henry Turner, despite the fact that Potter's prominence in the ACS in the early 1890s coincided with Turner's increased advocacy for emigration.

Unfortunately for all concerned, Potter was in Europe at the time of his election as ACS president and did not hear of it until some time later. In the meantime, in February 1892, one hundred twenty prospective colonizers arrived in New York. Unexpected and unwanted by the ACS, they were victims of a fraud and had fled rising racial violence in the hope of boarding ship to Liberia. With the sixty authorized colonizers who were already in New York, they awaited passage on a ship that could accommodate only fifty. The press widely reported the predicament of the stranded black emigrants and prominently mentioned Potter as head of the ACS. It seems that it was from these reports that Potter first learned of his election. Events thus conspired to make it difficult, perhaps impossible, for him to decline the election. After he returned from Europe in May 1892, Potter formally accepted the presidency and attempted to renew the ACS.[21]

At the January 1893 annual meeting, Potter admitted that he had sometimes thought that the criticism of the ACS as an anachronism was correct. In particular, he suggested that while "the institution of slavery prevailed over a large part of the land," it may have been appropriate to regard colonization as an appropriate response to the needs of free blacks. He went on to observe, however, that the "conditions which called [the society] into being have indeed largely changed; but the race which it aimed to serve is yet with us, and the land which it sought to colonize ... invites us as never before." Thus, rather than recommend that the society be dissolved, he recommended that its purposes and activities be reoriented. Noting the increasing European commercial interest in Africa, Potter argued that the society's task should be "to see to it that side by side with that commercial enterprise which is just awakening to its vast opportunities in Africa, there shall move the leavening influence of that force for good government and better morality, and personal industry and trained powers which make a great State." The society must therefore send to Africa not simply any who wish to go, but "only those, who, whether as day laborers or skilled artizans [*sic*] or men of a still higher culture," could provide this beneficial leaven.

> The day of indiscriminate colonization has long ago gone by. The motto of the Society needs henceforth to be *multum non multa:* in the matter of those whom it sends to the Liberian coasts, "*not quantity* but *quality.*" ... Amid all the growing interest, and often feverish eagerness, to conquer these new wildernesses, let it be the office of this Society to seize its chance to bear to Africa men and women who are well equipped to lay foundations, to build a society, to win the ignorant, to open a path for the light and the truth, and so to make straight in the desert at least one more enduring highway for the King and the Kingdom that are to be![22]

In Potter's view, Liberia was to be not a dumping ground for America's unwanted blacks, but a self-sufficient nation exercising a positive influence over the development of all Africa.

Potter remained active in the ACS through 1896, but his efforts to renew it were ineffective. In 1893 he unsuccessfully lobbied the American government to support Liberia in a boundary dispute provoked by French colonial activity in Africa. In February 1894, as a part of the society's attempt to educate the public about and raise money for its work,

Potter addressed a public meeting in Boston where several blacks in attendance openly criticized the society. One week later black leaders in Boston, in a meeting that attracted more attention than had Potter's, adopted a resolution denouncing colonization. In addition to declining support for colonization among both blacks and whites, and for racial reform in general among whites, Potter's efforts were hampered by the panic of 1893 and subsequent economic depression. The society raised no new money and sent only a few "quality" colonizers to Liberia in the mid-1890s. In 1910, two years after Potter's death, the American Colonization Society finally ceased operations.[23]

At about the same time as his leadership in the ACS, Potter seems to have become more interested in education for blacks, particularly the work of Booker T. Washington. By the turn of the century, support for Washington's conservative strategy of racial reform through industrial education was common among white social gospelers such as Lyman Abbott and white civic reformers such as Seth Low. The first contact between the Washington and Potter, however, had come in June 1875 on the occasion of Washington's graduation from Hampton Institute, Virginia, one of several schools for blacks established by the American Missionary Association. Potter heard Washington's graduation address and, according to Washington, "came across the platform, took my hand, and said to me: 'If you ever come to New York and want a friend, come in and see me,' and to the day of his death Bishop Potter kept that promise."[24]

Precisely when Potter first became interested in Washington's later work is not clear. In his 1908 memorial address, Washington suggests that Potter had supported him at least privately for some time. Potter certainly did so publicly no later than 1901. In March of that year, the same month that Washington's *Up from Slavery* was published, Potter addressed "a meeting in the interests of the Colored Schools, Tuskeega, Ala."[25] Potter probably delivered this address in New York rather than in Tuskegee, perhaps at the very meeting to which Washington refers in his memorial address after Potter's death. In that address, Washington said,

> I shall never forget how on one occasion, when I came to New York in quest of money, in quest of friends to carry on our work at Tuskegee, how I went to him and asked if he would not appear at a public meeting in Madison Square Garden Concert Hall and be one of the speakers. I remember how he looked over his programme for the evening. He had already upon that programme two other engagements for the evening, but he said to me, "If the meeting lasts long enough, I will appear on your platform," and I remember how at half-past ten in the evening, after a

hard day's work and a still more severe evening's work Bishop Potter appeared upon that platform to speak for us.[26]

A few months after that meeting, in October 1901, the *New York Times* quoted Potter's response to a reporter's question about President Theodore Roosevelt's recent and much publicized dinner with Washington.

> "I think," replied the Bishop, "that that question might best be answered, at least so far as I am concerned, by the statement that Mr. Washington has been on a number of occasions a guest at my table.
> "It is the man, not the color or the nationality, that counts. I can see no reason why a negro, if he be a man of intellect and culture, should not be received in the home of any man."[27]

This brief remark seems to be Potter's only published comment on Washington and, by implication, on Washington's conservative strategy of racial reform through education. This support is confirmed, however, by Washington's further remarks in his memorial address for Potter: "I not only had the gracious privilege of counting him as my personal friend but as the friend of my race. I had ample opportunity to test his friendship, to find out something of his deep and abiding interest in my race. . . . [I]t was my privilege to receive on several occasions the gracious hospitality of his home. . . . In him the negro race, ten million strong, always felt and always knew that it had a strong, consistent, and courageous friend."[28]

Immigration

In addition to the challenges to a Christian America posed by slavery and its legacy of oppression and injustice, the nineteenth century also presented the challenge of immigration. Chinese immigrants began arriving in the United States in the early 1850s, especially in California, where by 1852 there were already twenty-five thousand. Approximately two million Germans and Scandinavians and an equal number of Irish arrived by 1860; another five million immigrants came in the following twenty years. The immigration rate doubled in the next decade, with five million arriving from 1880 to 1890. A much larger proportion of these later immigrants were from central, southern, and eastern Europe, their customs and culture being less familiar to Americans of northern and western European ancestry. The immigration rate declined somewhat from 1890 to 1900, with only about three and one-third million arrivals, but it increased dramatically from 1900 to 1910, with the arrival of almost nine million.[29]

Before 1880 the relatively small numbers of immigrants and their general cultural similarity to the prevailing population presented few, but nevertheless troublesome, problems. In the west there was considerable anti-Chinese agitation in the 1870s, while in the east concern grew over German socialists and Irish Catholics. Protestantism's tendency to regard itself as true Christianity led many to regard an increase in the Catholic population as a threat to the realization of a Christian America. Immigration itself, however, was not generally perceived as a problem until the 1880s. Then the alien character and customs of the multitude of immigrants from China and central, eastern, and southern Europe seemed, to many, to threaten to undermine American life. Anti-Catholicism continued to function in the response of many Protestants, particularly as some two and one-half million Catholics arrived from 1880 to 1900.[30]

During this time the most significant symptom of and catalyst for alarm over immigration was Josiah Strong's *Our Country*, published in 1885. Strong portrayed the crisis confronting the nation and traced its sources to "seven perils": immigration, Romanism, Mormonism, intemperance, socialism, wealth, and the city. Protestants regularly blamed immigrants for most of the other six "perils." For Strong, the hope for addressing these problems lay in the Anglo-Saxonization of all who came to America, for to the Anglo-Saxons had been entrusted the mission of spreading Christian civilization throughout the world. Strong became secretary of the Evangelical Alliance in 1886 and through that office and later books continued to influence Protestant social thought.[31]

Under Strong's leadership, the Evangelical Alliance proved to be an influential force on Protestant social thought of the period. In an 1886 report on the many dangers facing the country, it included among them immigration and its consequent heterogeneous effect on American culture and religion. Immigration also figured prominently among the concerns raised at the alliance's 1887 meeting. The delegates enthusiastically received Samuel Harris, Episcopal bishop of Michigan, when he stressed the Anglo-Saxon character of American Protestantism and commended its "persistency of race type," whereby it "compelled other peoples to conform to that type and constrained them to accept its institutions, to speak its language, to obey its laws."[32]

Although alarmed at the possible consequences of an increasingly heterogeneous population, before the mid-1880s Protestant leaders generally did not argue for immigration restriction. At that time the demand for restriction was being made primarily by organized labor, which was concerned about the effect on the labor market of large numbers of immigrant workers and their willingness to work for wages lower than those received by American-born workers. Protestant leaders saw labor's demand as yet another example of its ill-conceived meddling with the laws of political economy; some openly regarded immigrant workers as a useful check on the demands of American-born workers and extolled the virtue and industry immigrant workers exhibited. By 1880, however, the perceived threats of immigrant-borne radicalism and irreligion began to turn Protestant thought in favor of immigration restriction.[33]

Henry Codman Potter first dealt with the challenge of immigration during his years at Grace Church from 1868 to 1883. Grace Church's programs for the nearby German immigrant population were strengthened in 1874 when the Episcopal Church established its Church German Society in New York to train German-speaking ministers for parish-based mission work. In 1877 Grace began holding two Sunday services in German, appointed a German assistant minister, and organized a German Missionary Association for lay support of this work and administration of aid to families in need. As a result of these and related activities, Grace Church "became known as a center for far-reaching missionary operations among Germans in all parts of the city."[34]

Like all institutional church work undertaken during this period, the motivation was in part charitable and in part socially and ecclesiastically conservative. Potter's 1877 observation suggests such mixed motives: "It is not easy to estimate the importance of doing all that can be done to bring under the influence of the Gospel and the Church the vast German population which is already so large an element in the life of New York. We may not dare longer to neglect or ignore it." This rationale was stated more directly, however, in the 1882 report of Grace Church's German Missionary Association. Recognizing that the German inhabitants of the East Side of New York "are for the most part a thrifty and hardworking class," the report notes that there are nevertheless circumstances, such as illness or unemployment due to "competition in labor," in which people "are reduced to great straits." In response, the association "after investigation, extends temporary aid," whether emergency food or prescription drugs, or partial payment of rent. Such "practical sympathy" functioned as "some proof to the poor that the religion of their more favored brethren is a reality" and as "a means of counteracting the evil influence of those who are laboring among them to subvert all social order." For Potter and his colleagues, at Grace and in the church at large, service to poor immigrants arose both from their sense of their responsibility to the less favored and from their fear of the social consequences of failing to Christianize and Americanize these immigrants.[35]

After becoming bishop in 1883, Potter continued to support mission work among immigrants, particularly Germans, Italians, and Chinese. In addition, his plans for construction of the Cathedral of St. John the Divine recognized the heterogeneous character of New York's population and "provided for seven chapels, each devoted to the use of a different race of people." The chapels were dedicated to saints associated with various "races," namely those of Spain, Italy, France, Ireland, Germany, the Scandinavian countries, and the countries of eastern and orthodox traditions such as Russia, Greece, and the Balkans. Notably unrepresented, however, were the peoples of Africa and Asia as well as aboriginal peoples of the Americas.[36]

One issue around which Protestant American concern about immigration coalesced was Sunday observance, a key element of the campaign to maintain the country's Christian character. To protect Sunday while respecting the separation of church and state, sabbatarians distinguished the religious from the civil sabbath. They argued that while it was inappropriate to enforce the former, it was not only appropriate but beneficial to society to enforce the latter. Before the war and in the context of a culturally homogeneous population, the rationale for Sunday observance had consisted largely of religious reasoning and historical appeals to the "Puritan sabbath." As the century drew to a close and the population became more heterogeneous, however, the rationale shifted to a more humanitarian focus as sabbatarians argued for the legal protection of Sunday as a day of rest and hoped that those benefiting from this rest might spend some of their time in the churches. They attributed the decline in Sunday observance to various causes, including the Civil War, the consequent decay in moral standards, and general human sinfulness. More prominently in their cries of alarm, however, figured immigrants, whom they held responsible for the country's heterogeneous population and the introduction of dangerous foreign ideas, especially the idea of the festive "continental Sabbath."[37]

In May 1878, at the request of and before the New York Sabbath Committee, Henry Potter preached "A Plea for the American Sunday." Significantly, the original edition of this address included a preface that noted the Sabbath Committee's concern for "the preservation of our free institutions and the rights and liberties of all classes" and argued that the "presence of our large foreign population and other influences occasion constant aggressions which it requires constant vigilance to detect and energetic action to resist." In Potter's plea, he employed the by-then-standard argument for the "consecration of one day in seven to uses other and more sacred than those of the rest" based on a "law imbedded in the very constitution, physical, mental, and moral of human nature." He credited the Anglo-Saxon peoples of the world with observing this law most fully and thereby attaining "the loftiest achievements in arms, in literature, in science, in philanthropy, in missionary enterprise, and in social advancement." This Anglo-Saxon heritage, he argued, was the distinguishing characteristic of American civilization as evidenced in its language, laws, and religion; the "reverent observance of the Lord's-day" was an indispensable element of this last.[38]

Potter went on to note the challenge to Sunday observance arising from the "enormous immigration," especially in the previous twenty years. Of the "Irishmen, Germans, Swedes, Norwegians, Italians, French and Chinese, not to mention scores of other nations" who had come to America, he wished to be understood to "speak of every one of them with heartiest respect" in light of "the indebtedness of a land like ours to these strangers of various speech and divers faiths." He affirmed that all should be accorded "cordial greeting and equal protection." Nevertheless, he decried "that somewhat imperious demand that our foreign-born brethren shall have liberty to take our American Lord's-day and convert it into a Berlinese or Parisian Sunday."

> Call it fanaticism, call it intolerance, call it political infatuation, what you will, I venture to declare that it is high time that our brethren of other lands, and other races, and other religions, or no religion at all, understood clearly and distinctly that while we welcome them to assimilation to our national life, America is for Americans, and that while we will welcome every foreigner, Christian or Jew, Pagan or Positivist, to our shores, they are our shores, not his, and are to be ruled by our traditions, not those of other peoples.

Despite such "fanatical" language in defense of the American Sunday, Potter did not recommend immigration restriction as a means of securing this defense. He advocated as strategies only "the influence of our personal example" and "an earnest and wider dissemination of a sound teaching and literature."[39]

A memorandum from about 1880 also shows Potter's qualified rejection of immigration restriction. In it Potter criticized legislation restricting Chinese immigration on the grounds that it discriminated against the Chinese as a people and thereby violated America's role as "a refuge for the downtrodden and oppressed, of every nation, race and creed." He acknowledged that such laws might be necessary to preserve the nation's political traditions, but he argued that they must have "absolute freedom from racial prejudice" and be based on "certain requirements which demand *equally of all, and every race* certain qualifications for American citizenship." Similarly, in 1890 he observed that "at present, under existing laws, we can do little—indeed, almost nothing—to regulate the character and the quality of foreign immigration" but suggested no measures for such regulation.[40]

The 1892 reprinting of his "Plea for the American Sunday" suggests that Potter held this view of immigration and Sunday observance for some time. In his introduction to that edition he maintained that "the gradual secularizing of the day once so largely consecrated to rest and worship is not the least grave among our higher social problems," and he pointed to immigrants unfamiliar with the American Sunday as the primary cause of this problem. In light of a recent study to which he only alluded, however, he retreated somewhat from his earlier representation of the thoroughly Anglo-Saxon character of the nation's founders. He maintained, nevertheless, that although among the founders "were indeed Celts as well as Saxons, Frenchmen and Irishmen as well as Englishmen and Hollanders," they "were not divided nor in doubt as to what they wanted to do, for instance, with the Lord's-day or the ten commandments."[41]

In his charge to the 1905 New York diocesan convention, Potter again spoke on the American Sunday. On this occasion he warned that without adequate time for rest and reflection, both the family and the state would crumble, but he laid the responsibility for neglect of Sunday observance not only on immigrants but also on the commercial and material spirit of the times. With regard to the former, he regarded the essential problem as how to reach agreement on protected hours in the face of cultural heterogeneity. In addition, he retracted his earlier effort to "reproduce the Sunday of our Puritan ancestry." "Once, and that not so long ago, we were a tolerably homogeneous people, and we, who believed strongly as to the duty and necessity of safe-guarding Sunday, could say to the foreigners—I have said so myself in a sermon published some thirty years ago—'If you don't like our Sunday traditions, you can stay away where they will not irk you. We mean to maintain them, as we have inherited them.' Well, we cannot say so any longer!" He argued that those concerned about Sunday observance "must recognize elements in the situation which are absolutely new," namely the overwhelmingly heterogeneous character of the population. Rejecting the efficacy of legislation, he recommended a dual strategy of cooperation and example. Those concerned to protect Sunday must cooperate with labor organizations for the establishment of a common rest day and show by the example of their practice "the incomparably higher privilege, and dignity, and *potentiality* of the Lord's Day." Without such recognition, "the very foundations of all our measurements of conduct may be slowly and unconsciously *eaten away,* unless, from time to time, we restore them at the feet of the Source of all standards." With regard to Sunday observance, Potter thus maintained his concern about immigration throughout his working life. Earlier he had spoken, by his own admission, in "fanatical" and "intolerant" terms of the need for resistance to the diverse traditions of more recently arrived Americans, but he never translated this resistance into legislated immigration restriction. Later he continued to advocate strategies of education and example, in addition to cooperation with organized labor, while also moderating his xenophobia in recognition of a legitimate greater diversity of peoples.[42]

Anglo-Saxon Superiority and the Brotherhood of Humanity

Essential to understanding Potter's response to racial reform and immigration is the background of white race thinking in the late nineteenth century, especially the widespread conviction of Anglo-Saxon superiority. This race thinking reflected the basic values and assumptions of the dominant white middle-class culture and was employed by learned people from a variety of disciplines. It also reflected the European etymological history of the term *race,* which from the fourteenth into the twentieth century could be variously used to denote a breed of animals; all of humanity; a social and cultural collective such as a tribe, nation, civilization, or religion; or almost any discernible class of living beings. "As a consequence," Curtis Grant observes, "the salient trait of race-thinking in the nineteenth century was its ambiguity."[43] A key element of this ambiguity was the failure to distinguish between biology and culture in the use of *race,* a distinction not commonly made until well into the twentieth century. In the late nineteenth century, social scientists and those influenced by them used *race* to denote social, cultural, or biological groupings later recognized as quite distinct sorts of groups. Particularly common was the confusion of races with cultural collectives such as tribes, nations, religions, or civilizations. Potter's usage, in various sermons and addresses, reflects this confusion.[44]

Chief among the collectives considered a "race" were the Anglo-Saxons. The assumption of Anglo-Saxon superiority was one of the ruling ideas of nineteenth century Anglo-American thought. It had its roots in the centuries-old attribution of some form of superiority to those peoples variously described as Teutons, Aryans, Germans, or Franks. Whereas early-nineteenth-century discussions of the Aryan hypothesis had viewed the hypothetical Aryans as the common ancestors of all Europeans, later nationalist historians in France, Germany, and England claimed Aryan descent exclusively for their particular peoples. In England, historians made much of the supposed Germanic origins of English political institutions and social virtues, while popular writers helped implant the idea of Anglo-Saxon superiority and world mission in English thought. As Grant observes, in the late nineteenth century such race thinking "was a respectable and scientifically supported philosophy of history. It was a ready-made tool for the propagandists of imperialism who sought to rationalize and justify Britain's territorial and economic expansion in the last quarter of the nineteenth century; in their hands, race-thinking was on the verge of racism, if indeed it had not already become so."[45]

North Americans of English descent also widely adopted the conviction of Anglo-Saxon superiority. Early in the nineteenth century this conviction was motivated by a defensive response to attacks on the institution of slavery, as well as by their need to justify their continuing domination of aboriginal Americans. Later, increasing immigration by non-English Europeans reinforced the cause of Anglo-Saxon superiority, as did rising American expansionist aspirations at the end of the century. Among reform-minded Christians, Josiah Strong seems to have made the most prominent and regular appeals to Anglo-Saxon superiority, but its sources and manifestations were many. It was part of the stock of ideas upon which many white Protestant social gospelers relied.[46]

Like many of his contemporaries, Henry Potter regularly appealed to Anglo-Saxon superiority and never questioned its veracity. For example, in 1878 he argued for the maintenance of Sunday observance by claiming that "the loftiest achievements in arms, in literature, in science, in philanthropy, in missionary enterprise, and in social advancement, belong to that Anglo-Saxon people whose observance of Sunday is to-day the wonder and the admiration of every intelligent traveler." And in his controversial 1889 address on the centennial of George Washington's inauguration, he described the first president as having "incarnated in his own person and character every best trait and attribute that have made the Anglo-Saxon name a glory to its children and a terror to its enemies throughout the world."[47]

Potter's approach to the issue of immigration is more similar to Horace Bushnell's than to Josiah Strong's, and his view of Anglo-Saxon superiority likewise seems to have been influenced primarily by Bushnell. In his 1896 address "The Chicago-Lambeth Articles," delivered at Union Theological Seminary, New York, Potter referred favorably to "what Dr. Bushnell called the out-populating power of Anglo-Saxon Christendom, especially since the days of the Reformation" and went on to ask, "Have we ever stopped to consider the larger question,—what this is which this amazing reproduction upon all sorts of foreign soils of the Anglo-Saxon really stands for?" For Potter, this "remarkable quality of adaptation like which I do not hesitate to say there is nothing else in all the earth" clearly signaled one of the key elements of Anglo-Saxon superiority.[48]

At the same time, however, the conviction of the "fatherhood of God and the brotherhood of man" was equally or perhaps more important to white Christian social reformers. Against both religious and social individualism, the former seen in Calvinist soteriology and the latter in various forms of laissez-faire social and economic theory, social Christians maintained that both the temporal and ultimate fate of persons was intimately bound up with that of all people. This "vital unity of the race," as Washington Gladden termed it, they derived from the universal "fatherhood of God" and understood to be realized in the consequent universal "brotherhood of men."[49]

Henry Potter regularly appealed to human brotherhood under a divine father, particularly when addressing the issue of social alienation. Appearing in his sermons as early as 1872, the role of the church in witnessing to and establishing this brotherhood became one of his stock arguments for the value of free chapels and churches. In 1877, for example, he decried the growing "spirit of caste" in the nation and warned of "the bitter and bloody fruit the growth of social alienation may bring forth." "And for what does the Church of God exist in the world, if not to resist and rebuke this hateful spirit of caste? What is the meaning of her Master's teaching, if it is not that, whatever inevitable distinctions exist elsewhere, inside the household of the common Father, and in the dear fellowship of the Divine Elder Brother, they are to be obliterated and forgotten."[50] Fifteen years later, in one of many sermons offering his rationale for the Cathedral of St. John the Divine, he suggested that the cathedral as a free church was necessary "to teach the great lesson of Christian brotherhood, of the absolute equality of all men before their Father who is in heaven." In addition, as noted above, plans for the cathedral included seven chapels devoted to different races in recognition of New York's diverse population. Over the years, Potter regularly invoked the brotherhood of humanity when discussing concerns such as the relation of Christianity to social science, church unity and ecumenism, the relation of European American to Asian peoples, the enduring principles of the Order of Masons (to which he belonged), and the need for members of the middle class to recognize the importance of recreation for those of the working class. On at least one occasion, Potter used a biblical metaphor other than brotherhood in support of his conviction of human solidarity. In his reply to a committee of Jewish leaders who had sought his views on ways to combat anti-Semitism, Potter wrote that "any race prejudice is, on the mere score of race, inexcusable, since 'God hath made of one blood all nations to dwell on the face of the earth.'" Although the available evidence on this point is not substantial, Potter seems to have exhibited a sensitivity to Jews atypical among his white Protestant contemporaries.[51]

Potter and his white contemporaries seem to have been unaware of the contradiction between their convictions regarding Anglo-Saxon superiority and the brotherhood of man. That they were able to hold these beliefs despite their contradiction is explained through their relation in a larger complex of ideas. The salient elements of this complex were, first, the ideological link between the sense of Anglo-Saxon world mission and the commitment to Christianizing the world and, second, the assumption of human inequality. Many reformers saw the tasks of Anglo-Saxonizing and Christianizing the world as virtually coextensive. This link was made possible in part by their view of Anglo-Saxon Christianity (that is, generally English and Protestant) as the purest extant form of Christianity. The link was also established through the grounding of Anglo-Saxonism and this form of Christian triumphalism in understandings of history and progress that explicitly included a pivotal role for a chosen people. White social reformers saw Anglo-Saxons as the bearers of progress in much the same way that Christians were bearers of the kingdom of God. Indeed, many saw the two as highly compatible if not identical. The superiority accorded Anglo-Saxons, however, was based on their past accomplishments, present greatness, and future promise, not upon any supposed exclusive biological or ontological quality. To the extent that they acknowledged that in earlier times the Greeks, Hebrews, and Romans had borne the responsibility now entrusted to Anglo-Saxons, these historians, social scientists, and reformers regarded such superiority as historically contingent. Similarly, the corollary of race development, the view that "inferior" peoples had the potential for attaining civilization, distinguished these thinkers from those who maintained that certain peoples were permanently inferior.[52]

Potter's 1896 address on the Chicago-Lambeth articles most clearly shows his conflation of the election of Anglo-Saxons and that of Christians. While arguing for an increase in efforts toward church unity, he confessed his hope in the establishment of a united, scriptural, and comprehensive church. He based this hope on his "profound faith in the mission to the whole world of a Christianity which is not Greek or Roman, Oriental or Italian, but Anglo-Saxon." Potter acknowledged this contradiction but, citing both Horace Bushnell and Edward Washburn, justified it by arguing for the superiority of Anglo-Saxon Christianity on the grounds of its adaptability to varied places and circumstances. Anglo-Saxon Christianity, he suggested, had demonstrated its character as a comprehensive Christianity, not simply another narrow variant. He argued further that the Chicago-Lambeth articles on church unity would prove to be vital to the cause of church unity, for they "are the product of a race which, arrogant as it may sound to say so, has revealed itself to many men in many lands as having more than any other the future of Christendom in its hands." Adding unintended irony to acknowledged contradiction, Potter concluded his address by urging that the unity of the "Christian brotherhood of man" was required to provide "the solution of the growing social riddles," including "the inequality of caste" and the "curse of serfdom."[53]

White reformers' reconciliation of Anglo-Saxon superiority with human brotherhood was also influenced by the prevailing assumption of the inevitability of human inequality. As Grant notes, although the brotherhood of humanity was "the *sine qua non* and hallmark of the coming Kingdom of God on earth," in the reformers' understanding it "did not necessarily signify the equality of men." The contradiction between the conviction of human brotherhood and the assumption of actual inequalities of people may have been the product of a lingering "this world/next world" dualism operative despite religious liberalism's efforts to overcome such dualisms. Whatever the causes, most social Christians took human inequality for granted. In Grant's words: "Although the idea of human inequality often exercised as much an influence on their thinking as did the doctrine of brotherhood, the Social Gospelers never thought human differences worthy of serious or sustained reflection. They did not theorize about inequality; they assumed it—for the very good reason that it was the only intellectually respectable alternative open to most educated men at the turn of the century."[54]

The import of this assumption is seen clearly in the social gospelers' response to social Darwinism. Most Christian social reformers rejected social Darwinists' acceptance of the operation of natural selection in human society but nevertheless accepted the existence of unequal classes of people. The key difference between the two social theories was in the norms they prescribed. Over against natural selection, social Christians set sacrificial service as the law by which "the fittest" were to operate and by which human progress was to be realized. While social Darwinists asserted the right of the strong to dominate or even destroy the weak, social Christians required that the strong care for and raise up the weak. Like the social Darwinists, however, social Christians assumed the existence of stronger and weaker, of unequal classes of people. Christian responsibility was to be exercised not through attempts to eradicate inequalities of ability and social condition, but through attempts to mitigate the worst effects of these inequalities. The law of love by which they lived was certainly as paternalistic as it was altruistic, but *noblesse oblige* was a significantly different ethic from survival of the fittest.[55]

Potter clearly worked with such an inequalitarian social theory. Throughout his ministry he prescribed for his affluent and powerful constituents an ethic of responsibility and service to the poor and weak, implicitly and sometimes explicitly invoking the principle of *noblesse oblige.* Responding to social Darwinist criticism of Christian philanthropy, he acknowledged that the unrestrained operation of natural selection in the social order might result in humans of remarkable abilities. He denied, however, that such a state of affairs was desirable, since it would result also in the "deification of selfishness." He interpreted the crucifixion of Jesus as the "one sublime and matchless act, in which the Perfect One gave Himself in eager sacrifice for imperfect ones, and in which there was proclaimed a law not of natural, but of supernatural, selection." And he exhorted the "wise and good" to follow this example, not forgetting that "there are still sufferings to be alleviated and want to be relieved, and above all ignorance and hopelessness and unbelief to be enlightened and uplifted." Further, in various contexts he explicitly appealed to the role of a favored elite, endowed with exceptional moral or intellectual abilities, in uplifting and ennobling the social whole.[56]

The conflicting convictions of Anglo-Saxon superiority, the brotherhood of humanity, human social inequality, and the development of races set the conceptual limit within which Henry Codman Potter addressed the problem of racial reform, a problem inherited from the country's flawed colonial foundation and challenged, however incompletely, by the consequences of emancipation and the failure of Reconstruction. These convictions also set the limits for his treatment of the new challenges of immigration and, especially at the start of the twentieth century, American imperialism. With regard to all three problems, Potter's overriding concern was with the "uplift" of weaker races through their Americanization, Anglo-Saxonization, and Christianization.

With respect to blacks, this concern translated into support for educational efforts, specifically Booker T. Washington's program of industrial education. Potter could regard blacks as equal to whites as children of a

common divine father, but at the same time could hold that they needed further preparation before assuming the full rights and responsibilities of American political and economic life. Combined with the common perception articulated by Washington Gladden that in emancipation
much had been done for blacks,[57] this thinking led Potter and others to
be less than enthusiastic about efforts to secure civil rights for blacks and
less than concerned about the increasing threats to freedom and safety
for blacks as the nineteenth century drew to a close. Potter and other
whites seem to have too readily assumed that black rights and freedoms
would be fully secured when, in the view of the "stronger" white race,
"weaker" blacks were ready for them.

Similarly, Potter tended to think that immigrants also required such
uplift, specifically training in American, Anglo-Saxon, and Christian
values and traditions. Indeed, one may see the programs operated at Grace
Church and other institutional churches as motivated by the concern of
the middle class and affluent to improve not simply the living and working conditions of the poor and immigrants, but the character of the poor
and immigrants themselves. Further, as I discuss in chapter 4, this concern for uplifting the weak played a pivotal role in Potter's reversal of his
initial opposition to American annexation of the Philippines in the wake
of the Spanish-American War. The combined conviction of human brotherhood and assumption of human inequality resulted in an ethic that was
overwhelmingly paternalistic. As Grant observes, white social gospelers'

> belief in brotherhood may have made them more sensitive to racial prej-
> udice and injustice in some instances, but their assumption of human
> inequality precluded serious consideration of means to achieve social or
> political equality for supposedly inferior races, whether at home or
> abroad. On the premise that undeveloped peoples possessed latent capac-
> ities for civilization, the Social Gospelers preached the Christian respon-
> sibility of advanced races and nations to prepare their backward fellows
> for eventual manhood and self-government. Under these circumstances,
> brotherhood lost its fraternal connotations and acquired a paternalistic
> character; brotherly love came to mean not so much fellowship among
> equals as service and sacrifice on behalf of the less fortunate.[58]

Nevertheless, compared to contemporary social Darwinism, this ethic
was decidedly benevolent.

If one understands racism, as does Grant, as the conviction of the
inherent and permanent superiority of one group over others and the
coercive system of exploitation and domination of supposedly inferior
groups based on that conviction, then it is clear that Potter and many of
his colleagues cannot be considered white racists. As Clyde Griffen ar-

gues, Potter's "conviction that backward peoples might be re-educated to American standards of citizenship excludes him from the racist camp." Nevertheless, the ideology of Anglo-Saxon superiority and the gradual development of supposedly inferior "races" perpetuated unjust social relations through systemic racial and ethnic discrimination, as well as through domestic and foreign imperialism. On the one hand, as Grant claims, the idea of race development was progressive in the context of late-nineteenth-century America. On the other hand, unfortunately albeit unintentionally, the views of Potter and many of his peers aided the continuation of racial and ethnic discrimination. Thus, the interaction of religious and moral traditions of human brotherhood and social and cultural conceptions of human inequality in late-nineteenth-century social Christianity offers a caution on the need to criticize those traditions in order to illuminate the unfortunate influence of our often unacknowledged assumptions.[59]

3 The Work and Well-Being of Women

Women were instrumental in the social and ecclesiastical reform movements of the nineteenth century. In the first decades of the century, women were active in the antislavery, peace, and temperance movements; after emancipation they continued to work in these latter two crusades. Women also formed a major part of the workforce for the postwar "Protestant religio-social system." Laywomen, sisters, and deaconesses staffed the day nurseries and industrial schools of the institutional churches; formed and operated domestic and foreign mission societies; founded and administered settlement houses and women's and girls' clubs; and staffed rescue missions, hospitals, and orphanages. As Eleanor Flexner has noted, the reform ferment of the nineteenth century "produced new forms of organization through which women could achieve greater participation in social action."[1] During the same period the movement for improving women's legal and political status grew and became focused on woman suffrage. The relation between this movement and the Protestant churches was ambivalent. One the one hand, women such as Frances Willard and Anna Howard Shaw were deeply religious, and the churches depended upon women for much of their labor and regarded women as a preeminent force for the moral regeneration of society. On the other hand, the churches generally regarded public leadership in church and state as inappropriate for women, and some women, including religious women, recognized that prevailing clerical practice and use of the Bible and doctrine were means of discrimination against women.

84

Despite their differences, many Protestant reformers and women's advocates united in the temperance movement, a prominent item on the agendas of both evangelicals working for a Christian America and women working to improve the conditions of their own lives and of the larger social order. These constituencies combined in the Women's Christian Temperance Union, which was both a vital instrument of mission and reform work and a means for women to exert their influence in public life. Both the temperance and the women's movements achieved significant victories with the passage of the Eighteenth and Nineteenth Amendments in 1920. Also by 1920, significant gains had been made in securing women's roles in the churches and in improving the conditions under which women worked. While not attributable exclusively to the churches, some church people made significant contributions to these gains.[2]

Henry Potter was among the men who addressed the needs of women, and in doing so he adopted new and sometimes surprising positions and strategies. Like his father, he advocated increased roles for women in church work and initiated and supported measures to secure such roles. As a result both of his concern with the rights of working people and of his recognition of the realities of working women's lives, he also advocated women's right to work to support themselves, supported measures to improve their working conditions, and argued for expanding the roles and occupations available to women. Neither Potter's published writings nor later treatments of his life and views, however, provide evidence of his view of woman suffrage. Like his father, Henry Potter was concerned throughout his life with temperance reform. The temperance movement directly influenced women's well-being, both in terms of the effect of alcohol on women's lives and of women's participation in temperance reform work, but Potter's approach to "the liquor problem" was significantly different from that of most women temperance workers.[3]

The Unemployed Agency of Christian Women

In the nineteenth century the terms of public debate on women's work and well-being were set by what has been described as the "Victorian family ideal" or the "urban-industrial cult of genteel womanhood."[4] Although elements of this ideology were present in earlier North American and European social thought, its later dominance was a product of the nineteenth-century shift from a rural agricultural economic order to an urban industrial one. Where women's participation in both production and consumption had been prevalent in rural European and North American societies, women's role in production became increasingly restricted as industrial capitalism took hold. As a result, the myth of women's special nature, while having precedents in earlier Western thought and practice, became normative with the advent of industrial capitalism. As Beverly Harrison observes: "What the rising bourgeois class did was to lock the myth into western consciousness so deeply that the conceptions of women's experience as unchanging, as totally child-centered and domiciled became axiomatic." As employed by white social Christians, the urban-industrial cult of genteel womanhood had three central characteristics. First, they sharply differentiated men's and women's labor, with the former relegated to the public, industrial sphere and the latter to the private, domestic sphere. Second, and as a consequence of the first, they construed the social ideal of the good woman on the model of the middle-class wife and mother, the happy practitioner of the domestic arts; those who did not conform to this ideal they regarded as failed women. Third, reinforced late in the century by social Darwinist thought, they regarded the family unit as the most Christianized of social institutions and thus the foundation and model for the Christianization of the rest of the social order.[5]

The realities of most women's lives, however, were markedly different from the image portrayed by the Victorian family ideal. Many urban women, both married and unmarried, depended on their own wage labor for their survival and that of their families. Indeed, before the great increase in immigration late in the century provided a larger number of male workers, factories were decidedly dependent upon women's labor. While decreasing somewhat in the late nineteenth and early twentieth century, this dependence by no means completely discontinued, as is demonstrated by legislation in the early 1900s regulating the labor of women and children. Further, women without either work or men who would marry or support them were frequently compelled to support themselves by one of the few means available to them, namely, prostitution. It is no coincidence, then, that the "vice trade" was a major concern for reformers and social Christians, although few made the connection between the ideology of domesticity and the realities of women's lives.[6]

One factor that limited the hegemony of the cult of genteel womanhood was the churches' midcentury need for laborers to undertake their growing mission and service work. The expanding role of women in the churches during this period was consistent with the urban-industrial ideology because that ideology conceived religion as an element of the domestic sphere. Nevertheless, women's participation and leadership in church and reform organizations provided them with opportunities for labor outside the home and helped to limit the ideology's complete hegemony. Women's role in the evangelical churches had been somewhat enhanced early in the nineteenth century by the "new measures" revivalism of Charles Finney, but the churches generally, and vehemently, opposed calls for women's rights at and in the wake of the 1848 Seneca Falls convention in upstate New York. The onset of the Civil War and disagreement among reform forces on the priority to be given women's rights further undermined efforts to secure such rights and expand the range of women's social roles.[7]

During the war, however, both church and society were compelled to rely on, in Alonzo Potter's phrase, "the unemployed agency of Christian women" for service in hospitals and congregations. Alonzo Potter's interest in women's work in the church was directly related to his support of the Memorial Movement and to its concern for adapting the church's "present canonical means and appliances" to the requirements of doing "the work of the Lord in this land and in this age." As bishop, he explored and encouraged several ways to enlist laypeople in this work. As early as the 1850 General Convention he proposed, unsuccessfully, that the church begin planning to better use "intelligent and pious persons of both sexes" in its work.[8] His concern for increasing the "laborers in the vineyard" and his view of women's special gifts for certain types of church work led him to propose the revival of the order of deaconesses and the establishment of sisterhoods. He argued for these measures in his 1862 address to the diocesan convention.

> There are many women of education, refinement and earnest piety who yearn for a sphere in which they can work for God and for the afflicted. There are those whose characters and whose enjoyments would be vastly improved by such occupation. Everywhere, but especially among the suffering and hardened of *our* sex, does woman carry the sunshine of patience and of hope. In proportion as she has lofty Christian aims, and the delicacy which comes from refined associations, she is better qualified to command respect and inspire affection; and, in proportion as she possesses the experience and the ready resource which spring generally from nothing but *training*, will her agency be permanent and useful. We have, it seems to me, but to weigh considerations like these; we have but to remember what a vast amount of talent and hearty zeal among women waits to be employed; we have but to contrast the homes of our poor in sickness, and too often, alas! in health; our prisons, asylums, our reformatories, our almshouses, our hospitals, *as they are, with what they might be, if pervaded with a higher feminine and religious influence,* and we shall perceive that nothing but *organization* and a wise and directing spirit is needed to achieve this mighty and beneficent revolution.[9]

The role of women in church work, both in England and in the United States, had increased in the two decades prior to Alonzo Potter's address. William Muhlenberg had helped establish the Sisterhood of the Holy Communion in 1845, although for its first eight years it had only one member, Anne Ayres, and was formally organized only in 1853 after a second member joined. The Sisterhood of St. John the Baptist founded its House of Mercy at Clewer, England, in 1849 and in subsequent years initiated other institutions including an orphanage, a convalescent hospital, and a penitentiary and house of refuge for women. An order of deaconesses was established in the Diocese of Maryland in 1855, and what was to become the Sisterhood of the Good Shepherd was begun in Baltimore in the following year. In 1860 the Mildmay Deaconesses Home was established in London, providing training for women for various types of domestic and foreign missions. While Alonzo Potter was not among those who pioneered this work, he was among those who, in the face of widespread suspicion about the introduction of Romish practices and questions about the suitability of women for such work, aided the acceptance and institutionalization of the work of women in the Episcopal Church. In its report to the 1856 General Convention, likely written by Potter, the commission formed in response to the 1853 memorial called attention "to the wasted or misdirected energies of the women of the Church" and pointed to the Roman Catholic Sisters of Charity (founded by former Episcopalian Elizabeth Seton) as a model for women's work in the church.[10]

In the Diocese of Pennsylvania, efforts to utilize the "unemployed agency of Christian women" began in two ways. First, after meetings of the bishop and the rectors and leading laypeople of the urban parishes convened in 1859 to consider "the best means of incorporating the more neglected classes into the Church," the diocese developed a system of parish visitation by women. In this system, a rector would select a "judicious, intelligent and experienced matron to act under his observation, with liberty to select her associate workers as needed," and these women would bring spiritual and physical relief to the homes of the poor and draw them to the churches for "social, educational and industrial Mother's Meetings, and for a free Sunday Service." After its success had been demonstrated, Bishop Potter authorized use of the Episcopal Hospital's chapel as an additional base for this system of outreach to working people.[11] Second, Alonzo Potter initiated the training and employment of women in the Philadelphia's Episcopal Hospital, a plan made more urgent by the outbreak of the Civil War in 1861 and the consequent wider use of women volunteers in army hospitals. The success of these efforts confirmed Potter's conviction of the importance of women's work. He later wrote, "Properly trained, this agency of Woman would be most benign in all our public institutions—in our prisons, almshouses, reformatories, and asylums for the sick and afflicted of every name. God bless the noble women who have given themselves to the work! The Lord make his face to shine upon efforts to extend and systematize it; and the Good Spirit rouse our sex—too slow to engage in such works—to emulate the example."[12] After Alonzo Potter's death, the diocese made a significant effort "to extend and systematize" this work by establishing in 1866 the Bishop Potter Memorial House for the training of women for work in hospitals, parish schools, and domestic and foreign missions.

Other evangelical Protestants, women and men, realized the potential for women's church work at about the same time. Women became increasingly involved in the oversight and support of domestic and foreign mission work and somewhat more directly involved in the churches' mission and reform activities. At the end of the war, however, this involvement was still limited, as suggested by the 1866 report on urban mission work prepared by the newly formed American Christian Commission. This report suggested "that the poor missionary showing of Protestant churches issued from ignorance and lack of organization as well as from social indifference." In addition, "as an example of the mischievous effect of this condition," it cited "the low esteem in which the churches held women missionaries. Despite the usefulness of female assistants, all the cities visited except New York and Boston could muster only twenty-eight women in actual service—a fact due not merely to prejudice but to the absence of information and training."[13]

The prominence given to the potential of women church workers in this report and in subsequent commission conferences helped to advance efforts in the churches, both to combat the prejudice and to provide the required training. At the commission's 1868 convention in New York, for example, "Nearly all speakers strongly favored free churches and women church workers. In the course of an eloquent plea for sisterhoods and deaconess institutions on the German Protestant model, the Reverend George W. Washburn stated that the 'theory that woman has no place in the Church deprives America of two-thirds of its Christian force.'"[14] Muhlenberg had demonstrated the importance of this German Protestant model with the founding of the Sisterhood of the Holy Communion. An order of deaconesses had been established at Kaiserwerth, Germany, in 1836, but Muhlenberg may not have been aware of it until after an American Lutheran pastor who had visited Kaiserwerth in 1846 returned to Pittsburgh and established a hospital staffed by four deaconesses. Muhlen-

berg, and Henry Potter after him, subsequently cited the Lutheran deaconesses in response to charges of Romanism in the establishment of
sisterhoods and deaconesses in the Episcopal Church. Writing in 1873,
Henry Potter called the Sisterhood of the Holy Communion "the first
Protestant association of the kind in this country, and anterior also to the
first of the English Sisterhoods." At the start, the sisters' work consisted
of teaching in the parish school and visiting the poor, but it gradually
shifted to include administration of an infirmary, dispensary, and, by
1858, St. Luke's Hospital. By 1866, the same year that the Bishop Alonzo
Potter Memorial House was opened, membership in the Sisterhood of the
Holy Communion had increased, which enabled resumption of their original work in addition to administration of the hospital.[15]

Thus, when Henry Potter became rector of Grace Church in 1868,
women were already responsible for important work in the Episcopal
Church. Such work, however, was neither universally accepted nor officially sanctioned. Potter labored to achieve both those ends in his work
at Grace Church, in the national church through its Board of Missions,
and as bishop of New York. In 1868, laywomen of Grace Church were
already operating the parish's Industrial School, which taught sewing and
provided clothing for poor children. Within a year, enrollment in the
school more than tripled, and two new women's organizations were added: the Ladies' Benevolent Society and the Ladies' Domestic Missionary
Relief Association. Over the next several years, the work of these organizations expanded and other organizations were added to Grace's institutional church program.[16]

Women, including Eliza Jacobs Potter, constituted the major component of the unpaid labor force of the institutional church programs established at Grace Church. In addition, several wealthy women provided substantial financial support for those programs. One such supporter
was Lucy Kimball Morton. After her death and to honor her commitment
to Potter's plans for expanding the parish's work, her husband, Levi P.
Morton, financier and later vice president of the United States under
Benjamin Harrison, purchased for Grace Church in 1872 the building that
came to be known as Grace Memorial House. From this building, the
church operated many of its outreach programs, including, temporarily,
Grace Chapel. Another woman who generously supported Potter's plans
was Catherine Lorillard Wolfe, who donated the funding for the construction of Grace House, the parish hall completed in 1880 from which the
church operated its greatly expanded programs.[17]

During his early years at Grace, Potter also participated in the effort
to secure official recognition and general acceptance of various modes of

women's church work. In 1869 the Episcopal Church's Board of Missions established a Committee on Organized Services of Women, the membership of which included William Welsh, a Pennsylvania layperson who had worked closely with Alonzo Potter. The following year the committee made its first report to the Board of Missions, which in turn authorized the formation of a larger committee, the Women's Work Committee of the Board of Missions, to consider the "best means of associating the organized or individual efforts of women with the missionary and educational work of the church."[18] Henry Potter was among those appointed to this larger committee, and he prepared and presented its report at the October 1871 meeting of the Board of Missions. That report recommended, and the Board of Missions adopted, three resolutions, one of which urged that "measures be immediately taken for engrafting such associations as may hereafter be organized under the constitutional provisions of this Board, upon the already existing missionary organizations of this Church, whether by the formation of 'Sisterhoods auxiliary,' or otherwise."[19] The committee envisioned not only parochial and diocesan sisterhoods, but also orders of deaconesses and associations of laywomen for support of foreign, domestic, and parochial missions. Shortly after the Board of Missions accepted this report, the 1871 General Convention also approved it. In addition, the 1871 Pastoral Letter of the House of Bishops, for which Henry Potter was then serving as secretary, cautiously endorsed "the revival of the Scriptural diaconate of women."[20]

In Potter's somewhat exaggerated view, these actions "committed the Church both to the recognition and adoption of associations of women for work in the Church, in Sisterhoods or otherwise, and also placed its stamp of approval upon the commissioning of godly women for service, in parishes or elsewhere, as Deaconesses."[21] One result of these actions was the 1871 formation of the Woman's Auxiliary to the Board of Missions. The auxiliary provided a churchwide structure for existing parochial women's missionary associations (such as those Potter had helped to establish at Grace) and for the expansion of such associations among other churches. It also provided a forum for women's leadership and participation in the mission work of the church and "became the primary avenue of support for the Board of Missions." It would be another eighteen years, however, before the Episcopal Church took further action on official support for women church workers.[22] After the 1871 General Convention, Potter attempted to build on these modest gains. In December 1871, he preached at Grace Church the sermon "Woman's Place and Work in the Church" and addressed objections to and offered arguments for increasing women's role in the church's work. Potter responded to objections not to the fitness of women, but rather to the fitness of *religious orders* for such work. Given Grace's Low Church traditions, this emphasis is not surprising. His parallel emphasis on the biblical foundation for formal associations of women is similarly intelligible. Potter also offered two practical arguments in favor of women's church work: first, women already were doing such work, and with notable success; and second, women were especially suited to such work.[23]

Like most of his contemporaries, including many women, Potter assumed that women possessed a special nature, one mark of the cult of genteel womanhood. While Potter and others ascribed unique traits to women's nature that suited them particularly to domestic work, they did not necessarily restrict women to work in the home and for the family. Indeed, Potter and others held that Christian women who were "free of domestic obligations" could best use their womanly skills in service of the church and their less fortunate neighbors. Potter believed that the church needed especially to employ "those winning, persuasive, and sympathetic gifts with which the Creator has supremely endowed woman." In this context, he acknowledged a recently published letter by prominent Congregationalist preacher Henry Ward Beecher (although Potter identified him only as "the eloquent, if somewhat erratic preacher who speaks from the platform of what is known as Plymouth Church"). Beecher had made women's special nature "the ground of an argument for admitting woman to the pulpit" and suggested that "no one can inculcate and illustrate that spirit of love which breathes through the New Testament as can a woman." In response, Potter maintained that the New Testament clearly opposed "any usurpation of the office of teaching in the congregation by woman," but also that "it is as clearly a fact that hers is a delicacy and tenderness of approach, and an intuitive wisdom of utterance that oftenest fit her most of all to deal with those whose ignorance, or vice, or prejudice make them hardest to reach and win." When this sermon was published in a collection of his addresses twenty years later, Potter, in an introductory note, repeated his defense of religious orders. He added to his case only the point that "modern society, with its unique and unprecedented exigencies would seem to be creating a situation and with it a demand for which religious orders furnish the only appropriate supply."[24]

In 1873 Potter published *Sisterhoods and Deaconesses at Home and Abroad*, a historical and practical description of Protestant associations of women in the United States and Europe. Potter intended the book to further the acceptance of women's church work, particularly among those still apprehensive about religious orders. More important, however, he offered it "to afford models of organization and to furnish more particular information as to details of work and rules of government for such persons in our own Church as may desire to labor in and through such organizations themselves, or to set them in operation for others."[25] Potter hoped to make direct use of such information at Grace Church. When he outlined his plans for Grace House in 1870, he expressed the hope that it would include, among other elements of an institutional church, "apartments for the two or three godly women, trained under such auspices as those of St. Luke's Hospital, or the 'Bishop Potter Memorial House,' in Philadelphia, who will be needed to carry on such a work." The following year, he expressed the hope that a deaconess association might shortly be formed at Grace. And in 1873 he raised the idea of establishing at Grace a "Home and Training House for Nurses." As a result in part of the Panic of 1873 and in part of continuing official ambivalence over sisterhoods and deaconesses in the Episcopal Church, these plans were not realized during Potter's tenure at Grace. After he became bishop, however, his successor, William Reed Huntington, established a Deaconess Home and Training School in 1890. In the previous year, Huntington had played a key role at the General Convention in securing official sanction for orders of deaconesses. Also during Potter's episcopate, plans for the Cathedral of St. John the Divine included a separate building for a training school for deaconesses. This building, however, was not completed until 1912, four years after Potter's death.[26]

During his episcopate, Potter visibly supported various women church workers. As I noted in chapter 1, his first official action after his consecration was to visit the Midnight Mission operated by the Sisters of St. John the Baptist. He continued to support various sisterhoods by officiating at the reception of new members and the opening of new buildings and by speaking publicly in their behalf. In late 1883 and early 1884 Potter also preached at services for women church workers at several New York congregations. Speaking of these services in his address to the 1884 diocesan convention, he expressed gratitude for the women undertaking this service. He also noted that for them "some more definite and explicit instruction has long been needed, and in initiating the services which I have this day reported to you, it is my hope that we have but begun a series of such instructions, to be continued from year to year, and in which I trust that I may have the help of my reverend brethren of the clergy and others." Potter continued to preach at such services annually for many years, and five of these sermons were published in 1887 as *Addresses to Women Engaged in Church Work*. Primarily instructional and inspirational in content, these addresses add little to our understanding of Potter's view of women's church work and could, indeed, have been addressed to any group engaged in mission work at that time.[27]

One address, however, suggests a major concern of many at the time, namely, that women engaged in church work be supervised by men. Potter's 1871 report to the Board of Missions had noted that both parochial and diocesan sisterhoods "should not only be subject . . . to the general supervision and *unreserved inspection* of the bishop, but also in a sense peculiar and exclusive, to his need and call." In this context, Potter's emphasis was primarily on having available to the bishop's direction an effective force capable of timely mobilization. In an 1886 address, however, Potter appealed directly to the need for subordination to authority. Discussing the conditions of the "realm of order," Potter exhorted women church workers to adopt a proper subordination, for "there must be some ultimate dispenser of authority, some ultimate voice that shall give the word of command, in matters of duty and service, in every company, little or great." His argument was not that women must always be subject to men. It was, rather, that those engaged in service must submit loyally to those in authority over them and must do so not because some are by nature inferior to others, but because an organization needs such subordination to operate effectively. Thus, while urging women church workers to respect the authority of their male superiors, Potter made no appeal to any supposed inherent superiority of men.[28]

Methodist churches ultimately outdistanced all other Protestant churches in employment of women church workers. The Episcopal Church's General Convention did not formally approve orders of deaconesses until 1889 and sisterhoods until 1913. This latter action thus came more than fifty years after Alonzo Potter had articulated his conviction of the importance of women church workers and more than forty years after Henry Potter had expressed his belief that the church was committed to the recognition and adoption of various associations of women for work in parishes, missions, and elsewhere. While the response of the Episcopal Church to women church workers was surely not what Henry Potter would have hoped, his efforts just as surely helped bring about what measure of their recognition and adoption was achieved by 1913.[29]

Women, Domesticity, and Labor

The effect of the urban-industrial cult of genteel womanhood on social Christians was most evident in their closely related discussion of women and labor and defense of the family. The ideology of domesticity maintained that the only sphere of women's labor was the home and, therefore, that those engaged in other forms of labor were less than ideal women. As the involvement of women in church work demonstrates, however, many women were engaged nevertheless in labor outside the immediate sphere of home and family. Henry Potter affirmed that women were by nature and divine design endowed with abilities different from those of men and supported the expansion of women's field of endeavor into such work. In his treatment of domesticity and women's wage labor, Potter further expanded women's field of endeavor.

Potter first articulated his views on women, domesticity, and labor in an 1877 address at the Packer Institute in Brooklyn. This address is notable both as an example of Potter's rhetoric and reasoning and as a critique of the ideology of domesticity. In it, while supporting the ideology of domesticity in principle, he nevertheless criticized its application under contemporary conditions, argued for women's right to labor in spheres other than the home, and urged women to support those of their sisters who sought both to exercise and defend that right. This address, moreover, demonstrates that perhaps because of his involvement with the various service programs of Grace Church, Potter had developed an understanding of the often harsh realities of working women's lives.[30] Taking as his text the story of the prophetess Deborah in Judges 4, Potter suggested that perhaps Deborah would not be of interest to most women because "a woman's idea of a happy and useful life is not usually a life of active effort on the platform or in public." Rather, he claimed, "A woman's idea of happiness and usefulness ordinarily centres (and who shall say that it does not rightly centre?) in a home. First of all to have a home, and then to make it fair and bright, and then, if it may be, to share it with another to whom it shall be a welcome haven of rest and sunshine,—such a longing, which is simply the outcome of that divine instinct in accordance with which God long ago set the solitary in families, is surely as right as it is natural." In addition, he commended the tendency of "the vast majority" of women to register their disapproval "when any woman or set of women, undertakes to break out of the restraints of home, to proclaim a larger liberty for her sex, or demand what are called 'Woman's rights.'" Further still, he observed that "such persons are called 'unwomanly,'— and sometimes they are, and women are wisely reminded that their proper sphere and their worthiest throne is in the home."

With a telling rhetorical question, however, Potter shifted his stand: "But is there not something to be said on the other side, and is it not time that it was said?" To this question he responded:

We have been accustomed to hear the constantly reiterated assertion that "woman's sphere is the home." I confess for one that in view of the actual facts of society, as they exist around us, there is often in such words a sound of cruel irony. Do not you and I know, that there are thousands of women to whom a home is as impossible a thing as a castle in Spain? Do we not know that there are thousands of young girls in these two sister cities of ours [Brooklyn and New York] who have no human being but themselves to depend upon, and who must somehow make their way and earn their own bread in life? Will you tell me how a home or any thing else than a room and a hard, stern struggle for life is possible to these?

From this recognition that the actual conditions of many women's lives was sharply at variance with the ideology of domesticity, Potter proceeded to cast doubt on the benefits of marriage for women and to cite a recent study to demonstrate that there were many more women than men in the population of the northeastern states. He also criticized an unqualified ideology of domesticity and defended not only women's right to labor but also their right to the support of men and women when they exercised it.

Doubtless some of them will marry and preside over households of their own, but even if the marriage relation were the one invariable, inevitable, infallibly blessed relation for women which some people account it, what do you propose to do when already on the eastern coast of this new country of ours we have reached that condition which Mr. Greg, in his social judgments, refers to under the interrogative title, "Why are women redundant?" In other words, what shall we do with our superfluous women? There are eighty thousand more women than men in the state of Massachusetts alone. Now then, unless these eighty thousand are all women of fortune, it is a solemn trifling with a very grave and very urgent problem to tell them that "woman's sphere is in the home." . . . It is Pharaoh commanding the captive Israelites to make brick without straw to bid the great army of solitary and dependent women back to the home, and when to this sort of exhortation there is added the sneer of ridicule or contempt for strong-minded women and women's rights and the like, it is adding mockery to heartlessness. Surely a woman has some rights as well as a man. Surely, too, among these is the right to earn her own living, and to maintain her virtuous independence if there be none other to maintain her in virtuous dependence. And most surely of all, in every such endeavor women deserve the most cordial sympathy of the more favored of their own sex, and not less the generous approval of men.

Potter avowed that he had "no sympathy with any radicalism of female reform more than with any other extravagance" (but offered no specific examples of such "radicalism"). Nevertheless, he contradicted his earlier commendation of women who criticized their more radical sisters and quoted with approval an unidentified Englishwoman:

> "I wish it were felt that women who are laboring for women are not necessarily one-sided or selfish or self-asserting. . . . When men nobly born and possessing advantages of wealth and education have fought the battles of poor men, and have claimed and wrung from parliaments an extension of privileges enjoyed by a few to classes of their fellowmen who were toiling and suffering, I do not remember ever to have heard them charged with self-seeking; on the contrary, the regard that such men have had for the rights of their fellowmen has been praised, and deservedly so, as noble and unselfish." And the same writer goes on to ask, in substance, why it is that the endeavors of men for men cease to become praiseworthy when they become the endeavors of women for women?

This view Potter justified by his interpretation of the contemporary socioeconomic situation as "a transition-period from the old state of labor for men and domesticity for women, to a period in which there must be found labor for women as well as for men." He therefore denied the legitimacy of "labor for men and domesticity for women" in the contemporary context and affirmed that what women ask is "that we shall so widen the sphere of woman that whatever work she can do modestly and well she shall be permitted and encouraged to attempt." By this qualification of "modestly" Potter meant not humbly, but decorously. Believing that womanliness entailed some limitation on women's labor, he affirmed that there were "some callings from which, as it seems to me, women must forever remain shut out." Such callings would be those that required "conspicuous publicity, masculine activities, and out-door leadership," examples of which were "hanging from a yard-arm, driving a steam-engine, digging in a coal mine, or vociferating in congress." These and like cases he regarded as exceptions, however, maintaining that "when we have eliminated from the question those occupations from which healthy self-respect would restrain any really womanly woman, there remain a vast range of employments on which women have not yet entered, but for which, nevertheless, they have singular and supreme qualifications." Potter's appeal to women's "singular and supreme qualifications" clearly indicates his assumption of women's special nature, an assumption further indicated by his example of women's facility in "the science of telegraphy." Women were, according to him, "more expert in it than men can possibly be" because they are superior to "almost any man" in their possession of "a quick ear, and a sensitive touch, and the art of rapid and exact manipulation."

In this context, Potter used the appeal to women's special nature to argue not for restricting their labor to the home, but rather for *increasing* women's opportunities for nondomestic labor. Potter further substantiated his argument through anecdotes of women reliably performing nontraditional jobs. Indicating that he was aware that the urban-industrial gender division of labor was not timeless, he also noted: "It is a curious and scarcely known fact that in the Middle Ages, the daughters as well as the sons in a family often inherited and carried on the family art or handicraft." Potter therefore concluded his argument: "Why should we deny any modest calling or handicraft, whether behind the counter or in the work-shop, to those whose maintenance and happiness would both alike be found in its pursuit? To this question there is really no answer. Unless we claim that men are a superior caste whose vocations must not be profaned by the entrance upon them of women, there is really no option for us but to proclaim the freedom of labor, and to contend for that freedom until it shall become complete and universal."

Potter then urged women to "awaken to the needs of her own sex" and, as Deborah roused Barak, "waken us men to the cruelties . . . in which too often and too widely the weak of your sex are to-day oppressed. Do not, then, be afraid to lift your voice in any good cause that aims to elevate women to equal chance and equal respect and equal emolument with men in the great struggle for life." Here again, Potter appealed to women's special nature, and again used it to expand women's sphere beyond, rather than restrict it to, the home. "It is our province who are men to reach a consciousness of wrongs to be righted and evils to be remedied by the slower process of reasoning. It is yours to see those wrongs with the more penetrating vision of an often unerring insight, and, not unfrequently, long before men have been awakened to them to burn with a sense of their oppression and their injustice."

Potter warned women that if they attempted to so raise their voices, many would call them rather "to be the 'angel of the house,'" limiting their concern for the care of those within their homes. Further, suggesting that he grasped some of the negative implications for women of the cult of genteel womanhood, he also warned that the woman who heeded such a call would "inevitably become a drudge, an idler, or a toy." Rather than urge women to abandon their domestic responsibilities, however, he urged that they not be limited by them. To justify both this "widening [of] the range of our vision" and the empowering of women to do so, Potter appealed to the example and work of Jesus Christ, "that Master whose footsteps, whatever human allegiance may come to be ours, we are supremely called to follow." Potter maintained that the work of Jesus Christ was especially characterized by the breadth of His sympathies for all, and their especial courageousness and explicitness in the interest of woman. He emancipates her, in one instance, from legal thraldom, in another from hereditary disabilities, in another from social exile, in another from masculine contempt. His words to one who came to Him merely for the healing of the body, 'Woman, thou art loosed,' are the key to every one of His acts and utterances toward the whole sex. Those acts and utterances are best described by the one word 'liberation,' and freedom,—freedom from the servitude of a despised inferiority, and the degrading relation of a chattel or a toy is the whole spirit of His Gospel.

Thus liberated by Jesus Christ from an inferior status, women, in Potter's view, were free to exercise their special gifts to further Jesus' work, specifically the realization for all women of the liberation he promised.

> If you see that there are wrongs, injustices, social tyrannies . . . in the punishments that are meted out to womanly, as distinguished from manly, errors, in the meagre opportunities that are afforded for a woman's virtuous and self-respecting independence, in the indifference that will not bestir itself to cheer and brighten and encourage a working woman's weakness, despondency, and loneliness—then resolve, I beseech you, that it shall be your high privilege to speak for these and to rouse others to speak and strive for them as well. Be, each one of you, a Deborah to cry to some slumberous Barak, "Up and do the Master's work, in the spirit of the Master's example!"

This closing exhortation suggests another element of the ideology of domesticity as employed by social Christians, namely, the conviction that the moral influence of women was essential for the Christianization of the social order. While Potter did not explicitly appeal to that conviction in this address, he did make use of it in his later writings and addresses on domesticity and the family.[31]

During his remaining six years at Grace Church, a primary means of Potter's continuing support for women beyond the limits of the ideology of domesticity were the church's outreach programs. By the time Potter became assistant bishop in 1883, programs that provided concrete aid to women, and largely administered and supported by women, included a chapter of the Girls' Friendly Association, providing "mutual help and assistance" for working girls and young women; a diet kitchen, providing "appropriate and nourishing" meals to poor people when sick; the Industrial School, teaching sewing to girls so that they might support themselves; the Ladies' Benevolent Society, which employed poor women as seamstresses who produced garments to be donated to charitable institutions; the St. Luke's Association, providing "temporal and spiritual ministrations" to the sick; the day nursery, providing day care for children of women working outside their homes; and the Fresh Air Fund, providing women and children with summer holidays in rural areas.[32]

In this period and later, Potter also worked in organizations with women in leadership positions. Such organizations included the State Charities Aid Association, under the presidency of Louisa Lee Schuyler; the Charity Organization Society and the New York Consumers' League, both under the leadership of Josephine Shaw Lowell; the New York Committee on Mediation and Conciliation, of which Josephine Shaw Lowell was a member; and the Church Association for the Advancement of the Interests of Labor (CAIL), of which Harriette Keyser was secretary and organizer. As bishop, he supported working women through his participation in the work of CAIL. In 1890, two years before Potter was named one of its honorary vice presidents, CAIL cooperated with the Working Women's Society of New York in convening a public meeting. At this meeting, according to Keyser, the "oppressive conditions in retail stores entailing much suffering on women and children passed under scathing review by the clerical speakers," with William Reed Huntington representing the Episcopal Church. The meeting led to the establishment of a "white list" of fair employers with whom consumers were encouraged to trade and to the formation of the New York Consumers' League, which expanded the effort to mobilize the buying public's power to compel fair employment practices.[33]

According to Keyser, Potter "was always interested in the efforts of the Society [CAIL] to minimize, and finally destroy, the sweating system," the practice of hiring workers, largely women and children, to produce goods out of their own homes for meager wages. In addition to undercutting the labor and wages of those regularly employed in shops, this practice was a primary means of exploiting women's and children's labor. When the Cloakmakers Union struck against the sweating system in 1895, Dr. Annie Bryan, a reform-minded Episcopalian, requested that the St. Michael's Church chapter of CAIL convene a meeting on the matter. Potter not only endorsed the meeting but presided at it, remarking on, in Keyser's words, "the unchristian character of underpaid labor." As a result of this meeting, the St. Michael's chapter formed a Committee on Sweating. This committee investigated employment practices among garment manufacturers in Manhattan and Brooklyn, issued a report of its findings, and circulated a list of manufacturers using fair employment practices. In 1899 Potter spoke at the annual CAIL supper and addressed, among other issues of labor reform, the inadequate staffing of sweatshop inspection by the State of New York.[34]

Potter's published work from 1878 until the turn of the century contains only a few references to women, labor, and domesticity. In an article published in *Century* magazine in November 1884, for example, he discussed the relation of Christian ethics to the social science that had arisen in the previous quarter-century. Among the elements of this social science he included "the devotion of women of wealth, leisure, and social refinement to the reform and improvement of our jails and hospitals and almshouses" as well as "the whole subject of the rights of women and their emancipation from restrictive and oppressive prejudices."[35] Potter devoted more attention to these issues when, in the 1890s, the middle-class family ideal was challenged both by socialists and feminists and by the increasing immigration of non-Anglo-Saxon peoples. Social Christians, including Potter, responded to these challenges with a defense of the family ideal that emphasized its importance for the stability and, ultimately, Christianization of the nation. Potter was among a group of six clergy who addressed these issues in 1898 in a series of lectures on Christianity and social issues delivered at the Divinity School of New Haven and published the following year. In his "Message of Christ to the Family," Potter appealed both to nature and history to demonstrate that the family was "an institution which is divine, and which, in the mind of God, is bound up forever with the progress and well-being of the race." Further, he maintained that Jesus had "consecrate[d] it forever by His own most intimate relation with it," as seen especially in the way in which he "turned to it more and more frequently, as the great crisis of His life and work drew on, to gather strength for that crisis."[36]

Potter also attended to the ways the influences of the times "combined to make the family more and more an institution to be indifferently regarded in itself, and distinctly disparaged as to its obligations and its authority." Citing Horace Bushnell, he attributed this state of affairs to the rise of individualism and the consequent loss of "the idea of organic powers and relations" among "the three great forces which God appointed for the race"—the state, the church, and the family. Against these trends, Potter commended "the preciousness and the sanctity of the family" and, specifically, the "sanctity of the marriage tie." He cited in this context Jesus' teaching on divorce (Matthew 5 and 19 and Mark 10), and quoted at some length from Shailer Mathews's "admirable volume," *The Social Teachings of Jesus*. Following Mathews, Potter argued that the foundation for Jesus' explicitness on divorce was the status of marriage as the basis of the family, and of the family as the basis of society. Thus, in Mathews's words: "To disclaim this first of human relations is to loosen the bonds of society; to lower present social ideals; to do injury to the essential nature both of the man and the woman." Indeed, as Potter observed, "no questions touch more closely or deeply the fundamental interests of human society" than those that bear on the family.

Potter justified the importance of the family for society by maintaining, again citing Bushnell, that "there is no school like it in all the world for educating high ideals, and developing a lofty type of character." Such, he maintained, was the example provided by the "American forefathers" whose "mutuality of love and service" produced "that fine race of mothers whose sons and daughters were the joy and glory of our earlier history." Potter also noted the confluence, recognized by those "American forefathers," of the images of the family and the kingdom of God. "God was a King, indeed, but He was most of all a Father. Christ was a Saviour and a Redeemer, verily, but He was to be no less our Elder Brother. The Church was His Kingdom, supreme and preëminent among all the kingdoms of the world, but it was equally and always His peerless and precious Bride. And the law which ruled within that Kingdom was to be forever the law of filial love and loyalty." Taking this image to be a "vision of the life that is to be," he maintained that "whatever else of earthly and human institutions vanishes out of the realm and the life that are to be, the family in its highest and most absolutely perfect type will still endure." With this view of the family, Potter concluded with a call to "honor its authority, reverence its sanctity, prize and cultivate its intercourse."

Part of the social background of this address and contemporary social gospel literature was the perception among middle-class, Anglo-Saxon Protestants that many of their contemporaries were shirking their social and familial obligations by having few or no children or by leaving the care of their children in the hands of others. In this address, delivered to an audience primarily of men, Potter emphasized the responsibilities of women and mothers. In other articles and addresses of this period, he repeated this emphasis but also attended to the responsibilities of men and fathers and qualified his uncritical glorification of the family ideal in his 1898 "Message of Christ to the Family."[37]

From 1901 through 1907 Potter published five articles on domesticity and the family in popular magazines. In the earlier two, he variously encouraged mothers to motherliness; decried the neglect of children by their fathers; and maintained that, for both men and women, "the only possibility of happiness in the last half of any life lies in children." He also warned of the social and economic pressures that were undermining home and family and repeated that the home was "the actual foundation of the nation; the bedrock upon which the national structure rests;

the only basis from which the national strength can be calculated. It is the only school of purity and of patriotism."[38] In the latter three articles, published in *Harper's Bazar* the year before his death, Potter displayed a more critical view of the ideology of domesticity. In the second of these, in the context of a discussion of the pace of modern life for women, he noted that "no more tremendous change has come to pass in the last half-century than that which has occurred in the realm of woman." This change Potter regarded specifically as the shift from a society where the ideal of domesticity for women prevailed to one where women were able to make significant contributions in various spheres.

> In other words, it is undeniable that half a century ago the ideal of woman was *domesticity*; and the virtues which find their fittest sphere in the retirement of the home were accounted of preeminent value. But all that is changed, and it can never be forgotten (and I pray Heaven that it never may be!) that such services as Dorothea Dix and Florence Nightingale and Sister Dora and their kind have illustrated were not rendered by staying at home.
>
> Indeed, history is full of memorable figures that, whatever the age and whatever the land, all the way from Deborah to Joan of Arc, have told men that the loftiest service and the highest heroisms, whether on battle-fields or in hospitals, might be achieved by women as truly as men. In a word, the race is coming, late and slowly, it is true, to learn that neither sex has a monopoly of those greater qualities upon which are built the triumph of nations and the victory of the truth.

Potter observed that although "there have never been wanting illustrations of women in every race and age and clime who have risen above their kind and have revealed the most splendid gifts in most splendid deeds," such illustrations, because of the restrictions imposed on women, have largely been exceptions. He suggested, however, that such exceptions would increasingly become the rule, for "the whole situation is changed, and is destined to be still more extensively changed during this twentieth century."

In this context, Potter related an anecdote about an encounter with "a masterful lady who, with imperious mien and strident voice, demanded, 'Sir! What is your opinion of woman's suffrage?'" On the one hand, his depiction of this encounter betrays a condescending attitude toward both the issue of woman suffrage and at least some of the women advocating it. On the other, upon referring to a prediction by a "learned American professor" that "in thirty-five years the reins of government in these United States will be in the hands of women," Potter did not repeat his 1877 opposition to women "vociferating in congress." His comment on this prospect, rather, was to observe that "whether in so short a time we are destined to see any such prophecy fulfilled, or not, this, I think, will be freely admitted—that our generation has seen a tremendous change in the relation of women to modern life." Potter took it as unnecessary to demonstrate this change but repeated here his earlier defense of women's right to labor for self-support, particularly against the charges that women had "unfairly forced themselves" into some occupations and that they were hired because they worked "not better, but more cheaply" than men.[39]

Near the end of this article, Potter praised "that magnificent advance which, in regard to women's service, our age has witnessed." He maintained that such service was rendered "not merely that in those departments of service which are especially feminine, such as nursing and the care and ministration of the sick," but also in "those various relations which women have assumed to public education, to the sanitary improvement of towns and villages, and to social and moral reform in many of their most difficult and delicate aspects." Potter not only defended this advance but criticized as "unintelligent" and "ill-natured" the ridicule of women's nondomestic work. "For when all the deductions which are demanded by women's overzealous enthusiasms have been made, there still remain the indisputable facts of her often mental and temperamental superiority. She has quicker intuitions than I have. She has a nicer touch than I. She has a larger patience than is mine. Shall not these gifts make her better fitted for certain tasks than I? To insist otherwise is not to be acute, but pig-headed and stupid. And, alas! that is what men have been for a great many centuries." Potter thus continued to rely on the ideology of women's special nature while upholding the value of women's work outside the home. He also maintained, then, that women's special gifts of "sympathy, delicacy, quickness of perception, and an undiscouraged faith in human nature" needed to be balanced by men's gifts of "a sane judgment and a wise reserve," in the same way that men's gifts needed to be balanced by women's.[40]

In the third of his 1907 articles for *Harper's Bazar*, Potter returned to an evaluation of the modern home and defense of the home and family as the source of "all nobility and character that the world has ever known." His argument here was substantially the same as that in his 1898 "Message of Christ to the Family" and again reflects the concerns that men and women were not fulfilling their social and familial obligations and that their failure to do so was a threat to the social and political order.

> It is because the *home* must forever be our supreme hope . . . that we may well look with dismay upon anything that threatens its fibre. From this

point of view every growth in luxury, every step in the direction of the relaxation of parental responsibility, every social usage or exaction that makes, upon father or mother, demands that involve disregard of the primal obligation of domestic responsibility, should be regarded as a menace to the nation. Once let it be admitted that a man or woman may put aside duty in the family for pleasure or ease or social demands of whatever kind, and we have taken the first step towards creating a re-public of fops and cads![41]

In the same month that this article appeared, the *American Journal of Sociology* published a discussion, to which Potter contributed, of the effects of the reduced birthrate in the United States. The author of the paper initiating the discussion, Edward A. Ross, acknowledged that there were some "disquieting effects" of this trend, including the "selfish eva-sion of all duties to the race" of men and women motivated by an "exag-gerated individualism." He maintained, however, that the reduced birth-rate was "at bottom salutary" because of its potential for reducing "famine, war, saber-tooth competition, class antagonism, the degradation of the masses, the wasting of children, the dwarfing of women, and the cheap-ening of men."[42] In his response, Potter defended the importance of fam-ily and home but condemned the glorification of large numbers of chil-dren. As in his earlier treatments of the family, he again referred to the ideals of the "founders of the Republic" and, especially, their "clear and profound conviction as to the august office, authority, and origin of the family." From this conviction, he noted, there proceeded the sense of the "sacred calling" of a large family which, by the turn of the century, had "widely ceased to prevail." Potter did not, however, call for a return to this view of the family. He regarded as more important than the ques-tion of how many children were being born the question of "under what conditions are they being born and reared, and what is the promise of their maturity to the well-being of the state?" He noted the supposed threat of rapid population growth among "immigrants from all parts of the world" but doubted that it would overcome the "higher ideals of the fam-ily" then prevailing in the country. As to the broader question of the re-lation of the family size to the welfare of the state, and perhaps recalling that his own mother had died shortly after she bore her seventh child, Potter criticized the unqualified ideology of domesticity for women on the grounds of its mortal consequences for women's lives. "It may be that we shall strive in vain to re-erect upon its throne that august sovereign-ty of the family which deified fatherhood, and which slaughtered wom-en in the interest of bearing sixteen children! I am not prepared, at any rate, to say that some of those earlier theories of huge families were anything better than the selfish incarnation of unconsciously hypocritical ideas (for there is such a thing as 'unconscious hypocrisy') disguising itself as religious duty." Nevertheless, he decried "what somebody has aptly called 'shirking the penalties of marriage'" because it had "begotten among us a group of nameless vices, of which prenatal infanticide is only one, and which deserve alike our indignant reprobation and our hostility." Potter thus upheld the ideal of domesticity, but in a form that enabled women to avoid some of its burdens and embrace some nondomestic opportunities.[43]

The Liquor Problem

Undoubtedly the most important aspect of women's religious and reform work in the nineteenth century, affecting nearly all elements of women's work and well-being, was the temperance crusade. As Ruth Bordin notes,

> Although temperance was not a new cause for women in the last quarter of the nineteenth century, the character of women's participation changed drastically in the 1870s, as did their relationship to the temperance movement as a whole. Temperance became a cause that large numbers of women actively embraced, and women in turn became the most important force in the temperance movement. Also, by the 1880s temperance had become the issue that drew tens of thousands of women to rally behind general women's and reformist causes and demand a more equal share in the political process. Through temperance, which women saw as protection of the home, women from many social and economic strata were caught up in feminist goals.

Especially as embodied in the Women's Christian Temperance Union (WCTU), the temperance movement gave women a mechanism to exercise their leadership, develop skills and self-reliance, and effect change on matters that directly influenced the quality of their lives.[44]

Alcohol consumption seems not to have been a major concern to the churches in the colonial and revolutionary periods, but it became one by the start of the nineteenth century and was linked with increases in crime and poverty. In response, evangelical Protestants added temperance to their reform agenda. By temperance some meant moderate consumption, but most saw total abstinence as the only sure approach. Revivalism and temperance reform reinforced each other: Revival methods were potent means for securing abstinence pledges, and temperance served as a rallying point for revivals. The movement lost some of its vitality by the late 1830s as a result of internal disputes between moderates and radicals, but by the start of the Civil War it had nevertheless secured prohibition or regulatory legislation in sixteen states and territories.[45]

Again, the work of Alonzo Potter offers a window onto this element of antebellum evangelical thought and practice. In the course of his duties as pastor to clergy of the diocese, Alonzo Potter wrote to one presbyter about whom he had heard a report, the latest in a series, suggesting that he had become inebriated at a party:

> I take it for granted that the story is false, but could it arise if you were as prudent as you ought to be? With your excitable temperament, are you not peculiarly liable to misconception if you drink at all? And without adopting my fanatical notions about abstinence, would you not do wisely to put an effectual estoppel on all misapprehension and misrepresentation by declining all intoxicating drinks? Such reports, though ever so much exaggerated, do you harm; they afflict your friends, they injure the Church, and therefore, dear—, *make them impossible!*[46]

While Alonzo Potter's views on total abstinence may have been "fanatical" in the context of the Episcopal Church, they would not have been so in the broader context of contemporary evangelical Protestantism.

Potter expressed his argument for total abstinence most fully in an 1852 address, which was reprinted in several editions by the Massachusetts Temperance Society and included among the literature later used by the Episcopal Church Temperance Society. The object of temperance reform, according to Potter, was "to prevent drunkenness, with its legion of ills, by drying up the principal sources from which it flows." Of these sources, he identified as the chief one the drinking customs of society, not of the poor and hard-pressed workers but rather of the upper classes. He argued that the example set by the privileged, even if they drank only temperately, was the source of intemperate drinking and its resulting misery and vice. Therefore,

> We must hold them answerable for maintaining corresponding usages in other classes of society; and we must hold them answerable, further, for the frightful amount of intemperance which results from those usages. We must hold them accountable for all the sin, and all the unhappiness, and all the pinching poverty, and all the nefarious crimes, to which intemperance gives rise. So long as these usages maintain their place among the respectable, so long will drinking and drunkenness abound through all grades and conditions of life. Neither the power of law aimed at the traffic in liquors, nor the force of argument addressed to the understandings and consciences of the many, will ever prevail to cast out the fiend drunkenness, so long as they who are esteemed the favored few uphold with unyielding hand the practice of drinking.

Those who temperately drink and are in a position to influence others, he argued, must instead practice total abstinence so that the evil effects of intemperance might not prevail. He undermined arguments in defense of temperate drinking by pointing out that it is neither necessary nor useful, adding nothing to strength of body, intellect, or character; that it is expensive, being "the most prolific source of improvidence and want" and a drain on one's personal income, "which is but a loan from God" entrusted to us for our own good and the good of others; that it is unreasonable, requiring that on social occasions people relinquish their personal freedom by allowing others to decide their drinking usages; and that it is unsafe, adversely affecting one's health and longevity.

Alonzo Potter was willing to admit, but only for the sake of argument, that it was possible to drink safely with oneself, but not that it was possible to drink safely with others. In this he showed that his fundamental concern with drinking was with its evil effects. He argued that one's own harmless indulgence, when practiced privately, *could* become "a stumbling-block,—ay, perchance, a fatal stumbling-block" for others when practiced publicly. In support of this principle, both, it seems, for illustration and for authorization, he cited Romans 14:21: "It is good neither to eat flesh, *nor to drink wine*, nor any thing whereby thy brother stumbleth, or is offended, or is made weak." Thus, in his view, it was far better to abstain than to risk causing another to stumble and fall through one's own moderation. And while he had held the "favored few" to account for their drinking usages, it was not only they whom he held to account. All people—parents, employers, husbands and wives, young women and men—had the potential for adverse influence on others and were thus all responsible.

From this argument for the importance of example in preventing another to fall and in preserving oneself from the charge of causing such a fall, Potter moved to a discussion of the circumstances of drinking in his day. "I do not maintain that drinking wine is, in the language of the schools, *sin per se*. There may be circumstances under which to use intoxicating liquors is no crime. There have been times and places in which the only intoxicating beverage was light wine, and where habits of inebriation were all but unknown. But is that *our* case?" He discussed in this context the particular intoxicating liquors available, citing the distinction in principle between those that were fermented and those that were distilled, but pointing out that the common practice of adulterating wines—so that their intoxicating effects were equivalent to those of gin or whisky—made this distinction useless in practice. The only sure course, he argued, was total abstinence from all alcohol. It mattered not what "may have been proper in other days or other lands, in the time of Pliny or of Paul." What mattered, given the specific conditions and usages of drinking in that time, was what was proper then, for "what may at one time be but a lawful and innocent liberty, becomes at another a positive sin." Thus, the responsibility of the Christian under the prevailing conditions was clear, that responsibility being nothing short of total abstinence.[47]

Robert Handy notes of nineteenth-century American evangelicalism that its "eagerness to enact its program into law reveals again something of the onesidedness of the evangelical understanding of freedom."[48] It also reveals the one-sidedness of most temperance reformers' view of the relation of intemperance to poverty and crime. In the first half of the century they tended to assume that all evils flowed from intemperance and that all goods would similarly flow from total abstinence and prohibition. These assumptions were challenged during the following decades, but the strategy of the temperance movement remained dominated by the emphases on total abstinence and prohibition. With rising national tensions and the outbreak of the war, the movement declined again. After the war temperance reformers renewed the struggle. The National Temperance Society and Publication House was established in 1865, and the Prohibition Party was formed in 1869. More important, however, was the "Women's Crusade," a series of revivals and demonstrations that began in Ohio in December 1873 and spread throughout neighboring states. One important result of this 1873–74 revolution was the formation of the WCTU in 1874.

Although not necessarily incompatible in terms of strict logic, in terms of the postwar social and cultural realities the perspective on temperance of Henry Potter and that of most women temperance workers were incompatible. Both men and women were victimized by the working conditions of early industrial capitalism and by the living conditions in the slums it spawned. Women and children, however, were further victimized by the financial deprivation and the physical and emotional violence resulting from alcohol abuse by the men upon whom they were dependent. By 1876 Frances Willard, then secretary of the WCTU, made explicit the connection between alcohol and its ill effects on the home in her appeal to home protection as justification for both temperance and woman suffrage. As Bordin notes, however, "the home-protection argument was implicit in women's participation in the temperance movement from the beginning. Many women had always seen the drunken husband as a threat to the home." Although the WCTU's official support for suffrage under the banner of "home protection" came only after Willard's

election as its president in 1879, home protection was the central rationale and by-word for temperance reform.[49]

Henry Potter's rationale for women's proper concern for public affairs
was consistent with that of Willard and the WCTU, but his approach to
temperance reform was significantly different. Like many women temperance reformers, Potter emphasized that the evil of alcohol was found
in its effects, and early in his working life he promoted total abstinence.
Unlike some in the WCTU and other elements of the temperance movement, however, Potter regarded purely restrictive measures as ineffective
and focused his attention on working people's legitimate need for recreation. As the need for recreation was, in his view, often met only by saloons, he maintained that no solution to intemperance was possible unless suitable preventive measures and recreational alternatives were
implemented. In doing so, he nowhere specifically considered women's
experience of their own and their children's suffering as a consequence
of alcohol abuse by men. And although he participated in other organizations in which women were prominent members or leaders, his participation in temperance organizations was limited to those whose membership was composed largely or exclusively of men.

Unlike some other churches, the Episcopal Church was not known
for advocating temperance reform. Prior to the war exceptions were found
in its Evangelical party, including Bishops Charles McIlvaine and Alonzo
Potter. After the war, because of increased interest in social reform and
the church's own Memorial and Broad Church movements, a greater
number of Episcopalians joined the ranks of temperance advocates. The
1876 Church Congress included a presentation titled "The Prevention and
Cure of Drunkenness" and heard R. Heber Newton propose an organization to include advocates of both temperance and total abstinence. In 1881
the Church Temperance Society was formed, with Henry Potter among
its founders.[50] In his earliest extant address on temperance, delivered in
1878 at a meeting of the National Temperance Society, he echoed his
father's moral reasoning on the subject. He also, however, raised concerns
that demonstrate his attention to the conditions of his day and his aware-
ness of the need for strategies appropriate to those conditions. Convinced
that "the Total Abstinence movement is the true Temperance movement,
and that the safety of the individual and the welfare of the land demand
that this movement be steadfastly maintained and carried on," Potter
considered how the movement's influence might be enlarged. He averred
that he was "both by precept and in practice, a Total Abstinence man,"
but he questioned the methods by which the movement had been promoted to date. He criticized the movement's emphasis on restrictive rath-

er than preventive strategies, especially measures that restricted alcohol only among poor and working people.

> There is no one of us, I presume, who does not believe that the city of New York will be better off for every corner-grocery that is closed and for every unlicensed dealer who is estopped from the illicit selling of liquor. But there is no one of us, I imagine, who does not recognize the fact that such a method of dealing with the evil of intemperance is not essentially curative; and has in it no feature which is genuinely preventive. It is restrictive, but, in the social gamut, it is mainly restrictive at the wrong end of the scale. . . . [I]t concedes to those who are in all respects, as the world estimates such things, most favored, privileges which it withholds from those who are least favored.

This line of reasoning, in its emphasis both on the responsibility of the "most favored" and on the importance of preventive measures, followed closely that of Alonzo Potter from a quarter-century earlier. Henry Potter also followed his father both in denying the authority of the biblical precedent of temperate drinking and in affirming the authority of self-abnegation and Paul's application of it.

> We hear him [Paul] say, in words that to my mind are the strongest Total Abstinence argument that was ever written, "If meat make my brother to offend, I will eat no meat while the world stands;" and we catch in them the echo of that spirit of utter self-forgetfulness. . . . It is the very spirit of the cross; and I venture to affirm that he who would win others to come up upon the ground of Total Abstinence must live it and illustrate it. . . . [T]here are multitudes of weaker ones who can only hope to triumph as they see Christ's pity, Christ's compassion, Christ's self-forgetting love and help incarnated in "the help of their brethren."

Potter argued further, however, that temperance reformers must take into account the miserable conditions in which poor and working people were compelled to live. He also suggested two points that were to become more important in postwar temperance reform efforts: first, that poverty was as much a cause as a result of intemperance, and second, that saloons were important for working people as places of companionship and escape from the misery of their homes and workplaces.

> Who that knows the lives and homes of the poor can wonder that they drink? I confess that when I have come out of one of those wretched tenement-houses in which some hundreds of thousands more or less of the people of New York are lodged, my wonder has been, not that the poor creatures who live in them drink so much, but that they drink so little. . . . There are men and women all over the land whose lives are dry and colorless. They lack the satisfaction of the play-element in their

natures, which is just as divine in its origin as the work-element. And if we want to make men temperate—if we want to save them from seeking in opium or strong drink the exhilaration which they can command in no other way, those who have wealth and taste and influence must meet the question, How shall we brighten the lives of such persons with wholesome and simple pleasures?

Potter's mention of the responsibility of "those who have wealth and taste and influence" for those less fortunate was an abiding theme in his social ethic. Other related principles here, upon which he built his treatment of temperance, were the reality of class alienation and the need for personal sympathy and individual effort to improve the homes and workplaces of the laboring classes. Such endeavor, he hoped, would introduce preventive strategies for strengthening the total abstinence movement.[51]

In 1882, one year after the formation of the Church Temperance Society, Potter preached on self-forgetting love that works for the well-being of others and cited as an example the pledge used by the society.

With a wise discernment of the needs of these times our *Church Temperance Society* has prepared for signature a pledge or declaration like this: "I recognize my duty to be always temperate myself and to do what I can by the help of God, to keep others from intemperance. Without binding myself to Total Abstinence, I engage, as a member of this Society, to be watchful over my own habits of indulgence and no less watchful of the influence of my example upon others, and I promise by my practice and example, in all ways that commend themselves to my judgment and my conscience, to discourage such drinking usages as are plainly at variance with the interest of good morals."[52]

Despite his 1878 profession of total abstinence, Potter seems not to have maintained this stance throughout his life. Implying that Potter was not always a total abstainer, Hodges observes that he "had at one time practised total abstinence for a number of years in order to encourage and continue the reformation of a man whom he was trying to save from the temptation of drink." More explicitly, Hodges acknowledges that "there was wine on his table on the occasion of formal dinners, and he found it under like conditions in the houses of his friends. It was a detail of the conventional life. Sometimes he tasted it; often not." Further, in August 1897 the *New York Times* reported that Bishop Potter had brought two cases of scotch whiskey when he returned to New York from a trip to Europe. The prohibition paper the *Voice* attempted to obtain verification from the bishop, but when he did not respond the controversy quietly died.[53]

Potter made no public comment on temperance in the fifteen years following his 1882 sermon. During this period he engaged in further study and discussion, particularly of preventive measures and "counter-attractions" to the saloon. In 1889 he became a member of a group of fifteen men who met to present and discuss papers on social questions. The group was expanded in 1893, came to be known as the Committee of Fifty, and devoted much of its energies to consideration of various aspects of the liquor problem. In addition to Potter, this group included noted reformers and social gospelers Felix Adler, William Dodge, Washington Gladden, William Reed Huntington, Seth Low, Theodore Munger, and Francis Peabody. On the basis of its studies, the committee published books on the legislative, economic, and physiological aspects of alcohol use, as well as on "saloon substitutes." This last topic was of particular interest to Potter, undoubtedly because of his early recognition of the positive as well as negative social functions played by saloons. Proponents of saloon substitutes, which offered nonalcoholic refreshment and wholesome amusement, intended them to provide all the positive and none of the negative functions of saloons. Such converted saloons, as they were called, had been tried in England, notably through the Public House Trust Company under Albert Henry George, the fourth earl Grey, and had met with some success.[54]

In January 1899 Potter addressed a benefit meeting in support of the Squirrel Inn, a saloon substitute sponsored by the Church Temperance Society. The inn had been made possible by the building's owner, Mrs. W. H. Bradford, who had closed the saloon operating there and offered the building to the Church Temperance Society, rent- and tax-free for five years, pending its success in raising $15,000 for building repairs. In his address at the inn's opening, Potter again maintained that the saloon was a social necessity because relaxation and amusement are human necessities, and because the more favored classes have provided no alternative for the less favored: "The man who keeps the saloon, and who says it is the poor man's club, tells the truth. Can anyone blame the poor laboring man, weary of his day's work, because he leaves his squalid home, his wife, his squealing children, and seeks in the brightly lighted, comfortable saloon the society of congenial companions?"[55]

Both favorable and unfavorable responses ensued. While the Episcopal reform organizations CAIL and the Brotherhood of St. Andrew defended the Bishop, some temperance reformers and rescue workers criticized him. Colonel Henry Hadley, speaking on behalf of the Christian Men's Union for Total Abstinence and Rescue Work, took issue with the "alleged declaration that 'the saloon is the poor man's club,' or that it is in 'any way necessary to the workingman or poor man.'" Potter avoided public debate on the matter, but his letter to an Ohio minister was printed in the *New York Times*. In it, Potter repeated his conviction that "something answering to the saloon, i. e., [a] place of inexpensive recreation and refreshment, would always be a necessity" and that providing such substitutes would prove more effective in eradicating the "mischiefs of the saloon" than had legislation and prohibition. Unfortunately, Potter failed to consider the typical ways in which the poor laboring man and his congenial companions, upon their return to their squalid homes, treated their wives and children.[56]

During the next six years, Potter continued to advocate rational temperance reform and to incur the ire of prohibitionists. In 1901, the same year that the Committee of Fifty's study on saloon substitutes was published, Potter addressed the Church Club of New York. The newspapers focused on his statement that prohibition was "a fraud and a failure," but his point remained that temperance reform could succeed only if it incorporated constructive and preventive strategies. Similarly, in his charge to the New York diocesan convention of 1902 Potter pointed to the hardships of industrial labor and urban life, the legitimate desire for relief from them, the lack of uplifting opportunities for such relief, and the need to provide such opportunities to combat the degrading effects of saloons and gin palaces. A *New York Times* editorial reported that "the more intemperate advocates of temperance" responded to Potter's remarks "with characteristic vehemence," but it nevertheless commended his approach. "That he recognises the social uses of the liquor saloon, and does not insist that an institution so clearly founded in human needs 'shall go,' may again make him a subject for public prayer on the part of the W. C. T. U. But the Bishop need not mind what the advocates of irrational and impossible temperance reform may have to say about his rational and cautious methods."[57]

In 1904 Potter again, and more than on any previous occasion, provoked the ire of some temperance workers when he presided at the dedication of the Subway Tavern. The idea for the Subway Tavern originated in the discussions of the Committee of Fifty and the work of W. S. Rainsford, who had been advocating reformed saloons for many years. Reformed saloons differed from saloon substitutes by serving alcoholic beverages while still offering a place for wholesome recreation for working people and their families. In an 1895 letter to Rainsford, Potter had called this idea "the wildest dream that was ever dreamed" and argued that the only course was "to destroy this agency of the devil, that will otherwise destroy us."[58]

By 1904, perhaps recognizing that efforts to provide saloon substitutes must be taken another step, Potter had changed his mind. Several men, some of whom were members of the Committee of Fifty, proposed an "ethical stimulant-selling establishment" on the model implemented in England by Earl Grey. They invited Potter to participate in the dedication of the Subway Tavern. Potter accepted and spoke again of the importance of constructive methods in fighting the evils of intemperance. Both his presence and remarks at the dedication offended many temperance workers. Some also objected to the suggestion, albeit incorrect, that Potter was a partner in the business, and to the impromptu singing of the doxology after his remarks (a feature of the dedication mentioned prominently in the press reports). Temperance reformers throughout the country and in most denominations, including his own, roundly denounced him. His old friend and Church Temperance Society colleague, Leighton Coleman, then bishop of Delaware, publicly questioned his action. Business at the Subway Tavern was good for a time, but after only thirteen months it closed and was considered a failure, as both a business enterprise and a temperance experiment.[59]

Unfortunately, none of the contemporary reports cites reaction from the WCTU or other women temperance leaders to the Subway Tavern or to Potter's earlier remarks on the means of combating the evils of drink. Even without such evidence, however, it is clear that Potter's perspective on and approach to the liquor problem emphasized the needs of working men. His criticism of merely restrictive measures would surely have included the 1888 platform of the Prohibition party, in the development of which Frances Willard and the WCTU were centrally involved. Potter undoubtedly would have agreed with the party that "the abolition of the saloon would remove burdens, moral, physical, pecuniary, and social, which now oppress labor and rob it of its earnings, and would prove to be the wise and successful way of promoting labor reform."[60] He insisted, however, that the saloon could be abolished not by legislation alone, but by providing working people with suitable and attractive substitutes.

Potter's treatment of issues pertinent to the work and well-being of women presents an ambiguous legacy. On the one hand, he substantially upheld the tenets of the urban-industrial cult of genteel womanhood, with its ideal of domesticity for women and its ideology of women's special nature; on the other hand, he at times explicitly criticized key aspects of the ideal of domesticity and regularly supported activities for women at variance with that ideal. On the one hand he glorified the family as divinely ordained, eternally valuable, and the source of personal and

social character; on the other, he recognized some of the negative consequences for women of a child- and home-centered life. On the one hand,
he ardently worked for temperance reform, a concern central to women's
well-being and on which many women labored; on the other hand, his
temperance writings and activities reflect no consciousness of why temperance reform was particularly important to women or of the ways in
which the consumption of alcohol adversely affected women and children differently from the way it did men. Potter vigorously defended
women's right to work outside the home, both in reform and mission
work and in industrial labor. Further, appealing to the ideology of wom-
en's special nature, he argued not only for their right to but also their
competence in nondomestic labor. Also on the basis of women's supposed
special nature, he wished to keep them out of certain types of work, but
by the end of his life he may have dropped his earlier opposition to women
in politics. Potter's view of the role of women in society implied the standard social gospel understanding of the potential for women's moral influence in Christianizing the social order, but nowhere in his work did
he make this view explicit. In addition, nowhere did he clearly indicate
either his support for or opposition to woman suffrage.

Consciously emulating antebellum and wartime initiatives to expand
women's church work, Potter's support for women's involvement in
mission and reform endeavors helped to expand the limits of women's
work and enhance their well-being. He went beyond some of his contemporaries but not as far as others in his support for women's right to and
competence in industrial labor. In this respect, then, he helped expand
the limits of women's work further still. Potter was not unique in this
regard. That he and others sometimes took positions at variance with the
urban-industrial cult of genteel womanhood, particularly in the early
postwar decades, suggests in part that its hegemony was achieved only
gradually over the late nineteenth and early twentieth centuries. That it
achieved such hegemony, however, suggests that the critique of the ideology of domesticity by Potter and others was insufficient to achieve
genuine equality and justice for women. Nevertheless, Potter and others certainly sought, within the limits of their assumptions and convictions, to achieve such justice and equality.

4 *Political Righteousness*

Writing in 1912, Walter Rauschenbusch argued that four major social institutions—family, church, education, and politics—had become Christianized because they had "passed through constitutional changes which have made them to some degree part of the organism through which the spirit of Christ can do its work in humanity." He admitted that including political life among the redeemed institutions might seem "a staggering assertion, for of all corrupt things surely our politics is the corruptest," and acknowledged that "the tattered clothes and questionable smells of the far country still cling to the prodigal." Because in this context his rhetorical intent was to emphasize the need to Christianize the one remaining major social institution, economics, he nevertheless maintained that the nation's "political communities are constitutionally on a Christian footing."[1] Rauschenbusch and many of his contemporaries affirmed this belief largely as a result of the reforms of the early years of the twentieth century, now somewhat imprecisely known as the Progressive Era. Social Christianity was an essential component of the intersection of political and religious reform impulses that gave rise to Progressivism. The transition from the antebellum reform agenda to the turn-of-the-century Progressive agenda was made possible in part by the efforts of postwar Christians to address the conditions wrought by industrialization and urbanization. Their socialization of a previously individualized gospel not only entailed an understanding of the involvement of the churches in the nation's political life that differed significantly from that of their predecessors but also helped establish the broad political constituency necessary for the success of Progressivism.[2]

Righteousness in Nation and City

From the earliest colonial settlements, the Protestant hope for Christian America included the extension of democracy and the Christianization of government. After religious disestablishment, this hope no longer entailed legal sanction and public support for Christian beliefs and practices. It did, however, entail an emphasis on Christian morality as the foundation for a reformed social order and its government. Advocates of a Christian America viewed morality as the essential link between religion and civilization, and the voluntary acceptance of such morality as the means of achieving the goal of Christianization. Church and state may have been separate, but there was to be no separation of religion and morality from the realization of the common good.[3] The close connection between religious and political affiliation in the nineteenth century reflects this relation between morality and government. In terms of the analytical tool developed by Paul Kleppner and employed by Robert Swierenga, "pietist" (evangelical) Christians tended to be Whigs and, later, Republicans while "liturgical" (nonevangelical) Christians tended to be Democrats. In the tradition established by Thomas Jefferson and continued by Andrew Jackson, the Democratic party emphasized a limited and secular government, individual autonomy, and cultural diversity. Liturgical Christians became Democrats in part because their theologies ascribed the process of salvation to extraworldly agencies and thus could more easily accommodate a secular government. In addition, especially after the Awakenings and to the extent that their constituencies consisted of primarily immigrant populations, liturgical denominations were minorities resisting conformity with the dominant evangelical Anglo-Saxon majority. Evangelicals tended to become Whigs and Republicans because these parties affirmed the positive role of an unofficially Protestant Christian government in regulating personal and social behavior for the purpose of establishing a Christian civilization.[4]

Of course, as with all such constructs, the application of this liturgical-pietist continuum to nineteenth-century American political life is not precise. The case of the Episcopal Church, for example, indicates that the various points on the continuum could find expression within a single denomination. One reason for this diversity is that within the Episcopal Church, not only the pietist Evangelical party but also the liturgical High Church party maintained a positive assessment of the state. This positive assessment is inconsistent with that of other liturgical denominations and can be regarded, as Swierenga argues, as an exception due to "cross-pressures and particular historic contexts [which] may change patterns or create unique situations."[5] For the Episcopal Church, such cross-pressures would include the heavily Anglo-Saxon character of the denomination and the influence of the Anglican social theory that had been developed in the context of that church's establishment in England. In the postwar Broad Church movement, perhaps uniquely in American Protestantism, both liturgical and pietist positive assessments of the state were united and a social theory employed that supported both social Christianity and Progressivism.

The development of Episcopal Evangelical and Broad Church political practice was related to the larger process by which evangelical Protestants helped form the Whig and Republican parties, a process that unfolded over several decades. "First they [evangelical Protestants] created the 'benevolent empire' in the 1810s to spread the gospel and teach the Bible. Then, in the 1820s, they established reform societies to eradicate slavery, saloons, Sabbath desecration, and other social ills. Finally, in the 1830s, they entered the political mainstream by joining the new Whig party coalition against the Jacksonian Democrats." In the early 1850s, the Whig party disintegrated, in part because its evangelical constituency "put ethical goals, such as abolition of slavery, above party loyalty." The Whig constituencies regrouped later in the decade to form the Republican party, which bore the standard of abolition and other reforms through the Civil War, Reconstruction, and into the Progressive Era.[6]

The evangelical emphasis on morality influenced not only the decline of the Whigs, but also the crusading character of the Republicans' conduct of the Civil War and Reconstruction and the postwar drives for reform of alcohol use, Sunday observance, uncontrolled immigration, dangerous working conditions, and other social perils. It also influenced the role of morality in the relation between religion and politics in two other key issues of the time: first, the reform of politics at all levels of government, and second, the expansion of national territory and responsibilities. While evangelicals like Alonzo Potter had regarded overt involvement in political affairs as a danger to be avoided, Henry Potter and many of his contemporaries found that postwar political life required a significant modification of antebellum approaches.

Commenting on the deplorable decline in public morality in the decades following the Civil War, a contributor to *Century Magazine* wrote in 1884

No feature of the present age is more displeasing to the moralist than the dishonesty that so widely prevails in commerce and politics. In whatever direction we turn, this phenomenon meets our eye; and there is no branch of business, no department of government, and no class in society in which it does not appear. The forms of commercial dishonesty are almost endless in variety. . . .

If, now, we turn to politics, we find a similar or even a worse state of affairs there. Fraudulent contracts, sinister legislation, bought and paid for by those whom it benefits, trading of offices and votes, and all the various methods of robbing the public for the benefit of a few, have become so common among us as hardly to awaken surprise when exposed to public view. There is, moreover, a close connection between the dishonest practices of politics and those of commerce, and collusions are constant between unscrupulous men in commercial business and equally unscrupulous men in public station.[7]

The influence of commerce on politics is the key to understanding the postwar moral decline. While the war itself surely influenced the deterioration of public morality, much more significant was the "cheerful and unstinted rapacity"[8] characteristic of the rising industrial capitalism. In their pursuit of wealth, the leaders of industry and finance observed as their only standard of conduct the potential for monetary gain. By this standard, they justified exploiting workers, defrauding consumers, swindling investors, and spying on and sabotaging competitors. Mark Twain's characterization of the era as the gilded age and the process of industrial growth as the Great Barbecue aptly capture the ethos created by this thinly veiled, if veiled at all, avarice.[9]

Especially after the financial panic of 1873 tarnished the public image of industrialists and financiers, many Protestant leaders commented on the deleterious influence of business morality upon the well-being of society. In a series of lectures delivered in 1875, R. Heber Newton decried the widespread mendacity in business practices that included dishonest advertising, adulteration of food, and other forms of fraud. Newton also argued that the morals of business were of great importance because commerce is the foundation of society. In the same year, Edward A. Washburn, another New York Episcopalian, also warned that the pervasive greed embodied in business practices was a threat to both personal and social well-being.[10] The contemporary judgments of Newton and Washburn are affirmed by the more recent evaluation of Richard Hofstadter. "From the business of industry the business of politics took its style. . . . Standards of success in politics changed. It was not merely self-expression or public service or glory that the typical politician sought— it was money. . . . The spoilsmen looked upon political power as a means of participating in the general riches, of becoming wealthy in their smaller ways and by their lesser standards, as did the captains of industry."[11] The notoriously corrupt presidency of Ulysses S. Grant, from 1869 to 1877, amply demonstrated the effect of the "business of industry" on the "business of politics." Following the lead of the wealth-seeking industrialists, many of those seeking political office were motivated by a desire for financial gain rather than a vocation to public service. Businesses seeking favorable economic and regulatory policies were happy to offer them the wealth they desired in exchange for agreeable regulatory and legislative consideration. As Hofstadter observes, "Fabulous sums were spent. . . . Between 1866 and 1872, for example, the Union Pacific spent $400,000 on bribes; between 1875 and 1885 graft cost the Central Pacific as much as $500,000 annually." In addition, after the war the Republican party was attempting to expand its constituency by supporting policies congenial to industrialists and financiers. Grant himself was an admirer and defender of the capitalist acquisitive ethos. The corruption of his administration, evidenced in such scandals as the Whiskey Ring bribes and the Crédit Mobilier stock fraud, was almost inevitable.[12]

A particularly influential response to this and other social perils came from patrician or genteel postwar reformers known as Mugwumps. Arising in the 1870s in response to what they saw as the vulgar avarice of industrialists, the crass corruption of politicians, and the coarse customs of immigrant workers, the Mugwumps advocated leadership by those whom they regarded as the enlightened and educated classes. They followed in the tradition of the antebellum religious and social reformers and provided continuity between them and the later Progressives. Typically they were Protestant middle-class and professional men, Republicans disaffected with corruption in their own as well as in the Democratic party. In the nineteenth century they looked exclusively to men to accomplish the desired social improvements, but by the early twentieth century reformers of this type supported extending the suffrage to genteel womanhood in order to fortify the diminishing political power of their class.

Both nationally and locally, Mugwumps criticized immorality and corruption in politics and opposed the reign of political machines based on the distribution of patronage in exchange for party support. Mugwump opposition to these machines, such as New York's Tammany Hall organization, was based as much on the machines' domination by immigrants (particularly Irish Catholics) as on their corrupt political practices. Mugwumps advocated appointment to government service based on merit; one of their major early accomplishments was the passage of the Pendleton Act of 1883, which established the federal civil service. In general, however, they sought to bring about change not by legislation but by individual education and moral persuasion.[13]

Henry Potter articulated his thinking on government and morality in this context. At midcentury his opposition to slavery and support of the federal government during the Civil War, combined with the broad reformist impulses he shared with his evangelical contemporaries, inclined him likewise to support the Republican party. Like many evangelical Protestants, however, he criticized the postwar decline in public morality generally and in government specifically. On Thanksgiving Day 1866, having become assistant minister at Trinity Church, Boston, Potter preached "Individual Responsibility to the Nation" and demonstrated a concern for "political righteousness" that was to be one of the principal emphases of his later work. He began this sermon by acknowledging the custom of religious gatherings on Thanksgiving "to speak of our history and destiny as a nation, and to be cheered or admonished by our past." He also acknowledged the potential abuse of that custom in "partisan harangues, or unfraternal and unseemly denunciations." Nevertheless, citing Jesus' tears upon his vision of Jerusalem's fate at the hands of the Romans, Potter argued that

> The pulpit cannot, therefore, change or ignore this time-honored custom if it would; and, for one, I freely own that I would not if I could. Until patriotism and the Gospel shall become, somehow, less indissolubly linked together than we have so long learned to believe them . . . we must needs obey the summons which calls us to speak to one another of the prosperity and of the perils which environ us as a people; to commune together of our past and of our present, and to gird ourselves for common prayer and effort, that so the land of our common love and pride may know a yet loftier and nobler future!

The "responsibility of the individual to the nation," he continued, is an appropriate topic for preaching, for it is included in a Christian's "circle of obligations" with those "to God, to yourselves, to the outcast and ignorant and benighted."

Potter then urged his hearers to take up their responsibility for "salting and leavening the nation's moral life," for without such a moral foundation "confidence in our institutions will be simply madness." "We may extend the borders of our territory; we may put down rebellion within ourselves; we may push forward the conquests of our civilization into yet vaster and remoter wildernesses, and yet have all the while the elements of ultimate decline and decay within ourselves, unless among the people there is not only a national purse but also a national conscience, a sense of reverence for righteousness, temperance, and truth." Potter saw two chief dangers to sustaining the national conscience: first, "a gradual deterioration in the standard of public morals," and second, the perils "that forever ensue with the incoming of an age of luxury."

On the first danger, he noted that the moral sensibilities of the nation had been blunted as a result of the war. "War, in no matter how holy a cause, is sure to be, somehow, deteriorating." One manifestation of this blunting was the "careless and superficial scrutiny" of those chosen for political office, with the result that some aspects of government had become disreputable. Potter identified the root of these evils as the failure of individuals to discharge their responsibilities as citizens. This appeal to the individual's responsibility to the nation was rooted in the assumption, typical of both evangelical Republicans and Mugwumps, that an enlightened few held in their hands the welfare of the nation. His remarks also reflect the characteristic distrust of Jeffersonian/Jacksonian democracy and suspicion of the influence of recent immigrants. "Invest the power of government in the hands of an ignorant or merely impulsive multitude, leave the control of that multitude in the keeping of an unscrupulous and self-seeking few, and you have an irresponsible oligarchy, beside whose possible tyrannies the wantonness of Nero might grow white! For, how can such a people help going astray, unless they have men bold and brave enough to tell them the truth?" Because of these dangers, then, he urged his hearers not to hold themselves aloof from politics. Without their participation, he feared, the decline of political morality would go unchecked. "Who shall be brave enough to tell our sovereign, the people, the truth, and how can we hope for a class of public servants who shall do otherwise than pander to their prejudices or their passions, unless the thoughtful and educated and reflecting element in our communities shall make itself felt as everywhere present and sympathetic— an unobtrusive but positive power in all the on-going of our national life?"

On the second danger, Potter argued that the material prosperity of the time, "a state of things which we have been disposed to view with no small complacency," in fact held within it "the seed of the gravest perils." Potter regarded the substance of the peril here to be the unavoidable function of the wealthy as social exemplars. He maintained, then, that the wealthy were responsible for using it in ways that were beneficial to the common good. "No man or woman," he argued, "has a right to indulge in habits of luxury or extravagance hurtful to the community around them. They are deteriorating the whole body politic by their bad example." In addition, he decried not only the unhealthy example of the use of wealth but also that of its acquisition. "Our people of all ranks and classes [are] fired by an unseemly ambition to vie, in their personal and domestic expenditures, with the habits of the wealthiest! Our business habits, how often are they those of an unhealthy spirit of speculation; a vain and silly eagerness to be rich by methods that are only by one step removed from those of the gambler or the adventurer." While not suggesting a causal link between greed for gain and the decline of political morality, Potter recognized that both threatened public welfare. As evidence he cited the historical lesson of the "great dynasties that once covered the earth with tokens of their wealth and strength" but that, despite their greatness, "rotted to death by the cancerous decay of an enervating luxury and extravagance." Such, he warned, was the fate of the country unless its citizens raised their voices in public and private and fulfilled their responsibility for maintaining "that peace and order and righteous serenity which are the fruits of a nation's chastened, virtuous, and simple habits!"[14]

Over the next twenty-five years, Potter continued to raise his warning voice in public and private. In his Thanksgiving sermon of 1879, for example, he reminded his congregation of "those ways in which gratitude may find its visible and substantial expression" and commended that expression that "strives to widen the horizon of human happiness, and to make our fellows sharers in that which has gladdened us." And in 1881, in a sermon preached upon the death of President James Garfield from wounds inflicted by an assassin, Potter praised Garfield as a model of fidelity, manly Christian faith, and Christian heroism and patience. These early reflections presaged Potter's later, more substantive efforts to imbue the virtues of political righteousness in federal and municipal governments.[15] After becoming bishop of New York, he presided at a meeting of working people at New York's Chickering Hall and addressed audiences at Lehigh and Johns Hopkins Universities. He also offered prayers at the Philadelphia ceremony commemorating the centennial of the Constitution. When the 1889 centennial of the inauguration of George Washington neared, the New York Centennial Celebration Committee asked Potter to preach at the ceremonies. At a service to be held on 30 April in St. Paul's Chapel, where Washington himself had worshiped, Potter was to deliver an address from which most observers expected little but comfortable platitudes about Washington's greatness and piety.[16]

The president at the time of the centennial was Republican Benjamin Harrison, who had defeated Grover Cleveland in 1888. Although a Democrat, Cleveland had been elected in 1884 in part because evangelical Protestants and genteel reformers, disgusted with political corruption, were appalled by the presidential candidacy of James Blaine, one of the Republican party's most influential machine bosses. Blaine had used his influence to his financial advantage and denied that he had done so despite published proof. During the 1884 campaign, however, it was also revealed that Cleveland, then the reform governor of New York, had fathered an illegitimate child. Faced with a choice between political corruption and sexual transgression, many church people had instead supported the Prohibition party candidate, Kansas governor John P. St. John. Mugwumps, including Henry Potter, had supported Cleveland.[17] In 1888 Potter voted Republican to support Harrison, whose vice president was Levi P. Morton, a former Grace Church parishioner of Potter's and a benefactor of both Grace and the Cathedral of St. John the Divine. During the campaign, Harrison endorsed civil service reform and appointment by merit. He thus gained a reputation as a reformer, at least in comparison to Cleveland, who was reluctant to expand the merit system. After his election, Harrison struggled with some success to limit the influence of patronage in his cabinet and civil service appointments. Nevertheless, some of his appointments—including James Blaine as secretary of state—drew substantial criticism both before and after Harrison's inauguration. By mid-April 1889, the *New York Times* described the process as a "patronage fair" that showed "no sign of closing." By the end of April, many were convinced that the new administration would not honor its promises or meet their expectations of political righteousness.[18]

The congregation gathered in St. Paul's Chapel at the end of April included President Harrison and Vice President Morton; former presidents Grover Cleveland and Rutherford B. Hayes; members of the Cabinet and of Congress; the governor and mayor; and numerous other officials and dignitaries. Notably absent, reportedly due to ill health, was James Blaine. As he remained one of the leading practitioners of the corrupt machine politics the Mugwumps abhorred, his appointment had undoubtedly provoked much of the public reaction against Harrison.[19]

Potter began his address predictably enough, praising Washington and saying that "he incarnated in his own person and character every best trait and attribute that have made the Anglo-Saxon name a glory to its children and a terror to its enemies throughout the world." The purposes of the celebration, he averred, were to thank God for Washington, to commemorate his inauguration, and "to recognize the responsibilities which a century so eventful has laid upon us." Potter emphasized this last task, building his remarks on an image of Washington's character and its embodiment in his administration. The commemoration of Washington's inauguration, then, was worthwhile because it celebrated "the beginning of an administration which, by its lofty and stainless integrity, by its absolute superiority to selfish or secondary motives, by the rectitude of its daily conduct in the face of whatsoever threats, blandishments, or combinations, rather than by the ostentatious phariseeism of its professions, has taught this nation and the world forever what the Christian ruler of a Christian people ought to be."[20]

Consistent with his characteristic concern for the importance of personal spirit for enlivening institutions, Potter stressed that, marvelous as was the Constitution crafted by the nation's founders, it was nevertheless "a dead and not a living thing." As with a ship, only "cool and competent mastery at the helm" could "under God, determine the glory or the ignominy of the voyage." From the image of government as a ship steered by a capable captain, Potter shifted his attention to another image, that of government as a "machine" functioning on the basis of "practical politics." Potter thereby also shifted from praising Washington to citing his example in criticism of the contemporary political ethic. "The conception of the National Government as a huge machine, existing mainly for the purpose of rewarding partisan service—this was a conception so alien to the character and conduct of Washington and his associates that it seems grotesque even to speak of it." But speak of it Potter did, quoting Washington's response to a friend who had written to him concerning a government appointment:

> In touching upon the more delicate part of your letter, . . . I will deal with you with all that frankness which is due to friendship, and which I wish should be a characteristic feature of my conduct through life. . . . Should it be my fate to administer the Government, I will go to the Chair under no preëngagement of any kind or nature whatever. And when in it, I will, to the best of my judgment, discharge the duties of the office with that impartiality and zeal for the public good which ought never to suffer connections of blood or friendship to have the least sway on decisions of a public nature.[21]

At this point in Potter's address, according to a *New York Times* report, "there was a marked movement indicative of surprise among the gentlemen who sat directly in front of the pulpit." The report continued, "President Harrison, who heretofore had permitted his eyes to wander about the church, fixed his eyes steadily upon the Bishop's face and never removed them until the address was ended. It was evident that that part of the Bishop's short talk had created a sensation of no mean proportions."[22] Potter proceeded to criticize the "steadily deteriorating process" from Washington's time to his own, and to identify two factors contributing to it. First, citing Bushnell and reflecting the typical Anglo-Saxon Protestant distrust of Irish Catholic participation in politics, he decried the "'constant importation . . . of the lowest orders of people from abroad to dilute the quality of our natural manhood.'" Second, he deprecated the dominant materialism of the times. "The growth of wealth, the prevalence of luxury, the massing of large material forces, which by their very existence are a standing menace to the freedom and integrity of the individual, the infinite swagger of our American speech and manners, mistaking bigness for greatness, and sadly confounding gain and godliness—all this is a contrast to the austere simplicity, the unpurchasable integrity, of the first days and first men of our Republic." Potter concluded by avowing that Washington's virtues exemplified "characteristics in her leaders of which the nation was never in more dire need than now."[23]

By all accounts, Potter's address was not only the most notable of the many addresses on the occasion, but also the most remarkable element of the entire two-day centennial celebration. It was the center of the discussion in the press. Some observers took his remarks as a critique of the dominant "practical politics" of both parties, others as a direct criticism of the Harrison administration. The Republican newspapers criticized Potter; the Mugwump papers praised him and reprinted the address.[24] *New York Evening Post* editor and fellow Mugwump E. L. Godkin, whom Potter had consulted before delivering the address, called it "the bravest, timeliest and most effective piece of pulpit oratory which this generation has heard." Carl Schurz, a noted Republican reformer who had served in the cabinet of Rutherford B. Hayes, wrote to Potter: "The more the newspaper discussion on your Centennial sermon spreads and the longer it continues, the more are you to be thanked for the brave and strong words with which you pointed out the contrast between the principles followed by Washington and those governing the 'practical politicians' of our days. We have celebrated the Centennial in vain if that is not understood."[25]

Potter denied any intention of admonishing President Harrison, perhaps having rather intended a broader indictment of contemporary political morality as practiced by both Democrats and Republicans. Whatever his aim, his plea for political righteousness before the country's assembled political leaders made him a national figure and established him as an authority on political and other reform issues. From 1889 until his death, newspapers regularly reported his addresses and sought his opinion on matters of public concern. Over the next two decades, he frequently repeated his insistence on political righteousness. In the next presidential election, he and most of the rest of the voters again chose the Democratic candidate, electing Grover Cleveland for the second time.[26] In 1897, when his Washington centennial address and several others were published as *The Scholar and the State*, one reviewer described it as "the very gospel of 'mugwumpery.'"[27] Having thus been attributed the status of an authority on political righteousness, Potter featured prominently in the reform of New York City politics and the debate over American acquisition of the Philippines.

Corruption and Reform in New York City

From the 1890s until his death in 1908, reflecting perhaps improvement in the conduct of federal politics during those years, Potter's concern for political righteousness focused on New York City municipal government. He regularly addressed civic reform organizations such as the City Club, the City Vigilance League, and Good Government Clubs (of one of the last of which he was a member). On Thanksgiving Day 1894 he preached on the defeat of Tammany Hall in the recent mayoral election, thanking God for the city's deliverance from "a reign of terror which has made New York a stench in the nostrils of the civilized world and citizenship in it a stain and a dishonor to every man who shared it." He also warned that "the safety of our institutions consists not in the vigilance of our official servants, but in our own." The following year, in another municipal election, he publicly allied himself with the Good Government Clubs in opposition to the Fusion Ticket, the latter an attempt to combine the anti-Tammany forces that Potter regarded as "a most mortifying surrender of the reform movement" because it had violated the principle of nonpartisanship in local politics.[28]

Potter also addressed young men at, for example, Harvard University, Union College, and a meeting of the New York State Association of YMCAs. He continued to criticize machine politics and the pursuit of wealth that was corrupting all aspects of social and political life. In those addresses delivered at colleges or universities, he focused on the social responsibilities of men of education and character, arguing that the scholar has his learning so "that he may serve and strengthen that civic order which underlies all that we call civilization."[29] In all his addresses from this period, he emphasized the need for those privileged few, distinguished by learning, character, and virtue, to stand against greed, immorality, and corruption. "In and age which is impatient of any voice that will not cry, 'Great is the god of railroads and syndicates, and greater yet are the apostles of "puts" and "calls," of "corners" and "pools"!' we want a race of men who by their very existence shall be a standing protest against the reign of coarse materialism and a deluge of greed and self-seeking."[30] Similarly, in 1895 he argued that "the men who are to lead in these reforms, the men whose right it is to lead . . . are the men who are ordained to be 'men of leading' because they are also 'men of light.'"[31]

In the mid-1890s, Potter added to these themes specific references to the corruption of New York City's government. In an 1895 address at Union College, he praised the model of the concerned scholar who "persists in obtruding himself into politics, as into all other burning questions, and turning the eye of his pitiless lantern of truth upon partizan leaders and placemen with equal searching and impartiality." Of such a scholar there was an example close to hand. "We have had our modern Elijah lately, in the great metropolis yonder, facing the modern Ahab of Tammany Hall as he sneered, 'Art thou he that troubleth Israel?' and answering as of old, 'I have not troubled Israel; but thou, and thy father's house.' And we sleep easier in New York because of his brave and splendid crusade."[32] The "modern Elijah" was the Reverend Charles Parkhurst. President of the New York Society for the Prevention of Crime, Parkhurst also led the People's Municipal League that had been organized in 1890 by R. Heber Newton. In 1892 Parkhurst investigated corruption in New York's police department and charged that the police were running a protection racket with gambling and prostitution rings. These charges, and the resulting state investigation, led to the defeat of the Tammany Hall machine in the 1894 municipal election. As a result, Potter could maintain that "the insolent pride of office needs forever to be taught, sharply and humblingly if need be, all the way from Chief Magistrate to policeman, that our rulers are the servants of the people."[33]

Reform governments came and went over the next several years as Tammany Hall and its variously constituted opponents traded elections. Potter himself played a central role in the reform victory of 1901, having unintentionally prepared for that role in 1895 when he undertook one of his more distinctive endeavors by living and working for six weeks at the Stanton Street Mission in the heart of New York's East Side tenement district. For many years St. George's Church, whose minister was W. S. Rainsford, had been supporting the mission and the Brotherhood of St. Andrew had been staffing it. By 1893, however, St. George's could support it no longer and the Brotherhood proposed to Bishop Potter that the cathedral assume responsibility for the mission. Coming only a few months after the cornerstone for the cathedral had been laid, Potter saw this proposal as a demonstration of his vision for the many-sided mission of the cathedral. He approved the proposal and in his address to the 1893 diocesan convention urged the clergy to "go in turn, for a month or two at a time, with a few faithful laity, and live sparely and work faithfully and pray earnestly with and among our brethren."[34]

To provide an example of such service (and to respond to clergy complaints about what they regarded as their bishop's unreasonable request), from 10 June to 8 August 1895 Potter lived at and assumed direct responsibility for what was now known as the Cathedral Mission. As Hodges notes, "It was impossible to enter upon this undertaking quietly, as he had hoped." Seeing a bishop living among the poor as a novelty, the newspapers took a keen interest in and reported extensively on Potter's arrival and work at the Cathedral Mission. To a suggestion that he was "going slumming," Potter replied: "I am not going to undergo martyrdom, nor am I to suffer any great hardships. This will be nothing new in my experience." Over the next several years he frequently preached and conducted baptisms, confirmations, and special services at the Cathedral Mission. While at the time he seems to have disliked the attention from the press to his 1895 visit there, a few years later his widespread public identification with the Cathedral Mission would prove to be instrumental in Potter's work against municipal corruption.[35]

In 1899 Potter appointed Robert Paddock vicar of the Cathedral Mission. Paddock was intensely concerned with the physical as well as the spiritual well-being of the area's residents. He readily cooperated with reformers and philanthropists Felix Adler and Jacob Schiff when, in the winter of 1899–1900, they initiated a campaign against houses of prostitution on the Lower East Side. Because of their economic vulnerability, women and children were regularly coerced into prostitution, often being abducted and sold for twenty-five dollars each. In the late summer of 1900 Paddock rescued a fourteen-year-old girl from the house to which she had been taken and sought police action against those responsible. Rather than assistance, however, Paddock received only abuse. As in the case of Parkhurst's investigations of 1892, it again became apparent that the police were complicit in and benefiting from the vice traffic.[36]

Paddock reported the incident to Bishop Potter. In consultation with diocesan clergy including William R. Huntington and Percy S. Grant, Potter investigated further and presented his findings to the diocesan convention in September. Huntington offered a resolution, passed unanimously, requesting that the bishop investigate "the alleged indignities" against Paddock and, if warranted, "to make a formal protest, in the name of the Church, to the Mayor of New York." The resolution suggested that the church's outrage was primarily due to the offense against one of its clergy, but it was in fact a slender pretense for a sweeping critique of municipal corruption. Bishop Potter's own association with and supervision of the Cathedral Mission certainly contributed both to the sense of outrage and to the impact of Potter's subsequent response. In the first report in the *New York Times* of the diocese's unprecedented action, Potter focused on "the awful conditions this metropolis shelters" rather than on the insult to Paddock and remarked that if these conditions were widely known "there would be such a storm of indignation as would shake the entire social structure."[37]

Potter helped precipitate that storm. After further investigation, he wrote in mid-November to Mayor Robert Van Wyck, a Tammany Hall functionary. Newspapers throughout the country printed the letter; the *New York Times* featured it in a front-page article headlined "Police Uphold a Reign of Vice." In it, Potter acknowledged his direct and personal responsibility for the Cathedral Mission but asserted that the insult to his representative there was "of the very smallest consequence." What mattered, rather, was the exploitation of the women and children of the district.

> Before God and in the face of the citizens of New York I protest, as my people have charged me to do, against the habitual insult, the persistent menace, the unutterably defiling contacts, to which, day by day, because of the base complicity of the police of New York with the lowest forms of vice and crime, they are subjected. And, in the name of these little ones, these weak and defenceless ones, Christian and Hebrew alike, of many races and tongues, but of homes in which God is feared and his law reverenced, and virtue and decency honored and exemplified, I call upon you, sir, to save these people who are in a very real way committed to your charge, from a living hell, leprous, deadly, damning, to which the criminal supineness of the constituted authorities, set for the defence of decency and good order, threatens to doom them.

That week, attempting to preempt the criticism generated by Potter's charges, the Tammany machine launched its own Anti-Vice Committee and investigation of the police officers involved in the original incident. Also, some of the city's clergy—including Episcopalian W. S. Rainsford, Congregationalist Lyman Abbot, and Roman Catholic Thomas Ducey—addressed the problem of vice and corruption in their sermons.[38]

Ten days after his letter to Van Wyck, Potter preached his sermon "God and the City" in a service at St. Paul's Chapel, the same venue as his address on the Washington inaugural centennial eleven years earlier. Announcements of the address invited "men of prominence in professional and mercantile life" to attend. Trinity Church rector Morgan Dix presided at the service, and Lyman Abbott attended. The chapel, as the *New York Times* reported, was "crowded to the doors" with "old men and young men. Women, aged and decrepit, with heads bowed down in constant prayer, were seated alongside daintily dressed girls, many of them with typewrit-

ers. Men of business and brokers from Wall Street stood alongside of mechanics in their working clothes." Potter took as his starting point Jesus'
tearful reaction upon looking down at Jerusalem, suggesting that Jesus'
sorrow was prompted in this instance "because of the moral apathy, because of the appalling spiritual insensibility, because of the deadness of the
soul which is the doom and damnation equally of a nation or of a man."

To overcome this spiritual blindness and confront the evils facing the
city, he proposed a four-point strategy. The first need was "the awakening and enlargement of the spiritual vision of man as the foundation of
all civic, social and natural regeneration." Second was the need for organized endeavor, for "every man and woman" to take his or her place in
the "great alignment of service." Having taken up their responsibilities,
citizens would then "find three or five men whom all of us trusted and
believed in" and entrust them with guidance and coordination of efforts
for "the betterment of New York." Third, all must remain vigilant against
vice and corruption: "if you and I had our eyes open, and kept them open
and stood where God calls us to stand to-day, New York would ere long
be a redeemed and regenerated city!" And fourth, he maintained, these
efforts must be characterized by persistence. "In this warfare, men and
brethren, if it is to be a triumphant warfare, we must enlist for life. Get
yourselves then on your knees in the noonday meetings of this chapel,
or in whatever way you may, pray God that he will open your eyes; pray
to Him for the power of His Son; let His Spirit kindle in you the flame of
a divine indignation, and keep it burning with the enduring power of a
divine and unflinching sacrifice!"[39]

Potter hoped to inspire the formation of a reform organization on the
model of the San Francisco Vigilance Committee, to which he had referred in his address. By January, however, no such organization had
materialized, and in an address at the City Club of New York, on a platform shared with Mark Twain and others, Potter expressed his disappoint-
ment. Convinced that "personal sacrifice and vigilance" were essential
to bringing about the desired reforms, he pointed to the example of Theodore Roosevelt, who had been president of the New York City Police
Commission from 1895 to 1897 and was at the time of Potter's address
vice president–elect to William McKinley. "Nothing better was ever done
by Mr. Roosevelt when he was Police Commissioner, than the nightly
tours he made through the city watching the police and seeing that they
performed their duty. It brought the men to a sense of feeling that they
were being watched. Every man charged with official duties ought to have
the same feeling." He also repeated his view of the link between political corruption and greed, maintaining that a "condition of society where

gain excuses all doings must naturally affect the mechanism which runs a city such as this. There must be some higher aim."[40]

Although the citizens of New York failed to organize a vigilance committee, they did undertake several initiatives for the elimination of corruption. One of them was the formation in late 1900 of a Committee of Fifteen men—merchants, financiers, and lawyers—to lead the campaign to oust the Tammany machine in the 1901 election. The elitism of this approach, characteristic of the efforts of the genteel reformers, did not go unnoticed. W. D. P. Bliss, Potter's more radical colleague in CAIL and the Christian Social Union, criticized the narrowness of the Committee of Fifteen's constituency and argued that it should also include representatives of labor. Potter agreed with Bliss on this point. Addressing a January 1901 meeting of Brooklyn's Get-Together Club, he said that he had advised those forming the Committee of Fifteen that "at least two representatives of labor should be placed on the committee, and that the committee should recognize all classes." His sense of the need for a broadly based effort is also reflected in his criticism of the club's decision, made that same evening, to continue to exclude women. Consistent with his convictions on women's appropriate concern with and competence in public issues, he noted, "I had hoped that in Brooklyn a vote on the question of the presence of ladies would have been unanimous in favor of admitting them. I think the time will come, and more speedily than you believe, when the counsel of both sexes will be essential in all forward movements."[41]

Through the rest of 1901, Potter regularly spoke in support of municipal reform, even in his remarks to the New York diocesan convention of 1901. Potter's political reform strategy was chiefly to persuade and inspire by public appeal, rather than to play a direct leadership role in reform organizations. As in the case of his contemporaneous work in support of recognition for organized labor, it seems likely that he also worked privately to counsel, advise, and encourage other reformers. In October he publicly, and correctly, predicted the victory of the reform ticket in the imminent election. As a result of the various efforts that Potter's leadership had helped initiate, Tammany Hall was defeated once again and Seth Low, president of Columbia University and former mayor of Brooklyn, was elected mayor of New York.[42]

Intervention, Expansion, and National Responsibility

At the same time that he was involved in this campaign for municipal reform, Potter was also involved in the heated public debates over American acquisition and administration of the Philippines in the wake of the Spanish-American War. What Paul Toews has noted of social gospelers generally is also true of Potter: "While devoting most of their energy to reform activity within the boundaries of the national state, the social gospelers never lost sight of the universal dream inherent in their kingdom theology. Reform of the nation only presaged international reform." At the end of the nineteenth century, the national ethos of isolation from world affairs was showing signs of strain, caused largely by a rapidly growing industrial economy. The new economic need for expansion of markets and sources of raw materials conflicted with the old national self-image of a democratic, noncolonial society.[43]

Interwoven with the economic drive for expansion was a powerful religious drive, manifest in the century-long tradition of foreign mission work. Those engaged in the missionary enterprise tended to regard the civilizing and Christianizing of the world as mutually sustaining. Foreign missions embodied the same attitudes and employed the same approaches that had been taken in domestic mission work among blacks, aboriginal peoples, the poor and working classes in the cities, and the unchurched on the frontiers. Various participants differed on the strategic priority of civilizing or Christianizing, but all agreed that both were essential elements in the campaign to "win the world for Jesus Christ." The link between Christianity and Anglo-American civilization, then, provided the means by which many Christians could regard the expansion of American commerce and political influence as a necessary component of the establishment of a world Christian civilization.[44] The hope for a world Christian civilization, however, did not necessarily entail the expansion of American territory and influence. Until well into the 1890s, most Protestant leaders adamantly maintained American anticolonial ideals in the face of rising expansionist fervor. They assumed that the United States would expand the Christian civilization through the force of its example for good and the influence of Christian missionaries. Further, they also tended to maintain that "the natural or God-given boundary of the nation within which freedom could be practiced and liberty made secure did not extend beyond the water's edge nor the Rio Grande."[45]

Henry Potter shared and publicly endorsed this view of both the extent of and limits to the nation's "natural or God-given boundary." In December 1895 he signaled his antiexpansionist sentiments in his criticism of President Grover Cleveland's message to Congress on the longstanding boundary dispute between Great Britain and Venezuela. Cleveland had threatened military intervention, under the authority of the Monroe Doctrine, if Great Britain unjustly appropriated any territory in its dispute with Venezuela. Potter strongly objected to such saber-rattling and argued that American attempts to arbitrate the dispute were motivated not by a desire to settle the issue impartially, but rather by hostility to British territorial claims. He therefore exhorted the nation,

> May no lust of conquest, no base passion inflaming us to humiliate a powerful rival, no blind following of demagogues eager to pander to the worst, eager not to appeal to the best in their fellow-men; and above all, no tolerance of a leadership crazed with the love of place, and eager to outwit a political adversary, persuade us to forget our duty as a Christian Nation to cultivate the graces of patience, forbearance, and a lofty self-restraint—which are the best graces of strong men—and so to "study the things that make for peace!"[46]

The dispute was ultimately settled by means of international arbitration, to the process of which all parties had agreed. In March 1897, one month after ratification of a treaty establishing the arbitration tribunal, Potter delivered a public address at New York's Cooper Union in support of international arbitration. During the subsequent three years, however, circumstances tested Potter's antiexpansionist convictions.[47]

The United States had an economic interest in preventing the expansion of British trade in Latin America, perhaps in the hope that expansion of American trade there might alleviate the 1895 economic depression. Cleveland's actions seem to have been motivated, however, as much by his concern to preserve national honor as by fear of extension of British economic and strategic power in the Americas. In any event, Cleveland's appeal to the Monroe Doctrine to validate American involvement in the Venezuelan boundary controversy was a step toward the similar assertion of American prerogatives in relations between Spain and Cuba. In the latter case, however, American actions did lead to war and to unintended and unexpected consequences. The Cuban insurrection had begun in late February 1895, several months before Cleveland's bellicose message to Congress on the Venezuelan boundary dispute, and raged on over the next three years. Lacking sympathy for the Cubans or the Spanish, Cleveland proclaimed American neutrality in June 1895. Others in the country, including many newspaper editors and members of Congress, regarded "the insurrectionists as Cuban replicas of the Minutemen of Lexington and Concord." Some Protestant leaders preached the duty of American intervention to liberate the Cubans from Spanish tyranny, but at this point in the conflict they were a minority. Domestic business interests viewed the acquisition of Cuba as a means of expanding markets for their products and sources for the raw materials they required.

Cleveland tried but failed not only to restrain the country's warmongers but also to end the rebellion by securing Spanish concessions.[48]

In the 1896 presidential campaign, Cleveland lost the Democratic nomination to William Jennings Bryan, who in turn lost the election to Republican William McKinley. Unlike Cleveland, McKinley readily combined policies of economic, political, and territorial expansion. As the Cuban crisis continued, however, and as American interventionist sentiment increased, McKinley proceeded cautiously. He obtained concessions from Spain on treatment of political prisoners and limited political autonomy for Cuba, but he irritated Spain by insisting on the right of the United States to monitor conditions in Cuba. By January 1898 the situation deteriorated and McKinley ordered the battleship *Maine* to Havana harbor. On February 16 it exploded and sank, killing 266 men. The possibility that Spain had caused the disaster provoked a frenzy of war fever. While awaiting the results of an inquiry that ultimately but, it is now clear, mistakenly concluded that the explosion had been caused by a submarine mine, McKinley increased diplomatic pressure on and prepared for war with Spain.

As public clamor for war mounted, most Protestant leaders nevertheless resisted the interventionist tide. The situation changed on 17 March when Senator Redfield Proctor reported on his recent visit to Cuba. Proctor's report described the brutal "pacification" campaign waged by the Spanish. As he was not regarded as an interventionist, Proctor's views carried some weight and brought about a shift in Protestant opinion. The 19 March issue of the *Churchman,* for example, argued that while a war for national gain was unjustifiable, a war of disinterested intervention was a clear national duty. Thus, while Protestant opinion had heretofore successfully resisted justifying imperialist endeavors, it came to justify what it regarded as an anti-imperial military intervention. With overwhelming popular and congressional support, McKinley declared war on Spain on 25 April 1898.[49]

The war of liberation, however, quickly became a war of territorial acquisition. Six days after the declaration of war, and nearly two months before the American invasion of Cuba, American naval forces under Commodore George Dewey destroyed the Spanish fleet at Manila Bay and occupied the Philippines for the United States. The United States invaded Cuba in late June; the war ended in mid-August. In less than six months, the problem for the nation had shifted from "What should we do about Cuba?" to "What should we do about the Philippines?" As Hudson observes, Protestant opinion was deeply divided. Potter and others insisted that the nation maintain its anticolonial traditions; others developed what Hudson called pious justifications for the recently accomplished territorial acquisition. By Thanksgiving Day 1898, and although Protestant opinion remained divided, Lyman Abbott noted that an "imperialism of liberty" had received substantial justification, largely on the grounds of the responsibility of stronger nations for weaker ones. About two weeks later, on 10 December 1898, Spain and the United States signed the Treaty of Paris, in which Spain formally ceded the Philippines, Puerto Rico, and Guam to the United States.[50]

Through the fall of 1898 some Protestant leaders such as Lyman Abbot and Washington Gladden began to shift toward support for the imperialism of liberty, but Potter and others maintained their opposition. In his address to the New York diocesan convention in September 1898, Potter decried the prevalent "dream of colonial gains": "The things that this community and this nation alike supremely need are not more territory, more avenues of trade, more subject races to prey upon, but a dawning consciousness of what, in individual and in national life, are a people's indispensable moral foundations—those great spiritual forces on which alone men and nations are built."[51] At the Episcopal Church's October 1898 General Convention, the House of Bishops, in view of the country's enlarged territorial holdings, established the Commission on the Increased Responsibilities of the Church. Before the bishops voted, however, Potter demonstrated his displeasure at the war's outcome by moving to strike from the resolution the phrase "by the extension of the sovereignty of the flag in new regions." The House of Bishops adopted the resolution as amended by Potter and appointed him to the commission.[52]

In a November 1898 letter to *Harper's Weekly*, Potter criticized the commercial, colonial, and religious arguments for territorial expansion and for American administration of the Philippines. To the proposition that the United States could benefit "subject races" by ruling, enfranchising, and ennobling them, he replied: "What now are the indications that we have any single qualification for such a task?" He answered this question by pointing to the dismal history of the nation's dealings with blacks, aboriginal peoples, and Chinese immigrants, regarding it as "one long record of cruelty, rapine, lust, and outrage." He also noted the "infamous results" of American civic and military administration "which have turned the glory of our victories into the shame of our most criminal incompetency." In the following year, Potter publicly supported the anti-imperialist Continental League and delivered an address against imperialism at the meeting of the Episcopal Church Congress held in Minneapolis. In his Church Congress address, he criticized American dealings with the people of the Philippines: "It would seem at least reasonable that the conquering or purchasing republic should inaugurate its relations to the new possessions by some conference with its dominant people. But no. Its first word is subjection, its first demand surrender, its first, second, and third conditions are, We will recognize nobody, we alone will dictate the terms."[53]

Events in the Philippines in 1899 transformed its relation to the United States yet again. Before and for a time after Dewey's victory Americans had maintained sympathetic contact with Emilio Aguinaldo, leader of the Philippine resistance to Spanish rule. As the American resolve to govern the Philippines hardened, tensions between American forces and Philippine insurgents increased. In February 1899, within a few days of Senate ratification of the Treaty of Paris, the tensions erupted into open hostilities, thus embroiling the United States in a colonial war. Anti-imperialists and some "imperialists of liberty" noted the similarity between this conflict and that between the Spanish and Cubans. Soon American troops were employing against Filipinos the very pacification tactics for which Americans had criticized the Spanish in Cuba only one year earlier. It became difficult to maintain the pious justification of benevolent administration following a war of liberation when the liberated clearly wanted no part in that administration and when the administrator required nonbenevolent means to subdue the liberated.[54]

In April 1899 Henry Potter discussed the gains and perils of expansion in an article in the *North American Review*. With respect to the expansion of commercial opportunities, he replied that American export business has thrived without territorial acquisition; with respect to the accession of peoples, he asked whether such new peoples might not make the American population, already greatly diverse, too heterogeneous to govern effectively. Turning to the likely perils, he listed first the extraordinary cost of maintaining military forces sufficient to govern "these alien, and, in some instances, utterly uncivilized peoples." In addition, he doubted, because of its own political corruption, America's ability to create and maintain an effective civil service for colonial administration. Finally, he pointed to the possible negative effect of not only Philippine but also increased Chinese immigration upon the life of the nation.

Such, in Potter's view, were the implications of the "path of bigness." Rather than take that path, he urged the nation to take the "path of greatness" based on the American ideal of "government of the people, by the people and for the people." By renouncing territorial expansion, he argued, the country could still extend its beneficial influence through the expansion of its leadership in technology and commerce, arts and letters, morals and missions. "These are the things which have interpreted us to the rest of the world, and these are the things which are the true notes of a nation's greatness." Thus, to the immediate question of the disposition of the Philippines, Potter proposed the establishment of an international tribunal of arbitration.[55]

In November 1899, after the Philippine insurrection had been raging for nearly a year, Potter embarked on a fact-finding mission to Hawaii, the Philippines, Japan, China, and India on behalf of the Commission on the Increased Responsibilities of the Church. By the time he returned in March 1900, he had reversed his position. While he had previously maintained that the United States was neither practically prepared nor morally justified to assume government of the Philippines, he now reasoned—to the great dismay of his anti-imperialist colleagues—that although the annexation of the islands was a blunder, it was the country's duty to execute its responsibilities honorably.[56]

The first hint of Potter's shift had come during his trip, in mid-December 1899, when the *New York Herald* reported some of his views on the Philippines. Included in this report was the suggestion that, unlike their British and German counterparts, American merchants had not yet appreciated "the commercial opportunities opened by American administration in the islands." Potter's first assessment after visiting the Philippines appears in a letter written from Singapore, and in it he for the first time accepted American administration of the Philippines.

> If we are to retain these islands, and the undersigned are constrained to own, however they may differ from any of their associates as to the wisdom of originally entering upon them, that no other course seems for the present open to the United States, these wrongs [as summarized earlier in the letter] and the righting of them lie at the foundation of the whole Philippine problem. . . . We must do justly in the Philippines, or God will have no use for us, and our presence there will inevitably redound to our national dishonor.[57]

Upon his return to New York in March 1900, the full scope of his shift became apparent. The *New York World* quoted Potter's revised view:

> We must accept the inevitable. . . . The question now is "What are you going to do now that you have got it?" We have got the responsibility of governing the Philippines, for better or worse. If it is for the worse, all the greater is our responsibility. . . . I went there in an attitude of hostility to the whole business, but that did not prevent the military authorities from extending every courtesy and facility that would aid me in comprehending the situation. I must say that my mind has greatly altered as to the relation of the higher civilization to the lower civiliza-

tion. We have got those islands and we have got to hold on to them. . . . The matter of their acquisition is now an academic question purely.[58]

Potter's reversal horrified his anti-imperialist colleagues. By the end of March, the *New York Times* observed: "On the whole it would appear that no event since the triumph of our land and sea forces in the war with Spain has so deeply disgusted the anti-imperialists as the Bishop's avowal that he has succumbed to the light of knowledge and reason and become a supporter of the policy of maintaining order in the Philippines."[59]

Potter had not, however, changed his view on the question of American expansion. He remained until his death opposed to any policy of territorial acquisition and always maintained that the acquisition of the Philippines had been a colossal blunder. After his visit there, however, he argued that despite this blunder the country must accept its responsibility for the well-being of the islands' people. The key to understanding Potter's reversal is his altered view of "the relation of the higher civilization to the lower civilization." Potter also illustrated this view in a revealing anecdote in a May 1900 address to the New York Military Order of the Loyal Legion. "Suppose my son were to come to me and say, 'My dear father, I am thinking of marrying a creole woman with seven children,' I am perfectly free to say that I should reply to him, 'My son, you are a fool.' But if he had actually married a creole woman with seven children, I should try to behave toward him as if I still sustained some blood relationship to him. . . . [W]hether we like it or not, what we have done is to establish some such relationship as that with the Filipinos."[60] Potter developed this perspective more fully in an essay published in November 1900. On the basis of research, his own visit to the Philippines, and correspondence with "responsible and impartial witnesses of all classes," he provided a historical context for American acquisition and a rationale for continuing American administration of the islands. In this discussion, Potter's sense of Anglo-Saxon cultural superiority proved ultimately stronger than either his conviction that America was ill-equipped for colonial administration or his commitment to the self-determination of peoples.[61]

Potter criticized Spanish colonial administration, specifically its military, civil, and ecclesiastical elements. He argued that Spain's bleak record there was due in part to the evils of its colonial practice, but also, in his view, to the low level of Philippine civilization as compared to that in India at the start of British colonial rule. His criticism of Spanish colonial administration functioned to make American administration more acceptable, but it also functioned as an example of the evils American rule should avoid. American domestic history, he suggested, provided plentiful evidence of tendencies toward ill-treatment of the governed, abuse of public office for personal gain, and corruption throughout the civil service. With this evaluation of the Philippine situation at the time of American acquisition, Potter concluded that "there has been nothing in the past history of the Filipino to educate him to value or to imitate high ideals of official authority or civic, social, or domestic self-restraint." To the suggestion of some anti-imperialists that the Philippine struggle for independence compared favorably with the American Revolution, Potter responded that "whatever elements of equity there may be in the Philippine struggle for freedom, the leaders have not yet appeared who could be seriously considered as competent to lead and organize it."

Regarding the people of the Philippines as incapable of self-government, yet acknowledging the manifold inadequacies of the United States, Potter concluded that the country could only execute honorably its task of governing the Philippines. "To throw up our task now would be a cruelty to those whom we abandon, and a confession of our impotence which would disgrace us before the world. . . . Noblesse oblige. A great nation cannot abandon a weaker people which it has, before all men, adopted as its ward without confessing that, great as its claims to be, it has nothing to impart, nothing to sacrifice, in order to give freedom and good government to those who have not forfeited all claim to such gifts because they have looked for them in the wrong direction." Of the ultimate success of this task, Potter offered no assurances and implied that the responsibility for its success lay not with Americans, but with the people of the Philippines. "Time alone can demonstrate how far we may be able to persuade a fickle, restless, impulsive, unreasoning people, embittered by many wrongs received at the hands of those we have expelled, or ought to expel, to trust us, to learn from us, and under our patient tutelage to grow into the stature of competent citizens in a self-governing state."

Potter's reassessment of the relation of "higher" to "lower" civilizations may also have been influenced by one particularly influential person. When Potter's essays on his tour of Asia and the Pacific were published in 1902 as *The East of To-day and To-morrow*, its dedication read "To John Pierpont Morgan, Financier, Philanthropist, Friend, to whose munificence these opportunities for observation in the East were owing, and whose constructive genius, which upbuilds and never pulls down, has indicated the tasks which await western civilization in eastern fields." This dedication implies that Morgan, the prominent financier and Episcopalian with whom Potter was well acquainted, donated the money for Potter's fact-finding tour. Morgan's sense of "the tasks which await western civilization in eastern fields" would certainly have entailed a more positive assessment of the relation of commercial opportunities to territorial expansion than that held by Potter prior to his trip.

In his later view of American duty to the Philippines, however, Potter nowhere appealed to the potential for increased trade and remained unconvinced by, and indeed suspicious of, commercial arguments for expansion. At one point he noted that "in handicrafts, the mechanic arts, and kindred industrial pursuits the native Filipino has exhibited unusual aptitude." In this context, his point was to demonstrate that the people of the Philippines had aptitudes that the Spanish had done little to encourage and develop, that the Spanish had therefore betrayed their responsibility to the people they governed, and that such development was necessary for legitimate colonial administration. This comment, however, could also have suggested that the Philippines provided a source of cheap skilled labor for American industrial endeavors.[62]

That Potter intended no such suggestion is clear in his April 1902 addresses at Yale University, published that year as *The Citizen in His Relation to the Industrial Situation.* Repeating both his opposition to expansion and his rationale for American acquisition of the Philippines as a justifiable exception, he emphasized that territorial expansion could not be justified on economic grounds.

> It cannot be denied that a large part of what I think I may not unjustly describe as a policy of aggressive imperialism is also a policy of aggressive commercialism. The "market" is to the minds of a great multitude of people among us the word, to-day, of the most magic import. What can we buy more cheaply in the Hawaiian or Philippine Islands than anywhere else, and what can we sell more dearly there? These, and not other and more serious questions which ought to concern a Christian people, are the importunate interrogations of the hour.

Potter sought to show "what may be involved in a merely sordid and greedy answer" to such questions. To that end, and quoting at length from John A. Hobson's *Social Problem,* he pointed to the worrisome fact that nations "are no longer content to justify their territorial aggression and their interferences with foreign nationalities, on the grounds of mere selfish expediency; but profess a certain mission of civilization, insisting, at any rate, that the attainment of their private ends is accompanied by a gain to the world, and, in particular, to the land or nation which is the object of the encroachment."[63]

Following Hobson, he rejected the economic argument for expansionism that maintained that the "utilization of the natural resources of each portion of the globe should be assigned to the people which can most effectively undertake it" and denied that "capacity for conquest" or "superiority in the present arts of industry" were adequate tests of a nation's fitness to utilize a territory's resources and govern another people. Instead, Potter argued, the only legitimate test was a nation's "competency to discharge any such responsibility or to administer any such trust." By this measure, he suggested that the United States might have something "to contribute to pagan lands and peoples" but argued that "as yet, its own standards, moral, social, industrial, are sorely below a worthy level, sorely below the level of either honorable or adequate achievement." To the question of how to "make ours a state meet to lead and to rule, at home or abroad," Potter answered, "We must not only affirm the brotherhood of man; we must live it. For then the state, and, in the state, the home, the church, and the individual, shall become the incarnation of a regenerated humanity, and earth, this earth, our earth, here and to-day, the vestibule of heaven!"[64]

Potter's justification for American administration of the Philippines was consistent with the official justification promulgated around the time of the publication of his *East of To-day and To-morrow*. In January 1903 journalist James F. Rusling published an interview President McKinley had held with a delegation from the Methodist Episcopal Church in November 1899 (the same month that Potter had departed for his tour of Asia). According to Rusling, McKinley told his ecclesiastical visitors that during the treaty negotiations with Spain he had prayed to God for guidance on the disposition of the Philippines. The answer to his prayer came in the form of the conviction that returning any or all of the islands to Spain "would be cowardly and dishonorable" and that the people of the Philippines were "unfit for self-government." McKinley concluded, therefore, "that there was nothing left for us to do but to take them all, and to educate the Filipinos, and uplift and civilize and Christianize them, as our fellow-men for whom Christ also died." Whether McKinley in fact used such religious language or Rusling later added it, Rusling's report demonstrates the public importance of the religious justification for continuing American administration of the Philippines.[65]

It also demonstrates that Potter's justification, while late in coming, ultimately reflected and contributed to public acceptance of this colonial role for the United States. His defense of continuing American rule, however, remained more cautious and restricted than that of other Protestant leaders. For example, Josiah Strong's *Expansion under New World Con-*

ditions, published in the same year as Potter's "Problem of the Philippines," went much further in justifying American expansion. Strong denounced the unscrupulous imperialism practiced by the European powers but recommended an "imperialism of righteousness" by which the nation would expand its moral influence throughout the world. In retrospect, it is evident that both Strong's imperialism of righteousness and Potter's international noblesse oblige have been used to justify the very ambitious and unscrupulous imperialism that they denounced. To Potter's credit, however, he seems to have perceived the dangers more clearly than most of those who accepted or gloried in the country's new international role.[66]

In the last years of his life, Potter continued to participate in discussions on international affairs in general and on the Philippines in particular. In May 1902, for example, he addressed a "private meeting of men" on American administration of the Philippines, and two years later spoke at a New York Chamber of Commerce reception for members of the Philippine Commission. At the end of 1904 he spoke on international arbitration at a public meeting at Carnegie Hall, and also there in April 1907 he presided at and addressed a meeting of the Peace Congress. In January 1908, six months before his death and again at Carnegie Hall, he presided at a meeting on constitutional government in Russia.[67]

From 1865 to 1908, Henry Codman Potter steadfastly argued for the necessity of the righteous practice of political life, whether municipal, national, or international. Like many of his contemporaries, he recognized the danger to public morality posed by the often unscrupulous means by which wealth was acquired as well as by the typically corrupting uses to which it was being put. Because he considered a largely homogeneous population a necessity for its governance and doubted the speed with which new immigrants could be Americanized, he also considered uncontrolled immigration a threat. Similarly, he saw the threat to American moral identity posed by the lust for commercial and territorial expansion at the turn of the century, as well as the threat to the governability of the country posed by the addition of the twelve million people of the Philippines. Against such threats to the public good, Potter encouraged citizens, particularly the country's "best men," to fulfill their responsibility for maintaining and strengthening the community's moral practice. Potter avowed that the nation would attain true greatness not by its accumulation of wealth or territorial expansion but by its moral fabric. Just as the righteous practice of politics would extend Christian democracy throughout the country by the force of its example, so too would it extend throughout the world.

Potter's conviction of the responsibility of what he regarded as the stronger to the weaker served as the thin edge of the wedge that ultimately brought about his reversal of his opposition to American administration of the Philippines. Whatever the role of commercial considerations in this reversal, his public reasoning clearly reflects his emphasis on the responsibility of (in his view and that of many of his contemporaries) the higher to the lower civilization. His treatment of this issue is thus consistent with his reliance elsewhere in his moral reasoning on an ethic of the responsibility of the strong for the weak. Potter did not, however, explicitly extend this responsibility to other, supposedly lower, civilizations, asserting that the case of the Philippines was unique because of the "original blunder" of Commodore Dewey and his superiors.[68] With this exception, he always maintained that the nation's responsibilities should be limited to its "natural or God-given" boundaries. At least implicitly, however, and despite Potter's criticism of the nation's treatment of aboriginal Americans, such a view similarly justified European American acquisition of territory occupied by and colonial governance of the continent's first peoples. That Potter nowhere addressed this question suggests the extent to which he, like most of his contemporaries, took for granted the righteousness of European, especially Anglo-Saxon, expansion into the Americas.

As Potter and many of his contemporaries were the link between the antebellum evangelical religious reform agenda and postwar social Christianity, so too were they the link between the political agendas of the earlier genteel or Mugwump reformers and the later Progressives. As Clyde Griffen has observed,

> The bishop's attitudes toward racism and imperialism, like his political and economic ideas, bridge the Mugwump convictions of his own generation and the outlook of younger men who became Progressives. His vision of the brotherhood of man, shared with the Social Gospelers, prevented him from accepting any theory of superiority based solely on racial difference and his Mugwump view of politics precluded any sympathy with the jingoes of 1898–1899. But his conviction that the English-speaking peoples, and especially Americans, possessed superior ideals and institutions and had a mission to civilize the rest of mankind allowed him to accept empire after it was an accomplished fact.[69]

By contributing to the establishment of the Progressive consensus, however flawed it and its ideological assumptions were, Henry Codman Potter helped make it possible for Rauschenbusch, with some justification, to claim at the end of the first decade of the twentieth century that the nation's political order had been Christianized. While hindsight suggests that Rauschenbusch's judgment was at best premature, that claim was necessary for Rauschenbusch to address the Christianization of the economic order, a task that Henry Potter had also taken up.

5 *Reconciling Labor and Capital*

The industrial problem was foremost among the interrelated social issues of concern to Henry Codman Potter and his contemporaries. In his 1876 book, *Working People and Their Employers,* Washington Gladden observed: "Now that slavery is out of the way, the questions that concern the welfare of our free laborers are coming forward; and no intelligent man needs to be admonished of their urgency. They are not only questions of economy, they are in a large sense moral questions; nay, they touch the very marrow of that religion of good-will of which Christ was the founder." Some scholars have read Gladden's observation as an indication not only of the importance of the relations of labor and capital to American social Christianity, but also of its shift away from concern for the welfare of black people after the Civil War. However one evaluates the social gospel on race relations, Gladden's comment accurately reflects, first, the historical relation between the elimination of slavery and the rise of free labor under industrial capitalism, and second, the growing tensions in the socioeconomic order as a result of the plight of free laborers in this new situation. That wage-earning laborers constituted a significant proportion of the American work force was itself a new phenomenon, produced in part by the elimination of slavery, but, more important, by the industrialization of manufacturing that began before and spread quickly after the Civil War. These new conditions and the problems they spawned prompted Henry Potter and many of his colleagues to develop and support strategies that, more than on any other social issue, distanced them from the strategies of their evangelical predecessors. In their responsiveness to these new conditions, however, they remained faithful to their broader evangelical heritage.[1]

Industrialization and the Rise and Fall of Clerical Political Economics

From colonial times until the 1820s, American economic life was based on agriculture and small-scale manufacturing, and on commerce in the goods thereby produced. Indentured servants, slaves, and apprentices were greater in both numbers and productive significance than the farmers, master craftsmen, and journeymen who owned or worked with them. In this period, many obstacles prevented the development of industrial manufacturing, including inadequate communication and transportation, insufficient population to support large markets, lack of capital for investment, and the efforts of English governments and manufacturers to inhibit development of American manufacturing. Also significant was American resistance to effects of industrialization such as child labor and slum housing that were obvious by 1800 in English manufacturing centers. By 1820 in the United States, however, significant changes had occurred in all these areas, and industrial manufacturing began to develop and spread.

Well underway by 1860, industrialization accelerated during the Civil War and, with the elimination of slavery and the destruction of the political power of the slaveholding states, the years immediately after the war. As mechanized manufacturing became more profitable, more capital was invested in it; as more capital was invested, mechanized manufacturing advanced in great strides; and as mechanized manufacturing advanced, its agents became larger and more concentrated. The concentration of vast sums of money in the control of relatively few people, already observable in the late 1860s, was a cause of public concern and provoked both secular and religious commentary on the perils of wealth and its corrupting influence on political and social life.

Contemporary observers noted other negative effects. The nation's overall wealth was increasing dramatically, but it was unequally shared between the captains of industry and the working people whose labor had helped produce it. The conspicuous consumption of the wealthy contrasted sharply with the daily struggle for existence of the working class, a struggle characterized not only by low wages, but also by unhealthy and dangerous living and working conditions. Such was the situation for working people in periods of economic prosperity. In periods of economic decline or depression, it was aggravated by widespread unemployment and its accompanying destitution, disease, and demoralization. Wage earners, only recently established as a significant sector of the American workforce, became alienated from and antagonistic toward those who so lavishly benefited from the socioeconomic revolution wrought by the rise of industrial capitalism. This industrial problem was singularly important for the development of social Christianity, but postwar social Christianity's attention to economic life was not a novel development in American Christianity. Political economy was, in fact, a major component of antebellum Protestant religious social thought.[2]

Henry May has characterized American Protestantism between the Revolutionary War and the Civil War as, in one important respect, a "battle with radicalism." Having surrendered, albeit reluctantly, both direct control of and financial support by the state, the churches steadfastly maintained their role as arbiters of a traditional strict morality. The defense of this morality included a defense of the status quo, not only in its religious and political institutions but also in its socioeconomic order. "When religion, the family, sound government and property rights seemed to be menaced by radical forces, Protestant conservatism became explicit and militant." In this period, Protestant conservatism was menaced first by forces of the Enlightenment, represented capably by Thomas Jefferson, and second by the radicalism associated with Jacksonian democracy. The struggle with this second wave of radicalism—which in its extreme forms included political atheism, anticlericalism, socialism, feminism, and freethinking—"fixed for a generation the pattern of Protestant social conservatism." An essential part of conservative Protestantism's defense was "an authoritative and well-knit body of conservative argument, derived from the highest academic quarters" and focused on political economy. May summarizes well its early development and ideological function:

> Collegiate education in America before the Civil War remained largely under the control not only of organized religion but of the most conservative sects. The oldest, most influential and most numerous colleges were those founded by Congregationalists and Presbyterians in New England and, as a part of the struggle for the western soul, in the northwest. . . . Partly in self-defense, partly from earnest devotion to inherited patterns of thought, the colleges had long mixed conservative political and economic precepts with their religious and moral indoctrination. In the first quarter of the nineteenth century such principles were

imbedded in the senior courses in moral philosophy. These culminating courses, often taught by the venerable white-bearded presidents themselves, instructed a generation of students in the sanctity of private property, checks and balances, limited suffrage and (as yet) free trade.

Confronted by the increasing militancy and popularity of radical doctrine in the Jacksonian years, college administrations, like other bulwarks of orthodox Protestantism, found it necessary to develop a more systematic, up-to-date defense. Relying on Whig businessmen for moral and financial assistance, the colleges needed a subject which would appeal by its practical soundness to these new allies. To meet these needs they turned toward the rising science of political economy.[3]

American Protestants did not automatically or uncritically accept the teachings of political economists Adam Smith and Thomas Malthus, because some of their tenets were at variance with Christian doctrine or American experience, or because political economy itself was associated with radical politics. Political economy was made acceptable to American Protestant leaders, however, through the efforts of both English religious leaders desirous of instructing industrial workers in correct political economy and Scottish moral philosophers reacting against David Hume's philosophical skepticism. These conservative adaptations of classical political economy provided the foundation for the efforts of American religious scholars. It is this school of political economy that May calls "clerical laissez faire," noting that for "at least a generation and in many institutions far longer, this body of doctrine dominated American economic teaching." Based on the Scottish school's reconciliation of natural and revealed religion, American clerical economists regarded the laws of political economy as not only compatible with but also part of natural religion. Thus, they argued, political economic laws were ordained by God. May summarizes the argument of Francis Wayland, president of Brown University, in *The Elements of Political Economy* in these words: "the Divine plan demands that all property must be divided and none held in common, that no charity must be given to any but the afflicted, and that the government has no right to levy protective tariffs, alter the value of specie, or 'oppress' banks."[4]

Of particular importance was the clerical school's support for the wages-fund doctrine, which asserted that a fixed and unchangeable fund exists from which wages are paid to workers and therefore that "artificial" means of increasing wages (such as action by labor unions) only served to decrease the wages-fund, which in turn decreased the number of workers who might be employed. Although he was to recant his support for this doctrine in 1869, John Stuart Mill expressed its classic form in 1848.

Wages, then, depend upon the demand and supply of labour; or, as it is often expressed, on the proportion between population and capital. By population is here meant the number only of the labouring class, or rather of those who work for hire; and by capital, only circulating capital, and not even the whole of that, but the part which is expended in the direct purchase of labour. . . . Wages (meaning, of course, the general rate) cannot rise, but by an increase of the aggregate funds employed in hiring labourers, or a diminution of the number of competitors for hire. . . . Since therefore the rate of wages which results from competition distributes the whole wages-fund among the whole labouring population; if law or opinion succeeds in fixing wages above this rate, some labourers are kept out of employment.

The ideological function of wages-fund doctrine (which in fact contributed to Mill's later recantation) was to refute demands by organized labor for increases in wages. Such increases, it was argued, would violate labor's own interests by decreasing the amount in the fixed fund and making it impossible for the capitalist either to employ as many workers or to devote sufficient profit to continuing production. On this view, the interests of labor and capital were inseparable. American clerical economists gave wages-fund doctrine the further sanction of divine law and thereby justified Protestant opposition to labor unions, one element of the radicalism they sought to contain.[5]

Having graduated from Union College in 1819, taught intellectual and moral philosophy there from 1831 to 1838 (nearly coextensive with the 1829 to 1837 presidency of Andrew Jackson), and served as the college's vice president from 1838 to 1845, Alonzo Potter fits May's profile of the antebellum clergy who developed and supported clerical political economics. Further, his 1840 book *Political Economy* demonstrates that he was an explicit and ardent proponent. Writing shortly after and in response to labor unrest arising from the 1837 depression, Potter "made a particularly rigid exposition" of the wages-fund doctrine and argued that labor unions "were bound to injure the interests of their own members because they disregarded the laws of nature 'which are nothing less than laws of God.'" Like other clerical economists, Potter's opposition to labor unions was based not only on the wages-fund doctrine but also on his view of the practices of the unions. He maintained "that unions were given to secrecy, that they tended toward class antagonism, and that their leaders were often foreign and atheistic." Further, he charged that they violated the rights of employers, farmers, and nonunion workers and debased their members. "They congregate workmen night after night in tumultuous assemblies, where their passions are inflamed and their principles poisoned."[6]

Other conservative Protestant political economists such as Henry Carey, Stephen Colwell, and John Bascom challenged the clerical laissez-faire of Wayland, Potter, and others, but it nevertheless dominated American political economy until the late 1880s.

> Small wonder that those who drew their whole stock in economic theory from these authorities were certain that the laws of political economy were as fixed and known as any other canons of natural religion. . . . The economic doctrines of the clerical professors constituted part of a general view of a world regulated by Divine Law, much of it codified and easily comprehensible. It was natural, therefore, that these principles occasionally found their way out of the classroom into the pulpit. Sermons on the correct principles of political economy served to supplement direct attacks on social and religious radicalism.[7]

When Christians in the postwar period questioned the goodness of the social order, they challenged the "correct principles of political economy" upon which their predecessors had based their defense of that order. Henry Codman Potter was among those who took up this challenge. That he did so is all the more interesting both because his father was a leading advocate of clerical laissez-faire and because in almost all other aspects of his work he consciously followed his father's example.

As late as the mid-1870s, based on its appropriation of clerical political economy as taught by Alonzo Potter, Francis Wayland, and Henry Ward Beecher, American Protestantism consistently denied both the legitimacy and efficacy of labor unions. By the middle 1880s, however, some Protestant leaders had begun, slowly and sporadically, to reject laissez-faire political economy, to endorse labor's right to organize and strike, and to praise the beneficial effects of labor organization. By the start of the twentieth century, Henry Codman Potter and others had effected a controversial but significant modification to American Protestantism's view of the relations of labor and capital. The factors producing this shift included both the internal religious and moral traditions of American Protestantism and the external challenges posed by the changing socioeconomic order. Prominent among the external challenges were the alienation of working people from the churches and the periods of sometimes severe social and economic disorder that rocked the country. Particularly significant were what May calls the "three earthquakes" that both exposed and exacerbated the cracks in the foundation of the American socioeconomic order. These earthquakes were the Great Upheaval and national railroad strike of 1877, the Haymarket Affair of 1886, and the socioeconomic disorder of the early 1890s, culminating in the Pullman strike of 1894.[8]

In the first decades of industrialization, American Protestants responded not so much to the development of industrialization itself, but rather to its effects. Many clerical and lay observers regarded the ostentatious living of individuals and the immoral business practices of companies—the by-products of the rapid accumulation of wealth in the hands of a few—as threats to public morality and political righteousness. In addition, arguments in the evangelical campaign for Sunday observance increasingly included consideration of working people's just need for a day of rest, while moderate temperance advocates recognized the role of the saloon in meeting their equally legitimate need for recreation. And the frightful living conditions working people endured in slums and tenements, the universal corollary of the rise of the factory system, provoked both condemnatory sermons and reformatory initiatives. Another effect of industrialization to which Protestant leaders responded was the alienation of working people from the churches. Although some preachers and editors had commented on this phenomenon in the early 1870s, many Protestants did not admit the problem for another twenty years. Even then, some saw this alienation not as a problem for the churches but the beneficial result of the process of distinguishing the educated, cultured, and religious from the unintelligent, uncouth, and unchurched. Others, however, recognizing that the project of Christianizing the nation included bringing the poor and working classes into the churches, responded with the development of institutional churches, free chapels and churches, and settlement houses.[9]

In the late 1880s, jolted by the severe labor conflicts of 1877 and 1886, some Protestants began to look into the causes of the alienation. They discovered that workers' alienation from the churches was related to another phenomenon, the growing alienation and antagonism between the workers and the wealthy. As the membership of established Protestant churches in the northeastern states was nearly coextensive with the capitalist and managerial classes, workers tended to be uncomfortable in and suspicious of the churches. Both labor leaders and rank-and-file workers widely held such views. For example, one of the respondents to Washington Gladden's 1880 survey of working people wrote: "when we see them so full of religion on Sunday, and then grinding the faces of the poor on the other six days, we are apt to think they are insincere. . . . When the capitalist prays for us one day in the week, and preys on us the other six, it can't be expected that we will have much respect for his Christianity."[10]

Related to this characteristic membership of established Protestant churches was their typical indifference or hostility to workers' demands for justice. Protestant preachers, writers, and editors regularly met such demands with exhortations to work harder, save more, and drink less and with appeals to the alleged futility of wage increases as demonstrated by clerical political economic teaching. As social crises multiplied and deepened, and as clerical and lay church workers came into more contact with working people, such platitudes and verities lost much of their appeal. Faced with a conflict between the social realities and the religious and moral principles of the churches, some Protestants reoriented the effort that had begun with the aim of Christianizing the working classes to include also the aims of Christianizing the socioeconomic order and socializing American Protestant Christianity. "The Christian social movement . . . owed its existence to the impact of labor conflict more than to any other single cause. Its formulations reflected many other influences, theoretical and concrete, but it could never have arisen had not the all-sufficient, optimistic formulae of Francis Wayland and Henry Ward Beecher been shattered by unanswerable events."[11]

In his work on the industrial problem, Henry Codman Potter demonstrated not only the responsiveness of American Protestantism, but also the particular ways in which it implemented its response and the continuities and discontinuities of that response with American Protestant religious traditions. While Alonzo Potter was among those whose "optimistic formulae" were shattered by "unanswerable events," Henry Potter was among those who sought to develop a new religious framework that might offer Christian answers to those events. In the process, he and like-minded contemporaries introduced into American Protestantism patterns of thought and action that were in some respects continuous and in others discontinuous with the antebellum traditions of Christian reform, but that sought to respond to the new challenges in ways faithful to those traditions.

Henry Potter contributed to this reworking of American Protestantism in three ways. First, he decried class alienation and proposed, in opposition to classical political economy and social Darwinism, an ethic of self-sacrificing paternalism as a means of alleviating that alienation. Second, as social crises multiplied and deepened by the mid-1880s, he explicitly supported labor's right to organize and negotiate its just demands, and he endorsed and participated in mediation and arbitration as alternatives to strikes. And third, from the mid-1880s until his death in 1908, he was a leading participant in the institutionalization of the social gospel in the Episcopal Church.

Alleviating Class Alienation

Henry Potter's response to industrialization grew, first, from the Memorial Movement's desire to adapt the agencies of the church to new demands, and from Alonzo Potter's vision of a Christianity that addressed the needs of the whole person. By the 1870s the interaction of these influences and the demands of the times produced in the Episcopal Church significant efforts to minister to the laboring classes. In the late 1860s Muhlenberg began to develop his St. Johnland project. Located on Long Island near what is now Smithtown, New York, St. Johnland was intended to provide affordable housing "for deserving families from among the working classes," a "home for aged men in destitute circumstances," education for "indigent boys and young men who desire literary education with a view to the Gospel Ministry," and above all "to give form and practical application to the principle of Brotherhood in Christ." By 1868 St. Johnland's directors and contributors included financier J. P. Morgan and Episcopal clergy Edward A. Washburn, John Cotton Smith, and Henry Codman Potter. In 1870 St. Mark's Church, Philadelphia, organized a workingmen's club, offering educational and recreational activities as well as temporary financial assistance. As I noted in chapter 1, the Church Congress met for the first time in New York in 1874 and became a forum for discussing social and economic concerns not discussed elsewhere in the Episcopal Church. And in the same year, Episcopal clergy and laypeople formed the national Free Church Association to promote common worship for all classes.[12]

Henry Potter addressed the effects of industrialization in his sermon on Thanksgiving Day 1871, "Our Brother's Blood." Preaching on Genesis 4:9–10, concerning the aftermath of Cain's murder of Abel, Potter spoke of "the dangers of social disintegration." Significantly, he noted that he had addressed the same topic three years earlier (perhaps in his first Thanksgiving Day sermon upon becoming rector of Grace Church). Already in the late 1860s, then, Potter was concerned about "the danger of the growth, in all large communities, and especially in communities where wealth is increasing rapidly, but not diffusively, of isolation between the rich and the poor, and so, sooner or later, of that spirit of caste, out of which comes haughty and heartless indifference on the one hand, and impatience, envy, and finally revolution, on the other."[13] As minister of a New York church engaged in outreach to the working classes, Potter was in a position to see at close hand the alienating effects of industrialization. He may have already observed them during his term at

Trinity Church, Boston, from 1866 to 1868. At that early date, however, few thought that there was cause for concern.

When Potter preached "Our Brother's Blood" in November 1871, however, the violent end of the Paris Commune a few months earlier had provoked alarm at the threat of similar events in the United States. Most Protestant commentators condemned the Communards and remained complacent about the economic injustices and class antagonisms developing in American life. Potter, however, took the "fierce and incontrollable hordes of the Commune" as an illustration of the result of social disintegration and warned that "in such days, no ruling or uppermost classes can afford to ignore what is due to the classes below them, not merely in the matter of legal justice, but also and equally, of living sympathy." While many Protestants expressed shock at the workers' violent response to their oppression, Potter averred that "if any man wonders that ignorance, poverty, under-paid labor, unrelieved suffering, uncorrected vice, rose up and ran riot in their cruel and vulgar strength, I for one do not. We shall always see such results, wherever neglect, indifference, and mutual distrust have been permitted long to precede them."

Citing the example of some English statesmen and nobles, Potter asserted that the way to ameliorate class alienation was for the rich and powerful to "reach forth the hand of manly and Christian brotherhood to the toiling millions that are below them." Such a strategy, he argued, was justified by the humanity that every person, however poor and lowly, "shares with the Christ of history, and which once for all made man the lasting creditor of all other men's sympathy and succor, when the Saviour of the race, pointing to its poor, its feeble, its imprisoned, its outcast ones, proclaimed, 'Inasmuch as ye have done it unto one of the least of these, ye have done it unto Me!'" The responsibility for the welfare of "the weak, the neglected, the outcast" rested squarely with the "so-called higher classes." The role of the church was to provide instruction in this responsibility and opportunities for them to fulfill it. He hoped that the church thereby would "pull down the barriers which wealth, luxury, and indolence, and selfishness, are rearing higher and higher, between the rich and the poor."[14]

Like that of many of his contemporaries, the ethic Potter expounded in the late 1860s to the early 1870s was predominantly an ethic of paternalistic charity, of noblesse oblige. This ethic assumed that the conflict had only two participants—the privileged and the neglected—and that the church was largely made up of the former. While this ethic exhorted the rich to exercise their responsibility to relieve the suffering of the poor and urged efforts to ameliorate class antagonism, it did not

advocate effecting changes to the socioeconomic order that would eliminate the causes of that antagonism. As social crises multiplied and deepened, however, Potter and many of his contemporaries significantly revised this ethic.

The catalyst for the first such crisis was the September 1873 failure
of the Jay Cooke and Company Banking House, which precipitated the
Panic of 1873 and the long depression that followed it. Cooke was an
Episcopalian and warden of St. Paul's Church, Philadelphia. As his company was one of the main financiers of railroad construction, its collapse
had a devastating impact on further construction and, in consequence,
the production of iron. The resulting wave of business failures and tide
of unemployment produced widespread impoverishment and suffering.
It also generated some doubts about the beneficial effects of the new industrial capitalism, which was supposed to have ushered in an era of
unchecked progress and material well-being. As George Hodges noted,
"These conditions increased the difficulties of Dr. Potter's work, but they
served also to emphasize his interest in the problem of the poor and to
lead him to study it more carefully."[15]

Potter's sermons and activities during this period reflect his increasing concern with problems of class alienation, the perils and responsibilities of wealth, charity and the right methods for delivering it, and the
role of the churches in meeting social needs. In May 1877, for example,
preaching on the anniversary of the Free Church Association, he emphasized the dangers of class alienation and importance of eliminating class
distinctions in the churches, and he appealed to "the brotherhood of
humanity in the liberating and ennobling bond of a common Saviour and
Redeemer."[16] In the month after Potter's Free Church Association address,
the social crisis deepened yet again. After several years of employer actions against labor during the depression, the Pennsylvania Railroad's June
1877 announcement of an additional 10 percent wage cut provoked
strikes by railroad and other workers in virtually all parts of the country. Employers successfully requested the assistance of municipal and
state militia; while in some cases the militia refused to act against the
strikers, in others they killed and wounded scores. Where local militia
were ineffective, as in West Virginia, Maryland, and Illinois, state gover-
nors requested and received federal troops from President Rutherford B.
Hayes.

In the early weeks of the strikes, the workers had considerable public support because of the common hatred of the railroad companies'
practices and the prevalence of hardship during the depression years. By
the end of July, however, as clashes between troops and strikers inten-

sified, many in the country became alarmed at the conflict and critical of the striking workers. Some Protestant commentators were particularly harsh. The *Independent* typified the dominant view of the Protestant press, maintaining that when workers prevented others from working, they "are then criminals in intent and criminals in fact. They are rioters and public enemies, and worse than wild beasts turned loose upon society." Further, it also recommended harsh measures for dealing with strikers. "If the club of the policeman, knocking out the brains of the rioter, will answer, then well and good; but if it does not promptly meet the exigency, then bullets and bayonets, canister and grape . . . constitute the one remedy and the one duty of the hour. . . . Napoleon was right when he said that the way to deal with a mob was to exterminate it." Henry Ward Beecher, a proponent of Spencerian social Darwinism, added derision to the prevalent condemnation of the strikers:

> It is said that a dollar a day is not enough for a wife and five or six children. No, not if the man smokes or drinks beer. It is not enough if they are to live as he would be glad to have them live. It is not enough to enable them to live as perhaps they would have a right to live in prosperous times. But is not a dollar a day enough to buy bread with? Water costs nothing; and a man who cannot live on bread is not fit to live. What is the use of a civilization that simply makes men incompetent to live under the conditions which exist.

Confronted with such attitudes, working people grew increasingly disaffected from the churches.[17]

The events of the summer of 1877, coming as they did after nearly four years of a severe economic depression, nevertheless shook the confidence of many Protestants and intensified their reevaluation of the socioeconomic order. One of those who undertook this task was Henry George. Greatly affected by that summer's events, George began writing *Progress and Poverty* in the fall of 1877. Upon its publication in 1879, it became one of the most influential works of the social movements of the late nineteenth century, and George himself became an international figure.

Also in the fall of 1877, the Episcopal Church's House of Bishops approved a report of the General Convention's Joint Committee on Church Work among the Laboring Classes. The report argued, in part, that

> The people need to be reminded that property and culture, and social and official position, have no rights that do not impose equivalent obligations. The first and highest of the obligations connected with these great gifts is the duty of teaching the people, by precept and example, those cardi-

nal principles of religion and morality which are the basis of social order. Not only our own recent history, but all history, teaches that unless these principles are embedded in the heart and exemplified in the
conduct of the people, mere physical force will be powerless to protect
and preserve the most cherished interests of society.

More important is that the report suggested two key elements of contemporary Episcopal social thought. First, it addressed "the privileged possessors of power and influence," indicating that this class composed the
church's membership. Second, its recommendations were concerned only
with evangelizing working people. In considering "the increasing desecration of the Lord's Day by unnecessary work," the report did note its
effect in both hindering "evangelizing of all the people" and exacerbat-
ing "the antagonism between labor and capital." Its main concern, however, was for employers to "remove many obstacles in the way of reaching the people" and was not to have employers pay a fair wage and
improve working conditions. Thus in the late 1870s, while on the one
hand many in the churches responded to workers' cries with condescension or condemnation, on the other hand some in the Episcopal Church,
as in other churches, responded with a benevolent paternalism that was
as yet oblivious to the justice of workers' demands.[18]

In his treatment of class alienation in this period, Henry Potter shared
the benevolent paternalism evident in the 1877 report, but he did not rely
exclusively on evangelization of the masses as the solution. In the two
years following the Great Upheaval, he addressed the problems of the poor
and unemployed and the conflict between employers and working people. His sermons and parish reports emphasized the responsibilities of the
powerful for the welfare of the lowly but included in those responsibilities not only evangelization but also the recognition and amelioration of
the material needs of poor and working people. In "One Another's Burdens," the first of his published sermons preached after the strikes, Potter explicitly criticized the social Darwinist response to the crisis. Delivered in early November 1877, this sermon may have been Potter's
response to the sermons that Henry Ward Beecher had delivered three
months earlier. In any case, it was certainly a direct repudiation of the
Spencerian views advocated by Beecher and others. This "school of thinkers," as Potter saw it, proposed that the correct way for "the wise and
good" to deal with the "the drunken and dissolute, or indolent or diseased
or vicious" was to "draw a line around them and leave them to become
extinct by the self-destroying power of their own vices, while the wise
and good devote themselves to bettering and uplifting their own kind."
In criticizing this view, Potter appealed to the "one sublime and match-

less act, in which the Perfect One gave Himself in eager sacrifice for imperfect ones, and in which there was proclaimed a law not of natural, but of supernatural, selection." On this basis, Potter urged his hearers to bear one another's burdens, rather than to leave one other to be crushed under their weight.[19]

Later the same month Potter also preached "Owe No Man Any Thing," in which he advocated—contrary to common speculative investment practices—"the payment of every honest debt in honest coin" by businesses as well as by individuals. In early 1878, he cautioned against faithlessness in one's fellow humans, pointing out that "after all, the foundations of human society are laid in the cement of mutual trust, not of mutual suspicion." Shortly afterward he delivered the sermons "The Perils of Wealth" and "The Impotence of Money." In these sermons he maintained that wealth, "like other dangerous powers, may be subjected to a wise discipline," and that the measure of this discipline was "how many lives have been brightened and how many sorrows have been healed" by its exercise. And in a sermon advocating Sunday observance he followed the reasoning of the previous year's report by the Joint Committee on Church Work among the Laboring Classes and appealed to the need to protect working people's "day of rest from being perverted and revolutionized into a day of toil." Unlike the committee's report, however, he did not appeal to the need for preserving Sunday as an opportunity for evangelizing the unchurched.[20]

The most fully developed statement of Potter's views during this period is his November 1878 sermon, "The Social Indifferentist." Here he maintained that "divine unselfishness" was central to the practice of Christianity: "Not to care when the feet of other men and women, no matter how obscure or remote from us, are going down to hell, this, disguise it as we may, is not Christianity, but paganism blank and heartless." He also denied the efficacy of the violent suppression of strikes, took seriously the hardships of the poor, affirmed the responsibility of the church for alleviating such hardships, and maintained the interrelation of social solidarity and divine unselfishness in a universal brotherhood.

> The social problem now confronting us is one of the gravest and most threatening problems of our time. The laborer does not love the capitalist, and the capitalist does not always understand the laborer. But we shall not finally silence the heresies of the communist with the bullets of the militia. Over against unreason, the crudeness of thought and the extravagance of speech that fever the life of the working-man, we must rear something better than the stern front of a stony indifference. If his misfortunes are not our fault, none the less he himself is our brother. And

somehow—anyhow—we must make him feel that we account him so. It is for this most of all, that we should prize every good work that brings us into personal intercourse with the unfortunate. It brings the parted ends of our great social nerve together. It helps to make Christ real to those who, if they even believe in Him at all, must begin to believe in Him, because they see His divine unselfishness reflected in His disciples.[21]

In his remaining years at Grace Church, Potter continued to preach on the perils and duties of wealth. He stressed the need to provide working people with opportunities for religious expression and the responsibility of the privileged for lifting up the neglected. Unlike some of his contemporaries, however, he insisted that this endeavor was as much for the benefit of the former as for that of the latter. These efforts to address the needs of the poor, understood both as a means of effecting their evangelization and of maintaining the church's own faithfulness, provided Potter with a greater appreciation for those needs. That appreciation engendered in turn the growth of an ethic for which the meeting of those needs was not so much a means to other ends, but an end in itself.[22]

Justice for Labor

Upon becoming assistant bishop in 1883, Potter continued to demonstrate his concern about class alienation and the welfare of working people. As noted in chapter 1, his support for the founding of the Order of the Holy Cross in 1884 and the Advent Mission of 1885 was motivated in part by concern about the disaffection between labor and the churches. An 1885 editorial in the *Churchman* observed, "The alienation has been allowed to progress too far already, and the situation is one that must enlist our best energies, if we do not wish the Church to suffer for generations."[23] As economic and social crises multiplied over the next twenty years, however, Potter and many of his contemporaries shifted from primarily attempting to ameliorate class alienation to recognizing and dealing also with workers' demands for just wages and working conditions. In doing so, they first developed arguments for justice for labor, including fair wages and working conditions and the right to organize; second, they organized themselves for analysis of and action on economic matters; third, through these organizations they proposed and implemented alternative strategies such as mediation of labor disputes and consumer boycotts for fair labor practices; and fourth, they developed a broader political economic critique.

The most important element of Potter's work in the mid-1880s was his May 1886 pastoral letter to the clergy of the Diocese of New York. By the early 1880s, the long depression had ended and the alarm over the strikes of 1878 had begun to recede. With the return of prosperity, some regarded the Great Upheaval as an exception to the smooth course of progress promised by industrial development. And although the strikes of 1878 had resulted in losses for organized labor in terms of its immediate demands, unions learned valuable lessons about their power to effect change and the best means of doing so. The combination of economic abundance and the successful strategies of conservative labor organizations such as the Knights of Labor led many in the churches to look more favorably upon labor unions and, in some cases, the right to strike. Church response to the 1883 strike by telegraph operators, for example, displayed the continuing, but weakening, grip of clerical laissez-faire upon Protestant commentators. While maintaining that strikes were generally objectionable and that wages were to be determined by supply and demand, the *Independent* acknowledged that there were "cases in which great and merciless monopolists . . . leave to their employees no other remedy."[24]

In 1883, however, the economic situation again deteriorated. Another depression led to further strikes, the most notable of which was the bitter, unsuccessful railway strike waged by the Knights of Labor in early 1886. In these difficult times, more radical leaders became more prominent in the labor movement and more strident in their demands. The 1883 Pittsburgh Manifesto, for example, called for the complete destruction of capitalism and its instruments of class domination, the state, the church, and the schools. At the same time, moderate labor initiatives focused on the campaign for the eight-hour day, which was to be inaugurated by nationwide strikes beginning 1 May 1886. Although initially opposed to the eight-hour day as a mere reformist measure, radical socialists and anarchists came to regard the eight-hour campaign as an opportunity to build a mass movement for a more revolutionary program.[25]

On 3 May 1886, during a strike at the McCormick Harvester factory in Chicago, police fired on striking workers, killing four and wounding several others. The following day, workers attended a peaceful rally at Haymarket Square to protest the killings and hear speeches by socialist and anarchist labor leaders. When the police attempted without provocation to break up the rally, someone in the crowd threw a bomb at them. In response, they shot and clubbed the assembled workers. The bomb killed one policeman, and seven others died subsequently from wounds inflicted, most likely, by their own comrades' gunfire; the injuries of most of the sixty police less seriously wounded were similarly inflicted. The exact number of civilian casualties is unknown, but it may be conservatively estimated at seven or eight killed and thirty to forty wounded.

Such details, however, were willfully ignored or deliberately hidden in the subsequent hysteria. Public reaction to the Haymarket "riot" united the country in its first red scare, in which employers, elected officials, church leaders, and working people alike called for the suppression of all radicalism. Many regarded all advocates of labor rights as guilty by association with socialists and anarchists of the crimes the latter were supposed to have committed. Nor was this lapse the only breach of justice. The eight men arrested and tried for conspiracy to commit murder were not accused of throwing the bomb. Rather their crime was having, by their writings and speeches, caused an unknown person to throw the bomb. Their conviction and death sentence only ratified that which had been pronounced by the secular and religious press from the days immediately after the tragedy. An international defense movement succeeded in having the sentences of two of the men commuted to life imprisonment; they and a colleague originally sentenced to prison were later pardoned by Illinois governor John Peter Altgeld in 1893. One of those sentenced to death committed suicide in prison; the remaining four were hanged in November 1887.[26]

Many in the churches participated heartily in the sweeping condemnation of radicalism, renewed opposition to labor unions, and uncritical support for the death sentence for the convicted men. Only a few radical clergy, such as Hugh O. Pentecost and J. M. L. Babcock, condemned the blatantly prejudicial character of the trial and opposed the verdict as well as the death sentence. Henry George, whose 1886 campaign for the New York mayoralty followed closely upon Haymarket, at first criticized the conduct of the trial but later, perhaps for political reasons, defended its verdict.[27] Somewhat common in the churches, however, was a condemnation of anarchism combined with a defense of working people and their aspirations. Washington Gladden, for example, had made such an argument in an address in the spring of 1886 to an audience of both workers and employers in Cleveland and repeated it subsequently on several occasions in Boston. These addresses provided the foundation for his essay, "Is It Peace or War?" published in *Century Magazine* in May 1886 shortly after Haymarket. In this essay, Gladden spoke of the condition of war between labor and capital but distinguished between "men who . . . are simply destroyers" and "sober, industrious workingmen." Referring explicitly to the Haymarket anarchists, he argued: "It is a cruel injustice to identify these miscreants with the army of labor. The labor forces sometimes make sad mistakes and commit serious offenses, but nothing like this fiendishness can be charged upon them. It is not with such weapons that they are waging war."

Gladden also defended labor's right to organize and strike, contending that, like capital, labor should combine for its own advantage, specifically to prevent the permanent social degradation of working people. In support of this view he noted that leading "students of political economy" generally agreed on "the right of the workmen to stand together in trades unions for the defense of their own interests" and maintained that "the more reasonable of the employers" also held this view. On this point, he quoted an address by James Means, "a leading shoe manufacturer of Massachusetts":

> Labor is the poor man's commodity; it is the only thing he has to sell; he must get the highest price for it that he can by legitimate means. The price which labor will bring is the market price. What is the market price of any commodity? It is the point where the "bull movements" and the "bear movements" exactly counterbalance each other. . . . What is a trades union? It is a "bull movement" in the labor market. Can any one wish to see the price of that commodity which we call labor governed by the "bears" alone? The "bears" organized, and no one complains. Is it fair that the price of labor should be fixed by powerful organization opposed to weak individuals? Is it not rather to be desired that a more reasonable price should be fixed by organization met by organization?[28]

Gladden used this quote to demonstrate some employers' support for labor's right to organize, but his use of it also demonstrates, first, that this right could be justified *within* a laissez-faire political economic view of labor as a commodity, and second, that by 1886 even progressive Protestants had not yet developed a critique of labor as a commodity, that tenet of laissez-faire economic theory most regularly used to deny the legitimacy and efficacy of organized labor.

One week after Haymarket, and in the same month that *Century Magazine* published Gladden's essay, Henry Potter also stood apart from the prevailing antilabor hysteria but in doing so explicitly criticized the view of labor as a commodity. In a pastoral letter to the clergy of the Diocese of New York, he called their attention to the "grave emergency" of the emerging "class conflict, whose proportions it is daily becoming more difficult to measure." Noting that the conflict threatened "not only the peace and good order of society but the permanence of our free institutions" and criticizing the "terrorism of unscrupulous organizations," Potter nevertheless refused to call for repressive civil measures. Rather, he urged the clergy to preach on the issues underlying the crisis "with great plainness of speech." Noting that the diocese's congregations included many of those who controlled the capital that employed the laborers, he exhorted the clergy to make plain to them *their* responsibility both for causing and for resolving the crisis. This responsibility, Potter argued, rested squarely with the more favored classes. He called upon them to make the sacrifices necessary to resolve the conflict, sacrifices "not so much of money as of ease, of self-indulgent ignorance, or contemptuous indifference, of conceited and shallow views of the relations of men to one another." The clear teaching of Christianity, he argued, was that "they to whom is committed the stewardship of exceptional gifts, whether of rank, wealth, learning, or cleverness, are not to treat them as their own, but as a trust for the whole community." Such stewardship did not, however, "mean the mere giving of doles and indiscriminate distribution of alms." With regard to the relations between laborers and employers, it did mean "fair and fraternal dealing."

Although in subsequent years Potter continued to preach the stewardship of wealth in terms of its "right use," his 1886 pastoral letter represents a significant expansion of his understanding of both the cause and the required response to the worsening social crisis. Recognizing that the cause of the crisis lay in the inequitable distribution of wealth among those responsible for its production, Potter saw that the crisis could be resolved neither by antistrike or antilabor legislation, nor by the coercive suppression of strikes and unions by police or militia; "the safety and welfare of the State are not in these things, they are in the contentment and loyalty of its people. And these come by a different road." Potter pointed to that "different road" in the pivotal passage of his pastoral letter:

> When capitalists and employers of labor have forever dismissed the fallacy, which may be true enough in the domain of political economy, but is essentially false in the domain of religion, that labor and the laborer are alike a commodity, to be bought and sold, employed or dismissed, paid or underpaid, as the market shall decree; when the interest of workman and master shall have been owned by both as one, and the share of the laboring man, shall be something more than a mere wage; when the principle of a joint interest in what is produced of all the brains and hands that go to produce it is wisely and generously recognized; when the well-being of our fellow-men, their homes and food, their pleasures and their higher moral and spiritual necessities shall be seen to be matters concerning which we may not dare to say, "Am I my brother's keeper?" then, but not till then may we hope to heal those grave social divisions, concerning which there need be among us all, as with Israel of old, "great searchings of heart."[29]

Potter's repudiation of labor as a commodity was not based on a sustained critique of laissez-faire economic theory. Indeed, his repudiation is weak-

ened by the dualism he maintained between the domain of political economy and the domain of religion and by his acknowledgment that the
contention that labor is a commodity may be true in the one domain but
not in the other. This dualism, however, was not one of separate domains
that had no relation to each other. Rather, parallel to his view that religion had much to say about the conduct of political life, Potter maintained
that the domain of religion could and should stand in judgment on the
domain of political economy. Thus, while his method may not have been
sophisticated, it challenged the prevailing view of labor as a commodity.
This challenge was particularly significant because for the previous half-
century this economic dogma had enjoyed a religious sanction that
Alonzo Potter had helped to articulate and perpetuate. Henry Potter's
claim that the laborer is not a commodity, then, signaled a turning point
in social Christianity's relationship with its evangelical heritage and in
its treatment of the demands of working people and the relation between
labor and capital. While not a watershed in Christian social thought,
Potter's letter not only promoted greater, more sober reflection on the labor question but also enhanced the credibility and legitimacy of labor's
right to organize and to negotiate and strike for just terms of employment.
In addition to his own reputation as a socially concerned cleric, Henry
Potter had social status and legitimacy as a bishop—and son and nephew of respected bishops—of a leading diocese in a conservative and
wealthy denomination. By the seriousness with which he treated the
causes and symptoms of the social crisis he lent that legitimacy to the
cause of justice for labor.

In the weeks following the distribution of Potter's pastoral letter,
several New York Episcopal clergy responded by preaching on the labor
problem. The *Churchman* not only reported but also reprinted large por-
tions of sermons by W. F. Morgan, R. Heber Newton, Henry Y. Satterlee,
and W. S. Rainsford. While not in complete agreement with each other,
these preachers did agree on the legitimacy of organized labor, the repudiation of some of its methods, the need for those more favored to act
responsibly toward those less favored, and the relevance of Christianity
for guiding that action. Morgan went so far as to suggest that the "words
of truth and soberness" of the First Epistle of Peter were "in perfect harmony with words put forth" in Bishop Potter's pastoral letter.[30]

The secular press also commented on Potter's letter. The *New York
Times* praised it in editorials on the two days immediately after the edition in which it had printed Potter's letter. The first of these called the
letter "one of the most important contributions to the literature of the
present era of the conflict between capital and labor" and lauded the

balance with which Potter treated the errors of both workers and employers. It also agreed that the "very essence of Christianity is involved in the contest, since the one issue at stake is the proper treatment of man by his brother man." The second editorial went on to commend the letter to all public-spirited citizens, for "civic virtues are not exclusively Christian virtues." It recognized that the heart of Potter's appeal lay in his critique of the view of labor as a commodity and joined him in repudiating "the misapprehension of the laws of trade as the laws that must govern human conduct." And it looked to the voluntary practice of "courtesy, consideration, and benevolence" as the means of alleviating labor troubles. An editorial in *The Nation*, ardent proponent of free enterprise, was less sympathetic to Potter's approach. It criticized "moralists" and "philanthropists" for relying "too much on the extraction of more talent and virtue from the capitalist class," for that class was "at its wits' ends." It also criticized those who, like Potter, suggested that the stronger had a responsibility to lift up the weaker and argued against turning the United States "into a republic of kindly patricians charged with the board, lodging, washing, and amusement of a vast and discontented proletariat." The editorial did, however, commend Potter's remarks on the dangers of wealth, particularly with regard to the "moral, economical, and political mischief" worked by its pursuit.[31]

The most important short-term response to Potter's 1886 pastoral letter came one year later with the formation of the Church Association for the Advancement of the Interests of Labor. CAIL, as it came to be known, was "in many respects the most remarkable organization in the half century of social Christianity's growth, with the exception of the Federal Council of Churches."[32] In the early 1880s, several clergy working among the poor in East Side free chapels or mission churches had begun meeting to discuss poverty, its effects, and its causes. In May 1887, a meeting of this group was convened by J. O. S. Huntington, who at this time was also an enthusiastic supporter of Henry George and his single-tax proposal. Others in attendance included W. D. P. Bliss, an Episcopal priest and member of the Knights of Labor who, three years later, would found the first American branch of the Society of Christian Socialists; and B. F. DeCosta, a theologically evangelical and socially progressive priest who was elected chair of the new association. A second meeting was held the following month, at which time DeCosta suggested that Potter's 1886 pastoral letter be read, "stating that in the absence of the Bishop there were no better words in which to express the sense of the meeting."[33]

Among its important early activities, CAIL organized mass meetings of working people and cooperated with the Working Women's League of

New York in organizing a meeting that led to the formation of the Consumers' League. It also successfully petitioned the Diocese of New York to have all its printing work done by unionized print shops and organized observance of the first Labor Sunday in churches in the United States. Probably because he wished to distance himself from the single-tax campaigning of Huntington and other CAIL founders, Potter was not among its early leaders or prominent supporters. After Huntington left New York and CAIL diversified its activities, however, Potter became substantially more involved and identified with the association. In 1892, for example, he was among forty bishops who became honorary vice presidents of CAIL.[34]

Potter's increased participation in CAIL and the expansion of its activities also coincided with the start of the period's third great socioeconomic earthquake. Beginning with the Homestead Steel strike of 1892 and culminating in the Pullman strike of 1894, this episode of labor unrest and economic depression was "the most serious challenge to American political and economic institutions between the Civil War and the depression of 1929–37." The Homestead strike began in April 1892 when the Carnegie Steel Corporation, which had previously maintained good working relations with the Amalgamated Association of Iron and Steel Workers, declared a sharp reduction in wages for the upcoming contract renewal. Andrew Carnegie, whose essay "Wealth" had three years earlier extolled the virtues of the beneficent uses of wealth, had decided that the steelworks would henceforth "be necessarily non-union after the expiration of the present agreement." Carnegie entrusted operations during the strike to Henry Clay Frick, the corporation's general manager, who locked out the workers and hired three hundred Pinkerton guards. On 6 July the Pinkertons attempted to land by barge at the steel mill and the workers tried to stop them. A daylong battle ensued in which nine workers and three guards were killed. Although the skirmish ended with the surrender of the Pinkertons, who were besieged in their barges, the strike was ultimately broken when nonunion workers under the protection of the National Guard reopened the mill.[35]

In the wake of the Homestead struggle, the mill there remained non-unionized for many years and the Amalgamated Association was reduced to ineffectiveness. In addition, the violence at the mill and an anarchist's nearly successful attempt to murder Frick generated yet another round of national antilabor sentiment. As May notes, a significant portion of the Protestant religious press, including the *Independent* and the *Christian Advocate*, "condemned the union in the old whole-hog manner, accusing union members of coercing fellow employees and attempting to 'control' the plant." Editorials in these and other papers defended the company's use of Pinkerton guards and denied that it had any obligation to confer with its workers. The *Churchman,* deploring the prolabor sympathies of J. O. S. Huntington, maintained that no punishment would be too severe for those who "instigate or aid such a revolution." In addition to those like Huntington who supported the cause of the workers locked out at Homestead, other religious leaders attempted to openly and fairly discuss the issues at stake. Journals like the *Andover Review,* the *Congregationalist,* and the *Christian Union* criticized the violence of both labor and capital but also argued for increased protection of workers' jobs, questioned the long-term adequacy of the wage system, and advocated arbitration of disputes. Although, as May observes, such views "do not represent the permanent conversion of any major portion of the religious press to a Social Gospel point of view," it was nevertheless "a striking novelty for major church organs to discuss such fundamental questions *during* a bloody crisis."[36]

While the country was trying to come to terms with this latest crisis, the situation deteriorated still further. The May 1893 failure of the National Cordage Company was the catalyst for a general stock market crash, hundreds of bank failures, thousands of business failures, unemployment for more than three-quarters of a million workers, and destitution for at least three million people. Churches, private charities, and labor unions were unable to meet the demand for assistance, and calls for publicly funded relief efforts and employment programs grew. In an attempt to promote one plan for public relief, an "army" of the unemployed inspired by Jacob Coxey marched on Washington in the spring of 1894. Although, as Philip Foner notes, the march on Washington "proved ineffective in forcing legislation to provide for the unemployed," nevertheless it "thrust before the eyes of the country the stark and naked fact that there was something basically wrong in the nation." Working people also increased their calls for an eight-hour day, seeing it as a means of reducing unemployment and providing other benefits to both workers and employers. Simultaneously, however, employers attempted to undermine labor's previous gains by decreasing wages, increasing working hours, and withdrawing other rights and benefits.

The intensified conflict between labor and capital in the early 1890s led to numerous strikes with varying outcomes, culminating in the Pullman strike of 1894. Pullman Company employees struck against the 25 to 50 percent wage cuts imposed on them in early May 1894. After the company repeatedly refused to submit the dispute to arbitration, the workers' cause was taken up by the American Railway Union (ARU) and its leader, Eugene V. Debs. Late in June, ARU members throughout the country's west-central region began an extensive boycott of Pullman sleeper cars and trains carrying them. What had begun as local dispute quickly and unexpectedly became a massive conflict between the ARU and the railroad companies' General Managers' Association. As the strike spread to rail lines throughout the country, both its effectiveness for organized labor and its threat to employers were magnified. Pullman employees continued to urge that the dispute be submitted to arbitration. The General Managers' Association, however, argued that the strike unduly interfered with the mails and with interstate commerce. With the encouragement of Attorney General Richard Olney, they obtained a federal injunction against the strike and its leaders. To enforce the injunction, President Grover Cleveland, on questionable authority and in spite of the opposition of Illinois governor Peter Altgeld, sent federal troops to Chicago to break the strike. The soldiers shot and killed twenty-five workers and injured another sixty. Although the strike continued for a short time, this domestic military intervention and further legal action against its leaders ultimately broke the strike.[37]

As in their responses to previous disputes, Protestant preachers and editors were virtually unanimous in their denunciation of the strikers, and especially vehement in their criticism of the ARU and Debs himself. The *Churchman* suggested that the "inhuman and brutal selfishness of the leaders of the American Railway Union is something which disgraces modern civilization," while the *Outlook*, which had been previously sympathetic to organized labor, called the strike "monstrous." Significantly, however, the *Outlook* also repeated its earlier call for compulsory arbitration of strikes. This call was taken up by others, particularly those concerned Protestants who were seeking alternatives to strikes as means of reconciling labor and capital.[38] From the early 1890s until his death, Henry Potter focused much of his activity on economic questions. In 1892, for example, he presided at and addressed a meeting of the Christian Social Union in Baltimore and became an honorary vice president of CAIL. In the wake of these and other such activities, Potter's reliance on the "stewardship of wealth" weakened and was supplemented by greater attention to strategies for meeting working people's demands for justice. As Griffen notes, "appeals for philanthropy by the rich played a less prominent part in the bishop's social teaching in the nineties as he became more interested in the possibilities of trade unionism, arbitration and conciliation, limited state intervention in the economy, and the organization of consumers."[39]

Nevertheless, Potter still struggled in his analysis of the relationship between moral and economic matters. In his address to the 1894 New York diocesan convention, unlike his 1886 pastoral letter in which he had emphasized the responsibility of the clergy for addressing the legitimate rights of working people, Potter stressed the need for caution in advocating remedies to the social crisis. He noted that it was the "glory of the clergy" that they were "distinguished by a very noble enthusiasm for the cause of the workingman" but warned against "a fervor of speech not always consistent with coolness of judgment and exactness of expression." Making a distinction between justifiably "impassioned utterance" and "essentially erroneous teaching," and perhaps reflecting his concern about the views of particular but unidentified clergy, he nevertheless maintained that

> there are such things as unjust combinations of employers, a veritable tyranny of capital, and profound indifference to the hardships of the man of scanty wage and scantier privileges. I have myself, more than once, called attention to these things in terms which some of you may have thought unnecessarily strenuous. I should still maintain it to be not only my right, nay, my duty to do so, and that of every other minister of Christ. But it is a very different thing when the pulpit, or the religious teacher, passing on from his own province of rebuking things that are evil, becomes the advocate and defender of a new social philosophy which perilously misconceives the problem of which it proposes the solution.

Quoting at length an essay by an unnamed "eminent English divine" in the London *Quarterly Review,* he challenged as fallacious the Christian socialist critique of classical economics. This critique, according to Potter, commendably maintained that moral law was superior to economic law but failed to recognize that the two types of law operated "in different spheres" and dealt with "different subject-matters." In opposition to this view, Potter argued that the laws of economics were comparable to "the axioms of Euclid" and the "laws of arithmetic," and not subject to the control of morality. In conclusion, Potter endorsed this mechanistic view of economic laws by arguing that the

> religion of Jesus Christ is here in the world to mitigate the hardships which arise out of the seemingly inexorable operation of the laws of nature, whether they are laws of trade, or of disease, or of death. But it is not here to dismiss them out of existence, whether by arbitrary lawmaking or anarchistic violence. Our duty to the social fabric . . . is not to pull it down because its existence seems to us to involve certain intolerable hardships, but to make those hardships tolerable, as even the

hardest labor and the sorest privations may be made tolerable by an inexhaustible sympathy and a never-tiring helpfulness toward all within our reach.[40]

Potter's primary intent in this address seems to have been to caution and correct those whom he regarded as guilty of "essentially erroneous teaching." The address suggests, then, that in the wake of the crisis of 1892–94, dissatisfaction with the socioeconomic order and the traditional economic doctrine that supported it had sharply increased. In particular, it seems, some Protestant clergy were among those who advocated alternatives such as Christian Socialism. That such was the case is attested by the response to Potter's address in the *New York Times*, which commended his "needful and timely" warning in light of "the part that a considerable number of clergymen have been playing in aggravating the discontent of employed workmen with their lot and with the present condition of society."[41]

In another response to Potter's address, however, W. D. P. Bliss argued that Bishop Potter had too readily accepted the contention that economic laws are of the order of natural laws and therefore not subject to moral critique. In the Christian Socialist journal, *The Dawn*, Bliss expressed concern over Potter's address but maintained that, while the bishop had certainly erred, it was not Potter "but a nameless writer in the *Quarterly Review*, who is the enemy in this case." Bliss also argued that the issue at stake was not the fallacious comparison of mechanical and moral laws, a fallacy that he denied Christian Socialists committed, but in the fallacious assumption that economic laws were of the order of mechanical rather than moral law. "Undoubtedly economics obey inexorable laws, but they are the laws which concern men and not machines, are moral and not mechanical." Bliss also noted that the *Quarterly Review* essay included other arguments, including "all the stock arguments and old misstatements against trade unionism," and that to his credit, "even the bishop [did] not seem to have been misled by these." Nevertheless, he chided Potter for failing to recognize the essential relation between moral and economic law. "But while a bishop may be excused for being misled in economics, it does seem too bad that he should so easily brush aside *morals* in a matter where human choice and fashion has so large a part to play, as it does in matters of price. It is simply in its last analysis a question of righteousness and sin, and on these topics a bishop might be expected to be a little more keen." Bliss reported in the same article, however, that Potter had "atone[d] for his New York mistake" in his address to the annual convention of the Brotherhood of St.

Andrew the following month. In that address, Bliss maintained, Potter "came perilously near to advocating the very views he had officially condemned" in his diocesan convention address. Ultimately, Bliss concluded, Potter had in his earlier address "simply made a slip."[42]

Bliss may have been correct that Potter had, in his attempt to correct what he perceived as the erroneous teaching of some clergy, "made a slip" on the relation between moral law and economic law. Potter's treatment of this relation in his September 1894 address is in part consistent with his 1886 pastoral letter to the clergy of the diocese. In the earlier work, he took for granted that political economy and religion occupied distinct domains. Unlike his 1894 diocesan convention address, however, he argued there that religion could and should criticize political economy, at least on the matter of labor as a commodity. It is difficult to assess conclusively Potter's thinking on this matter at this point in time, for in neither the 1886 letter nor the 1894 address did he offer sustained analysis of this issue. Such an analysis appeared only in his later work, particularly his 1902 *Citizen in His Relation to the Industrial Situation.*

Bliss's observation that Potter had not been "misled" by arguments against trade unionism confirms that Potter, despite his ambivalence on the status of economic law, remained committed to defending labor's rights and seeking means of assuring them. His participation in the mediation of labor disputes also confirms that commitment. This work was one of the most important aspects of Potter's response to the industrial problem in general and to the economic upheaval of the early 1890s in particular, marked the start of his greater involvement and identification with CAIL, and provides an important example of how Potter and other concerned Christians addressed social and economic problems.

Faced with the crisis of the early 1890s, many Christians sought alternatives to strikes and lockouts for settling labor disputes. Some of them, perhaps, had noted that the Homestead lockout and Pullman strike might have been prevented if management had not rejected labor's request to submit the disputes to mediation. In any case, social reformers and social Christians began to promote the use of mediation panels composed of representatives of capital and labor and, if necessary, arbitration by a mutually acceptable outside person or agency. CAIL's leaders drew particular inspiration from *Industrial Arbitration and Conciliation* by Josephine Shaw Lowell, a social reformer and the founder of New York's Charity Organization Society. In 1893 CAIL formed a panel to which labor disputes could be referred, with the consent of both employees and employer, conceiving the panel as a disinterested third party. The panel's first members were, representing capital, Seth Low, former mayor of Brooklyn and at that time president of Columbia University; representing labor, John Newton Bogart, member of CAIL and of Typographical Union No. 6; and representing the public, Henry Codman Potter, who also served as the panel's chair. Because of its early successes, the panel expanded and reorganized in 1894. Under Potter's leadership, but independent of CAIL, it became the New York Council on Mediation and Conciliation. Its new members included Josephine Shaw Lowell and Felix Adler, the latter a civic reformer and founder of the Society for Ethical Culture. In a letter signed by Potter and seven other members, the council stated that its intention was "to prevent or to settle, if possible, some of the disputes that so often arise between employer and employe, on questions of wages and other matters." The letter also outlined the council's proposed methods: first, to indicate to employers and employees "the best methods of forming boards of conciliation"; second, to help "bring about a friendly conference" between employers and employees; and third, when requested by both employer and employees, to act "as arbitrators in any case where trouble has already occurred."[43]

Potter figured prominently in the reorganized council's mediation of several disputes. In the New York City marble trade dispute of 1896, which involved several thousand working people, representatives of employees and employers met with council delegates at Potter's home for two weeks. These meetings produced a settlement and a wage increase satisfactory to both parties. According to Harriette Keyser, one participant in these discussions felt that Potter "had done probably more than any one other individual to break down the old-fashioned prejudice against organized labor, and to bring large employers of labor to a recognition of the advantages of conciliation over strikes and lockouts in the settlement of trade disputes." Potter also helped settle the New York lithographers' strike of the same year. After the strike began in February 1896, a mediation board consisting of both employers and employees was formed. As their efforts were minimally successful, they decided to call in someone outside the lithographers' trade, "and the choice fell upon Bishop Potter." In early April, Potter met with both parties to the strike and received their permission to refer the matter to the New York Council on Mediation and Conciliation. After reviewing the briefs submitted and consulting with council members, in early May 1896 Potter issued his decision, one that provides an instructive example of his practical moral reasoning.[44]

When the disputants first requested Potter's assistance, three issues remained to be resolved: first, payment by a piecework or wage work system; second, setting a minimum weekly wage; and third, setting the weekly hours of work at forty-seven or forty-four. On the last issue, Potter decided in favor of the employers for a forty-seven-hour week. In support of this decision, he argued that lithographers' work "is not especially exacting or exhausting, and, compared with many other kinds of labor, is done under agreeable conditions." On the other two points, however, Potter decided in favor of the workers and devoted the majority of his report to evaluating the issues and presenting his argument. Recognizing that the issues of piecework and a weekly wage were closely related, he maintained that they must necessarily be treated together. After summarizing the disputants' differing claims on these points, Potter weighed those claims in light of the conflicting demands of worker solidarity and worker isolation, and of his understanding of the requirements of arbitration:

> The gist of the matter seems to be this: There is a tendency at the present day among the working classes toward increasing solidarity. There is a strong movement among the employers of labor to resist this tendency. The conditions implied in the wage-work system are favorable to solidarity. Hence, the workmen demand it. The conditions implied in the piecework system allow the employer to deal with his men separately, and to isolate, more or less, the interest of each from his fellows. What should be the position of the arbitrator in such a conflict? If arbitration means compromise, I do not see how it is possible in these circumstances. There can be compromise as to hours of labor, as to amount of wages to be paid, as to number of apprentices to be allowed, etc. In fact, wherever the difference can be stated numerically, compromise seems clearly in order. But I do not see how there can be any compromise between opposing principles. If, nevertheless, the arbitrator or referee is required to give a decision, it seems to me he must consult his highest conscience as to which of the opposing tendencies make for the social good and side with one or the other of the parties accordingly.

Because the wage work system tended to increase labor solidarity, and because labor solidarity enhanced the social good, Potter concluded that piecework should be abolished. While noting that the workers acknowledged that, in some cases, a joint committee might decide that an employee's work was worth less than the agreed standard, he also endorsed the principle of a "minimum wage." On this point, he affirmed the substance of the workers' demand that a barrier be erected "against the excessive cheapening of the product of their labor by competition." Like employers' attempts to isolate workers, Potter viewed the tendency to cheapen the product of labor as "prolific of evil results to the working class." Concluding that the abolition of piecework and the establishment of a fixed wage were "measures in harmony with the tendencies that make for social progress," he decided in favor of the employees on these two points.[45]

Two aspects of Potter's reasoning in this decision are worthy of note. First, his primary criterion was that which enhances the social good, and a secondary criterion was that which enhances the well-being of workers. He used these criteria to evaluate workers' and employers' conflicting demands on piecework and minimum wage and decided that a wage work system incorporating a minimum wage was more conducive to the good of workers and the broader social good. This decision does not make clear, however, the grounds on which he argued or assumed both that the social good commanded such priority and that the well-being of working people enhanced the social good. That Potter did not articulate such considerations, and that both parties approved the decision, suggests that they may have generally shared his assumptions on these points. In light of other aspects of his broader social ethic, his concern for the social good was likely grounded, on the one hand, in the theological conviction of the fatherhood of God and the brotherhood of humanity and, on the other hand, in a closely related organic social theory. Second, it is important to note here that Potter's reasoning, by pointing to observed or expected "evil results" of a possible course of action, included appeals to the practical effects of decisions as well as to principles and norms.

Potter continued to demonstrate his commitment to working people through his mediation work and through public addresses, notably at occasions sponsored by CAIL. At the 1897 CAIL supper, Potter remarked that some regarded the association as "dangerous and revolutionary" because it "tends to unite the Church with the workingman in his great struggle." Against such criticism, Potter proclaimed: "I for one announce that from today on the Church of God is with the laborer." At the May 1898 service on CAIL Labor Sunday, Potter preached on the application of Christian principles to the labor question. Citing Paul's counsel in Philippians 4:5 regarding moderation, he commended the value of forbearance to the working people who constituted the majority of his audience. Such forbearance, however, was to be employed within a context where labor's right to organize was acknowledged and the mutual interests of labor and capital recognized. Potter maintained that these interests

> *are not antagonistic, but one and the same. . . .* [N]either one of them can do without the other. Capital can paralyze labor by withholding itself from it; but the process by which it does so paralyzes capital as absolutely and as utterly as it does labor. In spite of what fierce voices on the one side or the other are fond of shouting, it is not a question which

of the two shall be "on top." *Neither can be on top*—healthfully, fruit-
fully, or permanently. There is absolutely only one relation which they
can surely sustain to one another, and that is—THEY MUST WALK
HAND IN HAND.

Potter also credited the trade union movement with educating both capital and the public on this point by its employment of "that great principle which subordinates minor differences for the greater good of all."[46]
In such remarks, Potter reflected the perspective of the leadership of CAIL
and indeed of many moderate social Christians. In particular, Potter's
view of the mutuality of interests between capital and labor and his endorsement of trade unionism were key tenets of moderate social reform
and social Christianity.

Shortly after his 1898 Labor Sunday sermon, Potter became involved
with another organization with a similar orientation to the industrial problem, the National Civic Federation. Potter's work with the federation
would expand well beyond New York City the scope both of his efforts
and his reputation in settling industrial disputes. The National Civic Federation had its origins in the Chicago Civic Federation. Under the leadership of Ralph Easley, crusading journalist and all-around reformer, the Chicago Civic Federation had established a committee on mediation at about
the same time that CAIL did. The Chicago Civic Federation's activities,
however, were as broad as Easley's interests and encompassed all aspects
of civic reform. When Easley determined to make the Civic Federation a
national organization he intended to maintain this broad scope. Labor crises, however, compelled him to focus the federation's energies on the industrial problem. Easley was aware of Potter no later than May 1898, when
Easley mentioned the bishop among the "solid, unselfish, humane, Christian, educated element of the nation" he hoped to gather for a conference
on foreign policy held in Saratoga in August 1898. Easley also organized
two subsequent conferences (one on trusts in September 1899, and another
on trade agreements and conciliation in December 1900), and from these
the National Civic Federation took shape.[47]

At the December 1900 conference, a committee on industrial conciliation was formed with six representatives each of capital and labor.
Notable among the latter were Samuel Gompers of the American Federation of Labor and John Mitchell of the United Mine Workers. In January 1901 this committee was expanded to forty members, with Henry
Potter representing the public. He was a featured speaker at the federation's May 1901 meeting on industrial conciliation, at which it an-
nounced its intent to assist in the prevention and settlement of labor
disputes. In his remarks at that meeting, Potter defended the legitimacy

of the public's involvement in labor disputes and commended working people for their reasonableness. In addition to its various organizational and educational activities, the federation mediated, with mixed success, several important labor disputes. Potter "rendered notable service" in its attempts to settle the steel strike of 1901 and the anthracite coal strike of 1902–3. This service apparently consisted of behind-the-scenes efforts to persuade the owners and operators, including J. P. Morgan, to meet and settle with the unions. In the few years remaining before his death, Potter remained on the federation's executive committee and regularly participated in its meetings and conferences.[48]

For its founders the National Civic Federation was an attempt to avoid destructive industrial conflicts by cooperation between labor and capital. For Theodore Roosevelt, it was the realization of his desire "to see radicalism prosper under conservative leadership." For contemporary socialists it was a capitalist conspiracy intended to deceive labor into thinking meaningful reforms were being implemented, while for contemporary antiunion employers it was dominated by its labor members. For labor historian Philip Foner, the federation embodied a strategy by some employers of coopting organized labor: "Rather than smash unionism, this section of the employing class sought to emasculate it, to ensnare the labor leaders into a conscious program of collaborating with the employers, robbing the workers of their vigor, militancy, and the spirit of their class." However one evaluates the federation, Potter's views on the relations of labor and capital and the means of establishing cooperative relations were consistent with those of the federation and the moderate labor leaders like Samuel Gompers and John Mitchell who likewise participated in it. At a time when many employers remained ardently antiunion, Potter and the federation insisted on labor's right to organize and negotiate with capital on an equal basis.[49] Potter's work in mediating labor disputes "won for him on the one side the affection and the confidence of the laboring men of this city, and on the other side made him increasingly conscious of the necessity of official action on the part of the Church for the solution of the labor problems of the day." This affection and confidence of working people was such that, according to Hodges, a contemporary later recalled "one night in Cooper Union when a vast audience cheered at the name of Henry C. Potter, realizing, perhaps for the first time, what he really was to them."[50]

While Potter worked to reconcile labor and capital in particular disputes, he also worked to develop and educate people in an understanding of the relation between Christianity and political economy that might significantly reduce such conflicts. Although many of his addresses and essays on these matters were brief and superficial, at the turn of the century Potter developed a more sustained treatment of his views on the relations of labor and capital. He began to articulate these views in three addresses delivered at Kenyon College in November 1901, later published under the title *Man, Men, and Their Masters,* and developed them more fully in a series of lectures at Yale University in April 1902. In these lectures, published later that year as *The Citizen in His Relation to the Industrial Situation,* Potter repeated many of the themes and principles that had characterized his thought over the previous four decades, but he elaborated them in greater detail and demonstrated their bearing on the industrial situation.[51]

Potter's discussion of the various responsibilities of the citizen in the context of the industrial situation encompassed five key areas of social Christian theory: first, the definition of the problems underlying the industrial situation; second, an elaboration of the relation of Christianity to the industrial situation; third, an evaluation of the theory and practice of industrial capitalism and of proposed alternative systems, such as socialism; fourth, the consideration and advocacy of specific strategies for change; and fifth, the articulation of a social ethic. These five topics are interwoven, yet clearly identifiable, throughout Potter's arguments in *The Citizen in His Relation to the Industrial Situation.* His arguments are sometimes neither persuasive, nor lucid, nor even internally consistent, but his convictions in these areas are clear. Nevertheless, his discussion illuminates further the contemporary public discourse on the industrial situation within social Christianity.

Consistent with his enduring concern with the problem of class alienation was Potter's definition of the basic problem of the industrial situation, first in terms of the alienation of working people from their employers. Potter regarded the prevailing "tendency toward mutual alienation" as the "first and most grave consequence" of the contemporary socioeconomic context. He added, however, that a "still graver situation" was the "sullen class hatred . . . whose menace threatens not only the relations which bind together certain industrial interests, but the whole social fabric." Potter attributed this alienation to "aggregations of wealth which have greatly accentuated to the working classes the enormous discrepancies between themselves and the capitalist classes." He also criticized political economists such as John Stuart Mill who attempted to minimize the importance of this alienation by blurring the distinction between labor and capital. The second aspect of the problem in Potter's view was the "essential cruelty" of working conditions and the failure of employers to alleviate these conditions except when compelled. He pointed to "that long and ghastly pathway which runs through so many of our domestic industries" and declared that "there are whole groups of manufactures which, in their effect upon the worker, are simply deadly." Further, he criticized the tendency to maximum mechanization and specialization, which increased the dreariness and irksomeness of the workers' labor and decreased their employability elsewhere during times of economic depression. "In any other mill, at any other task, with any other tool, this man is *worthless*—and this is what the great march of industrial progress, over which we are all wont to rejoice, has done for him."[52]

With regard to Christianity's relation to the industrial situation, Potter acknowledged that some "maintain that religion has nothing whatever to do with the social conditions of human life, unless it be to teach men to look forward to an existence when they and their fellows shall be delivered from them; and, meanwhile, to cultivate such patience and resignation as they may." Against such a view, he argued that "you and I must be able, in the face of all that confronts us in these problems, social, economic, and industrial, to show that religion has some warrant for being concerned with them, and that, in the great task of their solution, we may not, must not, withhold our hands." In addition, he maintained that the application of Christianity to social problems was essential for their resolution. For this task Potter drew primarily on the teaching and example of Jesus, urging that they be brought to bear "upon all those [relationships] in which human society is bound together. It is the divorce of that life and teaching from the life of today, the social problems of to-day, the capitalist and working man of to-day, of which we are most of all in danger."

For Potter, the life and teaching of Jesus consisted of three key elements: the conviction of the fatherhood of God and brotherhood of humanity; the this-worldly character of the kingdom of God; and the moral principle of sacrificial love and selfless service. Commending Shailer Mathews's *Social Teaching of Jesus* with specific reference to the Lord's Prayer, Potter affirmed that "the relation binding men to God was a filial relation, and the relation of men to one another was a fraternal relation." He also argued that "thy kingdom come" means that "the kingdom of God . . . has its place in this realm and on our stage of being. On the earth as it is done in heaven cannot mean that the kingdom of God is an unrealizable thing for humanity in this world, and with our ennobled powers and faculties, or else the words that bid us pray for it are a grotesque and monstrous mockery." Further, Potter appealed to the example of Jesus, who, by his care for and close association with "the lowliest humanity," emphasized that "the Fatherhood of God had no meaning as a principle of action unless it issued forever in the service and sacrifice that affirm the brotherhood of man."

Potter's understanding of the fundamental moral principle as sacrificial love is closely related to his assumption of the inevitability of human inequality. Indeed, he maintained that Jesus himself "frankly recognized and freely utilized [this] eternal fact." Jesus demonstrated that the role of Christianity in relation to various human inequalities was "to minimize them; to introduce into human society, in one word, 'that great principle of brotherhood, in and through a divine Fatherhood, which should take from them their sting, and transform them, always and everywhere, into divinest opportunities for divinest service and sacrifice.'" As in his advocacy of free churches and chapels, Potter criticized the church—"the divine society which Jesus Christ instituted, wherewith to efface the harsh and rigid distinctions that have divided men"—for its role in "reviving and emphasizing those distinctions." But Potter did not suggest that it was the office of Christianity to eliminate such distinctions. Rather, he maintained that the twofold responsibility of Christians was, first, "to understand the large problems with which they are called to deal," and second, "to illustrate the principles which can alone effect their solution." Potter clearly intended his series of addresses on the industrial situation as helping to discharge the first aspect of this responsibility; the second aspect, he affirmed, was discharged through service and sacrifice.[53]

Potter's view of the church's relation to the state was a significant specific application of the relation between Christianity and social conditions. He allowed that "individual citizens" or "the people of a state on its way to ruin under the leadership of blind or corrupt rulers" might legitimately act against the state for the public good, but he maintained, in light of the church's history of "grasping at external power, and aping the airs and pomps of earthly courts," that such is not the church's role. Its role, rather, is "to penetrate the civil order with its divine spirit. It is to transform the secular mind by the spell, in it and on it, of the divine mind. It is to regenerate character, not to break laws. It is, in one word, to re-create the social fabric by the bringing into it of a new soul," infused with the spirit of service and sacrifice.[54]

In his evaluation of the theory and practice of industrial capitalism, Potter offered a mixed assessment. On the one hand, against those "who view our present social problems with alarm, and look for their solution in the abolition of capital and the capitalist," he articulated a defense of private property and the accumulation of wealth qualified by his insistence that both the acquisition and use of wealth are subject to moral criteria. On the other hand, he strongly criticized the so-called inexorable law of supply and demand and its role in determining wages and working conditions, as well as the supposed moral neutrality of corporations and their activities. Potter's acceptance of human inequality operated again in his defense of property and the accumulation of wealth. Citing the work of political economists such as John Stuart Mill, he maintained that capital accumulation is the just reward of abstinence and ability and that such accumulation is necessary for economic progress. He acknowledged that there were evils associated with large accumulations of wealth, such as "the buying of legislatures, the corruption of judges, the stealthy enervation, first of the forces that answer to our physical, and then to our moral police, by systems of organized bribery and profit-sharing in connection with the most infamous forms of vice and crime." Nevertheless, he argued that such evils were "neither the fault nor the fruit of the existence whether of the capitalist or of capital." His defense of this point, however, was limited to a description of the failings of proposed alternatives rather than a demonstration of the strengths of capitalism.[55]

Although he did not distinguish them clearly, Potter seems to have recognized three alternatives to industrial capitalism: the single-tax, collectivism, and socialism. Potter offered no detailed description of the single-tax. His failure to do so might indicate that he assumed that his audience was familiar with its proposals, or that he regarded it as being of so little value that it did not warrant detailed analysis, or both. Potter observed only that a "favorite theory for the solution of our great disparities and our often injustices, as by some they are believed to be, to the laborer as distinguished from the capitalist, is the annihilation of the private ownership, *e.g.*, of land, . . . and to divide up the land among all the people." In response to this scantily characterized proposal, he explicitly chose to ignore the question of the equity of land redistribution and focused rather on what he supposed to be its results. Quoting W. H. Mallock's *Labour and the Popular Welfare*, he argued that redistribution would not produce the results desired by its advocates, for "so far as mere money is concerned, the land offers the most insignificant instead of the most important question that could engage us, and is, every year, in diametrical contradiction to the theories of Mr. Henry George, becoming more unimportant."[56]

Potter's treatment of collectivism, however, is more detailed and balanced. He defined it as that "theory or system of industrial organization under which all private property is taken over by the state and run for the public benefit,—or, rather, to be more precise, for the equal benefit of each individual in the whole community." Those who endorsed such a system, he noted, argued that it would eliminate "the mere struggle for existence," "the enormous disparities between wealth and poverty," as well as "the rivalries and competitions that so largely embitter life." Potter acknowledged the value of these aims, but argued against collectivism on the grounds of its impossibility. He noted, first, that the disproportionate number of laboring and managerial positions and impossibility of alternating these positions fairly makes inevitable the violation of the "fundamental principle of absolute equality." Second, he argued that state control of industry would not eliminate economic fluctuations, for there remained "influences which are wholly outside the control of the state as are the motion of the heavenly bodies," such as "failure of crops, fluctuations in trade, commercial rivalries in other nations, war, famine, pestilence." Third, and undoubtedly based on his experience of political patronage and corruption, he maintained that "the erection of the state or communal authorities, of whatever name, into an employer introduces possibilities of corruption which the most humiliating experience has taught us to be almost inseparable from such a system." Various kinds of state-controlled employment "afford a temptation for corrupting the official employer of labor by bribe for 'soft places,' which, as the employer has no personal interest in the thoroughness or excellence of the work, he has no slightest motive of self-interest for refusing, and every sordid motive for accepting." And fourth, Potter contended that like other forms of monopoly, state monopoly extinguished not only the evils but also the benefits of competition, such as building character and stimulating progress.[57]

Potter understood socialism as "the collective ownership and control of the means of production, distribution, and exchange." It is significant that he made a point of distinguishing between socialism and anarchism, a distinction blurred by many of his more conservative or less reflective contemporaries. He drew on the work of Edward and Eleanor Marx Aveling and of Geoffrey Drage and pointed out the differences and similarities between the two political philosophies. In Potter's view, while socialists and anarchists agreed on the need for common ownership of property and a common system of production, anarchists also demanded a system of common consumption. They also differed on strategy, with socialists employing the "propaganda of word" and anarchists the "propaganda of deed" in addition. Both agreed, however, in their repudiation of the "bourgeois moralist" view that "individual good men make healthy social conditions" and maintain rather that "it is healthy social conditions that make good men." Perhaps assuming that anarchism was self-evidently objectionable, Potter confined the remainder of his remarks to socialism. He suggested that, given the socialist view of the relation between morality and social conditions, "it ought not to be surprising therefore that it has so often passed on into those extremer forms of a godless atheism" and cited the work of Michael Bakunin as illustration.[58]

Potter also criticized socialism for its economic analysis. He acknowledged that the "development of industrial activities in the century that has just closed has resulted in a vast increase in the world's wealth; and, especially in our own country, in aggregations of wealth which have greatly accentuated to the working classes the enormous discrepancies between themselves and the capitalist classes." Nevertheless, he criticized the socialist "invective" that claimed "that the product of labor, which belongs of right to the laborer, is, by some adroit but essentially dishonest process, diverted from his pocket, and goes—the vast proportion of it—not into the laborer's wage but into the employer's profit." Potter cited Karl Marx as the leader of the "whole school of social economists" who held this view, and Potter rejected it as being "as false as it is vicious." Against the claim that labor creates all wealth and that it has been unjustly deprived of its due share, Potter argued that "incomparably the largest part of wealth" is created not by "muscular force, or physical strength, or bodily energy, . . . but intelligence, foresight, ability, mental cleverness, the genius of invention, the genius of organization." In addition to this hierarchy of intellectual over physical labor, Potter also argued, citing a variety of statistics, that over the previous twenty-five years labor's share of the wealth produced had increased while capital's share had decreased. In a telling anecdote, Potter illustrated his view of the relation between labor and capital in the production of wealth. Recalling having seen elephants stacking lumber in the shipyards of Rangoon, Burma, he observed that although they could move large timbers and stack them precisely, they worked under the guidance of their riders. "The brute obeys the man. The clever intelligence and gentle touch of the Burmese rider's heel guides, directs, restrains, constrains, energizes, the enormous living bulk beneath him, and converts it from a destroying monster into a faithful and untiring servant."

Despite his negative evaluation of socialism's social theory and economic analysis, Potter recognized that "there is a very different kind of socialism, having indeed, substantially, the same ends in view, but resting its endeavors upon a very different basis, and inspired by a very different spirit." Thus, while critical of some of its proponents, Potter nevertheless appreciated the work and vision of Christian Socialism.

If the modern socialist movement rose with Robert Owen in 1817 . . . it owed its greatest impulse to the labors of such men as Frederick Dennison [*sic*] Maurice, Charles Kingsley, Thomas Hughes, Ludlow, Vansittart, Neale, and their like, who touched a dark and perplexing problem with the transforming word of Christian self-sacrifice. The best in some of our more modern teachers, Robertson, Bushnell, Westcott, and their like, who brought to the miseries, the maladjustments, the socio-industrial hardships and injustices of our modern life, a vision so clear, a touch so tender, and a scrutiny so patient and penetrating, that, step by step, up out of the caverns of despair in which some of the horrors of our nineteenth-century industrialism had plunged them, multitudes of all but despairing souls climbed upward toward the light, came from these great teachers!

For Potter, the means of addressing the problems of the industrial situation lay in following their example of "turn[ing] upon the perplexing problems of our social disorders the light of a divine life."[59]

Having criticized these alternatives to capitalism, Potter continued his defense of private property and accumulated wealth with a sweeping claim that their abolition was neither equitable, feasible, nor "scriptural and primitive and Christian." On the last of these points, he contended that "there is no slightest warrant for maintaining" that Acts 4 (regarding the selling of property and its use for the common good) provided, as some of his contemporaries held, "the disclosure of a social law for the kingdom of God." It was rather "simply a special provision for a special emergency." He based his case against the feasibility of eliminating private property on a higher estimate of intellectual over physical labor and the association of the former with progress and civilization, arguing that "a social order based upon the annihilation of property means a reversion to barbarism." And in rejecting the equitability of eliminating property, Potter demonstrated, with an intensity and unreflectiveness surprising for "the people's friend," a strong correlation of property and wealth with virtue and temperance. "By what rule of equity are the industrious called upon to surrender their earnings to the idle, the virtuous to the vicious, the temperate to the intemperate? . . . And when you have communized all the wealth in the land, can you give me any encouragement to believe that by that revolution you will have transformed human nature so as to make such a revolution an equitable thing?"[60]

Having concluded that there were no equitable or feasible alternatives to capitalism and that modern civilization could not "dispense with either capital or the capitalists," Potter's next task was to determine the means of mitigating the undeniably evil effects of capitalism and industrialization. In approaching this task, he suggested that capital should be treated similarly to any natural force. With capital, as with water or electricity, "mere aggregation may become dangerous because, with the growth of accumulation, . . . the possibilities of mischief from their unrestrained action are almost infinitely increased with the increase of volume." Large capital accumulations could thus be "a menace to society." "They make it possible for the unscrupulous strong to buy, corrupt, or crush the timid weak. They make it possible for vast organizations . . . to create fictitious values, on the one hand, and to destroy those that are real on the other. They make it easy, often, to produce a fictitious scarceness of the necessaries of life where there is none, and practically to annihilate values when weaker men refuse to yield to their decrees." Despite the seriousness with which he regarded this menace, Potter was confident that it could be held in check. Just as the nations of the world prevented any one of their number from growing too strong, he believed, "that other mighty multitude, the *people*, will surely say to capital grown too great and powerful, 'Thus far shalt thou come and no farther; and that thy power may no longer be a menacing giant or a corrupting cancer, we will see to it that, except as the common servant and common possession of all the people owned in common, employed in common, and dispensed in common, you shall exist no more.'"

Potter's justification of property and wealth perhaps blinded him to the fallacious character of this analogy, for what power the people may have had was by no means comparable to that of a collective of nations. Indeed, Potter himself recognized the corrupting influence of wealth on the people's primary instrument, the state, and expressed considerable doubt about its potential as a means of achieving economic justice. Nevertheless, he argued that the citizen and the church should subject capital and the capitalist to two moral criteria, namely, the just acquisition and the right use of wealth. On the former criterion, Potter argued that when wealth has been accumulated by "manipulations of values," "directorial chicanery," or abominable treatment of workers, the resulting fortunes "do not honestly belong to their possessors." On the latter, he decried alike those who would use wealth for self-indulgence, for the care only of themselves and those nearest them, or for power and influence.[61]

Implicit in Potter's remarks was a criticism of the view that the possessors of wealth could do with it as they wished, and that the production of wealth was not subject to moral evaluation. Potter made this criticism explicit in his discussion of the purported "inexorable laws" that regulated the conditions of economic activity and, it was supposed, "with which mere benevolence is powerless to interfere." Primary among these was the "law of supply and demand." According to its proponents in the Manchester School of political economists, supply and demand governed the prices of commodities, the profits of employers, and the wages and working conditions of employees. Because of the workings of supply and demand, they maintained, all efforts to improve wages or working conditions were ill-advised and futile. Against this view, and not on the basis of a discussion of economic laws but on a depiction of the evil results of the economic practices associated with the Manchester School's theory, Potter maintained that economic activity was not exempt from moral assessment. "This policy in our industrial life has been baptized with many names: whatever they are, *laissez faire*, necessarian, or the good of the greatest number, they are of the devil, and deserve, as Jesus did with devils, to be cast out." By thus challenging the inexorable character of economic laws and maintaining that all economic activity is subject to moral evaluation, Potter revised the position expressed in his address to the 1894 diocesan convention.[62]

Potter did not only challenge laissez-faire economic theory. He also challenged prevailing economic practice as embodied in the contention that corporations were not subject to moral standards.

If anything at all is clear concerning the mission of Jesus Christ to men, it is that he came to build here the temple of a regenerated society in obedience to the law of righteousness and love; to restore the divine equities; to rebuild the temples of justice, so that the humblest feet might enter into them; and over all human activities to arch the bow of a divine promise to those who loved their neighbors as themselves. Do I hear some one say that such a rule, however excellent it may be in our individual dealings with our fellow-men, has no place in, and can by no ingenuity be worked into, the fabric of a modern corporation? Why not? At what point does associated action cease to have a moral quality? . . . It is precisely the implied assertion of this moral irresponsibility on the part of corporations which threatens not only to put the greatest strain upon our institutions, but to destroy in the hearts of the masses all faith in a God who is the God of those who can acquiesce in, or connive at, or consent to be enriched by, practices and policies which transgress the plain principles of common honesty and equity.

In order to maintain the moral quality of corporate activity, then, Potter recommended the implementation of regular public reporting and independent auditing of financial records and the enforcement of legal penalties for the receipt of bribes by public officials and for stock speculation by corporate directors. "The evil of the corporation is not in its mechanism or its proportions," Potter maintained, "but in its temper and its morals." It is true that corporations have no souls, but it is also true that "those who compose them have consciences; and these they must

bring to the standard of a divine righteousness, to be touched by its quick-
ening hand, to be illumined by its spirit, and then to bear witness, in
king's palaces, at board meetings, at directors' meetings, not fearing the
face of man, because they have heard the voice of God."[63]

Potter's consideration of specific strategies for change was focused
both by his definition of the basic problem in the industrial situation and
by his judgment that industrial capitalism was both necessary and, despite its potential for evil, basically good. Those strategies for change that
he considered, then, aimed at the alleviation of two problems: the mutual alienation of working people and their employers and the conditions
under which working people labored. Potter therefore discussed four strategies: first, alternative means of distributing between labor and capital
the wealth produced by their joint efforts; second, some enlargement of
the role of the state in protecting working people; third, means by which
consumers might positively influence the working conditions of those
who produced the goods consumed; and fourth, the role of labor unions
in both protecting workers and alleviating class alienation.

Potter discussed industrial cooperation and profit sharing, two of the
"various specifics for remedying the injustice and inequalities of [work-
ing people's] present condition, on which from time to time social economists have built large hopes." Although different in some respects, in
both these strategies workers received a share of the profits in addition
to a fixed wage, a provision that was intended both to effect a more equitable distribution of wealth and to give workers greater commitment to
the success of the enterprise. Potter observed that industrial cooperation
"was born of a beautiful ideal" and had "appealed both to the just interests and the worthy ambitions of working men." It was hindered, however, by working people's lack of capital, which made them unable to bear
continued losses, and by the fact that working people often are "too im-
perfectly educated" in business to offer "anything else than an unintelligent and too often obstructive criticism." He similarly acknowledged
that there had been some successful implementations of profit sharing,
but he claimed that "the element of weakness in it lies in the inevitable
control of the business by others than the workman." Both strategies, he
maintained, "have, as their highest significance, a real note of sensitive-
ness as to what is due to the working man in connection with our industrial progress, and are, from this point of view, of large inspiration," but
he concluded that "in such methods as these the labor problem has not
yet found its sufficient solution."[64]

Although he maintained that the state's role was limited, Potter believed that it also had a role to play in addressing the problems of the

industrial situation. He defined the state as "a body corporate, sustaining a more or less clearly defined relation to other bodies corporate, and properly charged with certain definite responsibilities." He suggested that these responsibilities included not only protecting citizens' rights and maintaining peaceful relations with other nations, but also undertaking "certain additional responsibilities, such, *e.g.*, as that of public education, which experience has proven to be most advantageous to the common welfare." He recognized, then, especially in light of urgent social problems, that it was necessary to consider "How much farther in these directions may the state wisely go?" Although he had warned of the dangers of collectivism, Potter admitted that the state could and should act to protect its citizens, particularly its working people, from the otherwise unchecked power of commercial interests. If it is within the competence of the state to exercise guardianship for the common good in some areas, he reasoned, "it is difficult to see how the guardianship, the care, the beneficence, if you choose to call it so, of the state in behalf of the individual should not, in various directions of a kindred character, be equally extended."

Potter therefore advocated some government regulation to protect workers from exploitation in wages and working conditions and consumers from "fraudulent adulteration" of commodities. He also recommended that, while its efficacy was limited, legislation be employed to ensure such protection. Legal sanctions were necessary because, as the history of industrial development demonstrated, "all along, from first to last, whether in other countries or our own, those things that have been conceded to the working man for his protection and betterment—the prohibition of child labor, the sanitation of factories, the restriction of the work hours of women, and the like—were wrung originally from the employer by law, and rarely or never granted voluntarily." Legislation, however, could not only protect labor, but it could also educate capital. As Paul had suggested, Potter argued, so too was it true of the modern industrial world: "the law has been a schoolmaster to bring the reluctant employer, little as he may recognize it, to the recognition of those great principles of human brotherhood which are of the very essence of the divinest Teacher who has ever spoken to men."[65]

Potter had considerably more confidence in consumers than in legislation and regulation for effecting improvements in the conditions under which people labored. Building on his rejection of the inexorable character of the law of supply and demand as the determinant of wages and working conditions, he argued that consumption was, like other economic activities, subject to moral evaluation. It was, then, not only valid but necessary to ask how the production of what one consumed tended "either directly or indirectly to the betterment of the condition" of working people. Potter commended the practice of Consumers' Leagues who convinced their members "to abstain from buying goods at 'sweating' rates, in order to give the trade to a fair house." Further, he differed not only with those who argued that the moral evaluation of consumption was pointless but also with those who, while admitting the moral significance of consumption, minimized its potential for effecting change. On this point he cited John A. Hobson, who maintained that moral forces were ineffective against the powerful economic forces of competitive trade. Such a view, Potter objected,

> is asserting that powerful trade interests "are more intrinsically or inherently powerful" than "good-will and moral enlightenment," which, in effect, is saying that selfishness is more powerful than the religion and the principles of Jesus Christ, which are the principles of unselfishness. For one, I do not believe it; and it is because the ideal of foregoing a present gain to one's self for a greater gain to another is the Christ-principle which is behind the whole idea of the Consumers' League that we are bound, as I believe, to regard it as a wise and timely instrument for a present industrial emergency.

Potter also discussed the effect of one's patterns of consumption on those of others. "No one of us," he contended, "can indulge his own lust of ostentation or extravagance . . . without setting in motion a whole series of influences which reach down, and down, and down, until it fires the fierce covetousness and inflames the undisciplined passions of that vast substratum upon which, after all, the peace and prosperity of the republic must forever rest." Potter here echoed his early concern about the evil influence on the poor of the extravagant consumption of the wealthy. On this point, as on that of the impact of consumers upon producers, he demonstrated his commitment to social solidarity. His reference to "the undisciplined passions of that vast substratum," however, betrays the paternalism that nevertheless infused his social theory.[66]

Another strategy for change that Potter commended was the trade union movement. Like many contemporary proponents of social Christianity, Potter criticized some of unionized labor's tactics, rhetoric, and leaders, but he defended it as essential for the well-being of working people and for that of the social order as a whole. The combination of labor in unions was, in his view, as natural and inevitable a step as the combination of capital in corporations. Indeed, in the face of capital combinations, the combination of labor was essential: "If capitalists combined to economize the cost of production, the laborer must combine to protect himself against such applications of that economy as, to him, would be remorseless or fatal." Such protection was especially important "as the progress of the mechanic arts tended more and more toward the special- ization of labor," for this specialization had effected the deskilling of la- bor. Because "machinery went on usurping, one after another, the vari- ous earlier handicrafts," working people were increasingly deprived of the skills that would enable them to find alternative employment. "What is such a man worth when, dismissed from such a task, he is bidden to find another—having, it may be, no slightest resemblance to it—or starve? The only alternative . . . is in some such form of industrial combination as shall bind together him and his fellow-workmen in a common fellowship for mutual protection."

Potter acknowledged that labor unions had occasionally "lent them- selves to acts of violence for which there was no sufficient justification" and "broken explicit pledges with swift indifference and with scanty scruple," but he reminded his audience that unions too had been victims of such treatment by their employers. He encouraged all to recognize that in "the principles of their organization," labor unions "stand for all that society itself as an organized entity stands for,—the free consent of the governed." Potter maintained that the value of unions also consisted in their educational influence on working people. As they participated in governing their own affairs through unions, working people were trained in the responsibilities of citizenship. Underlying this view, of course, was the concern of Potter and many of his contemporaries for the American- ization of immigrants, particularly immigrants from countries other than those of northern Europe. On the one hand, to the extent that he assumed that immigrants and working people needed to be so influenced, his en- dorsement of the educational influence of unions reflects Potter's pater- nalistic ethic; but on the other hand it led him to suggest, in a signifi- cant departure from his dominant paternalism, that "the higher future of the working man must largely depend, finally, upon himself."[67]

One notable contemporary strategy for change that Potter did not consider was that of limiting or regulating the combination of capital in trusts. By the time Potter delivered these lectures, various forms of cap- ital combination, including trusts, had been controversial for at least two decades. In the 1880s trusts had provoked opposition not only by their ability, in the absence of competition, to maintain high prices for goods and services but also by the unrestrainable power of mammoth monop- olies. This early antitrust sentiment culminated in the 1890 passage of the Sherman Antitrust Act. The application of the act, however, was ambiguous at best, for new forms of capital combination quickly developed to replace the old, outlawed forms. In addition, the act itself was used against organized labor as well as against organized capital.[68] In the late 1890s, as the middecade depression waned, formation of trusts accelerated rapidly and their accumulated wealth expanded enormously. In response, antitrust sentiment also grew. Because organized labor's earlier fear that antitrust legislation would be used against them had proved justified, some labor leaders remained aloof from the turn-of-the-century antitrust movement. Some recognized the threat to organized labor that trusts posed: because the establishment of large trusts usually resulted in industrial mass production that made skilled labor marginal, and because much of the strategy and structure of organized labor revolved around skilled crafts or trades, such trusts directly undermined organized labor's viability. Others, such as Samuel Gompers, despite the dissent of many members of the American Federation of Labor, calmly viewed the renewed growth of industrial trusts and regarded trade unionism as an adequate defense against their increasing power.[69]

Potter's skepticism about the efficacy of legislation and his qualified defense of accumulated wealth likely contributed to his failure to consider the regulation of trusts. His rationale for organized labor was probably equally important. Since he held that the combination of labor in unions was as natural and inevitable as the combination of capital in corporations, arguing against capital combinations would have weakened his argument for labor combinations. Further, because his work with Gompers in the National Civic Federation suggests that the two men shared much in their view of the relations of capital and labor, it seems likely that Potter shared Gompers's view of trusts. In addition, his Yale lectures were delivered before Theodore Roosevelt made trust-busting a major part of his presidency's agenda and, as a result, a major topic of public debate. At this early point in the debate, the question of whether the federal government had the authority and power to regulate trusts remained unresolved. In addition, even Roosevelt distinguished between good and bad trusts and directed his regulatory efforts only against the latter. Roosevelt's efforts began producing significant results during his second term. Potter, who died in the last year of that term, nowhere publicly remarked on Roosevelt's trust-busting.

Although Potter did not explicitly develop a social ethical theory as a framework for his religious and moral reflections, elements of such an ethical theory are discernible in his treatment of the problems of the industrial situation and their potential solutions. That he defined the basic problems of the industrial situation as class alienation and working conditions is significant. First, it suggests a central element of his social theory, namely the inevitability of human inequality. In his discussion of the relation of Christianity to social conditions, he appealed to "the eternal fact—not to be altered or effaced by culture, by socio-economic legislation, or by bombastic pronunciamento—that all men are *not* born 'free and equal,' that there are diversities of gifts, of talents, of opportunities, and that so long as our human society exists, these will exist with it." For Potter as for many of his contemporaries, this inequality included not only natural talents but also the gifts of wealth and status; therefore the unequal distribution of such gifts was also inevitable. Potter named this assumption but, unlike contemporary secular and Christian socialists, nowhere questioned its adequacy for realizing his ethic of brotherhood. It permeated his consideration of the industrial situation just as it did his consideration of other social conditions. Second, by assuming the inevitability of human inequality and defining the problems as class alienation and poor working conditions, Potter narrowed his treatment of the means by which the evils of the industrial situation might be overcome to those that could be undertaken within the constraints imposed by his assumptions. Because he did not think it possible that inequalities could be eliminated, he did not—and perhaps could not—take seriously strategies for change that supposed that they could.

Potter's social ethic, then, was predominantly paternalistic, and the stewardship of wealth remained one of its basic tenets. He insisted that all forms of wealth were subject to moral evaluation, but he also defended its possession and unequal distribution. This defense included both economic warrants and religious warrants. It was consistent with his view of the relation between Christianity and social conditions that such warrants included appeals to the teachings and example of Jesus Christ:

> Christ did not denounce wealth any more than He denounced pauperism. He did not abhor money: He used it. He did not abhor the company of rich men: He sought it. He did not invariably scorn or even resent a certain profuseness of expenditure. With a fine discrimination, He, while habitually discouraging it, yet recognized that, here and there, there was a place for it. What He denounced was the *love* of wealth; the *lust* of riches; the vulgar snobbishness that chose exclusively the fellowship or the ways of rich men; the habit of extravagance; in one word, greed and luxury and self-indulgence. He taught men, first of all, and last of all, that they were stewards; that in the final analysis of men and things neither they nor theirs were their own.

Such stewardship meant not only that the possessors of wealth and privilege were responsible for using these gifts for the common good, but also that they bore the *primary* responsibility for alleviating the evils of the industrial situation. "A caste of capitalists, separated by practically impassable barriers from a caste of workers, means social anarchy and industrial war; and the only remedy for a situation so grave is in that unresting and self-sacrificing activity on the part of those who are outside of the working men's caste which shall first break into and then dissolve it by a temper and a service that shall transform hostile interests into common interests, and narrow and mean ambitions into higher and nobler aspirations." Thus, with the exception he allowed for the role of unionized labor, Potter placed his hopes for resolving the industrial situation in capitalists and consumers imbued with the spirit of sacrificial love. He seems not to have realized the contradiction between this position and his observation that improvements in working conditions had been implemented against the objections of the possessors of wealth and privilege who employed and exploited working people. Apparently, he distinguished responsible from irresponsible employers and assumed that there would be sufficient numbers of the former to diminish the significance of the latter. Similarly, he was optimistic about consumers' willingness to act against their immediate interests by spending more for goods produced under adequate working conditions.[70]

Institutionalizing Social Christianity

In addition to addressing the problem of class alienation and working by various means to achieve justice for labor, Potter also worked for the development of policy statements on the industrial problem and the establishment of permanent social-service structures in the Episcopal Church. Thus, in addition to his various other activities in response to industrial capitalism and its evil effects, Potter was also active in the process by which social Christianity, although still a minority perspective, was institutionalized within the Episcopal Church. C. H. Hopkins notes that the workings of that process within American Protestantism indicates neither "the full acceptance of social-gospel principles by the rank and file of American Protestants whom the national organizations represented" nor the "victory of a majority party." Nevertheless, the official sanction given social Christianity by the Episcopal Church and other Protestant churches "heightened the prestige of social Christianity, opened to it the resources of denominational educational machinery, and provided new access to an immense audience."[71] Potter participated in this process in two ways. First, his support for CAIL and the Christian Social Union encouraged and sanctioned the work of many other social Christians; these colleagues in turn worked to gain official recognition for their organizations and, thus, for the social Christian agenda. Second, Potter worked for the incorporation of social Christian concerns, especially with regard to the industrial situation, into official Episcopal Church documents and structures.

The Episcopal Church had responded in a variety of ways to the changing socioeconomic situation after the Civil War. In the years immediately after the war, these responses came primarily from individual leaders such as Frederic Dan Huntington and through local initiatives such as the Working Men's Clubs at St. Mark's Church, Philadelphia. The church as a whole first addressed the social crisis in the 1877 Report of the Joint Committee on Church Work among the Laboring Classes. This report, presented to and approved by that year's General Convention, focused on the symptoms of the crisis, particularly the "antagonism between labor and capital." In response, it proposed some means by which the church, composed largely of "the privileged possessors of power and influence," might both convey to its members their obligations for resolving the crisis and extend its outreach to working people.[72]

With the General Convention in 1883, the first in which Henry Potter participated as a member of the House of Bishops, the social problems of the day began to be addressed in the bishops' pastoral letters. Addressed to all clergy and laity of the church, the pastoral letters reflected the bishops' sense of urgent issues on which they felt an obligation to offer instruction and guidance. The pastoral letters both reflected and generated greater attention by the church as a whole to contemporary socioeconomic issues. In the 1883 pastoral letter, the bishops approached the problem by way of the alienation of labor and capital and the related alienation of working people from the churches. The church, they maintained, sought to reach out to "victims of social wrong, of unequal laws, of intemperance in drinks . . . and sometimes of merciless wealth" so that working people might "learn to love and bless the Ministry which they have cursed" and "capital and labor might worship side by side."[73]

The 1886 General Convention was held in Chicago just six months after the Haymarket Affair and Potter's own pastoral letter to the clergy of the Diocese of New York. Understandably, the bishops' 1886 pastoral letter devoted even greater attention to the social crisis and noted the "novel circumstances and untried conditions" that had compelled the church to face "new emergencies and perplexing problems." The bishops singled out as cause for concern the "rapid increase of wealth, the contempt of lawful authority, and the spread of unbelief" and suggested that such tendencies were "hazardous, not only to the spiritual life of the Church, but also to the tone of public morality and the highest interests in the State." Recognizing the intensification of social inequalities caused by the growth of both wealth and poverty, they asked, "How shall this discontent and misery be remedied, wealth recognize its stewardship, affluence own the brotherhood of man, and the less favored and success-ful of the community be rendered cheerful and contented with their lot?" The bishops criticized both individualism and collectivism as threats to the family, the church, and the state. In response to the "strife which has arrayed class against class," they maintained,

> These are not days to preach platitudes about doctrine, or to philosophize about religion. The Church must, in the spirit of Christ, be the media-tor to re-unite these sundered bonds. The rights of labor are primary rights, with which neither the tyranny of mobs nor the oppressions of capital may interfere. The rights of capital are not less sacred, to enjoy the reward of honest labor and wise forethought, and use it for the benefit of others. Every form of misfortune has, by virtue of the Incarnation, a claim to the help of its prosperous brother.

Thus the bishops looked to the religion of Jesus Christ, particularly in its affirmation of the brotherhood of humanity, as the means to the ulti-mate resolution of social strife and economic turmoil. Although not a member of the committee that wrote this pastoral letter, Henry Potter offered a resolution, adopted by the House of Bishops, that the letter be printed and its contents communicated to the church's clergy and laity.[74]

The Episcopal Church thus began to address in its highest councils the social evils introduced by the rapid rise of industrial capitalism. During this period, the concrete efforts to combat these evils were con-ducted largely by sisterhoods and orders of deaconesses and institution-al churches such as Grace Church, New York. As social needs and aware-ness of them grew in the years after the 1886 General Convention, however, concrete efforts expanded to quasi-official church organizations such as CAIL, the Christian Social Union, and the Church League for In-dustrial Democracy. Under the leadership of J. O. S. Huntington, Harri-ette Keyser, W. D. P. Bliss, and Vida Scudder, and supported by Bishops Frederic Dan Huntington and Henry Codman Potter, these organizations built a national network of social Christian activists and educators. While attempting to work out the church's response to the various aspects of the social crisis, they also built support for that mission within the church. As the new century neared, they sought official authorization for their work and the incorporation of the social Christian agenda into the work of the church.[75]

In 1898 CAIL petitioned the General Convention to increase the church's involvement in social questions and to obtain official recognition for itself. During the 1901 General Convention, against the background of that year's steel strike, CAIL convened a mass meeting, which Henry Potter attended and addressed. Five days later, Randolph McKim offered a resolution that proposed appointment of

> a Standing Commission upon the Relations of Capital and Labor and of employers and work-people, whose duty it shall be: First, to study carefully the aims and purposes of the labor organizations of our country; second, in particular to investigate the causes of industrial disturbances as these may arise; and third, to hold themselves in readiness to act as arbitrators, should their services be desired, between the men and their employers, with a view to bring about mutual conciliation and harmony in the spirit of the Prince of Peace.

The Convention passed the resolution and appointed to the Joint Commission on the Relations of Capital and Labor, from the House of Deputies, Randolph McKim, George Hodges, C. D. Williams, Seth Low, Samuel Mather, and Jacob Riis; and from the House of Bishops, Charles Anderson, William Lawrence, and Henry Potter.[76]

Potter was named chair of the new commission and presented its first report at the next General Convention in 1904. Since the previous General Convention, the country had faced the potentially disastrous anthracite coal strike of 1902, which had been settled largely through the intervention of President Theodore Roosevelt. The settlement achieved in early 1903 was of mixed value to the miners, but the process by which it was achieved enhanced public acceptance of labor unions. Most important, perhaps, were Roosevelt's unprecedented summons to both mine operators and miners to meet in Washington, his equal treatment of both labor and capital, and John Mitchell's admirable conduct of the miners' part in the discussion despite the virulent claims of the mine owners. Potter seems to have been involved in the attempt to settle the strike, primarily through his affiliation with the National Civic Federation, but the nature of his efforts and their outcome are unknown.[77]

In the joint commission's 1904 report, Potter explained that it had received no requests to act as arbitrator and that it had not yet "succeeded in studying in common the occasions of current disturbances." The report was consistent with the views expressed in Potter's Yale lectures, delivered less than two years earlier, and with contemporary Episcopal social teaching. It emphasized the moral causes of the alienation of and conflict between labor and capital, affirmed that "the capitalist and the laborer are alike sons of the Church," and suggested that the "Church helps to remove the moral causes of industrial strife when she brings these different members of her family into better acquaintance." Further, the report condemned organized labor's use of "tyranny and turbulence" but pointed out, "The laborer has learned from the capitalist to despise order and break law. He has learned from the churchman to pursue the dissenter with menace and violence." And it affirmed the necessity and value of unions: "The organization of labor is essential to the well-being of the working people. It is based upon a sense of the inestimable value of the individual man. . . . Its purpose is to maintain such a standard of wages, hours, and conditions as shall afford every man an opportunity to grow in mind and in heart. Without organization the standard cannot be maintained in the midst of our present commercial conditions." The report also decried the ignorance prevalent in the church of "the principles which are involved in the conflicts of the industrial world." It therefore recommended to church members several books, among them John Mitchell's *Organization of Labor,* Washington Gladden's *Tools and the Man,* Lyman Abbott's *Christianity and Social Problems,* and Francis Peabody's *Jesus Christ and the Social Question.* While explicitly avoiding detailed discussion of all aspects of the industrial problem, the report called particular attention to child labor and urged its abolition.[78]

In addition to presenting the joint commission's report, Potter wrote that year's bishops' pastoral letter. In it he called attention to "those two great problems," the industrial problem and the racial problem. Of the former, he repeated his support for labor unions and maintained that "in what they have attempted or accomplished, they have moved mainly along lines which are the glory of our democratic institutions." The 1904 General Convention included two other significant actions: first, it granted CAIL official recognition; and second, it authorized the continuation of the Standing Commission on the Relations of Capital and Labor for another three-year term.[79]

Nevertheless, by 1907 CAIL recognized that the structures and actions of the church were not yet sufficient to meet the demands of the situation. It therefore formally recommended to the forthcoming General Convention the establishment both of a permanent commission on labor and capital, modeled on the Department of Church and Labor established in 1903 by the Presbyterian Church, and of diocesan social-service committees. Potter, as both president of CAIL and chair of the Joint Commission on the Relations of Capital and Labor, was instrumental in conveying these recommendations to the convention. Indeed, these recommendations, supported in principle by several other social Christian organizations, constituted the most significant aspect of the commission's 1907 report. Presented again by Potter, the report treated in more detail the themes discussed in the previous report. It acknowledged the work of the Presbyterian Department of Church and Labor and commended the Presbyterian General Assembly's affirmation that "the labor question is fundamentally a moral and a religious question, and that it will never be settled on any other basis."

The report went on, however, to note the lack of coordination of the church's social-service efforts and recommended "that Diocesan Committees of Social Service and the like should be formed, and that they, with the local branches of existing organizations, be brought into mutual co-operation." More formally, the report also proposed that the joint commission be made a permanent structure of the church and that "its powers be extended to enable it to promote the co-ordination of the various organizations existing in the Church in the interests of social questions and to extend or add to them, to encourage sympathetic relations between Capital and Labor, and to deal according to their discretion with these kindred matters."[80]

The convention adopted both resolutions from the joint commission. The following month, at its November 1907 convention, the Diocese of New York established its Social Service Commission with Bishop Potter as its first chair. By the time of the next General Convention in 1910, thirteen such commissions had been established; by 1913, their number had grown to seventy-five. Also at the 1910 General Convention, the Joint Commission on the Relations of Capital and Labor was discharged and replaced with the Joint Commission on Social Service. The new commission was given an enlarged membership, expanded terms of reference, and, the following year, a full-time field secretary to staff its activities. Social Christianity had become institutionalized within the Protestant Episcopal Church. Henry Codman Potter had helped lay the foundation for this accomplishment, but he died in July 1908 and did not witness the fruition of this aspect of his work. At the start of its report to the 1910 General Convention, the Joint Commission on the Relations of Capital and Labor observed Potter's passing and paid tribute to his contribution.

> From the beginning of his Episcopate, identified with every important movement for social betterment, Bishop Potter was an admirable embodiment of the purpose for which this Commission was established. He was thoroughly versed in the great social problems of our time. His sympathy touched rich and poor alike. Fair in spirit, careful in judgment, fearless in utterance, he was trusted by all classes. His commanding influence was potent in removing from the Church the stigma of indifference to social and industrial conditions.[81]

The process by which American Protestantism shook off its "indifference to social and industrial conditions" is undoubtedly one of the most important aspects of its history. The problems arising from the industrialization of manufacturing and related changes in the socioeconomic order were, by the beginning of the twentieth century, central to the Protestant agenda for the Christianization of America. The work of the period's many social Christians was not limited to industrial problems, but their emphasis on industrialization and its effects was appropriate to their socioeconomic context. The changes wrought by industrial capitalism were the most significant and far-reaching of the many changes of the period. Increased dependence on the wage work system for material sustenance, relations of men and women and conceptions of the family, relations among the races, immigration, tenement housing, use and abuse of alcohol, unequal distribution of vast amounts of wealth, ostentatious consumption by the rich, corruption of political and commercial ethics, strains in the cohesion of the social fabric as a result of increased class alienation—all were affected by the rapid growth of industrial capitalism.

As they worked out their responses to this new situation, a growing group of American Protestants relied on the religious traditions of antebellum evangelical reform movements, on the vision of a Christian America, and on resources from English Christian Socialism, innovations in political economic theory, and experimental initiatives for meeting the material and spiritual needs of working people. Their conviction of the fatherhood of God and the brotherhood of humanity shaped much of this work. Although their idea of brotherhood did not necessarily entail material equality, it did require certain minimal standards of just treatment and decency in working and living conditions. This approach did not challenge the root causes of the period's conflicts. It did provide, however, a potent alternative to the powerful ideological alliance of social Darwinism and neoclassical political economy, according to which no person or agency should act to alleviate the sufferings of the weak and the poor.

As early as the late 1860s, Henry Potter was concerned about "dangers of social disintegration" and the "spirit of caste." In that he assumed that the unequal distribution of wealth and privilege was both inevitable and, at least to a certain extent, good, he focused his efforts on mitigating the evil effects of this inequality rather than on eliminating the inequalities themselves. Potter's early sermons on the stewardship of wealth exhibit clearly both his assumption of the unequal distribution of wealth and his conviction of the moral responsibility appropriate to its possessors, a responsibility grounded in the universal fatherhood of God and consequent brotherhood of humanity. His defense of private property thirty years later in *The Citizen in His Relation to the Industrial Situation* demonstrated the strength of this conviction, despite the weakness of his arguments. Throughout his work, then, Potter maintained that the possessors of power and privilege bore the primary responsibility for the welfare of those who possessed little or none of either. His fundamentally paternalistic ethic also initially assumed that there were two parties to the conflict, the rich and the poor, the strong and the weak, the privileged and the neglected. It also assumed that church membership was largely identified with the rich, strong, and privileged.

Although he never seriously questioned this ethic, Potter did qualify it in three significant ways over the course of his work. First, he modified the concern for evangelization of working people—a dominant note in his and others' early work—to include the provision of material needs of poor and working people and the commitment to meeting demands for justice in fair wages, fair treatment, and decent living and working conditions. Second, he altered the earlier assumption of a two-party conflict, with the church being largely identified with one of the parties, to a three-party scheme. In this view, the church was the mediator between labor and capital. This shift reflected the church's attempt to eliminate workers' alienation from it by minimizing its identification with the capitalist and managerial classes. It also reflected the experience of some social Christians who, like Potter, attempted to combat class alienation in concrete ways, especially through direct participation in the mediation of conflicts between workers and employers.

Third, Potter supplemented the stewardship of wealth with a critique of some fundamental tenets of clerical and classical political economic theory. By challenging the view of labor as a commodity and the inexorable character of the law of supply and demand, Potter helped to effect a major shift in the relation of Protestant thought to the theory and practice of commerce. Although for a time he seemed unclear about the relation of economic law to moral law, by the turn of the century Potter had unambiguously affirmed the relevance of moral criteria for economic activity, including the conduct of commerce as well as the production and consumption of commodities. For Potter, as for many of his contemporaries, the application of Christianity to social problems was essential to their ultimate solution. Related to this point is one of the crucial elements of Potter's attempts to apply Christianity to social and industrial conditions: his consistent, clear, and strong support for labor's right to organize and for the equality of status of organized labor with organized capital.

6 A Work for a Whole Life

In his address to the 1908 New York diocesan convention, delivered four months after the death of Henry Codman Potter, Bishop David Hummel Greer noted that Potter "loved his Church and served it, but his sympathies reached beyond it." As a result, "without regard to creed or race he loved his fellow men, and was always ready to work with those of every name who, like himself, were working for the common human good." In exercising those sympathies, Potter "believed that the Christian faith was something more than a theory, something more than a doctrine for esoteric tenure; it was, he held, a force to be practically applied, a force which should energize in all the common relations of our social life, and which as such should help to resolve all our social problems." Based on Potter's conviction of the nature of Christian faith, Greer also observed that

> this is one of the lessons, and not perhaps the least, which he has left and taught us—that religion is for life, for this life, and for the whole of this life. . . . He held . . . that Jesus Christ is the Lord of all human life, not only in the shelter and seclusion of the home, but in all the various ramifications of it, social and commercial, national and civic, or whatever other form and relation it assumed. That was what he stood for, and that was what persistently, in many ways and places, with his trenchant speech and pen, from first to last he taught—that Jesus Christ is the Lord and equally the Lord of all human life, and that not until His true and righteous claims were recognized and owned and practically obeyed would its evils be removed, its faults and vices cured, its bitter strifes and frictions terminate and cease. And to that end he saw it, slowly indeed, but surely and gradually moving on. For his was an optimistic faith,

which, while it did not overlook existing forms of evil nor underrate their strength, was not discouraged by them.[1]

Greer's apt characterization of Potter's life and work suggests much of his significance and the significance of the broader social Christianity of which Potter was an exemplar: a commitment to the church combined with a concern for matters outside the church's walls; an emphasis on the practical application rather than the theoretical formulation of Christian faith; and a conviction that the practical application of Christian faith entailed working for the transformation of all aspects of human life— wherever evil and injustice prevailed, wherever women and men were hungry, exploited, victimized, and alienated. Like many of his contemporaries in various white Protestant churches, Henry Codman Potter took the thread of nineteenth-century evangelicalism as the clue to discerning appropriate responses to the religious, economic, social, and cultural demands accompanying emancipation, industrialization, and urbanization in the decades after the Civil War. In the transition in the Episcopal Church from antebellum Evangelicalism to the postwar Broad Church movement, the lesson that Potter "has left and taught us" may therefore serve to illuminate the question of continuity and change in American Christianity. Further, his sense of "a work for a whole life,"[2] based on an optimistic faith and an affirmation of the universal sovereignty of Jesus Christ, may serve to illuminate the relation of theory and practice, theology and practical Christianity in American Protestantism.

Continuity and Change in American Protestantism

In that the demands postwar evangelicals faced were in some ways continuous and some ways discontinuous with those faced by antebellum evangelicals, so the responses they developed were in some ways continuous and some ways discontinuous with antebellum evangelicalism. Their very responsiveness to the demands of the day, however, was fundamentally continuous with evangelicalism. In the Episcopal Church, reflecting the process by which Evangelicals had helped to reinvigorate it in the early decades of the nineteenth century, Potter and moderate Evangelicals like him who came to be identified with the Broad Church movement were central to that continuing reinvigoration in the century's later decades. That process also was instrumental in the social awakening of the Episcopal Church and thereby of white American Protestantism.

Two theses in American church history have framed the debate about continuity and change in nineteenth-century Protestantism. On the one hand, in a 1931 essay Arthur M. Schlesinger Sr. contended that in the last

quarter of the nineteenth century American Christianity was characterized by its responses to the theoretical challenges of Darwinism, biblical criticism, and the comparative study of religion and to the social
challenges of industrialization and urbanization. Later studies by Aaron
Abell and Henry May reflected Schlesinger's "challenge-response" framework for understanding nineteenth-century Christianity by emphasizing
the influence of external social events rather than that of internal religious resources.[3] On the other hand, H. Richard Niebuhr, although he had
employed a method similar to Schlesinger's in his 1931 *Social Sources
of Denominationalism*, later diverged and dissented from it in his 1937
Kingdom of God in America. In his preface to the latter book, he acknowledged that while the "sociological approach . . . seemed relevant enough
to the institutionalized churches it did not explain the Christian movement which produced these churches; while it accounted for the diversity in American religion it did not explain the unity which our faith
possesses despite its variety; while it could deal with the religion which
was dependent on culture it left unexplained the faith which is independent, which is aggressive rather than passive, and which molds culture
instead of being molded by it."[4]

Similarly, Sidney Mead and Robert Handy have subsequently insisted on the significance of American Christianity's internal religious resources. Rather than viewing the social awakening of the churches as an
unprecedented result of their response to social challenges, they maintained
that various expressions of American Christianity from 1830 to 1930 were
characterized by the effort to "Christianize America." Antebellum revivalism and postwar social gospel were not discontinuous movements but
were different expressions of the same aggressive religious spirit. As Handy
argues, the churches' "response to the problems of an urbanized and industrialized society was shaped by the patterns of thought and action that
had long been characteristic of American Protestantism."[5] As White and
Hopkins observe, however, the two theses are not mutually exclusive, and
recent historical scholarship has acknowledged the value of both. Studies
in the history of American Christianity should attend both to the external social challenges and to the internal religious resources, both to the
novel character of the churches' responses and to the ways in which those
same responses are continuous with earlier efforts. Nevertheless, White
and Hopkins maintain that "accentuating continuity over discontinuity,
aggressive as opposed to defensive religion, Handy's viewpoint has implications for such issues as the theological precursors of the social gospel and
the movement's decline and revival."[6]

Historians may variously describe the relative importance of reliance on internal traditions or responsiveness to external challenges in American Christianity, but they or others may also evaluate these tendencies as either a strength or a weakness, as either faithful or unfaithful. Schlesinger himself seems to have regarded American Christianity's responsiveness to change as a strength, maintaining that "from early colonial times the life of American Christianity has been characterized by its adaptability and change. . . . However disturbing to defenders of the old-time religion, this ceaseless bending of creeds and practices to the changing needs of society has been the price of survival."[7] But however true it is that such "ceaseless bending of creeds and practices to the changing needs of society" has happened, historians and others may not necessarily regard paying the price of survival as legitimate warrant for doing so. They may have other reasons for preferring one way of bending creeds and practices to others. They may also differ on which particular expression of American Christianity is normative, on which old-time religion they choose to defend, and on their reasons for those choices. Such issues often accompany, explicitly or implicitly, discussions of continuity and change in American Christianity, including discussions of the relationship between Protestant evangelicalism and liberalism in the nineteenth century and, as one instance of it, the relationship between Episcopal Evangelicalism and the Broad Church movement.

In the introduction to his recent study of Reformed Episcopalians, Allen Guelzo discusses various competing alternatives for Anglican identity and notes that "as old High Churchmen, Anglo-Catholics, and Evangelicals were violently grappling with each other, yet another departure from the old identity developed in the German-inspired liberalism of *Essays and Reviews* and F. D. Maurice." Such a summary of Anglican liberalism serves Guelzo's entirely appropriate rhetorical requirements to introduce his study. By emphasizing external and neglecting internal influences on the development of Anglican and Episcopal liberalism, however, it inadequately describes the relationship between liberalism and Evangelicalism. In his account of the early development of the English Broad Church movement, Guelzo provides more information about that relationship. He not only notes the movement's Anglican sources but summarizes some key differences and similarities between it and Evangelicalism. Evangelicals regarded Broad Church theology as "shapeless," had little interest in Broad Church proposals for structural reform of the Church of England, and tended to be more dogmatic about matters such as scriptural authority and the atonement. Broad Churchmen regarded Evangelicals as having (in the words of Thomas Arnold) a "foolish fondness for their particular phraseology," were confident about the prospects for and efficacy of their proposals for ecclesiastical reform, and while less dogmatic than Evangelicals about some matters were equally so in their rejection of episcopal polity. Nevertheless, the two "shared the enthusiasm . . . for loosening the bonds of episcopal order" and were equally "energetic in their determination to Christianize England and to unite with any willing dissenter in the interests of achieving that end."[8]

Of course, Guelzo acknowledges that his book is not "about the Evangelical Episcopalians, but about what happened to them after they left the Episcopal Church in 1873" and that therefore what he says about them before that date is "of necessity sketchy." He further acknowledges that it "is also not a book about the Oxford Movement" and in his treatment of the movement he has "chosen to let the Evangelicals speak for themselves."[9] Neither, one might add, is Guelzo's a book about the Broad Church movement, and his treatment of it is similarly and justifiably from the perspective of the Evangelicals. Guelzo appropriately chooses which expression of Episcopal identity he takes as normative for the purposes of his study, and his treatment of alternative identities appropriately reflects that choice. He offers some helpful pointers on the relationship between Evangelicalism and the Broad Church movement, but other choices may suggest that there is more to be said about it.

In part because her book is about Evangelical Episcopalians before 1873, Diana Butler does say a great deal more about these matters. She more fully and somewhat sympathetically demonstrates the continuities between Evangelicalism and the Broad Church movement in the Episcopal Church, notably on their concern for Protestant ecumenism, use of the "rhetoric of liberality," and emphasis on religious experience. Taking the perspective of Evangelicals, especially in the example of Charles McIlvaine, she describes Broad Church liberalism (along with ritualism) as one of "the two great enemies of evangelicalism in the 1870s." She ultimately concludes, "When the younger Evangelicals abandoned the theology that empowered revivalism, the born again experience, personal holiness, and the 'preaching of Christ crucified,' they emptied their tradition of its life blood."[10] Perhaps. But in the late nineteenth and early twentieth centuries the vitality of the Broad Church movement and (in no small measure due to that movement) the vitality of the Episcopal Church strongly suggest that younger Evangelicals like Henry Codman Potter not only had retained their tradition's lifeblood but also with it had reinvigorated the Episcopal Church. Extending conversion and holiness from personal life to social life, and seeking to demonstrate in action the love of the crucified Christ, they helped the Episcopal Church to respond vigorously to the poverty, suffering, injustice, corruption, and oppression of the period.

Certainly, as Butler correctly describes it, this abandonment of Evangelical theology marks a significant point of discontinuity, but from the perspective of the moderate Evangelicals who became Evangelical liberals associated with the Broad Church movement, that abandonment may have been rather a faithful expression of internal elements of moderate Evangelicalism. For example, the Broad Church emphasis on practical Christianity rather than doctrine seems to have been in part an extension, from the realm of worship to the realm of theology, of what Butler describes as the Evangelical resistance to formalism in religious life. In short, Evangelical liberals seemed to have shared Arnold's assessment of Evangelicals' "foolish fondness for their particular phraseology." Further, this extension of Evangelical antiformalism, driven in part by the postwar failure of both the Evangelical and the High Church parties to demonstrate the spiritual vitality of their theologies or their ability to meet the demands of the day, was also consistent with the Evangelical emphasis on the importance of holy living and manifest in the Broad Church emphasis on practical Christianity.

Within contemporary American Protestantism more generally, the abandonment of evangelical theology seems to have been motivated in part by its failure to continue to do for some what it had done for so many in the eighteenth and nineteenth centuries, that is, inspire conversion and a commitment to holy living. The image of a God who requires the sacrificial torture and execution of his son as the means of effecting salvation had become a genuine spiritual stumbling block for many in the nineteenth century, in much the same way that orthodox Calvinist understandings of predestination had for many in the seventeenth and eighteenth centuries. The earlier Pietist rejection of predestination was mirrored in the later liberal rejection of vicarious atonement as Bushnell and others criticized the dominant evangelical view of the atonement for the sake of developing a theology that would continue to inspire conversion and discipleship. Henry Codman Potter reflected this understanding of Jesus' death in a sermon at Grace Church. "What is the power of Calvary over men? That it was an eternally necessary sacrifice—that in no other way could God have saved the race, than in the way which actually He chose? Once there was a theology which uttered a dogma so bold and so essentially presumptuous as this; but thank God, it has long ago found its way to the crowded limbo of outworn theological vagaries. No, the power of the cross over men lies in this, that it is the gift to men, by God, of His very best—'His well-beloved Son.'"[11] For Potter and other evangelical liberals, as God gave "His very best" to us, we were to give our best to God by service to others. In this way, their theology of salvation served to foster the evangelical emphasis on holy living even as it rejected an element of evangelical theology on which other evangelicals continued to insist. As evangelicals had resisted liturgical forms as impediments to life in the spirit, evangelical liberals resisted doctrinal forms in order to enable the spirit to animate genuine discipleship.

Another major point of discontinuity between antebellum evangelicals and postwar evangelical liberals was the authority and interpretation of scripture. Historians have often remarked on the influence of nineteenth-century German rationalism and historicism on the development of higher biblical criticism. In the history of Anglicanism, the publication in the early 1860s of *Essays and Reviews* and works of higher criticism by Bishop John Colenso are cited as evidence of the influence of such rationalism.[12] Nevertheless, by the late nineteenth century rationalism in its Enlightenment forms had long been prominent in evangelical thought. The question is not whether the use of rationalism was incompatible with evangelicalism, but on which rationalism evangelicals relied: while (in Butler's term) "proto-fundamentalist" Evangelicals continued to rely on Enlightenment rationalism as expressed in Scottish Common Sense philosophy, Evangelical liberals began to employ nineteenth-century German idealism. A readiness to employ rationalism was therefore characteristic of evangelicalism, and in this the Broad Church movement was continuous with it.[13]

Further, the Evangelical liberal acceptance of higher biblical criticism in response to the crisis in biblical authority was motivated not only by a readiness to employ rationalism but also by a problem within nineteenth-century American evangelicalism, namely, the difficulty of making a persuasive case against slavery from scripture. As noted in chapter 2, the 1863 controversy in the Diocese of Pennsylvania over the republication of Bishop John Henry Hopkins's defense of slavery, made in part on explicitly biblical grounds, was but one example of this problem. Other than his oft-stated commitment to "the unity of truth-seeking and the peace of a large charity," Henry Potter left no record of his specific rationale for supporting those like R. Heber Newton and Charles Briggs who helped advance the cause of higher criticism in American Protestantism. The absence of such explicit reflection in Potter's work may suggest that he had not made the connection between the reassessment of biblical authority and the use of scripture in arguments about slavery, that he was hesitant to question directly the deeply held Protestant conviction of *sola*

scriptura, or that he regarded that work as best left to others like Newton and Briggs. Nevertheless, by the outbreak of the Civil War debates
within evangelicalism about the relative weight to be given scripture or
moral intuition in assessing the evil of slavery had led, as Timothy Smith
has argued, to "the spread of a rational and historical approach to the
interpretation of Scripture, long before German scholarship became a
seminary fashion."[14] Evangelical liberals like Potter seem to have valued
higher criticism not only as a way of bringing Christian theology into
conformity with contemporary thought but also as a way of affirming
scriptural authority while reflecting how that authority had actually functioned for many evangelicals in relation to moral insight in the difficult
battle against slavery. As Robert Mullin observes, "For many an evangelical the formal exegetical method with its emphasis upon the objec-
tive text had been weighed in the balance in the great national crisis over
slavery only to be found wanting, because of the wedge it drove between
the Scriptures and the moral will."[15] To the extent that the Broad Church
acceptance of higher criticism diminished the sole authority of the Bible, it was discontinuous with Episcopal Evangelicalism; but to the extent that it thereby gave priority to moral reform and the eradication of
sin, it was also continuous.

The way in which the Broad Church movement fostered the reinvigoration of the Episcopal Church after the Civil War was itself in continuity with the role of Evangelicalism in the church after the Revolutionary War. The religious vitality that in the early decades of the nineteenth
century had done much to restore a beleaguered church also served in its
later decades to place the Episcopal Church at the forefront of the social
awakening of American Christianity. Appropriation of religious traditions, responsiveness to contemporary social events and cultural conditions, and the continuing interaction of this appropriation and responsiveness were central both to antebellum evangelicalism and postwar
social Christianity in general and to Episcopal Evangelicalism and the
Broad Church movement in particular. Henry Codman Potter explicitly
appropriated the traditions of white American evangelical Protestantism,
through its particular Episcopal expressions in the work of William
Muhlenberg and Alonzo Potter, especially as these emphasized practical
Christianity. The continuity of concern between Alonzo Potter and Henry
Codman Potter reflects the essential continuity between antebellum and
postwar white Protestantism. Nevertheless, postwar Protestantism, faced
with a radically different context from that faced by its predecessors,
adapted older methods and adopted new ones to meet the new demands.
The differences between Alonzo and Henry Codman Potter on religion

and politics and the relation of labor and capital similarly reflect this discontinuity.

William Reed Huntington observed shortly after Henry Potter's death that he was "no servile imitator" of his father. Rather, he sought "to adapt the tried principle to the changed condition, ever ready, like the instructed scribe, to bring forth out of his treasure things new and old."[16] The process by which Henry Potter engaged his religious traditions with the conditions of his day produced some surprising results in the eyes of some contemporary and subsequent observers. As Bernard Markwell observes: "Conservative fathers often beget liberal or even radical children, but the differences of opinion within the Potter family cannot be explained away on purely personal grounds. Neither man was an extremist in his own time; their differences reflect a change of attitude that took place in the Episcopal Church during the course of the nineteenth century. It was a remarkable transformation, and it is not difficult to understand why contemporaries were astonished."[17]

Henry Codman Potter's work included various practical, religious, and moral elements. Motivated by the spirit of the Memorial Movement, he emphasized in his work the practical usefulness of Christianity and deliberately and willingly experimented with methods for effecting such usefulness. In his development of the various institutional programs and services at Grace Church, his participation in the work of extra-ecclesiastical reform organizations, and his advocacy for and employment of sisterhoods, deaconesses, and brotherhoods, he embraced and adapted both Evangelical and High Church traditions for ministry among poor and working people and for awakening church to that need. In his work with the American Colonization Society and in his support for the Subway Tavern, where prevailing approaches to racial and temperance reform had showed limited effectiveness, he sought to develop new approaches to enduring problems. Similarly, realizing that opposition to the just demands and the organization of working people offered no hope of alleviating the evil of class alienation, he supported the development of labor unions, endorsed mediation and conciliation as alternatives to lockouts and strikes for settling labor disputes, and participated directly in the settlement of several such disputes.

Like most of his white predecessors and contemporaries, Potter assumed the inevitability of inequality of rich and poor, strong and weak, privileged and victimized. Against social Darwinism and laissez-faire political economy, however, he maintained that those with power were responsible for helping those without. While antebellum Protestantism had emphasized the limits to charity, the cycles of boom and bust that followed in the wake of the rapid growth of industrial capitalism led Potter and others to emphasize not the limits to charity but rather its right methods. Like Alonzo Potter, he maintained that individual efforts must be supplemented and directed by institutional, especially ecclesiastical, programs. He also maintained that institutional programs must never supplant individual charity, for direct personal contact between giver and receiver was necessary to maintain the bonds of human community. In contrast to suggesting *limits* to charity, Henry Potter and many of his contemporaries emphasized that the *goals* of Christian charity included decreasing the dependency of poor and working people and aiding in their attainment of self-sufficiency. In addition, he specifically repudiated the view that the wealthy deserved their riches and the poor their privation.[18]

Consistent with the white evangelical Protestant theology of his day, Potter grounded this concern for poor and working people in the religious conviction of the brotherhood of humanity. Many of his colleagues usually grounded this common humanity in the universal fatherhood of God, but Potter grounded it just as regularly in "the liberating and ennobling bond of a common Saviour and Redeemer." As savior of all people, Jesus Christ was elder brother, teacher, model, and example to be followed especially by the strong, privileged, rich, and educated—the "so-called higher classes."[19] For Potter, central to the life and teaching of Jesus were the conviction of the fatherhood of God and brotherhood of humanity, the this-worldly import of the kingdom of God, and the moral principle of sacrificial love and selfless service. By his care for and intimacy with "the lowliest humanity," Jesus emphasized that "the Fatherhood of God had no meaning as a principle of action unless it issued forever in the service and sacrifice that affirm the brotherhood of man." Further, Jesus' injunction to pray for the coming of the kingdom and the doing of God's will "on earth as in heaven" demonstrated that such service must be rendered in concrete ways in this world.[20]

Henry Potter addressed many of the same issues as were addressed by Alonzo Potter, in part because of his father's attention to them and in part because they remained urgent issues for the country and the church. In some cases, social and cultural changes late in the century subtly altered the character of these problems and, thus, required subtly different approaches to their solution. In other cases, social and cultural changes brought about more radical shifts and thus required similar transformations in efforts to respond to them. One of the major changes wrought by the Civil War was, of course, the abolition of slavery. For some ten years after the war, many hoped that Reconstruction and other initiatives would quickly bring about a significant measure of justice for black people. The retreat from Reconstruction and renewed discrimination and violence against blacks caused some white reformers to become discouraged and some to seek alternate means of achieving that justice. Of the latter, those who had been abolitionists before emancipation worked to protect the civil rights of black people; those who had been more moderate opponents of slavery worked to provide them with the education that, it was hoped, would help them to achieve equality. Protestant mission initiatives among black people thus manifested the prevalent concern that, as it was expressed, the more favored classes should lift up the less favored. Henry Potter supported such educational efforts, particularly that of Booker T. Washington. In addition, and unlike most of his contemporaries and perhaps motivated in part by the Episcopal Church's mission work in Liberia, he retained an interest in colonization. When called upon to help revive the American Colonization Society late in the century, he recognized that its purposes should be reoriented to reflect changed conditions in both the United States and Africa. Rather than promoting colonization as a solution to American race relations, then, he promoted it as a means of providing material assistance to Liberia and all Africa. Unfortunately, he seems not to have recognized that, by that time, many black people regarded colonization as promoted by whites, for whatever purpose, as objectionable.

Similarly, the mission to immigrants in the vicinity of Grace Church was motivated both by the perceived need to Christianize and Americanize them, in order to preserve the dominant religious and political traditions and to assure the cultural homogeneity necessary for governing the nation, and by the concern for exercising the responsibility of the stronger for the weaker. As immigration dramatically increased toward the end of the century, Potter tempered some of his early nativist views, opposed immigration restriction, acknowledged greater diversity among the European peoples who established the country's traditions, and celebrated New York's cultural diversity in the design of the Cathedral of St. John the Divine. Throughout his work, then, he affirmed like most of his white Protestant colleagues both Anglo-Saxon superiority and the brotherhood of humanity. Few recognized the contradictory character of this complex of ideas, but the ideological tension thus created served, on the one hand, to affirm the responsibilities of Anglo-Saxon world mission rather than any supposed biological or ontological superiority, and on the other, to impose limits on the justice attainable in a social order based on the inevitability of human inequality.

By 1870 the work and well-being of women had been significantly affected by their expanded public roles during the Civil War, the dependence of industrial manufacturing on their labor, and the continuing problem of alcohol consumption and its effect on domestic life. Relying on the ideology of women's special nature, Alonzo Potter had argued for expanding women's church work on the grounds of their competence and the church's need. Henry Potter adopted that reasoning but also extended it to justify women's work in nondomestic fields, including industrial manufacturing, in light of women's legitimate need to support themselves when they could rely on no man to support them. Such appeals to women's special nature were common among Potter's contemporaries, women as well as men, who believed that women's beneficial moral influence was essential to the project of Christianizing America. Although Potter and others regarded the home as the primary sphere for the exercise of that influence, by the start of the twentieth century they regularly appealed to it as a means of securing various public reforms and protecting white American Protestant traditions from the alien traditions of immigrants from Asia and central, southern, and eastern Europe.

Women's role in the temperance movement was the principal manifestation of this reasoning. Because for most people women had particular responsibility for the character of home life, and because alcohol consumption negatively affected the home, most acknowledged the legitimacy of women's efforts for temperance reform. Potter never explicitly supported women's temperance work, but his justification of women's nondomestic labor implicitly supported it. Further, by the first years of the twentieth century, he seems to have acknowledged that such roles for women should be extended to other reform efforts. The interaction of the traditions of women's special nature and role in Christianizing the nation, the labor demands of industrialized manufacturing, and the suffering of women and children as a result of unemployment and intemperance combined to extend women's proper work beyond the domestic sphere in practice, even though the ideology of domesticity continued to confine them to the home in theory.

Henry Potter's doubts about the efficacy of prohibition reflected his father's resistance to restrictive or legislative solutions to moral and social issues. In this respect, both Potters differed somewhat from the more prevalent evangelical Protestant confidence in the state's role in assuring a moral society. Nevertheless, that Henry Potter appropriated this element of Alonzo Potter's work, despite the dominance of the prohibition strategy in the late nineteenth century, demonstrates again the continuity between the two. Also, while Alonzo Potter advocated total abstinence but not legislation to assure it, Henry Potter retained the resistance to legislated solutions while shifting away from the advocacy of total abstinence in his support not only for saloon substitutes that served no alcoholic beverages but also for reformed saloons such as the Subway Tavern that did.

Henry Codman Potter also retained his father's caution about direct clerical and ecclesiastical involvement in political matters yet defended in principle and demonstrated in practice his conviction that all human activity, including politics, is subject to moral evaluation. Again, the particular postwar challenge of political corruption, fueled by the dramatic increases in wealth generated by industrialized manufacturing, created a substantially different context from that faced by Alonzo Potter's generation. In that new context, Henry Potter emphasized the need for political righteousness and the church's proper role in assuring it while declining to participate directly and publicly in any initiative, however reform-minded, that might be construed as partisan. In 1889 his address at the centennial celebration of the inauguration of George Washington, for example, he criticized not the objectionable conduct of the recently elected Republican administration, but rather the machine politics and consequent corrupt conduct prevalent among both Republicans and Democrats. In doing so, he explicitly drew on and upheld the continuing relevance of the religious and moral traditions of the nation's founders. Similarly, in his initial opposition to American acquisition of the Philippines in the Spanish-American War, he specifically appealed to these same traditions: "The things that this community and this nation alike supremely need are not more territory, more avenues of trade, more subject races to prey upon, but a dawning consciousness of what, in individual and in national life, are a people's indispensable moral foundations—those great spiritual forces on which alone men and nations are built."[21] When he reversed his position on continuing American administration of the Philippines, however, he did not repudiate those "indispensable moral foundations." Rather, he appealed instead to the responsibility of the more favored to the less favored, and to the demand of fulfilling a responsibility once assumed, regardless of the circumstances of its assumption.

By the mid-1870s, Henry Codman Potter and some others began to doubt the political economic verities produced as a result of evangelical Protestantism's antebellum campaign against radicalism. The conviction of the responsibility of the more favored to the less favored proved stronger than the appeals to natural and divine law in defense of private property, limits to charity, and labor as a commodity. Of course, Henry Potter's stewardship of wealth ethic functioned in part as a defense of private property. In that it subjected both the acquisition and use of wealth to moral evaluation, however, it also made more demands on the possessors of wealth than did the economic ethics of many of his predecessors and contemporaries. Similarly, Henry Potter's focus on the problem of class alienation—in his support for free churches, his insistence on personal contact in charitable work, his advocacy of organized labor—indicates that he envisioned no radical change in the social order, no classless society. On a few occasions, as in his 1902 Yale lectures, Potter defended the prevailing order against the challenges of socialists, but most often he assumed that changes such as those advocated by socialists simply were not possible.[22]

Nevertheless, like some of his contemporaries, Potter recognized that the social and economic realities of the late nineteenth century made it impossible to faithfully defend all aspects of the prevailing socioeconomic order by appeals to white American Protestantism's traditions. He and others may have undertaken the work of Christianizing the working classes in part to ensure that they would not undermine the accustomed privileges of the capitalist and managerial classes, but shortly after his arrival at Grace Church in 1868 he began to justify meeting their material needs as an end in itself. More important, by 1886 Potter directly challenged the view of labor as a commodity, a key tenet of the clerical laissez-faire political economy propounded by antebellum Protestants, including his father. He repudiated the commodification of labor because it aggravated the alienation of working people from their employers, alienated workers from each other, cheapened the value of their labor and of themselves as persons, and compelled them to work for minimal pay when industry required their labor and forced them into destitution when it did not. It is significant that, although he generally maintained that "they to whom is committed the stewardship of exceptional gifts, whether of rank, wealth, learning, or cleverness" were responsible to effect good, on this point he consistently argued that justice for working people was possible only if they could organize themselves in unions and negotiate with their employers as equals.[23] In this way, Potter's responsiveness to the sufferings of working people enabled him to adapt the religious traditions to the demands of the new situation. And by assisting in the institutionalization of this revised religious tradition in the Episcopal Church he helped to ensure its communication, however attenuated in subsequent decades, to succeeding generations.[24]

Theology and Practical Christianity

While Potter and many of his colleagues emphasized practical Christianity, their social gospel nevertheless entailed both explicit and implicit theological elements. White and Hopkins report that both contemporary and subsequent critics of the social gospel have charged that it was primarily a social rather than a religious movement, one that "coalesced more around action than belief." As they further observe, its "tendency to emphasize action culminated in the founding of the Federal Council of Churches in 1908. If there was any agreement by the various churches, it was on the famous Federal Council's 'Social Creed of the Churches' rather than on a more traditional theological creed." White and Hopkins do not, however, explain why a "tendency to emphasize action" is legitimate grounds for criticism, why such a tendency is necessarily symptomatic of the inferiority of such religious expressions to those that emphasize ideas.[25] Similarly, the neo-orthodox critique of the social gospel begun in the wake of World War I argued either that it had little or no theology or that what theology it had was faulty. Particularly problematic, on this view, were liberal theologians' optimistic assessment of the human capacity for good and its corollary neglect of the reality and power of evil. World War I and, later, the Great Depression and World War II were, to borrow Henry May's phrase, "unanswerable events" for the social gospel and its liberal theology in much the same way that the social and economic upheavals of the late nineteenth century were so for white American evangelicalism. Of course, neo-orthodox critics such as Karl Barth and Reinhold Niebuhr were as concerned as social gospelers with the practical, social implementation of Christian moral convictions; the aim of their critique was to correct the errors of theological liberalism in the interest of providing a more adequate theoretical framework for Christian action in the world. Nevertheless, because this critique tended to value faithful ideas more highly than faithful action and assumed that the latter would grow out of the former, it has led some scholars and church members to devalue all expressions of Christianity that value action more highly than ideas. In other words, the neo-orthodox emphasis on the ideational critique of the social gospel can function, and in some quarters has functioned, ideologically to delegitimize Christian social action. The relationship between thought and action, theory and practice, theology and social concern requires further consideration.[26]

Susan Lindley has observed that "when Walter Rauschenbusch asserted in 1917 that American Christianity had a social gospel and proposed to provide for it a theology—that is, systematic intellectual reflection—he sounded a distinctive note of the social gospel: practice and experience precede and are more consequential than theory."[27] Of course, the very distinction between theory and practice, ideas and actions is artificial. When Henry Codman Potter addressed an audience in a church or through an essay on temperance, he acted through the expression of his ideas, which in turn influenced the actions and ideas of others. Reciprocally, the experiences of Potter and others during the financial panic of 1873 caused them to reconsider prevailing ideas about the stewardship of wealth and methods of charity. As Lindley concludes,

> It is this critical relationship which suggests the concept of *praxis* as a fruitful approach to understanding a distinctive contribution of the social gospel in America. In one sense, the term is, of course, an anachronism; on the other hand, something similar to what liberation theologians point to in that concept was critical to the social gospel. . . . Historians have long since argued that personal, pastoral experience shaped the thought and careers of such social gospel giants as Washington Gladden and Walter Rauschenbusch, though it is perhaps worth emphasizing that experience is not a one-shot affair, that a continuing relationship of experience and theological reflection occurred: a kind of *praxis* in fact if not in name. Theology (in the sense of believed content) was not only to inspire action, it was shaped by the realities the Christian encountered in the world as he or she attempted to put faith into practice. For example, theological insights into the corporate and structural nature of sin affected social gospel critiques and participation in political and social causes, but the results and problems activist Christians met in turn reshaped their theological understandings. Walter Rauschenbusch's *A Theology for the Social Gospel* is the best-known and most systematic example of doctrine rethought in the light of social conditions and experiences, but the process and the theological results were not unique to him.[28]

If praxis, or lived faith, is central to the expression of religious convictions, then the social gospel's tendency to emphasize action is not a weakness but a strength, not a symptom of religious impoverishment but a sign that its practitioners have grasped the relationship between action and ideas in Christian life.

Recent historiography of the Episcopal Church in the nineteenth century also offers some insight on these matters. David Holmes suggests, for example, that the three defining movements in the church in the nineteenth century were focused not on theology but on worship, church unity, and social justice, and he therefore emphasizes these in his discussion of that period. And Robert Mullin maintains that by the second half of the century for the Episcopal Church, at least in its High Church and Anglo-Catholic expressions, "the worship tradition provided the continuity during the period of theological reorganization."[29] Their observations, the work of other historians, and the example of Henry Codman Potter suggest that in a period of theological reorganization—particularly one marked by widespread and sometimes severe human suffering and by challenges with far-reaching implications for deeply held assumptions—the relatively low priority of theological reflection need not be counted as an indication of religious inferiority, nor should this period in the life of the church be undervalued because theology was not its main focus. On the contrary, a concern for justice is, with worship and theology, among the enduring characteristics of Christianity that, while expressed in different ways in different contexts, may from time to time appropriately be more prominent than other characteristics.

It is therefore precisely because Potter's contribution was in the realm of practical Christianity that it is worth recovering, both for the importance of his contribution in itself and as a corrective to the idealist bias of much of today's Christian theology and ethics. Viewing Potter's work as a praxis, as a dynamically related complex of ideas and actions, illuminates how that work was composed of both theoretical and practical components and how these components were related in the larger complex. For Henry Codman Potter as for many of his predecessors and colleagues, the practical work of the church in mission and outreach preceded reflection on that work in theology and worship but functioned in dynamic relation to it. Reflecting in part the fruitlessness of decades of ecclesiastical partisanship in the Episcopal Church and in part an enduring element of Evangelicalism, Alonzo Potter had emphasized "Christianity as a *life*, not as a mere collection of dogmas" and maintained that faithfulness was best secured "by moral rather than by intellectual means, by proper culture and training in the duties of life, and in the hopes and services of religion, rather than through theological controversies." In addition, the Memorial Movement's emphasis on doing "the work of the Lord in this land and in this age" shifted the Episcopal Church's focus toward "preaching and dispensing the Gospel to all sorts and conditions" of people both inside and outside the church.[30]

Building on these foundations, the postwar Broad Church movement emphasized the practical work of the church, the tolerance of diverse theological beliefs and liturgical practices, and the vigorous pursuit of religious truth. Henry Codman Potter, a leading proponent and supporter of other proponents of the Broad Church movement, justified these emphases not only by pointing out the fruitlessness of ecclesiastical partisanship but also by acknowledging the limits to human understanding. "The moment that we have affirmed a truth we are bound to admit that there are, and rightly ought to be, various standpoints from which to look at it." Nevertheless, he maintained, "There is a divine doctrine, but let us take care that in defining it we do not make it narrower than Christ

Himself has made it! There is a divine order, but let us not seek only so inexorably to enforce it that, like those iron images of the middle ages, it shall crush the life out of the victim whom it embraces."[31]

Potter and other Broad Church proponents therefore insisted that the church should use its energies not for the definitive disposition of disputed ideas and rituals, but rather for the manifestation of God's saving love in concrete service to the poor, sick, and suffering. He did not neglect the doctrinal and ritual aspects of Christian life, but he valued them according to their usefulness in sustaining a life of service to others, which in turn witnessed to the truth of Christian beliefs and the efficacy of its worship. He affirmed that Jesus Christ had inaugurated a fellowship that ought to have a word of hope to all people oppressed by sorrow and want and argued therefore that it was the church's business "to take that word and carry it to men and translate it into deeds which they can not fail to understand. If this is not its business, then it has no business at all."[32]

Similarly, to the extent that Potter criticized contemporary religious and social theories, he evaluated them primarily according to their practical consequences for human well-being. He did so not because he regarded consistency with Christian doctrine as unimportant, but because he considered the enhancement of human well-being to be central to the teaching and example of Jesus Christ and, therefore, to the work of the church in the world. For Potter, the life and teaching of Jesus consisted of three key elements: the conviction of the fatherhood of God and brotherhood of humanity; the this-worldly character of the kingdom of God; and the moral principle of sacrificial love and selfless service. Commending Shailer Mathews's discussion of the Lord's Prayer in his *Social Teaching of Jesus*, Potter affirmed that "the relation binding men to God was a filial relation, and the relation of men to one another was a fraternal relation." He also argued that "thy kingdom come" means that "the kingdom of God . . . has its place in this realm and on our stage of being. On the earth as it is done in heaven cannot mean that the kingdom of God is an unrealizable thing for humanity in this world, and with our ennobled powers and faculties, or else the words that bid us pray for it are a grotesque and monstrous mockery."[33] Potter evaluated religious and social ideas, then, according to their tendency to produce either good or evil results for people. He professed the responsibility to "bear one another's burdens" and repudiated the social Darwinist ethic of leaving the weak to be crushed under the weight of those burdens; he defended women's right to labor for self-support and qualified the ideology of domesticity that limited their role to unpaid work in the home; he affirmed the val-

ue of labor and worker solidarity and rejected the political economic tenet of labor as a commodity; and he maintained that all economic activity was subject to moral evaluation and condemned the view that economic activity was governed only by its own inexorable laws. Potter's
practical engagement with the sufferings of people shaped his use of religious and social theory to work for the alleviation of such suffering.

Potter's attention to such suffering points to another aspect of the
relationship between theology and practical Christianity. Most of the
challenges faced by Potter and others in the second half of the nineteenth
century were produced by concrete human suffering—of recently eman-
cipated blacks who continued to be denied economic and political justice, many of whom faced persecution, torture, and lynching; of women
struggling under the burdens of an unrealistic ideology of domesticity or
of an exploitative sweating system; of unemployed and homeless wom-
en and children coerced into prostitution; of immigrants and other working people doomed to labor for meager wages in unhealthy and dangerous factories and mines, to unemployment according to the inexorable
laws of supply and demand, and to living in cramped homes without
adequate food, light, ventilation, sanitation, or recreation. As Potter and
others in this period shifted their strategies from outreach to the poor for
the sake of evangelizing them to programs, services, and organizations
to alleviate suffering and eliminate at least some of its causes, they effected a shift in the drive to Christianize America from the salvation of
individual persons to the transformation of the whole socioeconomic
order.

Implicit in this shift, and reflecting the optimistic faith of the postmillennialism of moderate evangelicals, is the conviction that redemption consists not simply in God's gracious forgiveness of our sins and
empowerment of us to avoid sin, but also in our concrete alleviation and
elimination of the sufferings of others—whether that suffering is a result
of their enslavement to their own sinfulness or their enslavement in a
socioeconomic order that systematically exploits their labor and their
lives. Potter and others also argued, both implicitly in their practical
activity and sometimes explicitly in their theoretical work, that Jesus'
salvific work included not only his death but also his teaching and his
activity or earthly ministry. This understanding of the saving significance
of Jesus, combined with their understanding that the church is commis-
sioned to carry on Jesus' redemptive work in the world, led them to develop ministries of care for the sick and the hungry, the underpaid and
the unemployed, the exploited and victimized, the outcast and the alien-

ated. Knowledge of God, then, consisted not in assenting to doctrines or precepts, but in experiencing human suffering and acting to alleviate it.

> I wonder if those who would so sharply confine the Church and the ministry to certain official and ceremonial functions, have ever read the New Testament. We may take the ministry of Christ, I suppose, as at once a prophecy and pattern of what the work and ministry of the Church should be to-day. But Christ did not merely preach the Sermon on the Mount and die on the cross. There was no disease so loathsome that He did not put forth His hand to touch it. There was no home that He went into, whether it was the home of that Pharisee whose dirty inhospitality He gently rebuked for giving Him no water wherewith to wash His feet, or the home of Simon's wife's mother, which He did not leave until He had expelled the fever which poisoned it and her;—there was no home, I say, which Christ entered, so far as we have any account of His ministry, which He did not leave, both physically and morally, sweeter and decenter and purer because He had entered it. And what He did, to the lame and the blind and the halt and the leper and the impure and the morally vile, I suppose that you and I who profess to be, in one sense or another, His baptized disciples, may wisely be concerned about doing also![34]

The later neo-orthodox criticism of the liberal social gospel's understanding of sin was substantially correct about its underestimation of the power of evil and overestimation of human ability to overcome it, but it missed the point that for social gospelers salvation is concerned with suffering as well as sin. A more complete assessment of the theological significance of the social gospel requires an evaluation of its broader understanding of soteriology, of which sin is but one part and in which the alleviation of suffering in central. Because explicit theological statements by Potter and some other social gospelers were brief and largely confined to sermons, addresses, and church reports, this implication of social gospel praxis is easily missed or misunderstood. Further, even most social gospelers seem to have been less than fully aware of this implication of their work. In his *Theology for the Social Gospel,* widely regarded as the most fully developed articulation of the theological framework of the social gospel, Walter Rauschenbusch defined salvation primarily in terms of salvation from sin.

> The new thing in the social gospel is the clearness and insistence with which it sets forth the necessity and the possibility of redeeming the historical life of humanity from the social wrongs which now pervade it and which act as temptations and incitements to evil and as forces of resistance to the powers of redemption. Its chief interest is concentrat-

ed on those manifestations of sin and redemption which lie beyond the individual soul. . . . Yet the salvation of the individual is, of course, an essential part of salvation.[35]

Certainly Rauschenbusch's reference to "redeeming the historical life of humanity from the social wrongs which now pervade it" suggests a concern for concrete human suffering, but his effort to provide "a systematic theology large enough to back" the social gospel seems to have been constrained by the definition of the basic problem from which God saves humanity dominant in Western Christianity, namely, sin. Rauschenbusch properly emphasized the need to overcome the dualism between the individual and the social but neglected the equally problematic dualism between the spiritual and the material. Broader social gospel praxis, however, suggests that sin is not the only religious problem with which Christianity is to be concerned. As important as suffering under sin is suffering under injustice and oppression, and not simply because such suffering makes evangelization difficult. Although they may not have made this point explicitly or articulated it fully, the praxis of Henry Potter and other social gospelers demonstrates their recognition that "good news to the poor" entailed more than just the forgiveness of sins and release from sinfulness, that Christianity is for "the whole of this life."

Beyond socializing the Christian understanding of sin, then, social gospel praxis also implied the *embodying* of the Christian understanding of salvation. In other words, in addition to drawing attention to, in Rauschenbusch's words, "super-personal" as well as personal sin, social gospel praxis also entailed alleviation of physical as well as spiritual suffering. In his memorial sermon after Potter's death, William Reed Huntington addressed this point while discussing Potter's early work at Grace Church:

> Those were the days when the methods of what it is the fashion to call "the institutional church" were just beginning to loom about the ecclesiastical horizon. Really, "the institutional church" is nothing in the world but a church which is trying to help the neighborhood in the midst of which it finds itself planted in just the sorts of ways in which Jesus Christ helped people when He was here among us. There is no blinking the fact that He cared for men's bodies as well as for their souls, that sympathy was the mainspring of his ministry, and that above all He sought to convince those among whom He moved that He was in very deed and truth their friend. If such was Christ, should not his Church be such? You remember that, after He had washed the disciples' feet, He said to them, . . . "For I have given you an example, that ye should do as I have done to you." That narrative is the perpetual justification of "the

institutional church." The words give an emphatic sanction to efforts to relate religion as we have received it to the needs and the demands of contemporary life.[36]

The institutional church and other elements of social gospel praxis, motivated by the concern to alleviate suffering and wherever possible eliminate its causes, effected in practice both the socializing and the embodying of soteriology. That Potter's practical work was addressed to the alleviation of suffering suggests that it may also be further specified as emancipatory practice. As defined by Beverly Harrison, "Emancipatory practice is precisely an ongoing struggle against structures of oppression and toward realization of the conditions for alternative social relations that enable nonexploitative relations to occur." For liberation theologians, Harrison notes, "only a praxis aimed at emancipation can yield 'truthful' theological interpretations and vision."[37] Again, while in this context the term is somewhat anachronistic, the idea of emancipatory practice helps to illuminate the work of Potter and other social gospelers not only because they emphasized practical activity focused on the alleviation and eradication of suffering, but also because they took such activity as the measure of the veracity of their faith.

Potter himself pointed in this direction when he acknowledged that some religious people "do not hesitate to maintain that religion has nothing whatever to do with the social conditions of human life, unless it be to teach men to look forward to an existence when they and their fellows shall be delivered from them; and, meanwhile, to cultivate such patience and resignation as they may." Against such a view, he argued that "you and I must be able, in the face of all that confronts us in these problems, social, economic, and industrial, to show that religion has some warrant for being concerned with them, and that, in the great task of their solution, we may not, must not, withhold our hands." In addition, he maintained that the application of Christianity to social problems was essential for their resolution. For this task Potter drew on Jesus' crucifixion, understanding it primarily as a model of sacrificial love to be emulated in our responses to others' needs, as well as on the teaching and activity of Jesus, urging that they be brought to bear "upon all those [relationships] in which human society is bound together. It is the divorce of that life and teaching from the life of today, the social problems of to-day, the capitalist and working man of to-day, of which we are most of all in danger."[38]

Henry Codman Potter therefore insisted that Christianity was to be comprehensively concerned with *all* aspects of human life. As he maintained in an 1870 sermon at Grace Church, the mission of the church must have "something to say to the bodies of those whom it would fain care for, as well as their souls; something to *do* for their physical and intellectual pains and hungers, as well as for that other and deeper hunger of the soul for the Bread of Life. No truly Christian endeavor can leave these physical and intellectual wants out of account; Christ never did; His Church may never dare to." Twelve years later, he reiterated that such a mission was neither optional nor secondary in the church's work: "Our Christianity must prove itself the helpful and saving power that it claims to be, or else it must get out of the way."[39] Throughout his work, Henry Codman Potter attempted to prove just that. This commitment grounded his various efforts to alleviate people's sufferings as well as his insistence that all aspects of human endeavor are subject to the reign of God. He expressed this comprehensive concern for all things human in a religious and moral praxis that was a work for a whole life.

NOTES

Introduction

1. Ronald C. White Jr. and C. Howard Hopkins, *The Social Gospel: Religion and Reform in Changing America* (Philadelphia: Temple University Press, 1976), xi–xix; William G. McLoughlin, *Revivals, Awakenings, and Reform: An Essay on Religion and Social Change in America, 1607–1977* (Chicago: University of Chicago Press, 1978), 1–44, 141–78.

2. Walter Rauschenbusch, *Christianizing the Social Order* (New York: Macmillan, 1913), 9–22.

3. *Churchman*, 8 March 1884, 262, *New York Sun*, 1894, and *Hammer and Pen* (September 1905) quoted by Clyde Griffen, "An Urban Church in Ferment: The Episcopal Church in New York City, 1880–1900" (Ph.D. diss., Columbia University, 1960), 56 and 76; Henry F. May, *Protestant Churches and Industrial America* (New York: Harper and Row, 1963), 182.

4. On the origins of CAIL, see Harriette Keyser, *Bishop Potter, the People's Friend* (New York: Thomas Whittaker, 1910), 18–21; Griffen, "Urban Church in Ferment," 390–415; Spencer Miller Jr. and Joseph F. Fletcher, *The Church and Industry* (New York: Longmans, Green, 1930), 52–76; and C. Howard Hopkins, *The Rise of the Social Gospel in American Protestantism, 1865–1915* (New Haven, Conn.: Yale University Press, 1961), 150–52. On HCP's 1886 pastoral letter, see Keyser, *Bishop Potter*, 21–26; and White and Hopkins, *Social Gospel*, 63–65, for a portion of the letter. On the Joint Commission on the Relations of Capital and Labor and diocesan social service commissions, see *The Journal of the Bishops, Clergy, and Laity Assembled in General Convention, 1901* (printed for the convention, 1902), 125–26; *Journal of the General Convention of the Protestant Episcopal Church in the United States of America, 1904* (printed for the convention, 1905), 95–98 [hereafter cited as *General Convention Journal*]; *General Convention Journal 1907*, 528; and *General Convention Journal 1910*, 110, 177, 534. See also Keyser, *Bishop Potter*, 140–49, 155–61; *New York Times*, 20 October 1904, 6; *Hammer and Pen*, 6.11 (November 1904): 90–91; and *National Civic Federation Review* 1 (15 November 1904): 1, 14.

5. James Sheerin, *Henry Codman Potter: An American Metropolitan* (New York: Fleming H. Revell, 1933), x. C. H. Hopkins, *Rise of the Social Gospel*, 35, 93, 102, 150–52, notes that in the late 1870s "the sensitive social conscience of Henry Codman Potter" led him "to preach on the perils of wealth, indifference to social need, the duties of citizenship, children in the slums, the tenement problem, and kindred topics growing out of his parish work." He also maintains that HCP's work on the conflict between labor and capital was particularly important, both because of his 1886 pastoral letter and his role in CAIL. Similarly, May, *Protestant Churches*, 132–35, notes the importance of HCP's letter, calling it "Perhaps the most striking Social Gospel reaction to

the dramatic events of 1886" largely because it was "a repudiation of the standard economic view of labor as a commodity, a theory that had been pronounced by clerical authorities consistently since of the time of Potter's father." May, *Protestant Churches*, 178–79, also cites HCP's response to Andrew Carnegie's 1889 essay, "Wealth." Aaron I. Abell, *The Urban Impact on American Protestantism* (Hamden, Conn.: Archon, 1962), 55, 113, 183–84, likewise notes HCP's significance. White and Hopkins, *Social Gospel*, 63–65, include HCP's 1886 pastoral letter in their anthology of social gospel texts; Ronald C. White Jr., *Liberty and Justice for All: Racial Reform and the Social Gospel (1877–1925)* (San Francisco: Harper and Row, 1990), 21–23, 211–12, 262, discusses HCP's work with the American Colonization Society in the context of the social gospel and racial reform; McLoughlin, *Revivals, Awakenings, and Reform*, 174, includes HCP among the moderates who were "probably the best-known Social Gospelers"; Donald K. Gorrell, *The Age of Social Responsibility: The Social Gospel in the Progressive Era, 1900–1920* (Macon, Ga.: Mercer University Press, 1988), 15, lists HCP first among those who "continuously challenged [the Episcopal Church] to social activity"; and Bernard Kent Markwell, *The Anglican Left: Radical Reformers in the Church of England and the Protestant Episcopal Church, 1846–1954*, Chicago Studies in the History of American Religion (Brooklyn, N.Y.: Carlson, 1991), 99, 100, 111, 132, cites HCP as a moderate reformer compared to radical Episcopalians J. O. S. Huntington, W. D. P. Bliss, and Vida Scudder. (Note, however, that Markwell's index incorrectly identifies HCP's father, Alonzo Potter, as the subject of these four references.) The only critical evaluation of HCP's work of any depth is provided by Griffen, "Urban Church in Ferment," 346–89, who examines both the ecclesial and the socioeconomic context for the activities of HCP and his colleagues in the diocese of New York, but Griffen does not treat in detail HCP's work prior to his election as assistant bishop in 1883.

6. Allen C. Guelzo, *For the Union of Evangelical Christendom: The Irony of the Reformed Episcopalians* (University Park: Pennsylvania State University Press, 1994), 48–49; David L. Holmes, *A Brief History of the Episcopal Church* (Valley Forge, Pa.: Trinity Press International, 1993), 118, 120, 128, 147; Robert Bruce Mullin, *Episcopal Vision/American Reality: High Church Theology and Social Thought in Evangelical America* (New Haven, Conn.: Yale University Press, 1986), 204–5; and Alvin W. Skardon, *Church Leader in the Cities: William Augustus Muhlenberg* (Philadelphia: University of Pennsylvania Press, 1971), 250, 265. Diana Hochstedt Butler, *Standing against the Whirlwind: Evangelical Episcopalians in Nineteenth-Century America* (New York: Oxford University Press, 1995), discusses the relation of Episcopal Evangelicalism with the rise of the Broad Church movement and the extent to which the children of Evangelicalism became Broad Church proponents, but she does not include the Evangelical Alonzo Potter, bishop of Pennsylvania, and his Broad Church son Henry Codman Potter among her examples.

7. Unfortunately for those wishing to recover the memory of Potter's work, Potter himself hindered that task by destroying his personal papers. In his preface to *Henry Codman Potter*, ix–x, Sheerin notes: "A recent letter from one of the Bishop's daughters, deprecates writing any life of her father, which she describes as 'an impossible task since my father had destroyed all the material which was needed to write a satisfactory one. Dean [George] Hodges had to rely on newspaper files for much of his information, and, though he did the very best he could, and with wonderful devotion to his task, we have sometimes since felt that we ought never to have undertaken it. . . . My father deplored publicity and really did not want his life written. He had to suffer from much personal adulation, and he hated it. His real self was the servant of his Master. Before he died I think that is all he wished to remember, or to have remem-

bered about him. But I grant you that there is great value and help to be gained from reading the lives of those who have been such servants, even of those whose ideal was such while feeling that they had fallen far short of it.'" Fortunately, however, almost all Potter's published writings are available. They include numerous sermons and addresses, most of which have been collected in books, and various articles and letters. The archives of the Episcopal Diocese of New York and of Grace Church, New York, also contain much useful unpublished material. The latter resource is especially important, for it records both Potter's activities and his theoretical reflections on them during his tenure as rector of Grace Church. Similarly important are Potter's "Detailed Account of Visitations and Acts" and his Bishop's Address to the diocesan conventions, both of which were published annually in the *Journal of the Proceedings of the Annual Convention of the Protestant Episcopal Church in the Diocese of New York* (cited hereafter as *New York Convention Proceedings*). Evidence of Potter's activities also exists in the contemporary records or accounts of organizations in whose work he participated, including various publications of the Charity Organization Society; *Hammer and Pen*, the journal of the Church Association for the Advancement of the Interests of Labor; and the *National Civic Federation Review*. The Episcopal journal, *The Churchman*, and the *New York Times* also contain much useful information. Three biographies of Potter, all of which were published within twenty-five years of his death in 1908, are also essential resources. Like many biographies of leading women and men of the period, these works belong more to the genre of hagiography than to that of critical scholarship; nevertheless, they form a central part of the record. Keyser's *Bishop Potter* was published in 1910. Keyser was for several years the secretary and organizer of CAIL, and her book is primarily a record of Potter's participation in its activities and includes extensive quotations from his sermons, addresses, and letters. George Hodges's *Henry Codman Potter, Seventh Bishop of New York* (New York: Macmillan, 1915), is the "authorized" biography, written at the request of Potter's family. Hodges, then dean of the Episcopal Theological Seminary in Cambridge and himself a leading progressive Episcopalian, provides the most comprehensive account of Potter's life and work. Sheerin intended his 1933 *Henry Codman Potter* "to set before a new generation a great and glowing religious personality," emphasizing the "social movements" of which he was a part.

8. For example, Butler, *Standing against the Whirlwind*, vii–viii, and Guelzo, *Evangelical Christendom*, 1–5.

9. White and Hopkins, *Social Gospel*, xvi–xix.

10. May, *Protestant Churches*, 3–160; Abell, *Urban Impact*, 3–26, 57–87; James M. McPherson, *Battle Cry of Freedom: The Civil War Era* (New York: Oxford University Press, 1988); Philip S. Foner, *History of the Labor Movement in the United States*, vols. 1–4 (New York: International Press, 1947–65); James T. Kloppenberg, *Uncertain Victory: Social Democracy and Progressivism in European and American Thought, 1870–1920* (New York: Oxford University Press, 1986).

11. McLoughlin, *Revivals, Awakenings, and Reform*, 1–178; May, *Protestant Churches*, 3–87, 163–265; Robert T. Handy, ed., *The Social Gospel in America, 1870–1920* (New York: Oxford University Press, 1966), 3–16, and Handy, *A History of the Churches in the United States and Canada* (New York: Oxford University Press, 1979), 162–227, 262–311; Sydney E. Ahlstrom, *A Religious History of the American People*, vol. 2 (Garden City, N.Y.: Image Books, 1975), 79–363; Janet F. Fishburn, *The Fatherhood of God and the Victorian Family: The Social Gospel in America* (Philadelphia: Fortress Press, 1981); C. G. Brown, "Christocentric Liberalism in the Episcopal Church," *Historical Magazine of the Protestant Episcopal Church* 37 (1968): 5–38.

12. Griffen, "Urban Church in Ferment," 1–345; James Thayer Addison, *The Epis-

copal Church in the United States, 1789–1931 (New York: Charles Scribner's Sons, 1951), 126–354; Raymond W. Albright, *A History of the Protestant Episcopal Church* (New York: Macmillan, 1964), 161–340; James Elliott Lindsley, *This Planted Vine: A Narrative History of the Episcopal Diocese of New York* (New York: Harper and Row, 1984), 102–204.

13. Hodges, *Henry Codman Potter*, 2–4; Frank Hunter Potter, *The Alonzo Potter Family* (Concord, N.H.: Rumford Press, 1923), 1–3. In relating HCP's ancestry, I do not assume that the men are more significant than the women, but, as women were largely confined to the home and their contribution there undervalued, the extant records offer little information about them. As F. H. Potter, HCP's youngest brother, said of their father's three wives (Sarah Nott, Sarah Benedict, and Frances Seton), *Alonzo Potter Family*, 11: "I wish I could tell you more about these three women, but the family traditions . . . dwell chiefly upon the men of the tribe." On the historiography of women, see Linda Gordon, Persis Hunt, Elizabeth Pleck, Rochelle Goldberg Ruthchild, and Marcia Scott, "Historical Phallacies: Sexism in American Historical Writing," 55–74, and Ann D. Gordon, Mari Jo Buhle, and Nancy Schrom Dye, "The Problem of Women's History," 75–92, both in *Liberating Women's History: Theoretical and Critical Essays*, ed. Berenice Carroll (Urbana: University of Illinois Press, 1976).

14. Hodges, *Henry Codman Potter*, 1, 5–7; F. H. Potter, *Alonzo Potter Family*, 4–5.

15. Guelzo, *Evangelical Christendom*, 25–32. Cf. Holmes, *Brief History*, 51–58.

16. Hodges, *Henry Codman Potter*, 10–13; F. H. Potter, *Alonzo Potter Family*, 9–10; Sheerin, *Henry Codman Potter*, 17–20; Addison, *Episcopal Church*, 170–76.

17. Skardon, *Church Leader*, 207–36; Butler, *Standing against the Whirlwind*, 140–41; Holmes, *Brief History*, 125, 148; Guelzo, *Evangelical Christendom*, 62–67.

18. F. H. Potter, *Alonzo Potter Family*, 10–11.

19. William Reed Huntington, "Henry Codman Potter, Rector, Bishop: In Remembrance," sermon preached in Grace Church, New York, 25 October 1908 (New York: printed at the request of the vestry, n.d.), 13. The similarities and differences between father and son provide a useful way to describe the transition in the Episcopal Church from antebellum moderate Evangelicalism to the postwar Broad Church movement, but it is no artificial construct. The influence of Alonzo Potter on his son illustrates the observation by historians of American Protestantism, expressed by White and Hopkins, *Social Gospel*, xiv, summarizing the view of Handy in his Introduction to *Social Gospel* and Handy, *A Christian America: Protestant Hopes and Historical Realities*, 2d ed. (New York: Oxford University Press, 1984), that "the period 1830–1930 can best be understood as a more or less continuous attempt by American Protestantism to 'Christianize America' first through revivalism and then through the social gospel." Huntington's observation also points not only to the influence of nineteenth-century Episcopal clerical fathers on their clerical sons (the Tyngs, Newtons, and Huntingtons, for example, as well as the Potters), but also to the extent to which, as noted by Butler, *Standing against the Whirlwind*, 23–33, the children of moderate Evangelicals in the last decades of the nineteenth century became members of the Broad Church movement.

20. HCP, "Scholarship and Service," in *The Scholar and the State* (New York: Century, 1897), 92–93. Cf. HCP, "The Witness of Our Fathers: A Sermon Preached at the Consecration of St. Mary's Memorial Church, Wayne, Pa., April 17, 1890" (New York: De Vinne Press, 1890), 15–17, 20–21; and HCP, "Mission and Commission," in HCP, *Waymarks, 1870–1891, Being Discourses with Some Account of Their Occasions* (New York: E. P. Dutton, 1892), 381–82; see also Sheerin, *Henry Codman Potter*, 100–103.

21. Lindsley, *This Planted Vine*, 146–64, 176; Mullin, *Episcopal Vision*, 163–65;

George E. DeMille, "The Episcopate of Horatio Potter (1802–1887), Sixth Bishop of New York, 1854–1887," *Historical Magazine of the Protestant Episcopal Church* 24 (March 1955): 68–69.

22. Lindsley, *This Planted Vine*, 176–204; DeMille, "Horatio Potter," 66–92; Guelzo, *Evangelical Christendom*, 70–73, 152–53; Skardon, *Church Leader*, 135–37, 202; Butler, *Standing against the Whirlwind*, 208–11; Albright, *History*, 307; Paul V. Marshall, "William Augustus Muhlenberg's Quiet Defection from Liturgical Uniformity," *Anglican and Episcopal History* 64 (1995): 156; Sheerin, *Henry Codman Potter*, 40–41, who quotes Horatio Potter's remarks on the Church Congress from his letter to HCP, 307.

23. Hodges, *Henry Codman Potter*, 14–15, 21–22, 24; F. H. Potter, *Alonzo Potter Family*, 31–32, Sheerin, *Henry Codman Potter*, 18–20, Griffen, "Urban Church in Ferment," 240, n. 3.

24. Hodges, *Henry Codman Potter*, 22–24. Cf. F. H. Potter, *Alonzo Potter Family*, 42, and Sheerin, *Henry Codman Potter*, 20–21. The work of Clara Boyd Jacobs at Spring Grove and her role in HCP's conversion perhaps bears out the observation of Leonard I. Sweet, *The Minister's Wife* (Philadelphia: Temple University Press, 1983), 6: "The Evangelical religious gestalt . . . defined women as responsible for conversion and permitted them to operate the machinery of evangelism."

25. For an account of Brooks's seminary experience, see John F. Woolverton, *The Education of Phillips Brooks*, Studies in Anglican History (Urbana: University of Illinois Press, 1995), 66–79. Alonzo Potter's view of the Fugitive Slave Law is quoted from an undated letter to the unidentified rector of a Washington, D.C., church by M. A. DeWolfe Howe, *Memoirs of the Life and Services of the Rt. Rev. Alonzo Potter, D.D., LL.D., Bishop of the Protestant Episcopal Church in the Diocese of Pennsylvania* (Philadelphia: J. B. Lippincott, 1871), 237. Cf. Hodges, *Henry Codman Potter*, 19–21, 24–33.

26. Hodges, *Henry Codman Potter*, 33, 36.

27. M. A. D. Howe, *Memoirs*, 230; Hodges, *Henry Codman Potter*, 38–39. The little evidence available suggests that Eliza Jacobs Potter's work may correspond to the "assistant" model described by Sweet, *Minister's Wife*, 7–9, 76–106.

28. Hodges, *Henry Codman Potter*, 340; F. H. Potter, *Alonzo Potter Family*, 31–44.

29. Hodges, *Henry Codman Potter*, 50.

30. HCP, *Reminiscences of Bishops and Archbishops* (New York: G. P. Putnam's Sons, 1906), 4–6.

31. HCP, "Individual Responsibility to the Nation: A Sermon Preached in Trinity Church, Boston, on Thanksgiving Day, November 29, 1866" (Boston: E. P. Dutton, 1867); Hodges, *Henry Codman Potter*, 63–64, 66–67; Sheerin, *Henry Codman Potter*, 24–26.

32. Hodges, *Henry Codman Potter*, 68–70; HCP, "Three Score Years and Ten: A Sermon Preached in Grace Church, New York, in Commemoration of Its Seventieth Anniversary" (New York: Vestry of Grace Church, 1878), 9–12, 29; HCP, "A Consecration Sermon," in *Waymarks*, 314–15; Hodges, *Henry Codman Potter*, 94–95; *Annual Report of the Various Departments of Parish Work of Grace Parish* (New York: Grace Parish, 1883) [hereafter *Annual Parish Report*]. The work of the parish organizations is recorded in these annual reports, begun in 1869 and continuing throughout Potter's tenure; a complete set is held at the archives of Grace Church, New York. These reports are essential for an understanding of HCP's ministry at Grace, for they document the needs deemed important, the programs formed to meet those needs, and, especially in HCP's annual introductory remarks, the theological and ethical rationale

for this work. As HCP noted in the 1882 annual report, 5, "A Parish Report . . . is a witness as to what those who make it understand by the Christian religion and the Christian life."

33. HCP, "The Perils of Wealth," in *Sermons of the City* (New York: E. P. Dutton, 1881), 84–87. Cf. HCP, "The Citizen's Twofold Stewardship," "The Impotence of Money," and "Cost and Beauty in Christian Worship," in ibid., 39–43, 246–47, and 295–308; HCP, "Sermon Commemorative of John David Wolfe" and "Sermon Commemorative of Adam Norrie," in *Waymarks*, 79–85 and 93–95; HCP, "The Relations of Science to Modern Life," in *Scholar and the State*, 140–42; and *Annual Parish Report 1883*, 7.

34. *Annual Parish Report 1874*, 6–9. Cf. *Annual Parish Report 1873*, 4–7; HCP, "Institutionalism: Its Dangers and Failures" and "One Another's Burdens" in *Sermons of the City*, 142–61, 220–33.

35. *Annual Parish Report 1882*, 7. Cf. *Annual Parish Report 1881*, 6–7.

36. HCP, "The Homes of the Poor," "The Slaughter of the Innocents," and "The Duty of Woman to Women," in *Sermons of the City*, 48–65, 96–110, and 125–41; HCP, "A Plea for the American Sunday," in *Waymarks*, 98–116 (all later citations to this sermon are to the *Waymarks* version, which is identical to the original published as "A Plea for the American Sunday; a Sermon, Preached at the Request of the New York Sabbath Committee, in Grace Church, New York, Sunday, May 19, 1878" [New York: New York Sabbath Committee, 1878]); HCP, "Some Ways of Strengthening and Extending the Total Abstinence Movement" (New York: National Temperance Society and Publication House, 1878); HCP, "Christianity and the Criminal," in *Scholar and the State*, 163–79; White, *Liberty and Justice*, 21–22; Anthony Jackson, *A Place Called Home: A History of Low-Cost Housing in Manhattan* (Cambridge, Mass.: MIT Press, 1976), 45–46; State Charities Aid Association, *Report of the Special Committee Appointed to Take Active Measures in Regard to the Erection of a New Bellevue Hospital* (New York: American Church Press, 1874); *Third Annual Report* (New York: State Charities Aid Association, 1875), 5–7, 47–49; *Report on Conference of Members of the State Charities Aid Association of December, 1880* (New York: G. P. Putnam's Sons, 1881), 3, 38, 57–59.

37. *The Election and Consecration of the Rev. Henry Codman Potter, D.D., LL.D., As Assistant Bishop of the Diocese of New York* (New York: James Pott, 1883), 5–19; Hodges, *Henry Codman Potter*, 123–29; Sheerin, *Henry Codman Potter*, 45; Griffen, "Urban Church in Ferment," 348–49.

38. Hodges, *Henry Codman Potter*, 146–65, 183–91; Sheerin, *Henry Codman Potter*, 79–80; Lindsley, *This Planted Vine*, 211–14; *Churchman*, 23 May 1885, 563.

39. *Churchman*, 22 May 1886, 565. See also Keyser, *Bishop Potter*, 21–26; *New York Times*, 14 May 1886, 3 (report and reprint of letter), and 15 May 1886, 4, and 16 May 1886, 8 (editorials); Charles F. Deems, ed., *Christian Thought: Lectures and Papers on Philosophy, Christian Evidence, Biblical Elucidation*, 4th ser. (New York: Wilbur B. Ketcham, 1886), 289–91, for a portion of the letter; and White and Hopkins, *Social Gospel*, 63–65, for the same portion. The letter has come to be known as "The Laborer Not a Commodity," but of the contemporary sources of its publication only the version in Deems bears that title. Presumably, as a letter it would have received no title from HCP, and the title given to it in Deems seems to have been adopted by subsequent scholarship. White and Hopkins cite Deems as their source, as does C. H. Hopkins, *Rise of the Social Gospel*, 90, 93, 113. See also May, *Protestant Churches*, 179, and *Churchman*, 29 May 1886, 593–94, for sermons of W. F. Morgan and R. Heber Newton, and *Churchman*, 5 June 1886, 621, 705–6, for those of Henry Y. Satterlee

and W. S. Rainsford. See also Griffen, "Urban Church in Ferment," 65–66, 287–88; Keyser, *Bishop Potter*, 21; and *Hammer and Pen*, special number (November 1908): 1–2. CAIL's journal *Hammer and Pen* and Keyser's book are the primary sources for CAIL's history and activities; useful secondary sources are Miller and Fletcher, *Church and Industry*, 52–76; and Griffen, "Urban Church in Ferment," 390–415. See also C. H. Hopkins, *Rise of the Social Gospel*, 150–52.

40. HCP, "Bishop's Address," in *New York Convention Proceedings, 1887*, 108, 114, 117; *New York Convention Proceedings, 1888*, 118–19, 121, 126; *New York Convention Proceedings, 1889*, 98, 100; *New York Convention Proceedings, 1893*, 104.

41. *New York Times*, 1 May 1889, 4, and 2 May 1989, 4; Hodges, *Henry Codman Potter*, 234–39; Sheerin, *Henry Codman Potter*, 45–57; Griffen, "Urban Church in Ferment," 362–67.

42. HCP, "The Gospel for Wealth," in *Scholar and the State*, 238; for his address at the dedication of Carnegie Hall, see "The Ministry of Music," in ibid., 215–30. On his remarks to the chamber of commerce, see *New York Times*, 18 November 1891, 2. For Carnegie's essay, see Andrew Carnegie, *The Gospel of Wealth, and Other Timely Essays*, ed. Edward C. Kirkland (Cambridge, Mass.: Belknap Press, 1962), 14–49. On HCP, the Century Association, and New York's social clubs and their membership patterns, see Hodges, *Henry Codman Potter*, 286; Griffen, "Urban Church in Ferment," 351–52; and David C. Hammack, *Power and Society: Greater New York at the Turn of the Century* (New York: Russell Sage Foundation, 1982), 72–76.

43. Keyser, *Bishop Potter*, 51–55; Griffen, "Urban Church in Ferment," 399–401. For dates of HCP's mediation sessions, see *New York Convention Proceedings 1895*, 95; *New York Convention Proceedings 1896*, 113, 118, 120; and *New York Convention Proceedings 1897*, 112, 114. Also in 1894, HCP discussed the role of the clergy in social problems in his address to the diocesan convention; see *New York Convention Proceedings 1894*, 129–33, and an editorial in the *New York Times*, 28 September 1894, 4.

44. HCP, "The Significance of the American Cathedral," in *Scholar and the State*, 321–35. White, *Liberty and Justice*, 21–23; *New York Convention Proceedings 1893*, 104; *New York Convention Proceedings 1894*, 96; *New York Convention Proceedings 1895*, 100; *New York Convention Proceedings 1896*, 114.

45. *New York Convention Proceedings 1893*, 99, 103, 110; *New York Convention Proceedings 1894*, 96; *New York Convention Proceedings 1895*, 98, 109–10; *New York Times*, 30 November 1894, 4, 11 July 1895, 9, 12 July 1895, 8, and 3 November 1895, 4; Hodges, *Henry Codman Potter*, 278–85; Griffen, "Urban Church in Ferment," 385–87.

46. *New York Convention Proceedings 1896*, 112, 115–16, 120; *New York Convention Proceedings 1898*, 108, 110; *New York Convention Proceedings 1899*, 101, 103; *New York Times*, 26 September 1896, 10, 17 November 1898, 2, and 21 December 1898, 7; Griffen, "Urban Church in Ferment," 101–2; Hammack, *Power and Society*, 77–78, 142–44.

47. *New York Times*, 24 December 1895, 4; *New York Convention Proceedings 1897*, 107, 112.

48. *General Convention Journal 1898*, 19, 26, 135, 138; *New York Convention Proceedings 1899*, 102; *New York Convention Proceedings 1900*, 99–100; *New York Times*, 23 January 1899, 1, 11 October 1899, 7, 19 December 1899, 8, 27 March 1900, 6, 2 May 1900, 2, and 16 November 1900, 2; Hodges, *Henry Codman Potter*, 313–25; Sheerin, *Henry Codman Potter*, 53–54; Griffen, "Urban Church in Ferment," 379–85. For HCP's

revised view, see his "Problem of the Philippines," originally published in *Century Magazine*, November 1900, republished in HCP's *East of To-day and To-morrow* (New York: Century, 1902), 41–69; all subsequent references are to the latter version.

49. For the text of HCP's letter to Mayor Van Wyck, see *New York Convention Proceedings 1901*, 119–21; "Letter to Mayor Van Wyck," *Outlook* 66 (24 November 1900): 732–33; Hodges, *Henry Codman Potter*, 328–31; and *New York Times*, 17 November 1900, 1, under the headline "Police Uphold a Reign of Vice." On his subsequent sermon, see HCP, *God and the City*, 2d ed. (New York: Abbey Press, 1900); on his remarks to the 1901 diocesan convention, see *New York Convention Proceedings 1901*, 118–21; and *New York Times*, 28 September 1901, 8. See also *New York Times*, 17 November 1900, 2, 19 November 1900, 2, 20 November 1900, 1, 21 November 1900, 2, 3 December 1900, 3, 5 January 1901, 1, 13 January 1901, 1, 15 January 1901, 1, 24 January 1901, 2, and 21 October 1901, 1. On the aftermath of Potter's letter, see *New York Times*, 29 September 1900, 9; *New York Convention Proceedings 1900*, 84; *Churchman*, 6 October 1900, 1; Hodges, *Henry Codman Potter*, 326–38; Keyser, *Bishop Potter*, 129–38; Sheerin, *Henry Codman Potter*, 57–61; Hammack, *Power and Society*, 154–55; and Jackson, *Place Called Home*, 124–25.

50. *New York Times*, 21 October 1901, 1; *New York Convention Proceedings 1901*, 127, and *New York Convention Proceedings 1902*, 118; People's Institute of New York, *Memorial to Henry Codman Potter by the People's Institute, Cooper Union, Sunday, December 20, 1908* (New York: Cheltenham Press, 1909), 60–67.

51. Hodges, *Henry Codman Potter*, 339–40; *New York Times*, 3 July 1901, 7.

52. Hodges, *Henry Codman Potter*, 353; Sheerin, *Henry Codman Potter*, 169–70.

53. HCP, "Some Ways of Strengthening" and "The Drink Problem in Modern Life" (New York: Thomas Y. Crowell, 1905); F. H. Potter, *Alonzo Potter Family*, 40; Hodges, *Henry Codman Potter*, 365–70; Sheerin, *Henry Codman Potter*, 110–13; *New York Convention Proceedings 1899*, 104; *New York Convention Proceedings 1902*, 115; *Hammer and Pen* 2 (February 1899): 1; *New York Times*, 17 January 1899, 9, 22 January 1899, 18, 26 January 1899, 5, 25 September 1902, 6, 5 October 1902, 30, 3 August 1904, 1, 5 August 1904, 7, and 14 November 1904, 7; William M. Hogue, "The Bishop's Saloon," *Historical Magazine of the Protestant Episcopal Church* 31 (December 1962): 341–50.

54. *New York Convention Proceedings 1898*, 114; *New York Times*, 9 May 1898, 9; *Hammer and Pen*, 1 (June 1898): 1–3, 5, 7; Keyser, *Bishop Potter*, 39–50.

55. Letter from Easley to Lyman J. Gage, 14 May 1898, quoted by Marguerite Green, *The National Civic Federation and the American Labor Movement, 1900–1925* (Westport, Conn.: Greenwood Press, 1983), 7; *New York Times*, 7 May 1901, 8; Hodges, *Henry Codman Potter*, 345–47; Keyser, *Bishop Potter*, 121–28; Sheerin, *Henry Codman Potter*, 47, 122–23; Griffen, "Urban Church in Ferment," 272–73; Green, *National Civic Federation*, 3–61; P. Foner, *Labor Movement*, 2: 384–87, 3: 61–110.

56. HCP, *The Citizen in His Relation to the Industrial Situation* (New York: Charles Scribner's Sons, 1902), 134; Hodges, *Henry Codman Potter*, 343–48; Sheerin, *Henry Codman Potter*, 104–5; Griffen, "Urban Church in Ferment," 371–76.

57. *General Convention Journal 1901*, 125–26; *General Convention Journal 1904*, 95–98; *General Convention Journal 1907*, 528; *New York Times*, 20 October 1904, 6; *Hammer and Pen* 6 (November 1904): 90–91; *National Civic Federation Review* 1 (15 November 1904): 1, 14; Keyser, *Bishop Potter*, 140–49, 155–61. The other commission members were Bishops William Lawrence and Charles Anderson; Revs. Randolph McKim, George Hodges, and C. D. Williams; and Samuel Mather, Jacob Riis, and Seth Low. The 1904 General Convention also, through its Committee on the State of the

Church, gave formal recognition to CAIL; Keyser, *Bishop Potter,* 157–59; *Hammer and Pen* 6 (November 1904): 90.

58. *New York Convention Proceedings 1904,* 134–35, 140; *New York Convention Proceedings 1905,* 163–66, 169; *New York Convention Proceedings 1907,* 137, 139, 141–42, 153; *New York Convention Proceedings 1908,* 154–56; *New York Times,* 20 October 1906, 9; Hodges, *Henry Codman Potter,* 352–57; Sheerin, *Henry Codman Potter,* 170–71; Lindsley, *This Planted Vine,* 243–45.

59. *New York Times,* 20 October 1906, 1.

60. HCP, "Women's Recreations," January 1907, 4–10; "The Social Pace," February 1907, 99–106; and "The Modern Home," March 1907, 203–9—all in *Harper's Bazaar; New York Times,* 22 July 1908, 1, 4; *Churchman,* 24 October 1908, 559–60, 570–74; *Hammer and Pen* Special Number (November 1908): 1–2; *National Civic Federation Review* 3 (September 1908): 13; Hodges, *Henry Codman Potter,* 378–81; Keyser, *Bishop Potter,* 177–82; Sheerin, *Henry Codman Potter,* 174–75.

61. Huntington, "Henry Codman Potter"; Century Association, *Henry Codman Potter: Memorial Addresses Delivered before the Century Association, December 12, 1908* (New York: Century Association, 1908); People's Institute, *Memorial to Henry Codman Potter;* Joseph Smith Auerbach, "Dedication of the Bishop Henry Codman Potter Memorial Buildings" (New York: City and Suburban Homes Company, 1912); and Andrew S. Dolkart, *Morningside Heights: A History of Its Architecture and Development* (New York: Columbia University Press, 1998), 369, n. 4.

62. Greer, "Bishop's Address," *New York Convention Proceedings 1908,* 144–46.

Chapter 1: A Many-Sided Mission

1. Hodges, *Henry Codman Potter,* 33; Sheerin, *Henry Codman Potter,* 30–31.

2. Guelzo, *Evangelical Christendom,* 19–32, 43, 53–61; Butler, *Standing against the Whirlwind,* 3–16, 94–103; Mullin, *Episcopal Vision,* 149–92; Holmes, *Brief History,* 46–77, 103–12.

3. Guelzo, *Evangelical Christendom,* 32–51; Butler, *Standing against the Whirlwind,* 32–49.

4. M. A. D. Howe, *Memoirs,* 249–50, cf. 172–73; Addison, *Episcopal Church,* 156–63; Albright, *History,* 226–51; Griffen, "Urban Church in Ferment," 161–65.

5. Quoted in M. A. D. Howe, *Memoirs,* 228. Howe refrained from identifying General Theological Seminary as the source of the graduates offensive to Alonzo Potter, but as it was known for tending to extremes of High Church ecclesiasticism, and as Alonzo had by this time seen to it that his son was enrolled at Virginia, it is certain that it is General to which he referred. Virginia Seminary was then regarded as the school for the Low Church party, and, in spite of the fact that he chose it for his son, Alonzo was also concerned about whether Henry might become ecclesiastically narrow in that direction. In this letter, then, Alonzo was not simply warning him of the dangers of one type of narrow ecclesiology, but of all narrow ecclesiology. Cf. Hodges, *Henry Codman Potter,* 20, 24–26, 28; and Sheerin, *Henry Codman Potter,* 21–22.

6. Quoted in M. A. D. Howe, *Memoirs,* 245.

7. H. Shelton Smith, Introduction to *Horace Bushnell,* Library of Protestant Thought (New York: Oxford University Press, 1965), 3–22.

8. Ibid., 121 and 38, quoting Bushnell, "Christian Comprehensiveness," *New Englander* 6 (1848): 81–111.

9. Woolverton, *Phillips Brooks,* 73–75.

10. Guelzo, *Evangelical Christendom,* 61, and Butler, *Standing against the Whirlwind,* 103–27, discuss the various strategies employed by Evangelicals in the struggle against Tractarianism but, I think, underrate the importance of comprehensiveness in Evangelicalism. Butler, *Standing against the Whirlwind,* 226–27, for example, discusses the continuity in the "rhetoric of liberality" between the Evangelical party and the Broad Church movement and argues that the latter "coopted the 'liberality' argument to introduce liberal theology and biblical criticism into the Episcopal Church." She acknowledges that the Evangelical party failed to respond to the various challenges of the nineteenth century and that the Broad Church movement inherited some of its central emphases, but her assessment of the Evangelical appeal to comprehensiveness as a *strategy* to combat High Church and Tractarian beliefs and practices diminishes its importance as an *element of* Episcopal Evangelicalism, at least in its moderate forms. Where Butler suggests that the Broad Church movement inappropriately employed Evangelical ideas of comprehensiveness and liberality, I suggest rather that it faithfully employed those ideas in ways that, while in some ways discontinuous with antebellum Evangelicalism, were nevertheless also continuous with it and responsive to the new demands of the last decades of the nineteenth century.

11. Hodges, *Henry Codman Potter,* 14–15, 21–22, 24; F. H. Potter, *Alonzo Potter Family,* 31–32; Sheerin, *Henry Codman Potter,* 18–20; Griffen, "Urban Church in Ferment," 240, n. 3. Skardon, *Church Leader,* 264–65, observes of Muhlenberg that "his most notable achievement was that he profoundly influenced a group of younger men who were to play an important part in the life of the Episcopal church in the years after the Civil War" and that "probably the best known of the Muhlenberg men was Henry Codman Potter."

12. Skardon, *Church Leader,* 1–99.

13. Ibid., 100–175, 195–98, including quotation from *Evangelical Catholic* 2.12; Marshall, "William Augustus Muhlenberg," 148–51; Dolkart, *Morningside Heights,* 85–96.

14. *General Convention Journal 1853,* 182. Skardon, *Church Leader,* 207–8, notes that in colonial Virginia, with the agreement of the Church of England, "the Lutheran parish required that its ministers be ordained in the Established English church so that the parish could be supported by taxation" and that "there had been a considerable interchange of Anglican and Lutheran clergymen in the colonial period." Muhlenberg was aware of such arrangements because his granduncle had been a Lutheran pastor who had also been ordained in the Anglican church.

15. M. A. D. Howe, *Memoirs,* 241–47; Alonzo Potter, ed. *Memorial Papers; The Memorial with Circular and Questions of the Episcopal Commission; Report of the Commission; Contributions of the Commission; and Communications from Episcopal and Non-Episcopal Divines* (Philadelphia: E. H. Butler, 1857); Marshall, "William Augustus Muhlenberg," 151–56. Hodges, *Henry Codman Potter,* 35–36, described Alonzo Potter as the "most able and influential champion of the Memorial Movement," and Skardon, *Church Leader,* 218, notes that he "took such an active part in the memorial movement that some sources regard him rather than Muhlenberg as its leader." On the Protestant revivals and reform societies, see Handy, *History of the Churches,* 171–73; May, *Protestant Churches,* 22–23; and White and Hopkins, *Social Gospel,* 5–13.

16. M. A. D. Howe, *Memoirs,* 241–47. Cf. Addison, *Episcopal Church,* 164–70, 177–88; E. Clowes Chorley, *Men and Movements in the Episcopal Church* (New York: Macmillan, 1946), 201.

17. Guelzo, *Evangelical Christendom,* 63–66; Butler, *Standing against the Whirlwind,* 139–41, 169, n. 9; Holmes, *Brief History,* 125.

18. M. A. D. Howe, *Memoirs*, 208, quoted from Dr. Caspar Morris, who also worked for the establishment of the hospital.

19. Skardon, *Church Leader*, 235–36, 264–66. In the generation of younger men influenced by Muhlenberg, Skardon includes Edward A. Washburn, Edwin Harwood, John Cotton Smith, R. Heber Newton, William Wilberforce Newton, Thomas Vail Hubbard, William Reed Huntington, and HCP. Skardon judges Huntington to be the one "who best typifies the continuing Muhlenberg tradition" even though he "was not, as far as can be discovered, associated with Muhlenberg during his lifetime." Skardon judges HCP to be "the best known of the Muhlenberg men," having "modelled that parish [Grace Church] after the Church of the Holy Communion taking Muhlenberg as his own model" and having demonstrated during his episcopate Muhlenberg's commitment to a comprehensive church.

20. Butler, *Standing against the Whirlwind*, 169, n. 19, notes that the Muhlenberg Memorial "has often been interpreted as the first document of the modern, liberal, and ecumenical Episcopal Church" and argues that "Muhlenberg and the memorial movement need to be more closely examined within the context of nineteenth-century American Protestantism, rather than that of what the twentieth-century Episcopal Church would become." Nevertheless, the fact that many in the twentieth-century Episcopal Church could trace their roots to 1853 argues for the memorial's long-term influence. While Butler's *Standing against the Whirlwind* and Guelzo's *Evangelical Christendom* correctly emphasize the importance of the context of mid-nineteenth-century American Protestantism that produced the 1853 memorial, the developments in the late-nineteenth- and early-twentieth-century Episcopal Church that the memorial helped produce are also important for interpreting its significance.

21. Richard M. Spielmann, "A Neglected Source: The Episcopal Church Congress, 1874–1934," *Anglican and Episcopal History* 58 (1989): 50–69; Griffen, "Urban Church in Ferment," 161–261; Holmes, *Brief History*, 117–20; Butler, *Standing against the Whirlwind*, 179; Guelzo, *Evangelical Christendom*, 120–21; Hodges, *Henry Codman Potter*, 82; HCP, "Christianity and the Criminal," in *Scholar and the State*, 165–79.

22. Guelzo, *Evangelical Christendom*, 43–46, 73; Lindsley, *This Planted Vine*, 146–64, 176; Mullin, *Episcopal Vision*, 161–65; Skardon, *Church Leader*, 184–88.

23. DeMille, "Horatio Potter," 68–69; Butler, *Standing against the Whirlwind*, 208–10; Guelzo, *Evangelical Christendom*, 70–73, 125–40; Skardon, *Church Leader*, 202.

24. *The Election and Consecration of the Rev. Henry Codman Potter, D.D., LL.D., As Assistant Bishop of the Diocese of New York* (New York: James Pott, 1883), 5–19; Hodges, *Henry Codman Potter*, 123–29; Sheerin, *Henry Codman Potter*, 45; Griffen, "Urban Church in Ferment," 348–49; Skardon, *Church Leader*, 120.

25. *New York Convention Proceedings 1885*, 141; *New York Convention Proceedings 1893*, 103; *New York Convention Proceedings 1900*, 99; Albright, *History*, 306–7, 314; Sheerin, *Henry Codman Potter*, 40–42.

26. Hodges, *Henry Codman Potter*, 135–41, 166–78; the 16 June 1885 *New York Tribune* editorial is quoted on 178. On the Ritchie case and its background, see also Albright, *History*, 288–89. While differing on some matters, Newton and HCP were both Broad Church sons of Evangelical clerics and shared many interests and convictions. On Newton's activities and views, on biblical criticism as well as social and economic reform, see Griffen, "Urban Church in Ferment," 239–61, and C. H. Hopkins, *Rise of the Social Gospel*, 32–33.

27. Butler, *Standing against the Whirlwind*, 166–67, 178–81; Mullin, *Episcopal Vision*, 205–7, and "Biblical Critics and the Battle over Slavery," *Journal of Presbyterian History* 61 (1983): 210–26.

28. Hodges, *Henry Codman Potter*, 260–61; HCP, "The Relation of the Clergy to the

Faith and Order of the Church: Third Triennial Charge to the Convention of the Diocese of New York" (New York: published by resolution of the convention, 1891), 187–88. For HCP's sermon at Brooks's consecration, see "Mission and Commission," in *Waymarks*, 361–83. HCP also preached a memorial sermon after Brooks's sudden death in January 1893; see "The Life-Giving Word," in *Scholar and the State*, 295–317.

29. HCP, "Relation of the Clergy," 23–27; Griffen, "Urban Church in Ferment," 36–37, 93.

30. While this passage echoes Horace Bushnell's understanding of the nature and limits of theological language, HCP did not cite Bushnell in this context.

31. Quoted by Mark S. Massa, *Charles Augustus Briggs and the Crisis of Historical Criticism*, Harvard Dissertations in Religion, no. 25 (Minneapolis: Fortress Press, 1990), 119, from Transcribed Ledger Books 9, letter of 11 November 1891, 268, Charles A. Briggs Collection, Union Theological Seminary.

32. Massa, *Charles Augustus Briggs*, 85–135; Hodges, *Henry Codman Potter*, 302–12; Griffen, "Urban Church in Ferment," 172–75; Mullin, *Episcopal Vision*, 205–7; Butler, *Standing against the Whirlwind*, 166–67, 178–81; Robert T. Handy, *A History of Union Theological Seminary in New York* (New York: Columbia University Press, 1987), 69–93. On Briggs and his work, see also M. James Sawyer, *Charles Augustus Briggs and Tensions in Late Nineteenth-Century American Theology* (Lewiston, N.Y.: Mellen University Press, 1994).

33. Hodges, *Henry Codman Potter*, 191–93; HCP, *Sisterhoods and Deaconesses at Home and Abroad* (New York: E. P. Dutton, 1873), 274–89; and HCP, *Addresses to Women Engaged in Church Work* (New York: E. P. Dutton, 1887).

34. HCP, "Bishop's Address," in *New York Convention Proceedings 1885*, 141; *New York Convention Proceedings 1886*, 102–4; White, *Liberty and Justice*, 22.

35. Hodges, *Henry Codman Potter*, 146–65, with Bishop Lee's and HCP's letters quoted on 150–58; Sheerin, *Henry Codman Potter*, 79–80; Lindsley, *This Planted Vine*, 211–14. See also Vida Dutton Scudder, *Father Huntington: Founder of the Order of the Holy Cross* (New York: E. P. Dutton, 1940), 91–101; and D. G. Paz, "Monasticism and Social Reform in Late Nineteenth Century America: The Case of Fr. Huntington," *Historical Magazine of the Protestant Episcopal Church* 48 (1979): 45–66.

36. *Churchman*, 23 May 1885, 563; Hodges, *Henry Codman Potter*, 183–91.

37. M. A. D. Howe, *Memoirs*, 210–11.

38. March 1861 letter from Alonzo Potter to William Welsh, a layperson of the diocese, quoted by M. A. D. Howe, *Memoirs*, 220, and by HCP, *Sisterhoods and Deaconesses*, 214–15. Cf. Sheerin, *Henry Codman Potter*, 100: "In Alonzo Potter's text book for what we now call normal schools, published by Harper & Brothers in 1842, and entitled, *The School and the Schoolmaster*, he emphasized education for the whole man."

39. HCP, "Young Men's Christian Associations: What Is Their Work, and How Shall They Perform It?" (privately printed, n.d.), 11; Hodges, *Henry Codman Potter*, 54–56; Sheerin, *Henry Codman Potter*, 24.

40. C. H. Hopkins, *Rise of the Social Gospel*, 154–58, 251–52; Abell, *Urban Impact*, 27–31, 85–86, 136–66; Griffen, "Urban Church in Ferment," 97–102; Lindsley, *This Planted Vine*, 196–201. Abell includes as elements of the Protestant religiosocial system: "(1) the humanitarian endeavor of various congregations; (2) the support of city missions through extra-parochial associations, denominational and undenominational; (3) the organizations for handling special groups in the population, especially youth; (4) the efforts to combat peculiar forms of evil, notably intemperance; and (5) the successful plans for the training of city missionaries." HCP's work included all five components of this religiosocial system.

41. While acknowledging the pioneering work of Muhlenberg and Beecher, C. H. Hopkins, *Rise of the Social Gospel,* 154, argues that "institutional features were significantly inaugurated in this country at St. George's (Episcopal) Church, New York, by the Reverend William S. Rainsford" upon his becoming rector of that church in 1882. Rainsford's skill at self-promotion has also perhaps influenced subsequent evaluation of his importance. Abell, *Urban Impact,* 42–43, notes that by 1877 Grace Church "became known as a center for far-reaching missionary operations among Germans in all parts of the city," but he does not sufficiently discuss its significance. On the other hand, Lindsley, *This Planted Vine,* 201, neglects initiatives at Grace during the ministry of Thomas House Taylor and overstates HCP's significance in his observation that "when Henry C. Potter became rector of Grace Church in 1868 he almost immediately jolted that parish into a shamefaced recognition of the shabbiness of city life only several blocks away." Lindsley is quite right, however, in his subsequent observation that William Reed Huntington, HCP's successor, "inherited a church of proven involvement in municipal affairs."

42. *Annual Parish Report 1869; Annual Parish Report 1874,* 6–9; Hodges, *Henry Codman Potter,* 68–70; HCP, "Three Score Years and Ten," 9–12, 29.

43. *Annual Parish Report 1870,* 40–43; *Annual Parish Report 1872,* 45–55; *Annual Parish Report 1876,* 5–10; *Annual Parish Report 1877,* 7–10; *Annual Parish Report 1880,* 7–10; HCP, "A Consecration Sermon," in *Waymarks,* 314–16; Hodges, *Henry Codman Potter,* 74–75, 80–81, 93–95, 100–104, 110–11.

44. *Annual Parish Report 1883; Annual Parish Report 1880,* 9.

45. Skardon, *Church Leader,* 112–15, 122–23, 157–58; Abell, *Urban Impact,* 27–30; C. H. Hopkins, *Rise of the Social Gospel,* 154–55; Addison, *Episcopal Church,* 282; Griffen, "Urban Church in Ferment," 220–21; Sheerin, *Henry Codman Potter,* 75.

46. HCP, "Our Brother's Blood; a Sermon, Preached in Grace Church, New York" (St. Johnland, N.Y.: Orphan Boys' Stereotype Foundry, 1872); HCP, "A Nation's Prayers," "A Nation's Sorrow," "A Consecration Sermon," and "The Free Church a Witness to the Brotherhood of Humanity," in *Waymarks,* 44–58, 312–26, and 327–41; "One Another's Burdens," and "Faith and Culture," in *Sermons of the City,* 100–103; *New York Times,* 26 September 1876, 2. Although it seems likely that HCP was a member of the Free Church Association, I have unfortunately found no evidence to substantiate this supposition.

47. HCP, "Free Church a Witness," in *Waymarks,* 327–35. According to HCP, 327, Grace "cheerfully welcome[d] strangers by hundreds to share in its sittings on every Lord's day," the cost of which sittings were eight dollars a year for single seats and twenty-five dollars a year for pews.

48. Ibid., 336, 341.

49. HCP, "Significance of the American Cathedral," 321–35; "The Cathedral Idea," "Sermon Preached at . . . Cathedral of the Incarnation," and "Sermon Preached at . . . All Saints Cathedral," in *Waymarks,* 153–208; HCP's 1887 appeal, "To the Citizens of New York," is reprinted in the first of these sermons. Cf. Hodges, *Henry Codman Potter,* 198–207, 222, 261–62, 273–74, 290–91; Griffen, "Urban Church in Ferment," 79–81; Dolkart, *Morningside Heights,* 37–57; and Lindsley, *This Planted Vine,* 202–4, 245–50. Lindsley incorrectly concludes, 202, that "only two of New York's bishops have devoted great energy to a diocesan cathedral: Horatio Potter and Bishop [William T.] Manning; the former by urging a cathedral at a diocesan convention, and the latter because he inherited, in prosperous times, a partially built cathedral. Henry C. Potter and Bishop [David H.] Greer [HCP's successor], viewed the cathedral as of peripheral importance."

50. *New York Convention Proceedings 1893,* 99; *New York Convention Proceedings*

1895, 109–10; *New York Times*, 11 July 1895, 9, and 12 July 1895, 8; Hodges, *Henry Codman Potter*, 278–85; Griffen, "Urban Church in Ferment," 385–87.

51. May, *Protestant Churches*, 51–52; C. H. Hopkins, *Rise of the Social Gospel*, 90, 97, 100–102.

52. HCP, "The Perils of Wealth," in *Sermons*, 84–87. Cf. HCP, "The Citizen's Two-fold Stewardship," "The Impotence of Money," and "Cost and Beauty in Christian Worship," in ibid., 39–43, 246–47, and 295–308; HCP, "Sermon Commemorative of John David Wolfe" and "Sermon Commemorative of Adam Norrie," in *Waymarks*, 79–85 and 93–95; HCP, "Relations of Science," 140–42; and *Annual Parish Report 1878*, 7–8, and *Annual Parish Report 1883*, 7.

53. Griffen, "Urban Church in Ferment," 351–52; Hodges, *Henry Codman Potter*, 293–94.

54. Andrew Carnegie, "The Gospel of Wealth," in Kirkland, ed., *Gospel of Wealth*, 14–49.

55. Kirkland, Introduction to *Gospel of Wealth*, vii–xx; May, *Protestant Churches*, 132–34; Griffen, "Urban Church in Ferment," 368–70; Herbert G. Gutman, *Work, Culture, and Society in Industrializing America* (New York: Alfred A. Knopf, 1976), 104–5; Richard Hofstadter, *The American Political Tradition* (New York: Vintage Books, 1957), 168–69. C. H. Hopkins, *Rise of the Social Gospel*, 97, observes, "If the proposal of the stewardship of wealth seems sentimental, it should be recalled that this was the era in which John D. Rockefeller asserted that God gave him his fortune and another spokesman for big business defended dictatorial and monopolistic practices on the ground that the wealth of the nation had been given into the keeping of its Christian businessmen."

56. HCP, "The Ministry of Music," in *Scholar and the State*, 217–30. HCP also favorably cites Carnegie's *Gospel of Wealth* in "The Rural Reinforcement of Cities," in ibid., 158–60. Griffen, "Urban Church in Ferment," 368, notes, "Ironically, the bishop was asked, two days after the [Carnegie Hall] address, to help the laborers who constructed the building to obtain the pay due them. One worker wrote, 'We have fallen among thieves and you are the only one who has shown us any sympathy.'" Unfortunately, the sources give no information on the final disposition of this matter.

57. HCP, "Gospel for Wealth," 238. Cf. HCP, "Introductory Note," *Annual Parish Report 1878*, 7, where he observes of those involved in the church's charitable programs: "They will own, I am sure, that their hearts have been kept tender, and their sympathies quick and warm, when otherwise they might easily have become hard and stiff and cold."

58. Abell, *Urban Impact*, 4–6, 84–86; May, *Protestant Churches*, 53–54, 121–23.

59. HCP, "Some Words Introductory," in *Annual Parish Report 1874*, 6–9. Cf. *Annual Parish Report 1873*, 4–7, and "Institutionalism: Its Dangers and Failures" and "One Another's Burdens," in *Sermons*, 142–61, 220–33.

60. A. A. Chevaillier, "New York Letter," *The Dawn* 1 (March 1890): 6. Ms. Chevaillier was a vice president of the New York Society of Christian Socialists. In an editor's note following and qualifying the "Letter," W. D. P. Bliss added, "It perhaps should be added that Socialists believe in organization, and organized charity, to wisely help, not arrest, the unfortunate."

61. Report of HCP's address in "The Way to Give Relief," *New York Times*, 21 December 1898, 7. Cf. *New York Times*, 26 September 1896, 10, and 17 November 1898, 2; *New York Convention Proceedings 1896*, 112, 115–16, 120; *New York Convention Proceedings 1898*, 108, 110; *New York Convention Proceedings 1899*, 101, 103; Hammack, *Power and Society*, 77–78, 142–44. Griffen, "Urban Church in Ferment," 101–2, notes, "Both the [Charity Organization] Society and the settlement house attempt-

ed to strengthen the old American virtue of self-reliance by abandoning the aristocratic and patronizing bias of previous charity which had conflicted with that virtue. In this respect, their purpose was truly conservative."

62. *Annual Parish Report 1870*, 40, and *Annual Parish Report 1881*, 6–7. Cf. *Annual Parish Report 1882*, 7.

63. HCP, "The Homes of the Poor," "The Slaughter of the Innocents," and "Duty of Woman to Women," in *Sermons*, 48–65, 96–110, and 125–41; HCP, "Plea for the American Sunday," in *Waymarks*, 98–116; and HCP, "Christianity and the Criminal," in *Scholar and the State*, 163–79.

64. Skardon, *Church Leader*, 119–20; State Charities Aid Association, *Report of the Special Committee; Third Annual Report*, 5–7, 47–49; *Report on Conference*, 3, 38, 57–59. Unfortunately, I have found no other information on the relationship between HCP and his brother Howard Potter.

65. Jackson, *Place Called Home*, 31.

66. Ibid., 45–58; Roy Lubove, *The Progressives and the Slums: Tenement House Reform in New York City, 1890–1917* (Pittsburgh: University of Pittsburgh Press, 1962), 28–32.

67. HCP, "The Homes of the Poor," in *Sermons*, 53–55. Cf. Hodges, *Henry Codman Potter*, 113–14, and Keyser, *Bishop Potter*, 12–14.

68. HCP, "Homes of the Poor," 58–59.

Chapter 2: Brotherhood and Inequality

1. Huntington, "Henry Codman Potter," 14.

2. M. A. D. Howe, *Memoirs*, 234.

3. Ibid., 231–32; Butler, *Standing against the Whirlwind*, 150–51; Public Broadcasting Service, *Africans in America: America's Journey through Slavery*, Part 3: "Brotherly Love," (Washington, D.C.: Public Broadcasting Service, 1998).

4. M. A. D. Howe, *Memoirs*, 231–34. This case, Howe notes, was "a solitary instance in the Episcopate of Alonzo Potter in which an overwhelming sense of right moved him to an assertion of privilege, and a freedom and fervency of expression quite beyond his wont, and which would be dangerous as a precedent for men of more impetuous temper." Unfortunately, Howe does not report the outcome of the vote, nor even the date of the convention at which it was held, likely in the years just before or after 1850.

5. Ibid., 237–38.

6. Ibid., 238–40; Mullin, *Episcopal Vision*, 206–7; Butler, *Standing against the Whirlwind*, 166; John Henry Hopkins, *A Scriptural, Ecclesiastical, and Historical View of Slavery, from the Days of the Patriarch Abraham to the Nineteenth Century* (New York: Negro Universities Press, 1969), 3–5, 44–51. This book, addressed to Alonzo Potter, included Bishop Hopkins's account of events leading to the controversy (3–5); the text of the disputed pamphlet (5–41); the protest from Potter and the Pennsylvania clergy with a list of its signatories (42–44); Hopkins's letter to Potter concerning the protest (44–49); and more than three hundred pages of "brotherly admonition" to his fellow bishop.

7. HCP, "Protest," in J. H. Hopkins, *Scriptural, Ecclesiastical, and Historical View of Slavery*, 42.

8. M. A. D. Howe, *Memoirs*, 239–40.

9. Hodges, *Henry Codman Potter*, 46. Although the sermons themselves were not preserved, Hodges had a journal from this period in which HCP kept a list of sermon

titles and the biblical texts on which he preached. Hodges's conclusion here is based only on this evidence.

10. Ibid., 41, 45–46; Sheerin, *Henry Codman Potter*, 23–24; F. H. Potter, *Alonzo Potter Family*, 21–28; Mcpherson, *Battle Cry*, 608–11, 653–65; Iver Bernstein, *The New York City Draft Riots: Their Significance for American Society and Politics in the Age of the Civil War* (New York: Oxford University Press, 1990), 3–72.

11. Addison, *Episcopal Church*, 189–99; Albright, *History*, 252–57; Holmes, *Brief History*, 80–82; May, *Protestant Churches*, 40–41; Mullin, *Episcopal Vision*, 202–11.

12. *General Convention Journal 1862*, 37–41, 51–53; Addison, *Episcopal Church*, 196–98; Butler, *Standing against the Whirlwind*, 166; Mullin, *Episcopal Vision*, 202–4; Robert E. Hood, *Social Teachings in the Episcopal Church* (Harrisburg, Pa: Morehouse, 1990), 65–66, and appendix B, 227–38, for the complete text of the 1862 pastoral letter.

13. Hodges, *Henry Codman Potter*, 47–50; Sheerin, *Henry Codman Potter*, 23–24; Mullin, *Episcopal Vision*, 204–5. See also James M. Donald, "Bishop Hopkins and the Reunification of the Church," *Historical Magazine of the Protestant Episcopal Church* 47 (1978): 73–91. Alonzo Potter had died in July 1865, before the convention met. Hodges notes that "Our Threefold Victory" was the second of HCP's sermons published, the first being, as Hodges describes it, "'Thirty Years Reviewed,' an historical and statistical discourse [on St. John's Church] preached and printed in 1861." I have been unable to locate a copy of "Our Threefold Victory" and thus rely here exclusively on Hodges.

14. HCP, "The Heroisms of the Unknown," in *Scholar and the State*, 48.

15. Huntington, "Henry Codman Potter," 14.

16. On the social gospel, its employment of these three strategies, and the status of blacks in the period under discussion here, see White, *Liberty and Justice*, 10–40, 61–90, 208–65; Ralph A. Luker, "The Social Gospel and the Failure of Racial Reform, 1877–1898," *Church History* 46 (1977): 80–99; Ralph A. Luker, *The Social Gospel in Black and White: American Racial Reform, 1885–1912* (Chapel Hill: University of North Carolina Press, 1991), 30–88, 125–58; Thomas Gossett, *Race: The History of an Idea in America* (New York: Schocken Books, 1965), 176–97, 253–86; Eric Foner, *Reconstruction: America's Unfinished Revolution, 1863–1877* (New York: Harper and Row, 1988). For HCP's comments on racial violence, see "The Policy of Expansion," *Harper's Weekly*, 5 November 1898, 1075, which includes his letter to the editor printed under the same heading with letters from Episcopal bishop Arthur C. A. Hall and Methodist bishop John F. Hurst.

17. Albright, *History*, 258–59; White, *Liberty and Justice*, 61–74; Luker, "Social Gospel," 84–89; H. Peers Brewer, "The Protestant Episcopal Freedmen's Commission, 1865–1878," *Historical Magazine of the Protestant Episcopal Church* (December 1957): 361–81; *New York Convention Proceedings 1888*, 118–19, 126. Why HCP attended the 1875 Hampton commencement is not clear. White, *Liberty and Justice*, 65–66, discusses the role of white social gospelers in the governance of black colleges and reports that the "first exposure for many came through a unique enterprise of businessman and philanthropist Robert C. Ogden. . . . In 1870 he began the practice of taking men and women from the North to the Hampton graduation exercises as his guests in a private railroad car. Later the railroad excursion was expanded to include Fisk and Tuskegee. Each year twenty-five individuals were exposed to black education. As we shall see, many of them returned to serve these same institutions in some governance capacity." Perhaps HCP was among those in Ogden's 1875 group. While Francis G. Peabody and others in such groups became trustees of black colleges, HCP apparently did not.

18. Letter from Hugh Douglass to William Coppinger, 27 May 1889, I-A, no. 274,

American Colonization Society Papers, quoted by Luker, *Social Gospel in Black and White*, 31.

19. Albright, *History*, 264; Addison, *Episcopal Church*, 148–49; Butler, *Standing against the Whirlwind*, 147–49; Holmes, *Brief History*, 81; Skardon, *Church Leader*, 238–39; Luker, *Social Gospel in Black and White*, 30–34; Edwin S. Redkey, *Black Exodus: Black Nationalism and Back-to-Africa Movements, 1890–1910*, Yale Publications in American Studies, no. 17 (New Haven, Conn.: Yale University Press, 1969), 16–23; John Hope Franklin and Alfred A. Moss Jr., *From Slavery to Freedom: A History of African Americans*, 8th ed. (New York: Alfred A. Knopf, 2000), 187–91. White, *Liberty and Justice*, 21, observes, "Among those who sought to grapple constructively with the race question, conservatives had long supported the various movements for colonization. . . . For the most part, the leaders of the Social Gospel were not involved in the colonization movement. They joined with the majority of Americans in recognizing that blacks were in America to stay. Social Gospel roots in the antislavery movement had been abolitionist and not colonizationist."

20. Redkey, *Black Exodus*, 99–118.

21. White, *Liberty and Justice*, 21–22; Luker, *Social Gospel in Black and White*, 43–44; Redkey, *Black Exodus*, 127–35; *New York Convention Proceedings 1886*, 103.

22. White, *Liberty and Justice*, 22–23; Redkey, *Black Exodus*, 127–35; "Address of President Potter," *Liberia* 2 (February 1893): 11–18; *New York Convention Proceedings 1893*, 104. HCP also used the principle of the leavening influence of a qualified few in other contexts. Almost three years earlier, in "The Rural Reinforcement of the Cities," *Scholar and the State*, 145–62, he argued that "because at present, under existing laws, we can do little—indeed, almost nothing—to regulate the character and the quality of foreign immigration into New York, [it is] of paramount importance that we should ennoble the quality of our own [rural immigrants to cities]. *Multum, non multa.* This is not so much a question of numbers as of character. Never more urgently than to-day did New York need a nucleus, a saving seed, of righteousness and integrity to stand the strain of its fevered and reckless life." He also used this principle in the municipal reform campaign of 1900–1901; see HCP, *God and the City*, 44–45.

23. White, *Liberty and Justice*, 22–23; Luker, *Social Gospel in Black and White*, 47–48; Redkey, *Black Exodus*, 127–35; *New York Convention Proceedings 1894*, 96; *New York Convention Proceedings 1895*, 100; and *New York Convention Proceedings 1896*, 114.

24. Booker T. Washington, "Bishop Potter and the Negro," in People's Institute, *Memorial to Henry Codman Potter*, 60–61; Franklin and Moss, *From Slavery to Freedom*, 293–306.

25. *New York Convention Proceedings 1901*, 127. Cf. *New York Convention Proceedings 1902*, 118, noting that in March 1902 HCP presided at and addressed a "meeting in the interest of colored people" at Carnegie Hall.

26. Washington, "Bishop Potter and the Negro," in People's Institute, *Memorial to Henry Codman Potter*, 61–62.

27. "Bishop Potter's Opinion," *New York Times*, 21 October 1901, 1.

28. Washington, "Bishop Potter and the Negro," in People's Institute, *Memorial to Henry Codman Potter*, 61, 63–64. Given Washington's reputed skill at public relations and the audience for his memorial address, it is possible that he may have exaggerated HCP's enthusiasm for the cause in order to claim for his work the legitimacy that the support of the eminent bishop would have given it in the eyes of wealthy white northeastern progressives. On Washington, his work, and the support for his work among white social gospelers, see White, *Liberty and Justice*, 91–129, and Luker, *Social Gospel in Black and White*, 125–58.

29. Handy, *History of the Churches*, 210, 216, 262; Gossett, *Race*, 290.

30. Handy, *History of the Churches*, 216–20; Gossett, *Race*, 287–309; Handy, *Christian America*, 58–59, 103–6.

31. Abell, *Urban Impact*, 91–94; C. H. Hopkins, *Rise of the Social Gospel*, 105, 113; May, *Protestant Churches*, 114–16; White, *Liberty and Justice*, 18–21; Griffen, "Urban Church in Ferment," 71–72; Handy, *Christian America*, 74–76, 179–81. HCP was aware of Strong's work but, like Strong, seems to have been influenced directly by Horace Bushnell. Thus, Strong's work tended to confirm views HCP held as a result of other prior influences.

32. White and Hopkins, *Social Gospel*, 202–3; Handy, *Christian America*, 105–6.

33. May, *Protestant Churches*, 123–24.

34. HCP, "Introductory Note," in *Annual Parish Report 1877*, 7–10; Abell, *Urban Impact*, 42–43.

35. "Introductory Note," in *Annual Parish Report 1877*, 8; "Sixth Annual Report of the German Missionary Association," in *Annual Parish Report 1882*, 81–82. The author of the report of the German Missionary Association was its president, one Rev. M. L. Woolsey. He and the association's other officers, all laywomen, formed an advisory committee that HCP chaired.

36. On HCP's episcopal support for missions to immigrants, see, e.g., *Churchman* (14 March 1885), 288; *New York Convention Proceedings 1884*, 148; *New York Convention Proceedings 1885*, 142–43, 145, 147; *New York Convention Proceedings 1886*, 99–100, 108; *New York Convention Proceedings 1887*, 113; *New York Convention Proceedings 1888*, 119–20, 122, 128, 130. On the cathedral and its chapels, see Hodges, *Henry Codman Potter*, 199–203, 262.

37. Handy, *Christian America*, 48–51, 84–88, 145–47; Handy, *History of the Churches*, 182–83, 283–84; May, *Protestant Churches*, 129–30.

38. HCP, "Plea for the American Sunday," 103–5.

39. Ibid., 105–9, 111–14. Cf. Hodges, *Henry Codman Potter*, 104.

40. "In re Restriction of Immigration" (typescript in Potter MSS) quoted by Griffen, "Urban Church in Ferment," 380; "The Rural Reinforcement of Cities," in *Scholar and the State*, 161. Griffen does not date the memorandum, and I have been unable to locate it; I date it to about 1880 on the assumption that HCP was responding to early discussion about this legislation, begun by the late 1870s, and because of a similar remark in his "Outlook and Its Promise: A Sermon Preached in Grace Church, New York, on Thanksgiving Day, Nov. 25, 1880" (New York: Thomas Whittaker, n.d.), 5: "We talk of excluding the Chinese, but unless we give the lie to all our past policy as a nation we cannot lift a hand to do so." This sermon also demonstrates HCP's perception of both the threat and the possibilities presented by the problem of immigration. Cf. HCP, "Western Civilization and the Birth-Rate," *American Journal of Sociology* 12 (March 1907): 626–27. The first Chinese exclusion act was passed by Congress in 1882, with subsequent legislation in 1888 and 1892. On this legislation, see Gossett, *Race*, 290–91.

41. HCP, "Introductory to a Plea for the American Sunday," in *Waymarks*, 98–99.

42. HCP, "Triennial Charge of Bishop Potter: The Lord's Day," in *New York Convention Proceedings 1905*, 136–52.

43. Curtis R. Grant, "The Social Gospel and Race" (Ph.D. diss., Stanford University, 1968), 4–7. For Grant, *racism* is characterized by the conviction of the inherent biological superiority of one group over others and by an enforced system of exploitation and domination of the groups perceived to be inferior. *Race thinking* is characterized by speculation about the nature of races and the origins and consequences of racial differences, while not *necessarily* assuming that such differences are immuta-

ble. On this and the discussion in the following pages, cf. Gossett, *Race*, 54–227, 310–38.

44. Grant, "Social Gospel and Race," 6–7, 109–13. Cf. White, *Liberty and Justice*, 19. For example, HCP calls for "a race of men who by their very existence shall be a standing protest against the reign of coarse materialism and a deluge of greed and self-seeking" and describes a "new race of employers" arising as a result of industrial capitalism. See, respectively, "Scholarship and Service," in *Scholar and the State*, 56, and *Citizen*, 227.

45. Grant, "Social Gospel and Race," 12–13; see 6–32 for his discussion of European American race thinking.

46. On Anglo-Saxon superiority in the thought of social gospelers such as Lyman Abbott, Theodore Thornton Munger, and Josiah Strong, see Luker, *Social Gospel in Black and White*, 120, 139, 268–75. Luker, ibid., 262–64, 293, 309–11, also discusses the contemporary critique of Anglo-Saxon superiority by black and white leaders.

47. HCP, "Plea for the American Sunday," 103; HCP, "Character in Statesmanship," in *Scholar and the State*, 33, 40–41. Cf. HCP, "Christianity and the Criminal," in ibid., 165; HCP, "Owe No Man Any Thing," in *Sermons*, 192–94; HCP, "India: Its People and Its Religions," in *East*, 188–89; HCP, "Modern Home," 205.

48. HCP, "The Chicago-Lambeth Articles," in Charles W. Shields, E. Benjamin Andrews, John F. Hurst, Henry C. Potter, and Amory Bradford, *Church Unity: Five Lectures* (New York: Charles Scribner's Sons, 1896), 186–90.

49. C. H. Hopkins, *Rise of the Social Gospel*, 125–26, 207–9; Grant, "Social Gospel and Race," 126–35; May, *Protestant Churches*, 146–47; Fishburn, *Fatherhood of God*, 92, 163–70.

50. HCP, "Free Church a Witness," in *Waymarks*, 328–32, 340–41. Cf. HCP, "Our Brother's Blood," 7–14, and "The Homes of the Poor," in *Sermons*, 60–61: "For what is, or ought to be, the burden of her [the church's] message? Is it not that God is the Father of all His children, and that, in Christ, humanity was meant to be one loving and self-forgetting brotherhood?"

51. HCP, "Significance of the American Cathedral," 334. Cf. HCP, "Life-Giving Word," in *Scholar and the State*, 306–8; HCP, "The Cathedral Idea" and "Sermon Preached at . . . Cathedral of the Incarnation," in *Waymarks*, 154–55, 162–63, 170; Hodges, *Henry Codman Potter*, 199–203, 262; HCP, "A Phase of Social Science," in *Scholar and the State*, 192–93; HCP, "Chicago-Lambeth Articles," 164–66, 194–96; HCP, "Impressions of India" and "India: Its People and its Religions," in *East*, 126–31, 190; "Bishop Potter's Address," *Proceedings of the Grand Chapter of the State of New York* (1903), 94–95; "Women's Recreations," 10; and Griffen, "Urban Church in Ferment," 379–80, citing a draft letter dated 24 February 1890; in this letter, HCP quoted Acts 17:26, from Paul's speech to the Athenians. On HCP's interaction with and views on Jews, see Griffen, "Urban Church in Ferment," 382, n. 3; *Churchman*, 28 March 1885, 343–44; and the memorial address of Rabbi Joseph Silverman of Temple Emanu-El, New York, "The Liberalism of Bishop Potter," in People's Institute, *Memorial to Henry Codman Potter*, 30–37. Cf. Egal Feldman, "The Social Gospel and the Jews," *American Jewish Historical Quarterly* 58 (March 1969): 300–320.

52. Grant, "Social Gospel and Race," 33–60; Handy, *Christian America*, 105–10.

53. HCP, "Chicago-Lambeth Articles," 184–96. HCP's concluding remarks quote from a writer he identified only as "Bossuet," perhaps meaning either Bishop Jacques Bossuet or the German scholar Wilhelm Bousset.

54. Grant, "Social Gospel and Race," 126, 190.

55. Ibid., 136–54.

56. HCP, "One Another's Burdens," in *Sermons*, 220–33; HCP, "The Scholar and the

State," "The Scholar in American Life," "Scholarship and Service," "The Rural Reinforcement of Cities," "Gospel for Wealth," and "The Christian and the State," in *Scholar and the State,* 1–29, 47–93, 147–62, 233–65; HCP, "Address of President Potter," 16–
18; HCP, *God and the City,* 43–47.

57. Handy, *Christian America,* 179, and Handy, *History of the Churches,* 274–75.

58. Grant, "Social Gospel and Race," 185.

59. Ibid., 4–7, 33–60, 166; Griffen, "Urban Church in Ferment," 381, who goes on to
observe that HCP's "use of 'race' reflects his sense of the tenacity of group characteristics rather than a settled belief in biological differences." See also Handy, *Christian
America,* 105–10.

Chapter 3: The Work and Well-Being of Women

1. Eleanor Flexner, *Century of Struggle: The Woman's Rights Movement in the
United States* (Cambridge, Mass.: Belknap Press, 1959), 204. Cf. Abell, *Urban Impact,*
13–15, 27–31, 50–51, 194–203, 219–22; Handy, *History of the Churches,* 183–85, 302–
3; Handy, *Christian America,* 92–93. The term "Protestant religio-social system" is
Abell's.

2. White and Hopkins, *Social Gospel,* 119–26; Beverly Wildung Harrison, "The Ear-
ly Feminists and the Clergy," in *Making the Connections: Essays in Feminist Social
Ethics,* ed. Carol S. Robb (Boston: Beacon Press, 1985), 193–205; Mari Jo Buhle and Paul
Buhle, Introduction to *The Concise History of Woman Suffrage,* ed. Mari Jo Buhle and
Paul Buhle (Urbana: University of Illinois Press, 1978).

3. Abell, *Urban Impact,* 47–50; Buhle and Buhle, Introduction, 1–12, 25–30; Handy,
Christian America, 88–92; May, *Protestant Churches,* 127–28; White and Hopkins,
Social Gospel, 119–26; Ruth Bordin, *Woman and Temperance: The Quest for Power
and Liberty, 1873–1900* (Philadelphia: Temple University Press, 1981), 3, 95–113.

4. These phrases are from, respectively, Fishburn, *Fatherhood of God,* 24, 121–25,
and Beverly Wildung Harrison, "The Effect of Industrialization," in *Making the Connections,* 49. I use Harrison's term in what follows because it conveys the relation
between the rise of this "cult" and that of industrial capitalism.

5. Harrison, "Effect of Industrialization," 45–49; Fishburn, *Fatherhood of God,* 24–
28, 53, 64, 96, 121–25, 169–70.

6. Harrison, "Effect of Industrialization," 49–50; Fishburn, *Fatherhood of God,* 87–
88, 118; Flexner, *Century of Struggle,* 212–15; Hammack, *Power and Society,* 147, 154–
56; Carroll Smith Rosenberg, *Religion and the Rise of the American City: The New
York City Mission Movement, 1812–1870* (Ithaca, N.Y.: Cornell University Press, 1971),
97–111, 118–19, 204–6, 226–28.

7. Butler, *Standing against the Whirlwind,* 34–35; Harrison, "Early Feminists," 194–
97; Fishburn, *Fatherhood of God,* 169; Handy, *History of the Churches,* 183, 302; Nancy
A. Hardesty, *Your Daughters Shall Prophesy: Revivalism and Feminism in the Age of
Finney,* Chicago Studies in the History of American Religion, vol. 5 (Brooklyn, N.Y.:
Carlson, 1991), 3–6, 131–41.

8. *General Convention Journal 1850,* 132, quoted by Mary S. Donovan in "Zealous
Evangelists: The Woman's Auxiliary to the Board of Missions," *Historical Magazine
of the Protestant Episcopal Church* 51 (1982): 371.

9. Quoted by M. A. D. Howe, *Memoirs,* 259–60, and HCP, *Sisterhoods and Deaconesses,* 217–18.

10. Skardon, *Church Leader,* 125–37; HCP, *Sisterhoods and Deaconesses; General
Convention Journal 1856,* cited by Alonzo Potter in his 1862 address to the Pennsyl-

vania diocesan convention and quoted by M. A. D. Howe, *Memoirs,* 259; Skardon, *Church Leader,* 129. Cf. Sandra Hughes Boyd, "The History of Women in the Episcopal Church: A Select Annotated Bibliography," *Historical Magazine of the Protestant Episcopal Church* 50 (1981): 423–34.

11. May 1864 letter from A. Potter to W. Welsh, quoted by HCP in *Sisterhoods and Deaconesses,* 218–19; December 1871 letter from W. Welsh to HCP, quoted in ibid., 210–16. Welsh noted, as quoted by HCP in *Sisterhoods and Deaconesses,* 214: "This experiment was not an individual enterprise, to end when its projector became enfeebled, but it was thoroughly incorporated into the Church's system and life. . . . More than eight thousand visits were annually made to five or six hundred houses, and these inexpensive home influences fed the Sunday-schools, Bible classes, Mothers' Meetings and night schools with those who had not been reached by any other instrumentality."

12. May 1864 letter from A. Potter to W. Welsh, quoted in HCP, *Sisterhoods and Deaconesses,* 220.

13. Handy, *History of the Churches,* 302; Abell, *Urban Impact,* 12–14. As Abell notes, the report was "based on personal investigation in thirty-five representative cities, assembled data relative to the growing need for humanitarian church work in cities, the American philanthropic situation as a whole, the activities of the churches as missionary congregations, and, finally, the question of using women as missionaries. Though not exhaustive, this report presented the first truly significant picture of Protestant prospects in urban America." On women in domestic and foreign mission work in the Episcopal Church, see Donovan, "Zealous Evangelists," 371–83, and Donovan, "Women and Mission: Towards a More Inclusive Historiography," *Historical Magazine of the Protestant Episcopal Church* 53 (1984): 297–305.

14. Abell, *Urban Impact,* 15, 194–97. The "German Protestant model" derived primarily from the deaconesses of Kaiserwerth, Germany; see HCP, *Sisterhoods and Deaconesses,* 297–344, and Hodges, *Henry Codman Potter,* 95.

15. HCP, *Sisterhoods and Deaconesses,* 92–94, 211–32; Abell, *Urban Impact,* 50–51; Addison, *Episcopal Church,* 164–70; Albright, *History,* 317–18; Lindsley, *This Planted Vine,* 187–88; Skardon, *Church Leader,* 130–31. HCP *may* have erroneously claimed historical priority for the Sisterhood of the Holy Communion: an English sisterhood, albeit short-lived, was also established in 1845 to work among the London poor.

16. Hodges, *Henry Codman Potter,* 32, 69–71; *Annual Parish Report 1869,* 8, 10–17. Cf. reports on these and other parish organizations in subsequent issues of the annual parish report.

17. Annual Parish Report 1870, 40–43; *Annual Parish Report 1872,* 45–55; Hodges, *Henry Codman Potter,* 80–111; Donovan, "Women and Missions," 298–99.

18. Quoted by HCP, *Sisterhoods and Deaconesses,* 7–8.

19. Quoted in ibid., 33.

20. Hodges, *Henry Codman Potter,* 75–78.

21. HCP, *Sisterhoods and Deaconesses,* 8. Cf. 10, where he claims that "such organizations as are described in this volume are placed within the lines of the Church's unequivocal countenance and approval"; and "Woman's Place and Work in the Church," in *Waymarks,* 212, where HCP notes that "it is gratifying to remember that the late General Convention of our Church, and especially the House of Bishops in its Pastoral Letter, have recognized not only the general expediency but also the Biblical authority for woman's work, and for the definite place in the organization of the Church which to-day it is proposed that woman should officially hold." As noted above, HCP also defended J. O. S. Huntington and the Order of the Holy Cross by explicitly citing the precedent of the church's acceptance of women's religious orders.

22. Addison, *Episcopal Church,* 130, 229, 339–40; Albright, *History,* 269; Donovan, "Zealous Evangelists," 371–83; Hodges, *Henry Codman Potter,* 78.

23. HCP, "Woman's Place and Work in the Church," in *Waymarks,* 212–23.

24. Ibid., 209–10, 213, 220–21. Suzanne R. Hiatt, "Women's Ordination in the Anglican Communion: Can This Church Be Saved?" in *Religious Institutions and Women's Leadership: New Roles inside the Mainstream,* ed. Catherine Wessinger (Columbia: University of South Carolina Press, 1996), 212, observes that in the nineteenth century, "the ordination of women was not an issue in the Episcopal Church. . . . Of course, women were active in ministry as they have always been in the churches, but ordination was not even considered. There was agitation enough about allowing women to serve as nuns or deaconesses, but women simply did not present themselves for ordination."

25. HCP, *Sisterhoods and Deaconesses,* 7–15; Hodges, *Henry Codman Potter,* 78.

26. *Annual Parish Report 1870,* 41; *Annual Parish Report 1871,* 52; *Annual Parish Report 1872,* 47–55; HCP, "The Cathedral Idea" and "Religious Orders" in *Waymarks,* 155, 211; Abell, *Urban Impact,* 203; Albright, *History,* 318; Lindsley, *This Planted Vine,* 247.

27. *New York Convention Proceedings 1884,* 119, 126, 143, 148–52; *New York Convention Proceedings 1886,* 89, 97–108; Hodges, *Henry Codman Potter,* 131–33, 146.

28. HCP, *Sisterhoods and Deaconesses,* 25; HCP, "The Realm of Order," in *Addresses to Women,* 36–40.

29. Abell, *Urban Impact,* 197–203; Albright, *History,* 316–25; Lindsley, *This Planted Vine,* 247.

30. HCP, "Duty of Woman to Women," in *Sermons,* 125–41. This address is the only one included in this volume that was not delivered at Grace Church. Cf. Keyser, *Bishop Potter,* 5–10, who introduces her quotation from it by noting that "At the early date when the sermons from which we are quoting were preached, there were few who realized that industrial emancipation depends upon political equality, and, that, the disenfranchisement of woman acts as a two-edged sword wounding both man and woman. . . . It will be refreshing to note what Bishop Potter had to say . . . about women in the political and industrial world."

31. HCP, "Duty of Woman to Women," in *Sermons,* 125–40.

32. *Annual Parish Report 1882* and *Annual Parish Report 1883.* Episcopal Girls' Friendly Societies paralleled the Working Girls Clubs and Associations of Working Girls Societies established under the leadership of Grace Dodge; see Flexner, *Century of Struggle,* 205–6.

33. Flexner, *Century of Struggle,* 205–9; Griffen, "Urban Church in Ferment," 399–400; Hammack, *Power and Society,* 77, 143, 301, 310; Keyser, *Bishop Potter,* 50–55, 67–69. Both Keyser and Griffen note that Josephine Shaw Lowell's published work on industrial arbitration and conciliation was a significant influence on CAIL's decision to work in this area.

34. Flexner, *Century of Struggle,* 208–9; Griffen, "Urban Church in Ferment," 398–403, 411–14; C. H. Hopkins, *Rise of the Social Gospel,* 248; Keyser, *Bishop Potter,* 34–36, 74–77; *Hammer and Pen* 2 (June 1899): 50–51. Writing in 1910, Keyser observed that, since its founding in 1887, "C.A.I.L. has seen a change in the sweating industries, because improved factory inspection and better labor laws have certainly produced better conditions; but the destruction of sweating has not yet been accomplished. The serpent is scotched, not killed."

35. HCP, "A Phase of Social Science," in *Scholar and the State,* 184–85.

36. HCP, "The Message of Christ to the Family," in *The Message of Christ to Manhood,* William Belden Noble Lectures for 1898 (Boston: Houghton, Mifflin, 1899), 185–

92 (the other contributors were Alexander V. G. Allen, Francis G. Peabody, Theodore T. Munger, William DeW. Hyde, and Henry Van Dyke). On turn-of-the-century social gospel views of the family, see Fishburn, *Fatherhood of God*, 22–28, 95–127.

37. HCP, "Message of Christ," 192–201. Cf. Fishburn, *Fatherhood of God*, 121–22.

38. HCP, "Mother and Child," *Harper's Monthly Magazine*, December 1901, 102–4; HCP, "Decline of the Home, 'The Foundation of the Nation,'" *Sunday Magazine*, 5 November 1905, 3–4.

39. HCP, "Social Pace," 100–102. As this reference to woman suffrage is the only one found in HCP's published writings, it seems clear that it was not an issue of major concern for him. That he devoted no time to arguing against it suggests that on this matter, at least, he did not follow Bushnell, whose *Women's Suffrage: The Reform against Nature* (New York: Charles Scribner's Sons) had been published in 1869.

40. HCP, "Social Pace," 105–6.

41. HCP, "Modern Home," 203–9.

42. Edward A. Ross, "Western Civilization and the Birth-Rate," *American Journal of Sociology* 12 (March 1907): 607–17.

43. HCP, "Western Civilization," 626–27.

44. Bordin, *Woman and Temperance*, 3; Abell, *Urban Impact*, 47–50; Buhle and Buhle, Introduction, 1–12, 25–30; Handy, *Christian America*, 88–92; May, *Protestant Churches*, 127–28; White and Hopkins, *Social Gospel*, 119–26.

45. Handy, *History of the Churches*, 181–82; Handy, *Christian America*, 51–54.

46. Quoted by M. A. D. Howe, *Memoirs*, 196.

47. Alonzo Potter, *The Drinking-Usages of Society* (Boston: Friends of the Massachusetts Temperance Society, 1861), 1–33. Cf. Sheerin, *Henry Codman Potter*, 100; F. H. Potter, *Alonzo Potter Family*, 10; Mark Lender, *Dictionary of American Temperance Biography: From Temperance Reform to Alcohol Research, the 1600s to the 1980s* (Westport, Conn.: Greenwood Press, 1984), 404–6.

48. Handy, *Christian America*, 92.

49. Bordin, *Woman and Temperance*, 56–63. Cf. Ruth Bordin, *Frances Willard: A Biography* (Chapel Hill: University of North Carolina Press, 1986), 97–111; Frances Willard is quoted from White and Hopkins, *Social Gospel*, 120–21.

50. Abell, *Urban Impact*, 48–49, 142–43; Markwell, *Anglican Left*, 247, n. 3; Sheerin, *Henry Codman Potter*, 109–10.

51. HCP, "Total Abstinence Movement," 7–24. Cf. Alonzo Potter, *Drinking Usages*, 1–14, and note that while Alonzo Potter had cited Rom. 14:21, HCP cited instead 1 Cor. 8:13. HCP's reference in this context to the importance of the "play element" in human nature again suggests the influence of Horace Bushnell, in this case his *Work and Play* (London: A. Strahan, 1864).

52. HCP, "The Branded Body: A Sermon Preached in Grace Church, New York, on the Morning of the First Sunday in Lent, February 26, 1882" (n.p., privately printed, n.d.), 8–9.

53. Hodges, *Henry Codman Potter*, 366; *New York Times*, 16 August 1897, 4. F. H. Potter, *Alonzo Potter Family*, 40, reports that HCP's daughter, Jane Potter Russell, later recounted a story about her father's pact with "an Irish clergyman of good family who had taken to drink" that neither man would "touch a drop of wine as long as his brother kept his pledge." Potter later "sent him out to Bishop Hare, to help with the work among the Indians," where he "did splendid work until he was accidentally shot a few years later." According to her, after he had met this man, HCP "gave up the glass of wine he occasionally took, and for years he never touched a drop, and not till much later did we know the reason."

54. Abell, *Urban Impact*, 99; Hodges, *Henry Codman Potter*, 366–68. Although I have

not located a complete list of the members of the Committee of Fifty, neither have I found any indication that any of its members were women.

55. HCP quoted in *New York Times,* 17 January 1899, 9; *New York Convention Proceedings 1899,* 104.

56. Letter of H. P. Ostrom, Brotherhood of St. Andrew, in *New York Times,* 22 January 1899, 18; "Bishop Potter on the Saloon," *Hammer and Pen* 2 (February 1899): 1; "A Reply to Bishop Potter" and "The Bishop Says He's Misquoted," *New York Times,* 26 January 1899, 5.

57. Hodges, *Henry Codman Potter,* 365–66, where he also observes that HCP "was opposed to mere negation. He felt that whether the matter in hand was the protection of Sunday or the prevention of the saloon, no merely destructive measures would suffice. Behind the evils were great, permanent, and wholesome facts of human nature which must be discovered and taken into account, and to which the reformer must minister. He saw no moral progress in repression without construction. He had no faith in a leadership whose sole formula was 'Thou shalt not.'" See also "Bishop Potter Sees Virtues in Saloons," *New York Times,* 28 September 1902, 6; "Rational Temperance Reform," *New York Times,* 5 October 1902, 30. The October 1902 editorial implies that HCP had earlier been a "subject for public prayer on the part of the W.C.T.U.," but I have found neither confirmation of such an incident nor any reference by HCP to the WCTU or its leaders.

58. Quoted in Hodges, *Henry Codman Potter,* 368.

59. Hodges, *Henry Codman Potter,* 368–70; Sheerin, *Henry Codman Potter,* 110–13; "Bishop Potter Helps Dedicate Model Saloon," *New York Times,* 3 August 1904, 1; "St. Louis Ministers Score Bishop Potter," *New York Times,* 5 August 1904, 7; "Bishop Potter Defends the Subway Tavern," *New York Times,* 14 November 1904, 7; Hogue, "Bishop's Saloon," 341–50.

60. Quoted in White and Hopkins, *Social Gospel,* 123.

Chapter 4: Political Righteousness

1. Rauschenbusch, *Christianizing the Social Order,* 147–55.

2. Mark S. Massa, "Social Justice in an Industrial Society," in *Church and State in America: A Bibliographical Guide,* vol. 2, *The Civil War to the Present Day,* ed. John F. Wilson (New York: Greenwood Press, 1987), 69–85; Stanley P. Caine, "The Origins of Progressivism," in *The Progressive Era,* ed. Lewis L. Gould (Syracuse, N.Y.: Syracuse University Press, 1974), 11–14.

3. Handy, *Christian America,* 23–24, 35–38, 42–49. On the coercive element in the evangelical crusade for a Christian America, Handy, 57–58, observes: "Believing that by the separation of church and state they had separated religious from secular concerns, they seem to have been largely unaware of how much specifically Protestant content they had in fact invested in their understanding of state and society. Groups which did not share their basic premises could become only too painfully aware of it." Cf. Nathan O. Hatch, "The Democratization of Christianity and the Character of American Politics," 101–3, and Handy, "Protestant Theological Tensions and Political Styles in the Progressive Period," 288–89, both in *Religion and American Politics: From the Colonial Period to the 1980s,* ed. Mark A. Noll (New York: Oxford University Press, 1990).

4. Daniel Walker Howe, "Religion and Politics in the Antebellum North," 121–45, and Robert P. Swierenga, "Ethnoreligious Political Behavior in the Mid-Nineteenth Century: Voting, Values, Cultures," 146–71, both in Noll, *Religion and American*

Politics. The distinction between evangelical and nonevangelical political behavior as a means of explaining the role of religion in nineteenth-century voting patterns and as conforming to a liturgical-pietist continuum was first developed by Paul Kleppner, *The Cross of Culture: A Social Analysis of Midwestern Politics, 1850–1900* (New York: Free Press, 1970), Richard J. Jensen, *The Winning of the Midwest: Social and Political Conflict, 1888–1896* (Chicago: University of Chicago Press, 1971), and Ronald P. Formisano, *The Birth of Mass Political Parties, 1827–1861* (Princeton, N.J.: Princeton University Press, 1971).

5. Swierenga, "Ethnoreligious Political Behavior," 154.

6. Ibid., 152, 158–59; Butler, *Standing against the Whirlwind,* 146–47; Guelzo, *Evangelical Christendom,* 46–48; Mullin, *Episcopal Vision,* 196–98.

7. "Dishonesty in Commerce and Politics," *Century Magazine* 28 (1884): 463, quoted in Leonard D. White and Jean Schneider, *The Republican Era, 1869–1901: A Study in Administrative History* (New York: Macmillan, 1958), 365–66.

8. The phrase is from Hofstadter, *American Political Tradition,* 165.

9. Ibid., 164–69; C. H. Hopkins, *Rise of the Social Gospel,* 11–13, 101.

10. C. H. Hopkins, *Rise of the Social Gospel,* 32–33, citing Newton's *Morals of Trade* and Washburn's *Social Law of God.*

11. Hofstadter, *American Political Tradition,* 169. Cf. ibid., 164: "There is no other period in the nation's history when politics seems so completely dwarfed by economic changes.... The industrialists of the Gilded Age ... behaved with becoming vulgarity; but they were also men of heroic audacity and magnificent exploitative talents—shrewd, energetic, aggressive, rapacious, domineering, insatiable. They directed the proliferation of the country's wealth, they seized its opportunities, they managed its corruption, and from them the era took its tone and color."

12. Ibid., 169–72; E. Foner, *Reconstruction,* 565–67; Wilbur Edel, ed., *Defenders of the Faith: Religion and Politics from the Pilgrim Fathers to Ronald Reagan* (New York: Praeger, 1987), 94. In 1992 dollars, the amounts cited by Hofstadter would be about $4,430,000 and $7,252,000 respectively; United States Bureau of the Census and Department of Commerce, *Historical Statistics of the United States, Colonial Times to 1970* (Washington, D.C.: U.S. Bureau of the Census and Department of Commerce, 1975), 210–11, and *Statistical Abstract of the United States, 1993* (Washington, D.C.: U.S. Bureau of the Census and Department of Commerce, 1993), 482.

13. Caine, "Origins of Progressivism," in Gould, *Progressive Era,* 19–21; Richard Hofstadter, *The Age of Reform: From Bryan to FDR* (New York: Alfred A. Knopf, 1961), 131–72; John G. Sproat, *"The Best Men"* (New York: Oxford University Press, 1968), esp. 111–41; Geoffrey Blodgett, "Reform Thought and the Genteel Tradition," in *The Gilded Age,* ed. H. Wayne Morgan (Syracuse, N.Y.: Syracuse University Press, 1970), 55–76. Scholars of American political history use *Mugwump* to refer either narrowly to liberal reform Republicans who voted for the Democratic candidate in the 1884 election or broadly to liberal reformers in the period between the Civil War and the Progressive Era; I follow the latter usage.

14. HCP, "Individual Responsibility," 5–18; Hodges, *Henry Codman Potter,* 63–64; Sheerin, *Henry Codman Potter,* 24–26. Hodges, *Henry Codman Potter,* 64, notes, "It is a true saying that most preachers, even very eminent ones, have only two or three sermons. These they preach over and over, from many different texts, with many changes of illustration and of application, throughout their ministry. This was one of Dr. Potter's sermons, this insistence on political righteousness."

15. HCP, "The Citizen's Twofold Stewardship," in *Sermons,* 31–46; HCP, "Outlook and Its Promise" and "A Nation in Its Sorrow: Two Sermons Preached in Grace Church, New York" (New York: Thomas Whittaker, 1881), reprinted as "A Nation's Prayers"

and "A Nation's Sorrow," in *Waymarks*, 44–70. Hofstadter, *American Political Tradition*, 172–73, describes Garfield as "essentially an honest and worthy soul" who was "tainted by a few minor scandals."

16. *New York Convention Proceedings 1887*, 108, 114, 117; *New York Convention Proceedings 1888*, 118–19, 121, 126; *New York Convention Proceedings 1889*, 98, 100.

17. Hofstadter, *American Political Tradition*, 174–78; May, *Protestant Churches*, 125–26; Sproat, *"Best Men,"* 111–41.

18. Griffen, "Urban Church in Ferment," 366–67, 378–79; Homer E. Socolofsky and Allan B. Spetter, *The Presidency of Benjamin Harrison*, American Presidency Series (Lawrence: University Press of Kansas, 1987), 19–45; *New York Times*, 18 April 1889, quoted in Socolofsky and Spetter, 34. Socolofsky and Spetter, 159, suggest that HCP was "a professed Republican all his life and not interested in the reform of Mugwump factions of the party." Griffen, "Urban Church in Ferment," 366–67, however, claims that HCP "bolted with other Mugwumps in 1884 to vote for Cleveland, but he returned to the fold when Harrison ran in 1888" and voted for Cleveland again in 1892. The evidence of HCP's political views and activities supports Griffen's characterization.

19. Hofstadter, *American Political Tradition*, 174–76; Socolofsky and Spetter, *Benjamin Harrison*, 19–29, 109–12, 158.

20. HCP, "Character in Statesmanship," in *Scholar and the State*, 33–43.

21. Ibid., 38–39.

22. *New York Times*, 1 May 1889, 1; quoted by Socolofsky and Spetter, *Benjamin Harrison*, 159–60, and Hodges, *Henry Codman Potter*, 234. Cf. editorials in *New York Times*, 1 May 1889, 4, and 2 May 1989, 4.

23. HCP, "Character in Statesmanship," in *Scholar and the State*, 40–43.

24. The Archives of the Diocese of New York contains three editions of the address, two of which were derived from the *Evening Post* reprint. One notes that "copies of this pamphlet may be obtained of The Evening Post, New York, at one cent each, in small or large quantities; postage extra"; another is a copy of the *Evening Post* reprint circulated as an advertisement "Compliments of J. S. Fry & Sons, Bristol and London, Eng., Manufacturers of the Finest Quality Chocolate and Cocoa." The Diocesan Archives also contains a political cartoon, identified only by the signature of C. J. Taylor and presumably from a magazine or newspaper, that bears the caption "A Sermon He Will Not Forget" and shows HCP pointing an accusing finger at a disgruntled President Harrison, quoting Potter's criticism of patronage politics.

25. Hodges, *Henry Codman Potter*, 234–39; Sheerin, *Henry Codman Potter*, 45–57; Griffen, "Urban Church in Ferment," 362–67; Socolofsky and Spetter, *Benjamin Harrison*, 159–60. Godkin and Schurz are quoted by Hodges, *Henry Codman Potter*, 235–37; Godkin is also quoted by Griffen, "Urban Church in Ferment," 365–66, from a letter to HCP of 28 April 1889 in *Life and Letters of E. L. Godkin*, ed. Rollo Ogden (New York: Macmillan, 1907), 2: 184.

26. Although Hodges, *Henry Codman Potter*, 238, suggests that HCP's 1889 address was a significant factor in Cleveland's reelection, the failure of Republican party bosses to support Harrison and some newspapers' continuing portrayal of Republican corruption were undoubtedly more significant.

27. *Evangelist*, 21 April 1898, quoted by Griffen, "Urban Church in Ferment," 363. The review continued, "The 'machines' should labor for its suppression. . . . For with such an engine of reform in the hands of the people, deriving its power from such a fountain of unfailing strength as the head and beating heart of the Episcopal Church, it is impossible for the unprincipled schemers for place and spoil, to continue their base endeavors to demoralize the masses."

28. *New York Convention Proceedings 1893*, 103 and 110; *New York Convention*

Proceedings 1894, 96; *New York Convention Proceedings 1895*, 98; *New York Times*, 30 November 1894, 4, and 3 November 1895, 4. On the political sympathies of HCP's colleagues W. S. Rainsford, R. Heber Newton, and Morgan Dix, see Griffen, "Urban Church in Ferment," 234–36, 260–61, 319–21, and Abell, *Urban Impact*, 81, 225–26. On the various New York City reform campaigns, their protagonists, and internal disputes, see Hammack, *Power and Society*, 109–81, 303–26.

29. HCP, "Scholar and the State," 4–5. Cf. "The Place of the Scholar in American Life: An Address Delivered at the Annual Commencement of the University of Michigan, Thursday, June 26th, 1884" (Ann Arbor: Board of Regents, University of Michigan, 1884).

30. HCP, "Scholar in American Life" [1889], in *Scholar and the State*, 56.

31. HCP, "Scholarship and Service" [1895], in ibid., 85.

32. Ibid., 84.

33. Ibid., 85. Cf. HCP, "Gospel for Wealth" and "The Christian and the State," in ibid., 247–48, 253. On Parkhurst, see Abell, *Urban Impact*, 81; Hammack, *Power and Society*, 147–48; C. H. Hopkins, *Rise of the Social Gospel*, 158–59; and May, *Protestant Churches*, 225–26.

34. *New York Convention Proceedings 1893*, 99; Hodges, *Henry Codman Potter*, 278–85; Griffen, "Urban Church in Ferment," 385–87.

35. *New York Convention Proceedings 1895*, 109–10; *New York Times*, 11 July 1895, 9, and 12 July 1895, 8.

36. Hodges, *Henry Codman Potter*, 326–38; Keyser, *Bishop Potter*, 129–38; Sheerin, *Henry Codman Potter*, 57–61; Hammack, *Power and Society*, 154–55; Jackson, *Place Called Home*, 124–25; *New York Times*, 29 September 1900, 9.

37. *New York Convention Proceedings 1900*, 84; *New York Times*, 29 September 1900, 9; *Churchman* 6 (October 1900): 1.

38. *New York Times*, 17 November 1900, 1–2, 19 November 1900, 2, 20 November 1900 1, 21 November 1900, 2; for HCP's letter to Van Wyck, see *New York Convention Proceedings 1901*, 119–21; Hodges, *Henry Codman Potter*, 328–31; and *New York Times*, 17 November 1900, 1.

39. HCP, *God and the City*; excerpted in *New York Times*, 24 November 1900, 3.

40. Quoted in *New York Times*, 5 January 1901, 1. On Roosevelt as police commissioner and governor, see Lewis L. Gould, *The Presidency of Theodore Roosevelt*, American Presidency Series (Lawrence: University Press of Kansas, 1991), 5–8.

41. *New York Times*, 3 December 1900, 3, 5 January 1901, 1, 13 January 1901, 1, 15 January 1901, 1; Hammack, *Power and Society*, 154. It is not clear what connection this Committee of Fifteen had to the Committee of Fifteen with which Potter worked on temperance issues; the two may or may not have been identical.

42. *New York Times*, 3 December 1900, 3, 5 January 1901, 1, 13 January 1901, 1, 15 January 1901, 1, 24 January 1901, 2, and 21 October 1901, 1. On HCP's remarks to the 1901 diocesan convention, see *New York Convention Proceedings 1901*, 118–21, and *New York Times*, 28 September 1901, 8; on the 1901 election campaign and Low's mayoral administration, see Hammack, *Power and Society*, 154–57.

43. Paul Toews, "The Imperialism of Righteousness," in White and Hopkins, *Social Gospel*, 114; Caine, "The Origins of Progressivism," in Gould, *Progressive Era*, 22.

44. James D. Beumler, "Church and State at the Turn of the Century: Missions and Imperialism, Bureaucratization, and War, 1898–1920," in Wilson, *Church and State*, 146–53; Handy, *Christian America*, 40–42, 82–83, 128–36; Handy, *History of the Churches*, 176–77; Winthrop Hudson, "Protestant Clergy Debate the Nation's Vocation, 1898–1899," *Church History* 42 (1973): 111–12.

45. Hudson, "Nation's Vocation," 111; note that this "God-given boundary of the

nation," as it specifies no northern border, could have included all of what is now Canada.

46. Quoted in "The Fury of Peacemakers," *New York Times*, 24 December 1895, 4, an editorial that admonished HCP and others critical of Cleveland's actions. On the boundary dispute and reaction to Cleveland's December 1895 message to Congress, see Richard E. Welch Jr., *The Presidencies of Grover Cleveland*, American Presidency Series (Lawrence: University Press of Kansas, 1988), 180–92. Welch's judgment, 190–91, tends to support HCP's assessment: "The Venezuelan diplomacy of Grover Cleveland, despite its self-assessed peaceful intentions, risked a war for which neither Cleveland nor the nation was prepared. A war with Britain over the eastern boundary of Venezuela was neither necessary for the national honor nor helpful to the national interest. It would have damaged both."

47. *New York Convention Proceedings 1897*, 112.

48. Welch, *Grover Cleveland*, 188–90; Hudson, "Nation's Vocation," 112; Hood, *Social Teachings*, 68; Lewis L. Gould, *The Presidency of William McKinley*, American Presidency Series (Lawrence: University Press of Kansas, 1980), 59–152.

49. *Churchman* 77 (19 March 1898): 414, cited by Hudson, "Nation's Vocation," 112–13.

50. Hudson, "Nation's Vocation," 113–18. Gould, *William McKinley*, 96, observes, "Dewey's victory transformed the military and diplomatic context of the war during its opening week. To the initial aim of ousting Spain from Cuba were now added the alluring possibilities of expanding America's economic and political influence in Asia and the role of being a genuine world power. . . . Equally vociferous were the spokesmen for the nation's Protestant churches, who saw the Far East as an arena for an evangelical effort."

51. Quoted in Hodges, *Henry Codman Potter*, 315.

52. *General Convention Journal 1898*, 19, 26, 135, 138; Hodges, *Henry Codman Potter*, 313–25; Griffen, "Urban Church in Ferment," 379–85; Sheerin, *Henry Codman Potter*, 53–54.

53. HCP, "The Policy of Expansion," *Harper's Weekly*, 5 November 1898, 1075; *New York Convention Proceedings 1899*, 102; *New York Times*, 23 January 1899, 1, 11 October 1899, 7.

54. Hudson, "Nation's Vocation," 118. Gould, *William McKinley*, 187–89, notes, "That the policy of the United States was not dictatorial, purposely oppressive, or genocidal under William McKinley is clear. That the conduct of the United States Army fell below the highest standards of the rules of war is also evident. Of course, it would not have mattered if the Americans in the Philippines had somehow managed to be truly benevolent and effectively imperial. The rule of one national group by another contradicted the nation's traditions, but it was an idea whose philosophical foundations were already crumbling. The Philippine episode in United States history was flawed and doomed, not because bad men carried out harsh and callous policies, but because good men, such as William McKinley, were trying to do the impossible."

55. HCP, "National Bigness or Greatness—Which?" *North American Review* 168 (April 1899): 433–44. A note to this article indicates that it was originally delivered as an address, but neither it nor other sources indicate on what occasion it was delivered.

56. *New York Convention Proceedings 1900*, 99–100. According to Hodges, *Henry Codman Potter*, 314, "The choice of Bishop Potter for this errand was obviously appropriate. Nobody else in the Church had concerned himself so notably and successfully with public affairs. . . . He had particularly interested himself in the discussion of the problem of the Philippines."

57. "Bishop Potter on the Philippines," in *New York Times*, 19 December 1899, 8.

This is an editorial about the *Herald*'s report on HCP's views; the *Times* editor noted, "There could be no more competent observer, and none whose remarks upon the political and social and commercial problems which confront us there could be more illuminating"; Hodges, *Henry Codman Potter,* 319–23, quotes at length from HCP's Singapore letter but does not identify the date it was sent or the name of the person to whom it was addressed.

58. Quoted in Hodges, *Henry Codman Potter,* 323–24.

59. Editorial "Punishing the Bishop," *New York Times,* 27 March 1900, 6. Cf. HCP's defense of the conduct of American soldiers in the Philippines, reported in *New York Times,* 3 May 1900, 2.

60. Quoted in Hodges, *Henry Codman Potter,* 324–25. Cf. *New York Times,* 3 May 1900, 2; Sheerin, *Henry Codman Potter,* 54; and Griffen, "Urban Church in Ferment," 384–85, who quotes a 4 April 1900 letter from HCP to Franklin Pierce: "I think it was ill-advised and unfortunate that originally we held the Philippines; but I think also that, to abandon them *now,* would be to abandon them to internal warfares of rival leaders and rival tribes. At present they are no more fit to lead themselves, or organize a government, than a parcel of children."

61. HCP, "Problem of the Philippines," 41–69. HCP nowhere mentions consulting Episcopal missionaries in the Philippines, but he may have done so. The 1898 General Convention constituted the Episcopal Church's missionary district of the Philippines, but its initial missionary workers were two army chaplains who remained in the islands after the war. Later, members of the Brotherhood of St. Andrew joined them; Addison, *Episcopal Church,* 238, 347–38; Albright, *History,* 336–39.

62. HCP, "Problem of the Philippines," 43–53, 62–69.

63. *Citizen,* 237–41; HCP here cites John A. Hobson, *The Social Problem,* 273–74.

64. HCP, *Citizen,* 242–47.

65. Lewis L. Gould, *The Spanish-American War and President McKinley* (Lawrence: University Press of Kansas, 1982), 108–10, citing Charles S. Olcott, *The Life of William McKinley* (Boston: Houghton, Mifflin, 1916), 2: 109–11.

66. Josiah Strong, *Expansion under New World Conditions* (New York: Baker and Taylor, 1900); on Strong, see Toews, "Imperialism of Righteousness," 114–18.

67. *New York Convention Proceedings 1902,* 121 (quotation); *New York Convention Proceedings 1904,* 142; *New York Convention Proceedings 1905,* 166; *New York Convention Proceedings 1907,* 141; *New York Convention Proceedings 1908,* 153. Unfortunately, there seems to be no record of HCP's remarks on these occasions. On the Philippine Commissions, see Gould, *William McKinley,* 180–87, 226–35.

68. Compare HCP's view with the editorial on HCP's "Problem of the Philippines" in *New York Times,* 16 November 1900, 2, which commends HCP's position but differs on whether the taking of the Philippines was a blunder.

69. Griffen, "Urban Church in Ferment," 378–79.

Chapter 5: Reconciling Labor and Capital

1. Gladden, *Working People and Their Employers* (Boston: Lockwood, Brooks, 1876), 3; on the assessment of the social gospel's record on race relations and on Gladden in particular, see White, *Liberty and Justice,* xi–xiii, 130–47. Cf. Preston Williams, "The Social Gospel and Race Relations: A Case Study of a Social Movement," in *Toward a Discipline of Social Ethics: Essays in Honor of Walter George Muelder,* ed. Paul Deats Jr. (Boston: Boston University Press, 1972); and Philip S. Foner, *Organized Labor and the Black Worker, 1619–1981* (New York: International Publishers, 1981).

2. P. Foner, *Labor Movement*, 1: 19–64; Robert L. Heilbroner, *The Making of Economic Society* (Englewood Cliffs, N.J.: Prentice-Hall, 1962), 72–140; May, *Protestant Churches*, 111; C. H. Hopkins, *Rise of the Social Gospel*, 245; Handy, *Christian America*, 159.

3. May, *Protestant Churches*, 3–13 (quotations from 6, 7, and 12–13, respectively); Hofstadter, *American Political Tradition*, 18–67.

4. May, *Protestant Churches*, 13–15; Phyllis Deane, *The Evolution of Economic Ideas*, Modern Cambridge Economics (Cambridge, U.K.: Cambridge University Press, 1980), 1–92; Maurice Dobb, *Theories of Value and Distribution since Adam Smith: Ideology and Economic Theory* (Cambridge, U.K.: Cambridge University Press, 1979), 38–120; Robert L. Heilbroner, *The Worldly Philosophers: The Lives, Times, and Ideas of the Great Economic Thinkers*, 5th ed. (New York: Touchstone Books, 1980), 40–101; Julián Marías, *History of Philosophy*, trans. Stanley Applebaum and Clarence C. Strowbridge (New York: Dover Books, 1967), 258–60.

5. John Stuart Mill, *Principles of Political Economy, with Some of Their Applications to Social Philosophy*, vol. 1, book 2 (London, 1848), 401–2, quoted in Dobb, *Theories of Value*, 132; see also Dobb, *Theories of Value*, 105, 131–34; and Deane, *Evolution of Economic Ideas*, 32, 38–40.

6. Alonzo Potter, *Political Economy* (New York: Harper and Brothers, 1840), 282, 289; May, *Protestant Churches*, 15–16; Markwell, *Anglican Left*, 1–2. May observes, in *Protestant Churches*, 15 n. 39: "This text is partly a revision of G. P. Scrope's British text, but the supplementary chapter on labor, to which the citations on these pages refer, is entirely Potter's own. The authorship of various chapters is established by [Michael] O'Connor, *Origins [of Academic Economics in the United States* (New York: Columbia University Press, 1944)], pp. 204–13."

7. May, *Protestant Churches*, 16, 21.

8. Ibid., 91–111.

9. Ibid., 119–24, 182, 193–94. C. H. Hopkins, *Rise of the Social Gospel*, 92–96, 280–81, observed that American social Christianity responded to the industrial problem in five typical ways. First, it demanded that employers treat workers justly in setting wages and maintaining working conditions. Second, it developed refutations of classical and clerical political economic theory. Third, it discussed the merits of trade unions, strikes, and other strategies. Fourth, it criticized some of labor's tactics, especially those involving violence and coercion. And fifth, it advocated arbitration of industrial conflict and cooperative means of distributing the proceeds of production, such as profit sharing. Further, it institutionalized the social gospel by establishing permanent commissions and departments and adopting official positions on industrial relations.

10. Washington Gladden, *Applied Christianity* (Boston: Houghton, Mifflin, 1886), 156–57.

11. May, *Protestant Churches*, 111; Abell, *Urban Impact*, 60–67; C. H. Hopkins, *Rise of the Social Gospel*, 82–85.

12. Skardon, *Church Leader*, 246–56; C. H. Hopkins, *Rise of the Social Gospel*, 38–39; Abell, *Urban Impact*, 29; Hood, *Social Teachings*, 70–73. Writing in 1995 Marshall, "William Augustus Muhlenberg," 170, noted, "Muhlenberg's Church of the Holy Communion has been sold by his diocese, and at this writing has been decommissioned from sacred employment and put to not merely secular but profane use. The Smithtown project (like St. Luke's Hospital) has fared much better. St. Johnland still stands, completely rebuilt on 110 remaining acres in the 1970s, its mission focused on ministry to the aged and now expanding to those with Alzheimer's disease and traumatic brain injury; some of its former land is a beachfront public park. Muhlenberg's grave,

along with that of Anne Ayers and other figures in its history sits atop a quiet knoll behind the director's residence at St. Johnland."

13. HCP, "Our Brother's Blood," 4–5. Although the publication date given is 1872, I date this sermon to Thanksgiving 1871 from internal evidence, from HCP's practice of preaching on social or political issues at Thanksgiving, and from the churches' regular practice of publishing HCP's Thanksgiving sermons.

14. Ibid., 5–16; on the development of industrialization and class conflict in New York City, see Sean Wilentz, *Chants Democratic: New York City and the Rise of the American Working Class, 1788–1850* (New York: Oxford University Press, 1984); on the Paris Commune, see Karl Marx, "The Civil War in France," in *The Marx-Engels Reader*, 2d ed., ed. Robert C. Tucker (New York: W. W. Norton, 1978), 618–52; on Protestant reaction to the Paris Commune, see May, *Protestant Churches*, 58, 72, 74.

15. Hodges, *Henry Codman Potter*, 86; Sheerin, *Henry Codman Potter*, 36; Griffen, "Urban Church in Ferment," 242; P. Foner, *Labor Movement*, 1: 439–74. Although HCP nowhere mentions Jay Cooke by name, Sheerin avers that HCP "knew and liked bankers of the Jay Cooke type, whose failure had helped make the panic a disaster. But he excused no man for his reckless financial mistakes, or his failure to set public interest before private gains. That such men were liberal contributors to church work, that they generously helped other public and ecclesiastical institutions by gifts of money, or even that their sons went into the ministry of the Episcopal Church, as Mr. Cooke's did in later years, had no retarding effect on his moral judgments or public ethical utterances."

16. HCP, "Free Church a Witness," in *Waymarks*, 327–41.

17. May, *Protestant Churches*, 92–96; P. Foner, *Labor Movement*, 1: 464–75; Robert V. Bruce, *1877: Year of Violence* (Indianapolis: Bobbs-Merrill, 1959); *Independent*, 26 July 1877, 16, and 2 August 1877, 16, quoted by May, *Protestant Churches*, 92–93; Beecher quoted by May, *Protestant Churches*, 93–94; Bruce, *1877*, 312–13, from *Christian Union*, 1 August 1877, 92–94, and 8 August 1877, 112–14.

18. On Henry George, see Bruce, *1877*, 312; C. H. Hopkins, *Rise of the Social Gospel*, 59–61; May, *Protestant Churches*, 154–56; and Eileen W. Lindner, "The Redemptive Politic of Henry George: A Legacy to the Social Gospel," *Union Seminary Quarterly Review* 42 (1988): 1–8. On the report of the Joint Committee on Church Work among the Laboring Classes, see *General Convention Journal 1877*, 267–69; C. H. Hopkins, *Rise of the Social Gospel*, 38–39; and Hood, *Social Teachings*, 67. When this report was approved, HCP had been secretary to the House of Bishops for eleven years but was not a member of this joint committee. Notable among the committee's members, however, were Frederick Dan Huntington, bishop of Central New York, and William Welsh, a layperson who had been a colleague of Alonzo Potter. See also May, *Protestant Churches*, 92–96.

19. HCP, "One Another's Burdens," in *Sermons*, 221–29.

20. HCP, "Owe No Man Any Thing," 204–5, "Faith in God and Man," 210–13, "The Perils of Wealth," 81–95, and "The Impotence of Money," 234–48, in *Sermons*; HCP, "Plea for the American Sunday," 110–13, and "Total Abstinence Movement," 23–24, in *Waymarks*; HCP, "Introductory Note," *Annual Parish Report 1878*, 7–8.

21. HCP, "The Social Indifferentist," in *Sermons*, 78–89.

22. HCP, "The Homes of the Poor," 48–65, "He Beheld the City," 15–29, "The Christian Life Organic," 249–66, "Faith and Culture," 310–24, "The Slaughter of the Innocents," 96–110, and "Related Life," 162–75, in *Sermons*; HCP, "A Nation's Prayers," 53–55, and "Sermon Commemorative of Adam Norrie," 94–97, in *Waymarks*. See also *Annual Parish Report 1880*, 7–10; *Annual Parish Report 1881*, 5–10; *Annual Parish Report 1882*, 5–8; and *Annual Parish Report 1883*, 5–10.

23. Hodges, *Henry Codman Potter*, 146–65, 183–91; Sheerin, *Henry Codman Potter*, 79–80; Lindsley, *This Planted Vine*, 211–14.

24. May, *Protestant Churches*, 96–99; *Independent*, 26 July 1883, 16, quoted in ibid., 97.

25. Abell, *Urban Impact*, 59–60; Henry David, *The History of the Haymarket Affair: A Study in the American Social-Revolutionary and Labor Movements*, 2d ed. (New York: Russell and Russell, 1958), 3–181; Paul Avrich, *The Haymarket Tragedy* (Princeton, N.J.: Princeton University Press, 1984), 68–78.

26. May, *Protestant Churches*, 100–104; Avrich, *Haymarket Tragedy*, 181–215; David, *History of the Haymarket Affair*, 182–392, 426–508; P. Foner, *Labor Movement*, 2: 93–114. The identity and motivation of the bomb thrower remain uncertain: David, 508–27, considers various suspects and concludes that it is impossible to identify the bomb thrower conclusively; P. Foner, *History of the Labor Movement*, 110–11, argues that the bomber was an agent provocateur in the employ of the police or employers who sought to discredit and defeat the eight-hour movement and organized labor itself; and Avrich, 437–45, argues that the bomber was indeed an anarchist acting alone and in retaliation for the police's shooting of workers on the previous day.

27. May, *Protestant Churches*, 100–104, 237–39; Avrich, *Haymarket Tragedy*, 297–312; David, *History of the Haymarket Affair*, 393–425.

28. Gladden, "Is It Peace or War?" in *Applied Christianity*, 114–15, reprinted from *Century Magazine*, May 1886; Handy, *Social Gospel*, 56, also reproduces the quote. Gladden orally delivered "Is It Peace or War?" on several occasions prior to Haymarket, but his clear reference in the published version to the Haymarket violence indicates that it appeared sometime after those events. I have been unable to determine whether it appeared before or after HCP's pastoral letter, which was distributed to the clergy on 13 May 1886, or whether HCP had seen published accounts of Gladden's address or even a manuscript of it before he composed his pastoral letter. On the one hand, the lack of direct textual or rhetorical parallels between the two essays and the continuity between HCP's letter and his earlier work tends to suggest that HCP did not rely on Gladden's work here; on the other hand, it is likely that HCP was well aware of Gladden and his work by 1886. The extent of the broader relationship between Gladden and HCP is similarly difficult to ascertain. Both men lived and worked in New York City from 1871 to 1875, when Gladden was editor of the *Independent* and HCP minister at Grace Church. Their views were similar on theological as well as social issues, both were consciously influenced by Horace Bushnell, and HCP was a member of New York's Century Association, whose *Century Magazine* published several of Gladden's articles. Nevertheless, HCP mentions Gladden nowhere in his work. The only demonstrable direct connection was their membership in 1893 on the Committee of Fifty on temperance-related issues.

29. HCP, "Duty of the Clergy," 565. See also Keyser, *Bishop Potter*, 21–26; report on and reprint of letter in "The Labor Disturbance," *New York Times*, 14 May 1886, 3; editorials in *New York Times*, 15 May 1886, 4, and 16 May 1886, 8; portion of letter in Deems, *Christian Thought*, 289–91; and White and Hopkins, *Social Gospel*, 63–65. The letter is called "The Laborer Not a Commodity" in the secondary literature, but of the contemporary sources only the version in Deems bears that title. Presumably, HCP would not have given a title to a letter, and the title given to it in Deems seems to have been adopted by subsequent scholars. I cite the "Duty of the Clergy" for all references to this letter, as it constitutes the most complete contemporary source, and cite parallel references as appropriate.

30. Morgan and Newton in *Churchman*, 29 May 1886, 593–94; Satterlee and Rainsford in *Churchman*, 5 June 1886, 621, 705–6.

31. "Bishop Potter's Letter," *New York Times*, 15 May 1886, 4; "'Labor Troubles' and Religion," *New York Times*, 16 May 1886, 8; "The Church and the Laborer," *Nation* 42 (1886): 419.

32. C. H. Hopkins, *Rise of the Social Gospel*, 150.

33. Keyser, *Bishop Potter*, 21. CAIL's journal *Hammer and Pen* and Keyser's book are the primary sources for CAIL's history and activities. Other useful sources include Miller and Fletcher, *Church and Industry*, 52–76; Griffen, "Urban Church in Ferment," 390–415; and C. H. Hopkins, *Rise of the Social Gospel*, 150–52. Hood, *Social Teachings*, 71, incorrectly identifies CAIL's founding leader as W. R. Huntington, who was in fact a cousin of J. O. S. Huntington and HCP's successor at Grace Church.

34. Keyser, *Bishop Potter*, 30–37; Hodges, *Henry Codman Potter*, 371–72; Griffen, "Urban Church in Ferment," 390–99; C. H. Hopkins, *Rise of the Social Gospel*, 151.

35. May, *Protestant Churches*, 105–6; P. Foner, *Labor Movement*, 2: 206–18; Almont Lindsey, *The Pullman Strike: The Story of a Unique Experiment and of a Great Labor Upheaval* (Chicago: University of Chicago Press, 1971), 9–10.

36. *Independent*, 14 July 1892, 18; *Christian Advocate* 14 July 1892, 460–61, and 28 July 1892, 507; *Churchman* 10 September 1892, 307, and 28 October 1892, 496; all cited in May, *Protestant Churches*, 105–7.

37. P. Foner, *Labor Movement*, 2: 235–78; May, *Protestant Churches*, 107–8; Lindsey, *Pullman Strike*, 11–18, 90–307. As Foner notes, 266: "Having served the railroad corporations for years as a lawyer and having been a railroad director and a member of the General Managers' Association before becoming a member of Cleveland's cabinet, Olney's interests were closely linked to those of big business. Moreover, Olney had sizable financial investments in the railroads."

38. *Churchman*, 7 July 1894, 7, and *Outlook*, 4 July 1894, 8–9, 4 August 1894, 170, cited and discussed in May, *Protestant Churches*, 108–11. Cf. P. Foner, *Labor Movement*, 2: 269, and Lindsey, *Pullman Strike*, 308–34.

39. *New York Convention Proceedings 1893*, 100; Griffen, "Urban Church in Ferment," 370.

40. *New York Convention Proceedings 1893*, 132–33.

41. "Bishop's Address," *New York Convention Proceedings 1894*, 131–33; "Christian Socialism," *New York Times*, 28 September 1894, 4. HCP cited the London *Quarterly Review*, July 1894, 6–7.

42. *The Dawn*, November 1894, 162–64. With regard to the "nameless writer" of the essay in the *Quarterly Review*, it is not clear whether the journal published the article without attribution or HCP failed to identify the writer so that Bliss, perhaps relying only on HCP's remarks, remained unaware of the writer's identity. Unfortunately, I have been unable to locate HCP's October 1894 address to which Bliss favorably refers, and that according to him was entitled "City and Nation."

43. Keyser, *Bishop Potter*, 51–56; Griffen, "Urban Church in Ferment," 399–401. HCP worked with Lowell in the Charity Organization Society and would later work with both Adler and Low in the 1900–1901 New York reform campaign. For dates of HCP's mediation sessions, see *New York Convention Proceedings 1895*, 95; *New York Convention Proceedings 1896*, 113, 118, 120; *New York Convention Proceedings 1897*, 112, 114.

44. Keyser, *Bishop Potter*, 61–66.

45. Ibid., 63–73; Hodges, *Henry Codman Potter*, 289; Griffen, "Urban Church in Ferment," 370–71. Griffen cites the typescript of HCP's "Decision in the Dispute between the International Lithographic Artists' and Engravers Insurance and Protective Association of the United States and the Lithographic Association of the Metropolitan District"; I have been unable to locate this source and assume that Keyser's complete quotation of the decision is accurate.

46. HCP's speech at 1897 CAIL supper quoted from editorial in *Brooklyn Eagle* and sermon at 1898 Labor Sunday service by Keyser, *Bishop Potter*, 102–3, 39–50. See also *New York Convention Proceedings 1898*, 114; *New York Times*, 9 May 1898, 9; *Hammer and Pen*, 1 (June 1898): 1–3, 5, 7.

47. Letter from Easley to Lyman J. Gage, 14 May 1898, quoted by Green, *National Civic Federation*, 7.

48. Hodges, *Henry Codman Potter*, 345–47; Keyser, *Bishop Potter*, 121–28; Sheerin, *Henry Codman Potter*, 47, 122–23; Griffen, "Urban Church in Ferment," 272–73; Green, *National Civic Federation*, 3–61; P. Foner, *Labor Movement*, 2: 384–87; *New York Times*, 7 May 1901, 8.

49. P. Foner, *Labor Movement*, 3: 61–110; Green, *National Civic Federation*, 482–96.

50. *Hammer and Pen*, special no. (November 1908): 1–2; Hodges, *Henry Codman Potter*, 373.

51. Hodges, *Henry Codman Potter*, 343–48; Sheerin, *Henry Codman Potter*, 104–5; Griffen, "Urban Church in Ferment," 371–76; HCP, *Citizen*.

52. HCP, *Citizen*, 15–21, 42–47, 59–61, 139–47.

53. Ibid., 29–40, 162–63; HCP does not identify the source from which he quotes regarding minimizing human inequalities by the principle of human brotherhood through a divine Fatherhood, but the context suggests that it may have been Mathews's *Social Teaching of Jesus*.

54. HCP, *Citizen*, 211–14.

55. Ibid., 87–97.

56. Ibid., 93–103. Cf. ibid., 35, where HCP criticizes "the extravagance of religious teachers who, having cast in their lot with the advocates of social reform, have accepted social theories as the basis of a regeneration of society which in truth but exchange one set of errors for another" and gives as an example of such theories "the restoration of the land to the people." While HCP in this context cited Christian socialist Stewart Headlam, it seems clear that Henry George's single-tax proposal lies behind Headlam's argument and HCP's criticism of it.

57. Ibid., 72–78, 223–25.

58. Ibid., 22–26; HCP referred to Bakunin's *God and the State*.

59. Ibid., 26–27, 35–37, 47–59.

60. Ibid., 98–102.

61. Ibid., 103–24.

62. Ibid., 125–38. On supply and demand in neoclassical political economy, see Deane, *Evolution of Economic Ideas*, 107–13, who elucidates the strong practical and ideological appeal of the supposed scientific character of the law of supply and demand. On the one hand, the "notion of an integrated system in which changes in prices and quantities, in demand and supply, could be interpreted as a system of opposing forces and handled with the techniques of static mechanics provided a remarkably effective technique of analysis and generated a whole range of fruitful though simple tools . . . which enabled the academic conceptual apparatus to be put to direct practical use in sorting out the crucial issues involved in many real-world policy problems." On the other hand, "a methodology which took as its central examplar a demonstration of the optimal allocation of scarce resources in a perfect market and substituted a 'scientific' concept of equilibrium for the out-dated philosophical assumption of the 'natural law' . . . permitted economists to justify an ideological bias toward the *status quo* of income distribution on ostensibly non-political grounds."

63. HCP, *Citizen*, 165–70, 188–205.

64. Ibid., 68–71.

65. Ibid., 207–33. HCP does not cite any particular passage from Paul's epistles, but he may have been alluding to Romans 3:22 and 7:7 or Galatians 3:24 in his reference to the law as schoolmaster.

66. Ibid., 152–60.

67. Ibid., 15–18, 62–68, 170–87.

68. P. Foner, *Labor Movement*, 2: 370, notes: "From 1892 to 1896 the government brought five cases under the act against labor and won four, and five against the trusts and won only one."

69. Gould, *Theodore Roosevelt*, 27–32, 49–53, 105–6, 212–18; P. Foner, *Labor Movement*, 2: 12–14, 231, 369–87.

70. HCP, *Citizen*, 38–39, 80.

71. C. H. Hopkins, *Rise of the Social Gospel*, 280, 284–86.

72. *General Convention Journal 1877*, 267–69; C. H. Hopkins, *Rise of the Social Gospel*, 38–39; Hood, *Social Teachings*, 67.

73. "Pastoral Letter," *General Convention Journal 1883*, 466–67; May, *Protestant Churches*, 183. HCP was not a member of the 1883 Standing Committee on the Pastoral Letter, but a notable member was Bishop Frederic Dan Huntington; see *General Convention Journal 1883*, 33.

74. "The Pastoral Letter," *General Convention Journal 1886*, 555–70; for HCP's resolution on its dissemination, see ibid., 119. Hood, *Social Teachings*, 67 and 72, suggests that this pastoral letter reflects a shift from a "theological model of the church as advocate for the weaker classes" to a "model of the church as mediator between opposing forces, labor and capital." I agree that the 1886 Pastoral Letter employs the latter model, but I find no evidence for an advocacy model in the earlier documents and, therefore, disagree that such a shift took place. The model operative earlier is one of paternalism, not advocacy, and continues alongside the mediator model in later documents (as seen, for example, in 1886 Pastoral Letter's discussion of mission work among black people). Both these models were operative also in HCP's work.

75. On these organizations and their activities, see Keyser, *Bishop Potter*; Miller and Fletcher, *Church and Industry*, 52–110; C. H. Hopkins, *Rise of the Social Gospel*, 150–52; and May, *Protestant Churches*, 184–86. May, *Protestant Churches*, 186, observes, "The fact that Bishops Huntington and Potter consistently backed the C.A.I.L. made it difficult for even the most conservative Episcopal laymen to believe it altogether bad."

76. *General Convention Journal 1901*, 125–26; Keyser, *Bishop Potter*, 139–49; Miller and Fletcher, *Church and Industry*, 111–13. C. H. Hopkins, *Rise of the Social Gospel*, 284, notes, "Both the General Convention of the Protestant Episcopal Church and the National Council of Congregational Churches took preliminary action leading toward official social-service programs at their meetings in 1901. By coincidence, the resolutions were passed within a few hours of each other by bodies in session on opposite sides of the continent."

77. Gould, *Theodore Roosevelt*, 66–72; Green, *National Civic Federation*, 43–56; "The Anthracite Miners and the Decision of the Commission," *Hammer and Pen* (May 1903): 1.

78. *General Convention Journal 1904*, 96–97.

79. *General Convention Journal 1904*, 95–98, 394–96. See also Keyser, *Bishop Potter*, 140–49, 157–59; "Episcopalians Defend Organization of Labor," *New York Times*, 20 October 1904, 6; *Hammer and Pen* 6 (November 1904): 90–91; and *National Civic Federation Review* 1 (15 November 1904): 1, 14.

80. *General Convention Journal 1907*, 165–66, 527–29; *Hammer and Pen* 8 (July 1907): 202–13 and 8 (October 1907): 218–19; Keyser, *Bishop Potter*, 155–72; Miller and

Fletcher, *Church and Industry,* 114–16; C. H. Hopkins, *Rise of the Social Gospel,* 285. In his address to the November 1907 New York Diocesan Convention, HCP commended the Report of the Joint Commission on the Relations of Capital and Labor presented to the General Convention in the previous month but noted that he had *not* written it; *New York Convention Proceedings 1907,* 178.

81. *General Convention Journal 1910,* 110, 534–38; Miller and Fletcher, *Church and Industry,* 116–28; C. H. Hopkins, *Rise of the Social Gospel,* 285–86.

Chapter 6: A Work for a Whole Life

1. Greer, "Bishop's Address," *New York Convention Proceedings 1908,* 144–46.

2. The phrase "a work for a whole life" appears as one of the headings in HCP's *God and the City,* 51–53.

3. Arthur M. Schlesinger, *A Critical Period in American Religion, 1875–1900* (Philadelphia: Fortress Press, 1967). Cf. May, *Protestant Churches,* vii–xv, and White and Hopkins, *Social Gospel,* xiii–xv.

4. H. Richard Niebuhr, *The Kingdom of God in America,* repr. ed. (Middletown, Conn.: Wesleyan University Press, 1988), xix–xx; *The Social Sources of Denominationalism* (New York: Henry Holt, 1931; reprint, New York: Meridian Books, 1960).

5. Handy, Introduction to *Social Gospel,* 3–5. Cf. Handy, *Christian America,* and Sidney Mead, *The Lively Experiment* (New York: Harper and Row, 1963).

6. White and Hopkins, *Social Gospel,* xiii–xv. Cf. May, *Protestant Churches,* vii–xiii.

7. Schlesinger, *Critical Period,* 1.

8. Guelzo, *Evangelical Christendom,* 1–13, 120–21. While Guelzo holds Anglo-Catholic historiography primarily responsible for the fact that the "names of Johns, McIlvaine, Sparrow, Eastburn, Tyng, Bedell, Milnor, Clark, Stevens and of course Cummins have simply been chiseled off the Episcopal monuments," liberals ignorant of or embarrassed by their evangelical heritage may also bear some of the responsibility.

9. Ibid., 15.

10. Butler, *Standing against the Whirlwind,* 235.

11. HCP, "Cost and Beauty in Worship," in *Sermons,* 308. On Bushnell's soteriology, see his *God in Christ* (Hartford, Conn.: W. J. Hamersley, 1852), *Christ and His Salvation* (London: R. D. Dickinson, 1880), and *The Vicarious Sacrifice: Grounded in Principles of Universal Obligation* (London: R. D. Dickinson, 1880).

12. For example, Butler, *Standing against the Whirlwind,* 179–83; and Holmes, *Brief History,* 116–21.

13. See, e.g., Sawyer, *Charles Augustus Briggs,* 25–37; and Mark A. Knoll, "The Evangelical Enlightenment and the Task of Theological Education," in *Communication and Change in American Religious History,* ed. Leonard I. Sweet (Grand Rapids, Mich.: William B. Eerdmans, 1993), 270–300.

14. Timothy L. Smith, *Revivalism and Social Reform: American Protestantism on the Eve of the Civil War* (Nashville, Tenn.: Abingdon Press, 1957), 217; Robert Bruce Mullin, "Biblical Critics and the Battle over Slavery," *Journal of Presbyterian History* 61 (1983): 210–26. Mullin well illustrates the issues at stake for many antislavery evangelicals by quoting S. W. S. Dutton, "Slavery and the Bible; Slavery and the Church; Slavery and Infidelity," *New Englander* 15 (1857): 134: "We must give up the point that the New Testament defends slavery, or we *must* give up a very large—and an increasingly large—portion of this land to infidelity; for they neither can, nor will, nor ought, to be convinced that a book that sanctions slavery is from God."

15. Mullin, "Biblical Critics," 223.

16. Huntington, "Henry Codman Potter," 18.

17. Markwell, *Anglican Left*, 2.

18. HCP, "Some Words Introductory," in *Annual Parish Report 1874*, 6–9; HCP, "Institutionalism: Its Dangers and Failures" and "One Another's Burdens," in *Sermons*, 142–61 and 220–33.

19. HCP, "Free Church a Witness," 327–35.

20. HCP, *Citizen*, 162–63.

21. Quoted in Hodges, *Henry Codman Potter*, 315.

22. HCP, *Citizen*, 98–104.

23. HCP, "Duty of the Clergy," 565; Keyser, *Bishop Potter*, 21–24; White and Hopkins, *Social Gospel*, 63–64; HCP, *Citizen*, 15–18, 38, 62–68, 80, 170–87; *General Convention Journal 1904*, 95–97.

24. HCP's contribution is similar to that of Charles R. Henderson, a Baptist pastor and professor of sociology, as described by Robert T. Handy, "Practical and Prophetic Aspects of the Social Gospel: Charles R. Henderson and Walter Rauschenbusch," *Chronicle* 18 (July 1955): 99–105. By comparison with Walter Rauschenbusch, whom Handy describes as emphasizing the prophetic and theoretical aspects of the gospel, Henderson "embodied the practical, the humanitarian, the sociological side of the gospel" and "led more by his participation in the work of committees and organizations." Handy's summary remarks about Henderson, 105, are also fitting for HCP: "His emphasis was always on the practical; his works and activities sprang from his understanding of Christian faith, and were an attempt to translate faith's directives into action. His efforts and writings were so directly related to the problems of his own day that it has been easy to overlook them; his understanding of Christian faith was so colored by the atmosphere of his time that it has been easy to minimize his sincerity. But any fair assessment of the important period of our history between Civil and first World Wars must take account of his contribution."

25. White and Hopkins, *Social Gospel*, xvi–xvii.

26. May, *Protestant Churches*, viii–xvii, 111, 231–35; White and Hopkins, *Social Gospel*, 259–72, 285–95; H. R. Niebuhr, *Kingdom of God*, 150–63, 183–98; W. A. Visser't Hooft, *The Background of the Social Gospel in America* (St. Louis: Bethany Press, 1928); Reinhold Niebuhr, *Moral Man and Immoral Society* (New York: Charles Scribner's Sons, 1932); Christopher Lasch, "Religious Contributions to Social Movements: Walter Rauschenbusch, the Social Gospel, and Its Critics," *Journal of Religious Ethics* 18 (Spring 1990): 7–25.

27. Susan H. Lindley, "'Neglected Voices' and *Praxis* in the Social Gospel," *Journal of Religious Ethics* 18 (Spring 1990): 75.

28. Ibid., 96. On the understanding of praxis in liberation theology, see Juan Luis Segundo, *The Liberation of Theology* (Maryknoll, N.Y.: Orbis Books, 1976), 7–38, 69–96; and Beverly Wildung Harrison, "Theological Reflection in the Struggle for Liberation: A Feminist Perspective," in *Making the Connections*, 235–63.

29. Holmes, *Brief History*, 92–142; Mullin, *Episcopal Vision*, 211–12.

30. A. Potter quoted in M. A. D. Howe, *Memoirs*, 245; *General Convention Journal 1853*, 182; M. A. D. Howe, *Memoirs*, 241–47; Addison, *Episcopal Church*, 177–88.

31. HCP, "Relation of the Clergy," 26–27.

32. *Annual Parish Report 1870*, 40; *Annual Parish Report 1881*, 6–7.

33. HCP, *Citizen*, 29–40.

34. HCP, "The Homes of the Poor," in *Sermons*, 59.

35. Walter Rauschenbusch, *A Theology for the Social Gospel* (New York: Macmillan, 1917; reprint, Nashville: Abingdon, 1981), 95.

36. Huntington, "Henry Codman Potter," 6–7.

37. Harrison, "Theological Reflection," 248. Cf. 282, n. 55: "In a feminist liberation perspective, praxis as resistance to concrete suffering is the norm for collaboration, not conceptual agreement. Solidarity and common accountability in resisting concrete human suffering are more important than intellectual agreement. In sum, *social theoretical* formulations are to be judged by how well they clarify the sources of oppression of poor black women. *Theological* formulations are to be judged by how profoundly they give voice to the sources of hope such women experience."

38. HCP, *Citizen*, 29–35.

39. *Annual Parish Report 1870*, 40; *Annual Parish Report 1882*, 7.

BIBLIOGRAPHY

Publications by Henry Codman Potter

"Address Delivered at St. Paul's Chapel, New York, on Tuesday, April 30, 1889, Being the One Hundredth Anniversary of the Inauguration of George Washington." New York: E. P. Dutton, 1889. A copy exists in the Archives of the Episcopal Diocese of New York as no. 10 in a volume of pamphlets under the title "Address at the Centennial Commemoration Service of Washington's Inauguration, St. Paul's Church, New York, April 30, 1889." Reprinted from the *New York Evening Post.*

"Address Delivered at the Service Commemorative of the One Hundredth Anniversary of the Consecration of the First Bishops for America, by Bishops of the Church of England in the Chapel of Lambeth Palace, February 4th, 1887." London: W. Ridgway, 1887.

"Address of President Potter." *Liberia* 2 (February 1993): 11–18.

"Address to the Convention of New York, 1884." New York: J. C. Rankin, 1884.

"Address to the Convention of New York, 1885." New York: J. C. Rankin, 1885.

"Address to the Convention of New York, Together with the Report of the Committee Thereon." New York: n.p., 1899.

Addresses to Women Engaged in Church Work. New York: E. P. Dutton, 1887.

"And Now, Why Tarriest Thou? Some Words to Men and Others of Adult Years Concerning Confirmation." New York: E. P. Dutton, 1877.

"Baccalaureate Sermon, Preached before the Columbia College Law School, May 14, 1871, at the Church of the Holy Saviour." New York: D. Van Nostrand, 1872.

"Bishop Potter's Address." *Proceedings of the Grand Chapter of the State of New York* (1903): 94–95.

"Bishop's Address." In *Journal of Proceedings of the Annual Convention of the Protestant Episcopal Church in the Diocese of New York.* New York: J. C. Rankin Jr., 1884–85; New York: J. J. Little, 1886–1907; New York: J. J. Little and Ives, 1908. [Potter's annual address as bishop to the diocesan convention.]

"The Branded Body: A Sermon Preached in Grace Church, New York, on the Morning of the First Sunday in Lent, February 26, 1882." Privately printed, n.d.

"The Building and the Builder: A Sermon Preached at the Church of St. John the Evangelist, New York, November 6th, 1872, at the Institution of W. T. Egbert As Rector." New York: American Church Press, 1872.

"The Call of Lent, to Say 'No.'" New York: Thomas Whittaker, n.d.

"The Cathedral and Its Uses; a Sermon Preached November 20, 1888, at the Dedication of All Saints' Cathedral, Albany, New York." Albany: Weed and Parsons, 1888.

263

"The Chicago-Lambeth Articles." Pp. 155–96 in *Church Unity: Five Lectures, Delivered in the Union Theological Seminary, New York, during the Winter of 1896*. New York: Charles Scribner's Sons, 1896.

"Chinese Traits and Western Blunders." *Century Magazine*, October 1900, 921–30.

"The Choked Life; Some Thoughts for Lent." New York: E. P. Dutton, 1873.

"Christianity and the Criminal: A Paper Read before the Church Congress at Richmond, Virginia, October, 1882." New York: Thomas Whittaker, 1883. Reprinted in *The Scholar and the State, and Other Orations and Addresses*, 165–79. New York: Century, 1897.

"Christmas, and After: A Sermon." *Forum* 12 (January 1892): 677–86.

"The Church and the Children: A Sermon in Behalf of the Church Home of the Protestant Episcopal Church of Boston, Preached on Wednesday Evening, April 18, 1868, at Trinity Church." Boston: E. P. Dutton, 1868.

The Citizen in His Relation to the Industrial Situation. New York: Charles Scribner's Sons, 1902. Reprint, New Haven, Conn.: Yale University Press, 1903.

"Columbia College Commencement, 1889; Baccalaureate Sermon Preached in St. Thomas' Church, Whit-Sunday, June 9, 1889." N.p., n.d.

"The Consecration of St. John's in Stamford, Connecticut. A Sermon Preached on All Saints' Day, 1898, in Memory of William Tatlock." N.p., n.d.

"Decline of the Home, the Foundation of the Nation." *Sunday Magazine*, 5 November 1905, 3–4.

"The Divorce Question; Comment on Article 'Some Social Tendencies in America,' *North American Review*." *Catholic World*, January 1890, 555–56.

"The Drink Problem in Modern Life." New York: Thomas Y. Crowell, 1905.

"The Duty of the Clergy in the Present Emergency." *Churchman*, 22 May 1886, 565–66.

The East of To-day and To-morrow. New York: Century, 1902.

"The Free Church a Witness to the Brotherhood of Humanity in Christ Jesus. A Sermon Delivered before the Free Church Association, Philadelphia, May 17, 1877." N.p., n.d. Reprinted in *Waymarks, 1870–1891, Being Discourses with Some Account of Their Occasions*, 327–41. New York: E. P. Dutton, 1892.

The Gates of the East: A Winter in Egypt and Syria. New York: E. P. Dutton, 1877.

God and the City. 2d ed. New York: Abbey Press, 1900.

"A Good Man's Burial: A Sermon Preached at Grace Church, New York." St. Johnland, N.Y.: Orphan Boys' Stereotype Foundry, 1872.

"The Gospel for Wealth." *North American Review* 152 (May 1891): 513–22. Reprinted in *The Scholar and the State, and Other Orations and Addresses*, 233–48. New York: Century, 1897.

"The Graves of Three Washingtons." *Century Magazine*, February 1907, 509–16.

"The Heroisms of the Unknown." In *The Scholar and the State, and Other Orations and Addresses*, 97–108. New York: Century, 1897. Originally published as "Oration delivered July 2, 1893, at the Dedication of the Monument Commemorative of the Men of New York Who Fell at Gettysburg, July 2, 1863." N.p., 1893.

"The Higher Uses of an Exhibition." In *The Scholar and the State, and Other Orations and Addresses*, 267–78. New York: Century, 1897. Originally published as "Sunday and the Columbian Exposition." *Forum* 14 (October 1892): 194–200.

"The Hymns of the Ordinal." Pp. 121–61 in *Lauda Sion; or, The Liturgical Hymns of the Church.* New York: E. and J. B. Young, 1896.

"Impressions of the Hawaiian Islands." *Century Magazine,* September 1901, 762–68. Reprinted in *The East of To-day and To-morrow,* 139–68. New York: Century, 1902.

"Impressions of Japan." *Century Magazine,* March 1901, 663–70. Reprinted in *The East of To-day and To-morrow,* 71–138. New York: Century, 1902.

"India: Its People and Its Religions." In *The East of To-day and To-morrow,* 169–90. New York: Century, 1902. Originally published as "Impressions of India." *Century Magazine,* August 1901, 622–30.

"Individual Responsibility to the Nation: A Sermon Preached in Trinity Church, Boston, on Thanksgiving Day, November 29, 1866." Boston: E. P. Dutton, 1867.

Introduction to *Annual Report of the Various Departments of Parish Work of Grace Parish, New York.* New York: Grace Parish, 1870–84.

Introduction to *The Pilgrim's Progress,* by John Bunyan. New York: Century, 1900.

"The Laborer Not a Commodity." Pp. 289–91 in *Christian Thought: Lectures and Papers on Philosophy, Christian Evidence, Biblical Elucidation,* 4th ser. Edited by Charles F. Deems. New York: Wilbur B. Ketcham, 1886.

"Law and Loyalty: A Charge Delivered to the One Hundred and Third Convention of New York, on St. Michael and All Angels' Day, 1886." New York: James Pott, 1886.

Law and Loyalty, with Other Charges and Sermons Preached at the Consecration of Bishops. New York: E. S. Gorham, 1903.

"Letter to Mayor Van Wyck." *Outlook* 66 (24 November 1900): 732–33.

"Letter to R. Heber Newton, February 4, 1885." New York: Privately printed, n.d.

"The Life-Giving Word; a Sermon Memorial of the Rt. Rev. Phillips Brooks." Boston: Damrell and Upham, 1893. Reprinted in *The Scholar and the State, and Other Orations and Addresses,* 297–317. New York: Century, 1897.

"The Liturgy, and Its Use: A Sermon, Preached in Grace Church, New York, on Sunday, May 14th, 1871." St. Johnland, N.Y.: Orphan Boys' Stereotype Foundry, 1871.

"Man: Men: and Their Master: Delivered at Gambier, Ohio, November, 1901." New York: E. S. Gorham, 1902.

"A Man after God's Own Heart; Loving Words to the Dear Memory of Francis E. Lawrence, for More Than a Quarter-Century the Pastor of the Church of the Holy Communion, Spoken at the Memorial Service, Sunday Evening, November 2, 1879." Printed for private circulation, 1879.

"A Martyr's Memorial: Sermon Commemorative of the Rev. R. Archer B. Ffennel, Missionary among the Indians." N.p., n.d.

"Mary and Martha." *Harper's Bazar,* 19 May 1900, 129–35.

"The Message of Christ to the Family." Pp. 185–203 in *The Message of Christ to Manhood.* William Belden Noble Lectures for 1898. Boston: Houghton, Mifflin, 1899.

"The Mission and Commission of the Episcopate; a Sermon Preached at the Consecration of Phillips Brooks." New York: E. P. Dutton, 1892. Reprinted in *Waymarks, 1870–1891, Being Discourses with Some Account of Their Occasions,* 361–83. New York: E. P. Dutton, 1892.

"The Mission of the Episcopate; the Sermon Preached at the Consecration of

Thomas F. Davies as Bishop of Michigan, at St. Peter's Church, Philadelphia, on St. Luke's Day, 1889." Philadelphia: Vestry of St. Peter's Church, 1889.

"The Modern Home." *Harper's Bazar,* March 1907, 203–9.

The Modern Man and His Fellow Man. The William Bull Lectures for 1902. Philadelphia: G. W. Jacobs, 1903.

"Mother and Child." *Harper's Monthly Magazine,* December 1901, 102–4.

A Nation in Its Sorrow; Two Sermons Preached in Grace Church, New York, on Garfield's Death. New York: Thomas Whittaker, 1881. Reprinted in *Waymarks, 1870–1891, Being Discourses with Some Account of Their Occasions,* 44–70. New York: E. P. Dutton, 1892.

"National Bigness or Greatness—Which?" *North American Review* 168 (April 1899): 433–44.

"The Offices of Warden and Vestryman; Triennial Charge Delivered to the Clergy and Laity of the Diocese of New York, September 24, 1890." 3d ed. New York: James Pott, 1899.

"Our Brother's Blood; a Sermon, Preached in Grace Church, New York." St. Johnland, N.Y.: Orphan Boys' Stereotype Foundry, 1872.

"The Outlook and Its Promise: A Sermon Preached in Grace Church, New York, on Thanksgiving Day, Nov. 25, 1880." New York: Thomas Whittaker, 1880.

"Papal Infallibility." Preached on Mark 12:17 at Grace Church, New York, on 13 December 1874. New York Diocesan Archives.

"The Passing of Victoria." *Independent* 53 (31 January 1901): 244–45.

"The Place of the Scholar in American Life: An Address Delivered at the Annual Commencement of the University of Michigan, Thursday, June 26th, 1884." Ann Arbor: Board of Regents, University of Michigan, 1884.

"A Plea for the American Sunday: A Sermon, Preached at the Request of the New York Sabbath Committee, in Grace Church, New York, Sunday, May 19, 1878." New York: New York Sabbath Committee, 1878. Reprinted in *Waymarks, 1870–1891, Being Discourses with Some Account of Their Occasions,* 100–116. New York: E. P. Dutton, 1892.

"The Policy of Expansion." *Harper's Weekly,* 5 November 1898, 1075.

"The Powers and the Power of the Episcopate; a Sermon Preached in St. John's Church, Detroit, on St. Matthias' Day, 1885, on the Occasion of the Consecration of George Worthington As Bishop of Nebraska." Detroit: n.p., 1885. Reprinted in *Waymarks, 1870–1891, Being Discourses with Some Account of Their Occasions,* 274–90. New York: E. P. Dutton, 1892.

"The Problem of the Philippines." *Century Magazine,* November 1900, 129–35. Reprinted in *The East of To-day and To-morrow,* 41–69. New York: Century, 1902.

"The Realm of Order." New York: E. P. Dutton, 1887.

"The Reconstructive Power of Christianity." In *Waymarks, 1870–1891, Being Discourses with Some Account of Their Occasions,* 119–32. New York: E. P. Dutton, 1892. Originally published as "The Reconstructive Power of the Religion of Jesus Christ: Sermon Preached at the Consecration of Trinity Church, Lenox." Pittsfield, Mass.: Press of the Berkshire County Eagle, 1888.

"The Relation of the Clergy to the Faith and Order of the Church: Third Triennial Charge to the Convention of the Diocese of New York, October 1st, 1891." New York: Published by resolution of the convention, 1891.

"The Relations of Science to Modern Life; a Lecture Delivered before the New York Academy of Sciences, on Thursday Evening, February 19, 1980." New

York: G. P. Putnam's Sons, 1880. Reprinted in *The Scholar and the State, and Other Orations and Addresses*, 111–44. New York: Century, 1897.

"Religion in Action; a Sermon Preached in Grace Church, New York, on Sunday, May 18, 1873, being the Sunday Following the Funeral Services of John Lloyd Aspinwall." New York: Thomas Whittaker, 1873.

Reminiscences of Bishops and Archbishops. New York: G. P. Putnam's Sons, 1906.

The Scholar and the State, and Other Orations and Addresses. New York: Century, 1897.

"Sermon, in Memory of the Late Abram Newkirk Littlejohn, Preached in the Cathedral of the Incarnation, Garden City." Brooklyn, N.Y.: Eagle Book and Job Printing, 1901.

"A Sermon Delivered in Christ Church, Hartford, Sunday Evening, June 21, 1891, before the Students and Authorities of Trinity College." Hartford, Conn.: Case, Lockwood, and Brainard, 1891.

"A Sermon Preached at the Consecration of Grace Chapel, New York." New York: McWilliams, White, 1876.

"Sermon Preached at the Consecration of the Cathedral of the Incarnation, Garden City, L.I., June 2, 1885." In *Waymarks, 1870–1891, Being Discourses with Some Account of Their Occasions*, 158–75. New York: E. P. Dutton, 1892. Originally published as "A Sermon, Delivered at Garden City, Long Island, June 2nd, 1885, at the Consecration of the Cathedral of the Incarnation." N.p., 1885.

"A Sermon Preached at the Consecration of the Rt. Rev. Alexander Hamilton Vinton, D.D., As Bishop of Western Massachusetts, All Saints' Church, Worcester, April 22nd, 1902." N.p., n.d.

"The Sermon Preached by the Bishop of New York at the Consecration of the Chapel of S. Peter and S. Paul, St. Paul's School, Concord, N.H., on Tuesday, June 5, 1888." Concord, N.H.: Republican Press Association, 1888.

Sermons of the City. New York: E. P. Dutton, 1881.

"Shams in Lent; or, The Real and False in Lenten Duties." New York: E. P. Dutton, 1875.

"A Shepherd Faithful and True; Being a Sermon Commemorative of the Right Rev. Henry Champlin Lay, D.D., LL.D., Delivered in Christ Church, Easton, Md., at the Special Diocesan Convention, November 18th, 1885." New York: American Church Press, 1885.

"The Significance of the American Cathedral." *Forum* 13 (May 1892): 351–59. Reprinted in *The Scholar and the State, and Other Orations and Addresses*, 321–35. New York: Century, 1897.

Sisterhoods and Deaconesses at Home and Abroad. New York: E. P. Dutton, 1873.

"The Social Pace." *Harper's Bazar*, February 1907, 99–106.

"Some Exposition Uses of Sunday." *Century Magazine*, November 1892, 138–41.

"Some Ways of Strengthening and Extending the Total Abstinence Movement." New York: National Temperance Society and Publication House, 1878.

"Some Words Valedictory. A Sermon Preached in Grace Church, New York, on Sunday Morning after Christmas Day, December 30th, 1883." Privately printed, n.d.

"The Teaching Office of the Church, a Charge Delivered to the Convention of the Diocese of New York, on Wednesday, September 26th, 1900." N.p., n.d.

"Thirty Years Reviewed; Being an Anniversary Discourse, Delivered in St. John's Church, Troy, New York." Troy, N.Y.: Budget, 1861.

"Three Score Years and Ten: A Sermon Preached in Grace Church, New York, in Commemoration of Its Seventieth Anniversary." New York: Vestry of Grace Church, 1878.

"Timely Words by Two Bishops of the Protestant Episcopal Church." N.p., n.d.

"Triennial Charge of Bishop Potter: The Lord's Day." *Journal of the One Hundred Twenty-Second Convention of the Diocese of New York*, 1905, 136–52. New York: J. J. Little, 1905.

"Twenty-Fifth Anniversary of the Consecration of the Right Reverend Frederic Dan Huntington." N.p., 1894.

"Two Africas." *Liberia* 4 (February 1894): 12.

"Ultimate Responsibility: A Sermon." *Outlook* 54 (19 December 1896): 1139–41.

"The Uses of a Cathedral." *Century Magazine*, February 1902, 565–71.

Waymarks, 1870–1891, Being Discourses with Some Account of Their Occasions. New York: E. P. Dutton, 1892.

"Western Civilization and the Birth-Rate." *American Journal of Sociology* 12 (March 1907): 626–27. [Response to a paper by Edward A. Ross with the same title.]

"The Witness of Our Fathers: A Sermon Preached at the Consecration of St. Mary's Memorial Church, Wayne, Pa., April 17, 1890." New York: De Vinne Press, n.d.

"Women's Recreations." *Harper's Bazar*, January 1907, 4–10.

"Young Men's Christian Associations: What Is Their Work, and How Shall They Perform It?" Privately printed, n.d.

Other Primary Sources

Annual Report of the Various Departments of Parish Work of Grace Parish, New York. 1869–83 vols. New York: Grace Parish, 1870–84.

Auerbach, Joseph Smith. "Dedication of the Bishop Henry Codman Potter Memorial Buildings." New York: City and Suburban Homes Company, 1912.

———. "The Lesson of Bishop Potter's Life." In *Essays and Miscellanies*. New York: Harper and Brothers, 1914.

Birdsall, Ralph. "A Village View of the Rt. Rev. Henry Codman Potter, D.D., Seventh Bishop of New York, Who Died at His Summer Home in Cooperstown, July 21, 1908." A Sermon Preached in Christ Church, Cooperstown, on the Sixth Sunday after Trinity, 26 July 1908. N.p., 1908.

Bishop, G. R. "Three Sonnets in Memory of the Late Bishop Henry Codman Potter." New York: Privately printed by the author, 1919.

Bushnell, Horace. *Christ and His Salvation.* London: R. D. Dickinson, 1880.

———. *God in Christ.* Hartford, Conn.: W. J. Hamersley, 1852.

———. *The Vicarious Sacrifice: Grounded in Principles of Universal Obligation.* London: R. D. Dickinson, 1880.

———. *Women's Suffrage: The Reform against Nature.* New York: Charles Scribner's Sons, 1869.

———. *Work and Play.* London: A. Strahan, 1864.

Century Association. *Henry Codman Potter: Memorial Addresses Delivered before the Century Association, December 12, 1908.* New York: Century Association, 1908.

Carnegie, Andrew. *The Gospel of Wealth and Other Timely Essays.* Edited by Edward C. Kirkland. Cambridge, Mass.: Belknap Press, 1962.

Douglas, George William. "The Right Reverend Henry Codman Potter." Pp. 71–85 in *Essays in Appreciation.* New York: Longmans, Green, 1912.

The Election and Consecration of the Rev. Henry Codman Potter, D.D., LL.D., As Assistant Bishop of the Diocese of New York. New York: James Pott, 1883.

Gladden, Washington. *Applied Christianity.* Boston: Houghton, Mifflin, 1886.

———. *Working People and Their Employers.* Boston: Lockwood, Brooks, 1876.

Hammer and Pen. Journal of the Church Association for the Advancement of the Interest of Labor. Vols. 1–10, 1898–1908.

Hopkins, John Henry. *A Scriptural, Ecclesiastical, and Historical View of Slavery . . . Addressed to the Right Reverend Alonzo Potter.* 1864. Reprint, New York: Negro Universities Press, 1969.

Howe, M. A. DeWolfe. *Memoirs of the Life and Services of the Rt. Rev. Alonzo Potter, D.D., LL.D., Bishop of the Protestant Episcopal Church in the Diocese of Pennsylvania.* Philadelphia: J. B. Lippincott, 1871.

Huntington, William Reed. "Henry Codman Potter, Rector, Bishop: In Remembrance." Sermon preached at Grace Church, New York, 25 October 1908. New York: printed at the request of the vestry, n.d.

Manning, William Thomas. "Henry Codman Potter, Seventh Bishop of New York; Sermon at the Commemoration of the Fiftieth Anniversary of the Consecration of Bishop Potter, Preached in Grace Church on Sunday, October 22, 1933." New York: n.p., n.d.

National Civic Federation Review. Vols. 1–3, 1903–8.

Nelson, George F. "Some Characteristics of Bishop Potter." Typescript in New York Diocesan Archives, n.d.

People's Institute of New York. *Memorial to Henry Codman Potter by the People's Institute, Cooper Union, Sunday, December 20, 1908.* New York: Cheltenham Press, 1909.

Potter, Alonzo. "Address on the Drinking-Usages of Society." Pp. 5–33 in *Massachusetts Temperance Society, Addresses . . . 1861.* N.p., n.d.

———. "An Appeal in Behalf of Missions. . . ." Boston: R. P. and C. Williams, 1829.

———. "Charge to the Clergy of the Diocese of Pennsylvania." Philadelphia: King and Baird, 1849.

———. "Christian Philanthropy . . . Discourses in St. George's Church, Schenectady, January 13, 1833, before the African School Society."

———. *Discourses, Charges, Addresses, Pastoral Letters, Etc.* Philadelphia: E. H. Butler, 1858.

———. *The Drinking-Usages of Society . . . Masonic Hall, Pittsburgh . . . April 3, 1852.* 1852. Reprint, Boston: Friends of the Massachusetts Temperance Society, 1854.

———, ed. *Memorial Papers; The Memorial with Circular and Questions of the Episcopal Commission; Report of the Commission; Contributions of the Commission; and Communications from Episcopal and Non-Episcopal Divines.* Philadelphia: E. H. Butler, 1857.

———. *Political Economy.* New York: Harper and Brothers, 1840.

———. "Third and Fourth Charges to the Clergy of the Diocese of Pennsylvania." Philadelphia: King and Baird, 1852.

Potter, Frank Hunter. *The Alonzo Potter Family.* Concord, N.H.: Rumford Press, 1923.

Protestant Episcopal Church in the Diocese of New York. *Journal of the Proceedings of the Annual Convention of the Protestant Episcopal Church in the Diocese of New York.* New York: J. C. Rankin Jr., 1884–85; New York: J. J. Little, 1886–1907; New York: J. J. Little and Ives, 1908.

Protestant Episcopal Church in the United States of America. *Journal of the Proceedings of the Bishops, Clergy, and Laity of the Protestant Episcopal Church in the United States of America Assembled in General Convention.* Philadelphia: King and Baird, 1854; Boston: E. P. Dutton, 1863; printed for the convention, 1878–1910.

Ross, Edward A. "Western Civilization and the Birth-Rate." *American Journal of Sociology* 12 (March 1907): 607–17.

State Charities Aid Association. *Report of the Special Committee Appointed to Take Active Measures in Regard to the Erection of a New Bellevue Hospital, February 18, 1874.* New York: American Church Press, 1874.

———. *Report on Conference of Members of the State Charities Aid Association of December, 1880.* New York: G. P. Putnam's Sons, 1881.

———. *Third Annual Report of the State Charities Aid Association to the State Board of Charities of the State of New York, March 1, 1875.* New York: State Charities Aid Association, 1875.

Strong, Josiah. *Expansion under New World Conditions.* New York: Baker and Taylor, 1900.

Secondary Sources

Abell, Aaron I. *The Urban Impact on American Protestantism, 1865–1900.* Cambridge, Mass.: Harvard University Press, 1943. Reprint, Hamden, Conn.: Archon, 1962.

Addison, James Thayer. *The Episcopal Church in the United States, 1789–1931.* New York: Charles Scribner's Sons, 1951.

Ahlstrom, Sydney E. *A Religious History of the American People.* 2 vols. New Haven, Conn.: Yale University Press, 1972. Reprint, Garden City, N.Y.: Image Books, 1975.

Albright, Raymond W. *A History of the Protestant Episcopal Church.* New York: Macmillan, 1964.

Avrich, Paul. *The Haymarket Tragedy.* Princeton, N.J.: Princeton University Press, 1984.

Bernstein, Iver. *The New York City Draft Riots: Their Significance for American Society and Politics in the Age of the Civil War.* New York: Oxford University Press, 1990.

Bordin, Ruth. *Frances Willard: A Biography.* Chapel Hill: University of North Carolina Press, 1986.

———. *Woman and Temperance: The Quest for Power and Liberty, 1873–1900.* Philadelphia: Temple University Press, 1981.

Boyd, Sandra Hughes. "The History of Women in the Episcopal Church: A Select Annotated Bibliography." *Historical Magazine of the Protestant Episcopal Church* 50 (1981): 423–34.

Brewer, H. Peers. "The Protestant Episcopal Freedmen's Commission, 1865–1878." *Historical Magazine of the Protestant Episcopal Church* 26 (December 1957): 361–81.

Brown, C. G. "Christocentric Liberalism in the Episcopal Church." *Historical Magazine of the Protestant Episcopal Church* 37 (1968): 5–38.

Bruce, Robert V. *1877: Year of Violence.* Indianapolis: Bobbs-Merrill, 1959.

Buhle, Mari Jo, and Paul Buhle, eds. *The Concise History of Woman Suffrage.* Urbana: University of Illinois Press, 1978.

Butler, Diana Hochstedt. *Standing against the Whirlwind: Evangelical Episcopalians in Nineteenth-Century America.* New York: Oxford University Press, 1995.

Carroll, Berenice A., ed. *Liberating Women's History: Theoretical and Critical Essays.* Urbana: University of Illinois Press, 1976.

Chorley, E. Clowes. *Men and Movements in the Episcopal Church.* New York: Macmillan, 1946.

David, Henry. *The History of the Haymarket Affair: A Study in the American Social-Revolutionary and Labor Movements.* 2d ed. New York: Russell and Russell, 1958.

Deane, Phyllis. *The Evolution of Economic Ideas.* Modern Cambridge Economics. Cambridge, U.K.: Cambridge University Press, 1978.

Deems, Charles, ed. *Christian Thought: Lectures and Papers on Philosophy, Christian Evidence, Biblical Elucidation.* 4th ser. New York: Wilbur B. Ketcham, 1886.

DeMille, George E. "The Episcopate of Horatio Potter (1802–1887), Sixth Bishop of New York, 1854–1887." *Historical Magazine of the Protestant Episcopal Church* 24 (1955): 66–92.

Dobb, Maurice. *Theories of Value and Distribution since Adam Smith: Ideology and Economic Theory.* Cambridge, U.K.: Cambridge University Press, 1973. Reprint, 1979.

Dolkart, Andrew S. *Morningside Heights: A History of Its Architecture and Development.* New York: Columbia University Press, 1998.

Donald, James M. "Bishop Hopkins and the Reunification of the Church." *Historical Magazine of the Protestant Episcopal Church* 47 (1978): 73–91.

Donovan, Mary S. "Women and Mission: Towards a More Inclusive Historiography." *Historical Magazine of the Protestant Episcopal Church* 53 (1984): 297–305.

———. "Zealous Evangelists: The Woman's Auxiliary to the Board of Missions." *Historical Magazine of the Protestant Episcopal Church* 51 (1982): 371–83.

Edel, Wilbur, ed. *Defenders of the Faith: Religion and Politics from the Pilgrim Fathers to Ronald Reagan.* New York: Praeger, 1987.

Feldman, Egal. "The Social Gospel and the Jews." *American Jewish Historical Quarterly* 58 (March 1969): 300–320.

Fishburn, Janet Forsythe. *The Fatherhood of God and the Victorian Family: The Social Gospel in America.* Philadelphia: Fortress Press, 1981.

Flexner, Eleanor. *Century of Struggle: The Woman's Rights Movement in the United States.* Cambridge, Mass.: Belknap Press, 1959.

Foner, Eric. *Reconstruction: America's Unfinished Revolution, 1863–1877.* New York: Harper and Row, 1988.

Foner, Philip S. *History of the Labor Movement in the United States.* Vols. 1–4. New York: International Publishers, 1947–65.

————. *Organized Labor and the Black Worker, 1619–1981.* New York: International Publishers, 1981.

Formisano, Ronald P. *The Birth of Mass Political Parties, 1827–1861.* Princeton, N.J.: Princeton University Press, 1971.

Franklin, John Hope, and Alfred A. Moss Jr. *From Slavery to Freedom: A History of African Americans.* 8th ed. New York: Alfred A. Knopf, 2000.

Garraty, John A., ed. *Labor and Capital in the Gilded Age: Testimony Taken by the Senate Committee upon the Relations between Labor and Capital, 1883.* Boston: Little, Brown, 1968.

Gorrell, Donald K. *The Age of Social Responsibility: The Social Gospel in the Progressive Era, 1900–1920.* Macon, Ga.: Mercer University Press, 1988.

Gossett, Thomas. *Race: The History of an Idea in America.* New York: Schocken Books, 1965.

Gould, Lewis L. *The Presidency of Theodore Roosevelt.* American Presidency Series. Lawrence: University Press of Kansas, 1991.

————. *The Presidency of William McKinley.* American Presidency Series. Lawrence: University Press of Kansas, 1980.

————, ed. *The Progressive Era.* Syracuse, N.Y.: Syracuse University Press, 1974.

————. *The Spanish-American War and President McKinley.* Lawrence: University Press of Kansas, 1982.

Grant, Curtis R. "The Social Gospel and Race." Ph.D. diss., Stanford University, 1968.

Green, Marguerite. *The National Civic Federation and the American Labor Movement, 1900–1925.* Westport, Conn.: Greenwood Press, 1983.

Griffen, Clyde. "An Urban Church in Ferment: The Episcopal Church in New York City, 1880–1900." Ph.D. diss., Columbia University, 1960.

Guelzo, Allen C. *The Crisis of the American Republic: A History of the Civil War and Reconstruction Era.* St. Martin's Series in U.S. History. New York: St. Martin's Press, 1995.

————. *For the Union of Evangelical Christendom: The Irony of the Reformed Episcopalians.* University Park: Pennsylvania State University Press, 1994.

Gustafson, James M. *Theology and Christian Ethics.* Philadelphia: Pilgrim Press, 1974.

Gutman, Herbert G. *Work, Culture, and Society in Industrializing America: Essays in American Working-Class and Social History.* New York: Alfred A. Knopf, 1976.

Hammack, David C. *Power and Society: Greater New York at the Turn of the Century.* New York: Russell Sage Foundation, 1982.

Handy, Robert T. *A Christian America: Protestant Hopes and Historical Realities.* 2d ed., revised and enlarged. New York: Oxford University Press, 1984.

————. *A History of the Churches in the United States and Canada.* New York: Oxford University Press, 1976.

————. *A History of Union Theological Seminary in New York.* New York: Columbia University Press, 1987.

————. "Practical and Prophetic Aspects of the Social Gospel: Charles R. Henderson and Walter Rauschenbusch." *Chronicle* 18, nos. 3–4 (July 1955): 99–110.

————, ed. *The Social Gospel in America, 1870–1920.* New York: Oxford University Press, 1966.

Hardesty, Nancy A. *Your Daughters Shall Prophesy: Revivalism and Feminism in the Age of Finney.* Chicago Studies in the History of American Religion, vol. 5. Brooklyn, N.Y.: Carlson, 1991.

Harrison, Beverly Wildung. *Making the Connections: Essays in Feminist Social Ethics.* Edited by Carol S. Robb. Boston: Beacon Press, 1985.

Heilbroner, Robert L. *The Making of Economic Society.* Englewood Cliffs, N.J.: Prentice-Hall, 1962.

———. *The Worldly Philosophers: The Lives, Times, and Ideas of the Great Economic Thinkers.* 5th ed. New York: Simon and Schuster, 1980.

Hiatt, Suzanne Radley. "Women's Ordination in the Anglican Communion: Can This Church Be Saved?" Pp. 211–30 in *Religious Institutions and Women's Leadership: New Roles inside the Mainstream,* edited by Catherine Wessinger. Columbia: University of South Carolina Press, 1996.

Hodges, George. *Henry Codman Potter, Seventh Bishop of New York.* New York: Macmillan, 1915.

Hofstadter, Richard. *The Age of Reform: From Bryan to FDR.* New York: Alfred A. Knopf, 1961.

———. *The American Political Tradition.* New York: Alfred A. Knopf, 1948; New York: Vintage Books, 1957.

Hogue, William M. "The Bishop's Saloon." *Historical Magazine of the Protestant Episcopal Church* 31 (1962): 341–50.

Holladay, J. Douglas. "Nineteenth Century Evangelical Activism: From Private Charity to State Intervention, 1830–50." *Historical Magazine of the Protestant Episcopal Church* 51 (1982): 53–79.

Holmes, David L. *A Brief History of the Episcopal Church.* Valley Forge, Pa.: Trinity Press International, 1993.

Hood, Robert E. *Social Teachings in the Episcopal Church.* Harrisburg, Pa.: Morehouse, 1990.

Hopkins, C. Howard. *The Rise of the Social Gospel in American Protestantism, 1865–1915.* New Haven, Conn.: Yale University Press, 1940. Reprint, 1961.

Hudson, Winthrop. "Protestant Clergy Debate the Nation's Vocation, 1898–1899." *Church History* 42 (1973): 110–18.

Jackson, Anthony. *A Place Called Home: A History of Low-Cost Housing in Manhattan.* Cambridge, Mass.: MIT Press, 1976.

Jensen, Richard J. *The Winning of the Midwest: Social and Political Conflict, 1888–1896.* Chicago: University of Chicago Press, 1971.

Johnson, James T. "On Keeping Faith: The Use of History for Religious Ethics." *Journal of Religious Ethics* 7 (Spring 1979): 97–115.

Keyser, Harriette A. *Bishop Potter, the People's Friend.* New York: Thomas Whittaker, 1910.

Kleppner, Paul. *The Cross of Culture: A Social Analysis of Midwestern Politics, 1850–1900.* New York: Free Press, 1970.

Kloppenberg, James T. *Uncertain Victory: Social Democracy and Progressivism in European and American Thought, 1870–1920.* New York: Oxford University Press, 1986.

Lasch, Christopher. "Religious Contributions to Social Movements: Walter Rauschenbusch, the Social Gospel, and Its Critics." *Journal of Religious Ethics* 18 (Spring 1990): 7–25.

Lender, Mark Edward. *Dictionary of American Temperance Biography: From Temperance Reform to Alcohol Research, the 1600s to the 1980s.* Westport, Conn.: Greenwood Press, 1984.

Lindley, Susan H. "'Neglected Voices' and *Praxis* in the Social Gospel." *Journal of Religious Ethics* 18 (Spring 1990): 75–102.

Lindner, Eileen W. "The Redemptive Politic of Henry George: A Legacy to the Social Gospel." *Union Seminary Quarterly Review* 42 (1988): 1–8.

Lindsey, Almont. *The Pullman Strike: The Story of a Unique Experiment and of a Great Labor Upheaval.* Chicago: University of Chicago Press, 1971.

Lindsley, James Elliott. *This Planted Vine: A Narrative History of the Episcopal Diocese of New York.* New York: Harper and Row, 1984.

Lippy, Charles H. "Social Christianity." Pp. 917–31 in *Encyclopedia of the American Religious Experience: Studies of Traditions and Movements.* 917–31. Edited by Charles H. Lippy and Peter W. Williams. New York: Charles Scribner's Sons, 1988.

Lotz, David W., Donald W. Shriver Jr., and John F. Wilson, eds. *Altered Landscapes: Christianity in America, 1935–1985.* Grand Rapids, Mich.: William B. Eerdmans, 1989.

Lubove, Roy. *The Progressives and the Slums: Tenement House Reform in New York City, 1890–1917.* Pittsburgh: University of Pittsburgh Press, 1962.

Luker, Ralph E. "The Social Gospel and the Failure of Racial Reform, 1877–1898." *Church History* 46 (1977): 80–99.

———. *The Social Gospel in Black and White: American Racial Reform, 1885–1912.* Chapel Hill: University of North Carolina Press, 1991.

Marías, Julián. *History of Philosophy.* Translated by Stanley Applebaum and Clarence C. Strowbridge. New York: Dover Books, 1967.

Markwell, Bernard Kent. *The Anglican Left: Radical Social Reformers in the Church of England and the Protestant Episcopal Church, 1846–1954.* Chicago Studies in the History of American Religion. Brooklyn, N.Y.: Carlson, 1991.

Marshall, Paul V. "William Augustus Muhlenberg's Quiet Defection from Liturgical Uniformity." *Anglican and Episcopal History* 64 (1995): 148–72.

Massa, Mark S. *Charles Augustus Briggs and the Crisis of Historical Criticism.* Harvard Dissertations in Religion no. 25. Minneapolis: Fortress Press, 1990.

May, Henry F. *Protestant Churches and Industrial America.* New York: Harper and Row, 1949. Reprint, 1963.

McLoughlin, William G. *Revivals, Awakenings, and Reform: An Essay on Religion and Social Change in America, 1607–1977.* Chicago: University of Chicago Press, 1978.

McPherson, James M. *Battle Cry of Freedom: The Civil War Era.* The Oxford History of the United States, vol. 6. C. Vann Woodward, general editor. New York: Oxford University Press, 1988.

Mead, Sidney. *The Lively Experiment.* New York: Harper and Row, 1963.

Miller, Spencer Jr., and Joseph F. Fletcher. *The Church and Industry.* New York: Longmans, Green, 1930.

Morgan, H. Wayne, ed. *The Gilded Age.* Syracuse, N.Y.: Syracuse University Press, 1970.

Mullin, Robert Bruce. "Biblical Critics and the Battle over Slavery." *Journal of Presbyterian History* 61 (1983): 210–26.

———. *Episcopal Vision/American Reality: High Church Theology and Social Thought in Evangelical America.* New Haven, Conn.: Yale University Press, 1986.

Niebuhr, H. Richard. *Christ and Culture.* New York: Harper and Row, 1951. Reprint, 1975.

———. *The Kingdom of God in America.* New York: Harper and Row, 1937. Reprint, Middletown, Conn.: Wesleyan University Press, 1988.

———. *The Social Sources of Denominationalism.* New York: Henry Holt, 1931. Reprint, New York: Meridian Books, 1960.

Niebuhr, Reinhold. *Moral Man and Immoral Society.* New York: Charles Scribner's Sons, 1932.

Noll, Mark A., ed. *Religion and American Politics: From the Colonial Period to the 1980s.* New York: Oxford University Press, 1990.

Ogden, Rollo, ed. *Life and Letters of E. L. Godkin.* Vol. 2. New York: Macmillan, 1907.

Olcott, Charles S. *The Life of William McKinley.* Vol. 2. Boston: Houghton, Mifflin, 1916.

Paz, D. G. "Monasticism and Social Reform in Late Nineteenth Century America: The Case of Fr. Huntington." *Historical Magazine of the Protestant Episcopal Church* 48 (1979): 45–66.

Public Broadcasting Service. *Africans in America: America's Journey through Slavery.* Washington, D.C.: Public Broadcasting Service, 1998.

Rauschenbusch, Walter. *Christianizing the Social Order.* New York: Macmillan, 1912.

———. *A Theology for the Social Gospel.* New York: Macmillan, 1917. Reprint, Nashville, Tenn.: Abingdon, 1981.

Reckitt, Maurice B. *For Christ and the People: Studies of Four Socialist Priests and Prophets of the Church of England between 1870 and 1930.* London: SPCK, 1968.

Redkey, Edwin S. *Black Exodus: Black Nationalism and Back-to-Africa Movements, 1890–1910.* Yale Publications in American Studies, no. 17. New Haven, Conn.: Yale University Press, 1969.

Rosenberg, Carroll Smith. *Religion and the Rise of the American City: The New York City Mission Movement, 1812–1870.* Ithaca, N.Y.: Cornell University Press, 1971.

Sawyer, M. James. *Charles Augustus Briggs and Tensions in Late Nineteenth-Century American Theology.* Lewiston, N.Y.: Mellen University Press, 1994.

Schlesinger, Arthur M. "A Critical Period in American Religion, 1875–1900." *Massachusetts Historical Society Proceedings* 64 (October 1930–June 1932): 523–46. Reprinted as *A Critical Period in American Religion, 1875–1900.* Historical Series (American Church), vol. 7. Edited by Richard C. Wolf. Philadelphia: Fortress Press, 1967.

Schweiker, William. "Tradition and Criticism: Problems and Approaches in the History of Ethics." Pp. 291–301 in *The Annual of the Society of Christian Ethics, 1992.* Edited by Harlan Beckley. Boston: Society of Christian Ethics, 1992.

Scudder, Vida. *Father Huntington: Founder of the Order of the Holy Cross.* New York: E. P. Dutton, 1940.

Segundo, Juan Luis. *The Liberation of Theology.* Maryknoll, N.Y.: Orbis Books, 1976.

Sheerin, James. *Henry Codman Potter: An American Metropolitan.* New York: Fleming H. Revell, 1933.

Shinn, Roger L. "Religious Faith and the Task of the Historian." Pp. 56–77 in *Liberal Learning and Religion.* Edited by Amos N. Wilder. New York: Harper and Brothers, 1951.

Skardon, Alvin W. *Church Leader in the Cities: William Augustus Muhlenberg.* Philadelphia: University of Pennsylvania Press, 1971.

Smith, H. Shelton, ed. *Horace Bushnell.* Library of Protestant Thought. New York: Oxford University Press, 1965.

Smith, Timothy L. *Revivalism and Social Reform: American Protestantism on the Eve of the Civil War.* Nashville, Tenn.: Abingdon Press, 1957.

Socolofsky, Homer E., and Allan B. Spetter. *The Presidency of Benjamin Harrison.* American Presidency Series. Lawrence: University Press of Kansas, 1987.

Spielmann, Richard M. "A Neglected Source: The Episcopal Church Congress, 1874–1934." *Anglican and Episcopal History* 58 (1989): 50–80.

Sproat, John G. *"The Best Men."* New York: Oxford University Press, 1968.

Sweet, Leonard I., ed. *Communication and Change in American Religious History.* Grand Rapids, Mich.: William B. Eerdmans, 1993.

———, ed. *The Evangelical Tradition in America.* Macon, Ga.: Mercer University Press, 1984.

———. *The Minister's Wife.* Philadelphia: Temple University Press, 1983.

Troeltsch, Ernst. *The Social Teaching of the Christian Churches.* 2 vols. Translated by Olive Wyon. New York: Macmillan, 1931. Reprint, Chicago: University of Chicago Press, 1976.

Tucker, Robert C., ed. *The Marx-Engels Reader.* 2d ed. New York: W. W. Norton, 1978.

U.S. Bureau of the Census. *Historical Statistics of the United States, Colonial Times to 1970.* Washington, D.C.: U.S. Bureau of the Census, 1975.

———. *Statistical Abstract of the United States, 1993.* Washington, D.C.: U.S. Bureau of the Census, 1993.

Visser't Hooft, W. A. *The Background of the Social Gospel in America.* St. Louis: Bethany Press, 1928.

Welch, Richard E. Jr. *The Presidencies of Grover Cleveland.* American Presidency Series. Lawrence: University Press of Kansas, 1988.

White, Leonard D., and Jean Schneider. *The Republican Era, 1869–1901: A Study in Administrative History.* New York: Macmillan, 1958.

White, Ronald C. Jr. *Liberty and Justice for All: Racial Reform and the Social Gospel (1877–1925).* San Francisco: Harper and Row, 1990.

White, Ronald C. Jr., and C. Howard Hopkins. *The Social Gospel: Religion and Reform in Changing America.* Philadelphia: Temple University Press, 1976.

Wilentz, Sean. *Chants Democratic: New York City and the Rise of the American Working Class, 1788–1850.* New York: Oxford University Press, 1984.

Williams, Preston. "The Social Gospel and Race Relations: A Case Study of a Social Movement." In *Toward a Discipline of Social Ethics: Essays in Honor of Walter George Muelder.* Edited by Paul Deats Jr. Boston: Boston University Press, 1972.

Wilson, John F., ed. *Church and State in America: A Bibliographical Guide.* Vol. 2: *The Civil War to the Present Day.* New York: Greenwood Press, 1987.

Woolverton, John F. *The Education of Phillips Brooks.* Studies in Anglican History. Urbana: University of Illinois Press, 1995.

INDEX

Sparrow, William, 27
Squirrel Inn, 20, 113
Stanton Street Mission, 17, 18, 38, 47, 129–30
State Charities Aid Association, 14, 53, 100
St. George's Church (New York), 44, 46, 47, 129
St. John, John P., 125
St. Johnland, 155
St. John's Church (Troy), 12, 32, 43, 62
St. Luke's Association, 44, 99
St. Luke's Church (Philadelphia), 9
St. Luke's Hospital, 7–8, 90
St. Mark's Church (Philadelphia), 155, 195
St. Michael's Church (New York), 100
St. Paul's Chapel (New York), 3–4, 124–25
St. Paul's Church (Boston), 7
St. Paul's Church (Philadelphia), 157
St. Peter's Church (Albany), 8
Strikes, 153–54, 157–60, 162, 168–70, 173, 174, 178, 197, 210, 254n9; anthracite coal, 20, 197; Cloakmakers', 100; Homestead Steel workers', 17, 20, 168, 173; Pullman, 17, 152, 168, 169–70, 173
Strong, Josiah, 1, 15, 65, 71, 77, 143–44, 242n31, 243n46; seven perils of, 71
Subway Tavern, 20, 114–15, 210, 214
Sunday observance, 5, 14, 53, 73–76, 77, 119, 153, 160
Supply and demand, 187, 201, 258n62
Sweating system, 100
Sweet, Leonard I., 229n24
Swierenga, Robert, 118

Tammany Hall, 17, 18, 121, 128–33
Taylor, C. J., 250n24
Taylor, Nathaniel, 26–27
Taylor, Thomas House, 13, 43, 44, 237n41
Temperance movement, 84–85, 106–16, 153, 213–14
Temperance reform, 2, 5, 8, 14, 19–21, 53, 71, 85, 106–16, 119, 216–17

Tenement housing, 14, 40, 53–55, 153, 200
Tertullian, 37
Theology, practical Christianity and, 215–24
"Third Great Awakening," 1
Toews, Paul, 134
Tractarianism, 25, 28–30, 33–34, 234n10
Tracts for the Times, 24
Trade union movement, 20–21, 164, 173, 176, 190–92, 215, 254n9
Treaty of Paris (1898), 137
Trinity, 26
Trinity Church (Boston), 12–13, 157
Trinity College (Hartford), 8
Trusts, regulation of, 191–92
Tucker, William Jewett, 50
Turner, Henry M., 67
Twain, Mark, 120, 132
Tyler, Bennet, 26–27
Tyng, Stephen H., Jr., 33, 43

"Unemployed agency of Christian women," 85–94
Unemployment, 149, 159, 169, 213
Union College, 7–9, 12
Union Theological Seminary, 38, 77
Unitarianism, 5, 26–27
Universalism, 5
Urban-industrial cult of genteel womanhood, 85–86, 92, 94
Urbanization, 5, 24, 117, 204

Van Wyck, Robert, 19, 131
Venezuela, 134–35
Victorian family ideal, 85–86
Violence against women, 109–10
Virginia Theological Seminary, 10–11, 25, 233n5

Wage work system, 174–75, 200
Wages, fair, 161, 169, 174–75, 189
Wages-fund doctrine, 150–51
Wainwright, Jonathan, 33
Washburn, Edward A., 32, 80, 120, 155, 235n19
Washburn, George W., 89

MICHAEL BOURGEOIS is an assistant professor of theology at Emmanuel College of Victoria University in the University of Toronto.

The University of Illinois Press
is a founding member of the
Association of American University Presses.

Composed in 9.5/12.5 Trump Mediæval
at the University of Illinois Press
Manufactured by Thomson-Shore, Inc.

University of Illinois Press
1325 South Oak Street
Champaign, IL 61820-6903
www.press.uillinois.edu